Praise for Peter Vronsky's
Serial Killers: The Method and Madness of Monsters

"This formidably comprehensive, brilliantly researched book must be the most wide-ranging work on serial killers that has been written so far. The fact that it sprang from the author's brief encounters with two serial killers lends it a sense of personal urgency."

—Colin Wilson, coauthor of *Killers Among Us* and author of *Written in Blood*

"*Serial Killers: The Method and Madness of Monsters* is one of the most complete books I have read on serial killers. If you are fascinated by the human mind and by those who are abnormal, this is the book for you."

—Roundtablereviews.com

Titles by Peter Vronsky

FEMALE SERIAL KILLERS: HOW AND WHY WOMEN BECOME MONSTERS

SERIAL KILLERS: THE METHOD AND MADNESS OF MONSTERS

FEMALE SERIAL KILLERS

HOW AND WHY WOMEN BECOME MONSTERS

PETER VRONSKY

BERKLEY BOOKS, NEW YORK

THE BERKLEY PUBLISHING GROUP
Published by the Penguin Group
Penguin Group (USA) Inc.
375 Hudson Street, New York, New York 10014, USA
Penguin Group (Canada), 90 Eglinton Avenue East, Suite 700, Toronto, Ontario M4P 2Y3, Canada
(a division of Pearson Penguin Canada Inc.)
Penguin Books Ltd., 80 Strand, London WC2R 0RL, England
Penguin Group Ireland, 25 St. Stephen's Green, Dublin 2, Ireland (a division of Penguin Books Ltd.)
Penguin Group (Australia), 250 Camberwell Road, Camberwell, Victoria 3124, Australia
(a division of Pearson Australia Group Pty. Ltd.)
Penguin Books India Pvt. Ltd., 11 Community Centre, Panchsheel Park, New Delhi—110 017, India
Penguin Group (NZ), 67 Apollo Drive, Rosedale, North Shore 0745, Auckland, New Zealand
(a division of Pearson New Zealand Ltd.)
Penguin Books (South Africa) (Pty.) Ltd., 24 Sturdee Avenue, Rosebank, Johannesburg 2196,
South Africa

Penguin Books Ltd., Registered Offices: 80 Strand, London WC2R 0RL, England

This book is an original publication of The Berkley Publishing Group.

PRINTING HISTORY
Berkley trade paperback edition / August 2007

Library of Congress Cataloging-in-Publication Data

Vronsky, Peter.
    Female serial killers : how and why women become monsters / Peter Vronsky.
        p. cm.
    Includes bibliographical references and index.
    ISBN: 978-0-425-21390-2
    1. Women serial murderers. I. Title.
    HV6517.V76 2007
    364.152'3—dc22

                                                            2007015094

PRINTED IN THE UNITED STATES OF AMERICA

10   9   8

FOR MEN AND WOMEN,

YOUNG AND OLD,

THE LIVING AND THE DEAD,

THE GUILTY AND THE INNOCENT.

VICTIMS ALL.

CONTENTS

SERIAL SPARTACISM

The Politics of Female Aggression

Can you name the serial killer who struck in the back of a military helicopter flying at 4,000 feet on a mission? Or the one who, at the age of eleven, killed two victims? Or the one who danced and socialized with a California governor? Some would know to name Genene Jones, Mary Bell, and Dorothea Puente—three females. But for the rest of us, we never even knew there *were* female serial killers. That is, except for that *Monster* lesbian hooker—the one they made the movie about—Aileen Wuornos. While the names of Ted Bundy, John Wayne Gacy, and Jeffrey Dahmer or the monikers of the Boston Strangler, Son of Sam, the Green River Killer, and BTK are familiar to all, ask us to name a few female serial killers and we usually stop right after Aileen. Were there others?

Yes, many actually. About one out of every six serial killers is a woman.[1]

As atonement for my past negligence in having overlooked them, along with Aileen, Genene, and Mary, I uncovered the legion of their serial killing sisters, and they are many.

I first came to writing about male serial killers in the wake of my own very brief and casual encounters with two of them before they were identified and apprehended. (One just behind St. Basil's Cathedral in Moscow in 1990 and another in a New York City hotel lobby eleven years earlier.)[2] At the time I did not know they were serial killers. I only learned who they were and what they had done months and years later through press reports and it made me wonder about the possibility that perhaps I had met more than just those two, and did not know it. Anything can happen *once*—that I understood and it did not surprise me. But discovering that I had met two—well, *twice* was entirely a different matter. It inspired all sorts of meditation on the statistical possibilities of life as we live it today. I wondered what the odds were for any of us to have at least once unknowingly sat next to a serial killer on a bus or a train, passed one in a crowd on the street, parked or shopped next to one, or stood behind one waiting in line.

As far as "my" two serial killers were concerned, I was living a relatively conventional heterosexual male middle-class existence, which I believed unfolded far away from the lonely corpse-littered road-sides, low-rent musty holes, and gloomy cellars where serial killers did their ugly horrible thing. I smugly asserted that my coincidental encounters had nothing to do with my being a potential victim for I was not in a preferred category for serial killer prey: I was not a young unaccompanied female or a late-night service employee, a street sex worker, a promiscuous player, or a child of any gender.

After encountering my first serial killer in a trashy part of town near a hookers' stroll in New York, I contentedly described myself as "trespassing" on a serial killer's hunting ground and getting "bumped" by a monster for going where I did not normally belong.

But I had gotten it all wrong. While I was vigilantly looking over my shoulder for a masculine threat from the seedier side of town, I should have been instead looking first closer to home—to whose bed I comfortably slept in and who slept in mine. If a white, heterosexual, middle-aged male ends up murdered, most likely his killer is a woman who he knows and knows intimately. When serial death comes calling on lonely, single middle-class guys with jobs and condos, or for that matter on horny old widower farmers, it comes with kisses and caring.

But all the serial killers I imagined myself randomly passing by on the street were always males, while women remained entirely off my paranoid radar as anything other than victims. I was conditioned to perceive the serial killer as a "he" and "she" as "his" victim.

That is not just a male point of view. Women until very recently had felt the same way. The presence of another female, even a stranger, still disarms many women's primal fears of finding themselves alone with a male stranger. Our belief in an intrinsic non-threatening nature of the feminine is deceiving both genders.

FEMALE SERIAL KILLERS: HOW MANY?

One in nearly every six serial killers in the U.S. is a woman, acting as a solo perpetrator or an accomplice. Of a total of about 400 serial killers identified between 1800 and 1995, nearly 16 percent were females—a total of 62 killers.[3] While that might not be an overwhelming majority, it is not an insignificant number either—those 62 women collectively killed between 400 and 600 victims—men, women, and children. Three female serial killers alone—Genene Jones, Belle Gunness, and Jane Toppan—might account collectively for as many as 200 suspected murders. Another study, which included cases from other countries, named 86 known female serial killers.[4] The appendix at the end of this book lists 140 known female serial killers and the number of their victims. More disturbing is that three-quarters of female serial killers in the U.S. made their appearance since 1950, and a full half only since 1975![5]

Yet somehow the notion of a female serial killer has not entered our popular consciousness of fear or into our alarmed imaginations in the same menacing way that the figure of the male serial killer has. Women serial killers seem to border on the comic or titillating for many of us. Compare the monikers we give male serial killers (Jack the Ripper, Boston Strangler, Night Stalker, Skid Row Slasher, Bedroom Basher, Slavemaster) with the female ones (Lady Bluebeard, Giggling Grandma, Lonely Hearts Killer, Lady Rotten, Black Widow, Angel of Death, Barbie Killer, Death Row Granny). We have not been taking female killers seriously enough.

Part of the explanation is found in who we think female serial killers have been murdering and where. Many female serialists kill at home and their victims have often been family members or intimates: husbands, lovers, and children. Where one first nursed is not necessarily the safest place to be, yet how many of us are even remotely prepared to imagine our mom as a serial killer?

Other female serial killers murder at work in their professional capacity as trusted caregivers—nurses, babysitters, bearers of medicine, food preparers, and trusted social services contractors.

Nurses killing on their job—killing where they belong: on the frontline of the war between life and death where people *do* die; nurses as angels of death with the catheter and syringe in their hands, nobody suspecting them, realizing that the death of their victim was anything but a medical emergency.

But in our popular imagination the serial killer lurks faceless after dark behind the wheel of *his* cruising car with a trunkful of rope and duct tape. We neglect to look beyond the sexy, cool cotton-white of the nurse who draws our blood, the cheery home-care worker calling on Granddad, the cute girl behind the deli counter slicing our bread, the miniskirted one with scissors cutting hair, or the one looking into our eyes from across the table while sipping her drink.

MONSTER—THE UNQUIET KILLER

Amazing how fast movies today can still change everything. Our collective awareness of female serial killers was recently taken up to a new level thanks to *Monster,* a 2003 movie starring Charlize Theron and Christina Ricci, along with a host of documentaries and television reports, all about Aileen Wuornos, a Florida roadside prostitute who was convicted of murdering seven men. A lot of promotion and commentary around the case suggested that Wuornos was "America's first female serial killer." Far from it—she was more likely somewhere around the fifty-seventh.

Wuornos was at best, perhaps, America's first mass media *celebrity* female serial killer—giving countless interviews to press, media, and documentary filmmakers before she was put to death by lethal injection in 2002. What made Wuornos so unique was that she appeared to murder just like a male serial killer—she killed strangers with a handgun in a car and left their bodies in public places.

The one thing most of us believe about female serial killers, if anything, is that they generally tend to use poison and that their victims are known or related to them. Male serial killers stalk and hunt strangers; females trap and poison intimates—kill on their own home territory or on that which they share with their victim. The only really popular conception that has endured of a female serial killer through the decades is of the one who kills a string of husbands or lovers for profit. We even have a readymade moniker for her: the Black Widow.

For some reason we imagine the Black Widow as a creature of the past, from a time long ago when poisons were readily sold over the counter, marriage was often contractually functional, and record keeping of identities was haphazard. She could lure, seduce, marry quickly, discreetly kill, and vanish several times over before anybody would notice. When the Black Widow appears today, we think she only does so in Hollywood films in the guise of Sharon Stone, Kathleen Turner, or Linda Fiorentino. *Mrrrrreow.* So titillating—sex to die for.

What we rarely saw was the type of predatory sexually charged Ted Bundy/Green River Killer–type of female perpetrator leaving an alarming trail of visible corpses in her wake. Wuornos came closest to that. She was "the unquiet killer." Unlike the typical female serial killer who leaves her victims expired in their beds or cribs or discreetly buries them in the garden out back, Wuornos dumped her victims' bodies by the rest stops and roadsides of Florida's interstate system. Corpses on the roads to Disney World! And unlike most female serial killers who historically murdered their victims in the capacity of a wife, lover, babysitter, nurse, or landlady, Wuornos barely had any relationship with her victims, other than hitchhiker, motorist in distress, or roadside prostitute with client, ironically the very same relationship that many male serial killers themselves exploit when they murder their female victims.

Wuornos, however, confuses our perceptions of *real* female serial killers by not only being a lesbian, but by being a particular *type* of lesbian. She was not the pretty and feminine *L Word* lipstick-lesbian, but a hard-edged dyke type, oozing a beefy, drunken-stoned, sloppy kind of muscular knucklehead violence we typically associate with males. As a serial killer, it is easier to correlate Wuornos's violence with an overabundance of the masculine rather than with any intrinsic femininity gone awry.

THE NATURE OF FEMALE VIOLENCE

Wuornos exposes the core of our perceptual problem—violence is still almost universally associated with the male and the masculine. It was thought to be implicit in the male physique, a function of testosterone. Men commit violence; women and children suffer from it.

When women commit violence the only explanation offered has been that it is involuntary, defensive, or the result of mental illness or hormonal imbalance inherent with female physiology: postpartum depression, premenstrual syndrome, and menopause have been included among the named culprits. Women have been generally perceived to be capable of committing only "expressive" violence—an uncontrollable release of bottled-up rage or fear, often as a result of long-term abuse at the hands of males: Battered Woman Syndrome or Battered Spouse Syndrome. It has been generally believed that women usually murder unwillingly without premeditation.

"Instrumental" violence, however, murder for a purpose—political power, rape, sadistic pleasure, robbery, or some other base gratification—remains the domain of the male. After all, every male is a potential killer in the form of a warrior—and he only becomes a murderer when he misuses his innate physical and socialized capacity to kill for ignoble, immoral, and impolitic reasons. While the male is built and programmed to destroy, the female nests, creates, and nurtures. Or so the story goes.

History, of course, is full of instrumentally violent women: Valeria Messalina, Queen Boadicea, Agrippina the Younger, Lucrezia Borgia, Catherine the Great, Elizabeth the First, Madame Mao, Golda Meier, Margaret Thatcher. Some of these women can be characterized as serial killers; many had on numerous occasions killed and tortured serially, or ordered it to be done in the name of political power, patriotism, vengeance, or material greed and lust—and they did it as ruthlessly and obsessively as their male contemporaries—and sometimes even more so.

But most of these women are cultures, centuries, and classes distant from the modern Western woman—from the welfare moms in the Laundromat to the soccer moms in the mall and those without kids at all. It could be argued that as empresses or high priestesses they were beyond the common distinction of gender—they were heirs to divine power as manifestations of their political state. Yet it is precisely that deadly divine power that so many serial killers obsessively attempt to replicate through murder:

power over life and death. It's almost always about the power. But in the end, when we negate the feminine, all that remains is a potential murderer.

THE STUDY OF FEMALE AGGRESSION

We really do not understand much about female violence because we have only recently begun to pay careful attention to it. Of 314 scientific studies on human aggression published by 1974 only 8 percent exclusively addressed violence in women or girls.[6] But that was *before* the frequency of female serial killers in the U.S. had dramatically doubled by 1975 over the previous two decades, and would double again by 1995![7]

. Proportionally there are more females among serial killers (16 percent) than females among total homicide offenders during the twenty-five year period from 1976–2002 (11.4 percent.)[8] In general, violent offenses by females have been rising significantly. In 1987, women's arrest rates for aggravated assault and robbery in the U.S. rose by 17.6 percent from 1978—and in some localities, like New York City, the rise was much more dramatic: 47 percent for aggravated assault and 75.8 percent for robbery. More recently, between 1992 and 1996, the rate of females arrested for violent crimes increased by 22.8 percent.[9]

THE DEPTHS OF SERIAL DEPRAVITY

Serial killing, whether perpetrated by male or female, has always stood in its own special corner of criminal depravity. Most of us can understand killing once—we can imagine a degree of jealousy, fear, desperation, rage, or even greed that could lead to taking a life. Most murderers do not know they are about to kill—it is not planned or intended. Many sincerely and deeply regret their act, make no attempt to evade justice, and rarely kill again. Serial killers, however, are opposite in every way from the common kind of murderer.

Serial killers are frequently aware of their intention to kill long before they commit murder—some fantasize about it for years and carefully plan it. After committing their first murder and "cooling off" from any emotions that led to it, serial killers are cyclically prepared to commit more murders, or—as some might argue—are *compelled* to kill again and again. (They become addicted to murder.) There is no regret or remorse—or certainly not enough to change their behavior. Many carefully review their actions, improving their plan for the next murder, going to extraordinary lengths to evade apprehension. A willingness or desire to kill repeatedly is something from the realm of evil—impervious to rational, scientific explanation. Our society can barely account for evil in males, let alone imagine it in females.

FEMINISM AND THE FEMALE SERIAL KILLER

If being killed by a female intimate is characteristic of a male middle-aged murder victim, then so is blaming feminism for it. The problem is that our understanding of the steady rise of female serial killers among us since 1950 has truly been confounded in its analysis by a new radical so called "second-wave" feminism, a form of "spartacism," a tendency to associate female criminality with an aspiration for freedom from slavery and oppression at the hands of "the patriarchy."

Ann Jones, a feminist historian of female-perpetrated murder proclaims, "A wave of attention to women's criminality follows thunderously on every wave of feminism and surely will continue to do so until we can grasp the truth that free people are not dangerous."[10] Slave revolt is the crime, she is saying.

The early first wave of feminism addressed the "liberation" and equality of females within the parameters of precise and specific legal and constitutional challenges—the right to vote, the right to equal pay for equal work, family law equity, fair hiring, equal status, equal opportunity, and so on.

First-wave feminists (so-called "liberal feminists") had associated the rise of female criminality with the notion of women becoming free to assert themselves *as equally* as men. Thus Freda Adler's *Sisters in Crime* in 1975 interpreted increasing female violence in the context of self-empowerment. As in business, sports, the arts or sciences, the female as a criminal was not content to take second place in the hierarchy of crime. According to Adler, women were ready to compete with men on male terms and by their rules and that meant necessarily being as aggressive and as violent as the male criminal. This became known as the "liberation hypothesis."

Adler's Vietnam War–era antiestablishment liberationist generation of feminism, however, was flagging by the time her book
came out. Moreover, the glee with which conservatives adopted
Adler's thesis in their opposition to female equality further alienated Adler's liberation hypothesis from new emerging feminism.
Adler was even seen as dangerous by some of the younger radicals
in the feminist movement because her work was so eagerly cited by
conservatives blaming feminism for the rise in female violence
along with other family and societal ills.

A more radical second wave·of feminists emerged, focusing on a
darker notion of a deeply seated systematic victimization of women
and womanhood by a biocultural conspiracy of a male "phallo
centric heteropatriarchy" or the "phallocratic state." According to
this school of feminism, women will remain oppressed until males
are transformed into something other than what they are collectively socialized to be today.

This second wave of feminism rejected the simple notion of
equality between male and female, claiming that inherent in first-
wave feminism is the proposition that all women want is to be *like*
men—share their opportunities, have access to their world, be able
to play by their rules, be equal to them—period. They maintained
that this was akin to arguing that all African-Americans just
needed and wanted to be white. Second-wave feminists called on
women to liberate themselves not as individuals but as a unique
collective feminine culture and to establish an identity of their own
in the pursuit of an overthrow of an unyielding and oppressive
male hegemony.

According to second-wave feminism, women are victims and
males are collectively oppressors and women's aggression should
not be equated with any kind of female aspiration for equality
with an oppressor.

Female violence, it was argued, was self-defense against sys-
temic male aggression against women: It was liberational. And it
was; the female murderer was transformed into the victim and the
victim into the aggressor. As one feminist argues, "Women do kill.
And their motives can usually be attributed to a very specific set of
circumstances, underlying which are American principles of eco-
nomics and property ownership, firmly legitimated by media

coverage . . . women in America appear to have a very specific orientation to murder. Motivations may loop and repeat as social, political, and judicial landscapes do, but the basic issue is almost always one of survival."[11]

As Patricia Pearson summarizes in her recent study of female violence, "By the 1980s, it was no longer a badge of honor to make a fist and wave it; it was more prestigious to weep in a therapist's office. Therefore women couldn't want to do something so antisocial and frankly offensive as crime. Women were not to be held as men's equals in villainy, they were to be shown as men's victims."[12]

The absence of studies on female aggression and violence prior to 1975 was soon remedied by new feminist analysis, which fundamentally argued that all women are systematically victimized by the "heteropatriarchy" and its "phallocentric" institutions. Its common currency was to explain female-perpetrated homicide as an act of self-defense and rebellion against a long-standing conspiracy of rape and battering at the hands of the "phallocracy." This vision was passionately popular among reading young women in the mid-1970s in bestsellers like *Against Our Will* by Susan Brownmiller in 1975 and *Battered Wives* by Del Martin the following year. *The Burning Bed*/Battered Woman Syndrome emerged in jurisprudence, explaining how wives can kill their husbands in "self-defense" even as their victims sleep soundly. The American Civil Liberties Union chimed in, saying, "Most death-row women have killed an abusive husband."[13] Could this be true?

A FEW TALES OF WOMEN ON DEATH ROW

Since the resumption of executions in the U.S. in 1977, a total of sixty-three women have been sentenced to death by 2005.* Eleven of them have been executed. (The last woman executed prior to 1977 was Elizabeth Duncan, back in 1962 in California's gas chamber for the contract murder of her pregnant daughter-in-law, who she had buried alive.) Here are the brief case histories of the eleven women actually executed. You be the judge.

---

* Department of Justice, Bureau of Justice Statistics, Capital Punishment Statistics http://www.ojp.usdoj.gov/bjs/cp.htm

- The first to be executed was in 1984. Fifty-two-year-old Margie Velma Barfield in North Carolina, a grandmother who not only killed her husband by poisoning him with arsenic, but also on separate occasions murdered two elderly men and one elderly woman who employed her as a home-care worker, her fiancé, and her own mother. A total of six victims, and perhaps a seventh one—her first husband whose fire death she might have staged to appear as a result of his careless smoking. (More on Velma later.)

- Second executed was 37-year-old Karla Fay Tucker in Texas in 1998. Karla and her boyfriend, both high on drugs, went to the apartment of an acquaintance, Jerry Lynn Dean, and attempted to steal the keys to his motorcycle. After her boyfriend knocked Dean unconscious with a hammer, Tucker found a pickax in the apartment and finished Dean off to stop him from making gurgling sounds. As she explained at her trial, "I just wanted to make the noise stop." She then noticed 32-year-old Deborah Thornton cowering in bed under a blanket, and proceeded to batter her to death with the pickax, eventually leaving it embedded in her torso. On police wiretaps, Tucker was heard saying that she had an orgasm every time she sank the pickax into her two victims.

- The same year, the state of Florida executed 54-year-old Judias "Judy" Buenoano, a successful beauty salon owner who drove a Corvette, for the arsenic poisoning of her husband. The murder came to the attention of the authorities only after they had arrested Buenoano for the car-bombing murder attempt of a boyfriend and discovered another murder in her background—that of her handicapped 19-year-old son. Buenoano first failed in her attempt to poison her son and instead caused partial paralysis, which required him to wear heavy metal leg braces. She then took him on a canoe trip during which she tipped them both over into a lake resulting in his "accidental" drowning and a lucrative insurance payout. All together, Buenoano collected $240,000 in insurance claims in the deaths of her husband and son, and in the death of a boyfriend in Colorado. But with her death sentence in Florida, Colorado authorities declined to prosecute.

- The fourth woman executed was 62-year-old great-grandmother Betty Lou Beets in 2000 in Texas, for shooting her fifth husband, Dallas fire captain Jimmy Don Beets. After burying his body in the yard of their house and setting her husband's boat adrift with his heart medicine spilled in it, Beets reported her husband missing. She then made a claim on his life insurance and fireman's pension. It took police two years to collect sufficient evidence to get a search warrant and discover her husband's body under the lawn. During the search, police discovered the body of another husband who had also disappeared, Doyle Wayne Barker, buried under the garage and shot with the same .38 handgun used to kill Jimmy. During her trial, Beets claimed that her husband had battered her and she had killed him in self-defense. On the eve of her execution Amnesty International described Beets as "a lifelong survivor of domestic violence and sexual assault" and claimed that "since her conviction, prominent psychologist Lenore Walker has diagnosed Ms. Beets as suffering from both Battered Woman's Syndrome and Post-Traumatic Stress Disorder."[14] No mention was made by Amnesty International of the discovery of the body of another husband buried under her garage.

- That same year, the state of Arkansas executed the fifth woman, 28-year-old Christina Marie Riggs, for the murder of her two children, Justin Thomas, 5, and Shelby Alexis, 2. Riggs attempted to kill her children by sedating them and then injecting them with potassium chloride. When she botched the attempt, she ended up smothering them with a pillow. She then attempted to commit suicide but failed. Riggs pursued the execution of her own death sentence.

- Wanda Jean Allen, age 41, was the sixth woman to be put to death when the state of Oklahoma executed her by lethal injection in 2001 for the murder of her lesbian lover. Allen had already been convicted and served a sentence for killing another woman, a childhood friend, in an argument. Five years after her release in 1983, she killed again, this time shooting her lover, Gloria Leathers, in the stomach. She was the first black woman executed in the U.S. since executions resumed in 1977.

- Oklahoma also executed the seventh woman in 2001—40-year-old Marilyn Kay Plantz, who hired her teenage boyfriend, Clifford Bryson, and his friend Clint McKimble to kill her husband, Jim, for about $300,000 in life insurance. Jim was ambushed on his arrival home from his night shift at work by Bryson and McKimble and beaten into unconsciousness with the children's baseball bats while Plantz pretended to sleep in the next room. Ignoring her husband's desperate pleas for help, Plantz got up from her bed and instructed the killers to "burn him" in his vehicle to make it look like a traffic accident. They drove the semi-conscious victim to a deserted location, doused him and his pickup with gasoline, and set it on fire. McKimble testified in the case for the prosecution and received a life sentence. Plantz and Bryson were tried jointly. Bryson was executed in 2000.

- Eighth executed, again in Oklahoma in 2001, was 61-year-old Lois Nadean Smith, convicted for the murder of a woman, 21-year-old Cindy Baillee. According to a description from a prosecutor's office, "Baillee was the former girlfriend of Smith's son, Greg. Smith, along with her son and another woman, picked up Baillee from a Tahlequah motel early on the morning of the murder. As they drove away from the motel, Smith confronted Baillee about rumors that Baillee had arranged for Greg Smith's murder—charges Baillee denied. Smith choked Baillee and stabbed her in the throat as they drove to the home of Smith's ex-husband in Gans. At the house, Smith forced Baillee to sit in a recliner and taunted her with a pistol, finally firing several shots. Baillee fell to the floor, and while her son reloaded the pistol, Smith laughed and jumped on Baillee's neck. She then fired four shots into Baillee's chest and two to the back of her head."[15] (A mother's love for her son knows no bounds.)

- The ninth woman to be executed, in 2002 in Alabama, and probably the last to die in the electric chair, was 54-year-old Lynda Lyon Block, a former Cub Scout mom, Humane Society volunteer, and Friends of the Library president who became involved with a faction of the right-wing patriot movement. She was traveling with her boyfriend, George Sibley, also a patriot militant, and her nine-year-old son, on the run after their conviction for assault in a property dispute involving the stabbing of Block's former husband. Both Block and Sibley were armed. When they stopped in a Opelika-area Wal-Mart parking lot so that Block could make a phone call, a passerby noticed that the pair appeared to be living out of their car, and concerned for the child, alerted Opelika Police Department officer Roger Motley who was shopping at the time for office supplies at the mall. The officer, unaware that Block was away from the vehicle making a phone call, approached it and demanded to see Sibley's driver's license. Sibley instead drew his weapon and a gunfight ensued between Sibley and Motley. Lynda Block dropped the phone and ran up from behind Motley and shot him with her Glock 9mm handgun. As the wounded officer crawled towards his cruiser she continued to fire several more shots into him. Because of budgetary shortages in Opelika, Motley had offered up his bulletproof vest to a rookie cop the week before. In letters to friends and supporters, Block later would describe Motley as a "bad cop" and a wife beater with multiple complaints against him. As part of the conspiracy against her, she said, she was prohibited from bringing up his record in court. His personnel file makes no mention of any misbehavior and his wife stated that her husband had always been a kind and patient man. Block's companion was executed in 2005 for his role in the murder.

- The tenth woman executed was Aileen Wuornos in 2002, when the state of Florida put her to death for seven serial murders. Aileen Wuornos's case is notorious and described in more detail later on.

- Finally, the eleventh woman to die was 40-year-old Frances Newton in Texas in 2005 for the .25 caliber handgun slaying of her husband and two children—her son, Alton, 7, and daughter, Farrah, 21 months. Newton attempted to claim the $100,000 insurance policy on their lives. She was the second black woman executed among the eleven.

Instead of the supposed abusive husbands, many of the victims in the above cases, in fact, turned out to be children, other women, or innocent men. Four, and perhaps even arguably five, of these eleven cases involved a serial killer and at least four to six involved a type of materialistic Black Widow killer we popularly associate with a bygone era or the movies. In three of these cases it was unsuccessfully argued by the defense that the male victims had been abusers of the killers.

In fact, historically more than half (53 percent) of known female serial killers in the U.S. have killed at least one adult female victim and 32 percent have counted at least one female child among their victims.[16]

Yet there persists a tendency to interpret homicide by women as "defensive" or to politically contextualize it. One study of fifty female-perpetrated homicide cases, for example, insists that murder for women was "a resource of self-protection."[17] Yet only eighteen of those cases featured any evidence of abuse by the victim. The other thirty-two cases involve the murder of other women, children, and innocent men. The authors of the report remain eerily silent about that majority as if these cases did not exist.[18]

In the late 1980s and early 1990s, at the height of new feminist rhetoric, it was asserted that women just could not be serial killers—period. Some argued, "Only men . . . are compulsive, lone hunters, driven by the lust to kill—a sexual desire which finds its outlet in murder."[19]

Another feminist critic, Jane Caputi, objected to gender-neutral language in the analysis of serial homicide because it "works to obscure what actually *is* going on out there, for the 'people' who torture, kill, and mutilate in this way are men, while their victims are predominantly females, women and girls, and to a lesser extent, young men."[20]

Caputi explains that, "as these hierarchical lines indicate, these are crimes of sexually political import, crimes rooted in a system of male supremacy in the same way that lynching is based in white supremacy.[21]

Ann Jones also objects to the gender-neutral term "domestic violence," arguing, "I suspect that some academic researcher coined the term, dismayed by the fact that all those beaten wives were *women*."[22] In the introduction to *Women Who Kill,* her "history of America's female murderers," Jones declares, "If this book leaves the impression that men have conspired to keep women down, that is exactly the impression I mean to convey . . ."[23]

According to Jones's history, "the same social and legal deprivations that compel some women to feminism push others to homicide . . . society is afraid of both the feminist and the murderer, for each of them, in her own way, tests society's established boundaries. Not surprisingly, the interests of feminists and murderers sometimes coincide . . ."[24]

Wow! They do, do they?

Put that together with her earlier quote about female criminality and free people not being dangerous.* How could one be but absolved of any culpability when killing for as noble a cause as freedom? What's the word; *femfascism*? Or put simply, as Ann Jones declares, "The story of women who kill is the story of women."[25]

Second-wave feminists view sexual violence against women as a political manifestation of the "patriarchy" and serial killers as its instruments. As one feminist theorist insists, female serial killers simply do not exist while the male serial killer is a martyr for the patriarchal state.

Just as the icon of the derogated eagle on the seal of the United State bespeaks this nation's rape of the wilderness, so too does the endemic spread-eagling of women in patriarchal culture—in sexual murder, pornography, gynecology, and obligatory "missionary position" intercourse—point to the persistent and systematic punishment of women.[26]

---

* "A wave of attention to women's criminality follows thunderously on every wave of feminism and surely will continue to do so until we can grasp the truth that free people are not dangerous."

Politicized terms are substituted for "serial homicide" and imply that the offender was exclusively male and the victim female: "gynocide,"[27] "phallic terrorism,"[28] and "femicide."[29]

But then in 1990 along came Aileen Wuornos with her year-long serial spree of roadside murders of seven middle-aged and elderly men including a missionary evangelist, a child abuse investigator, a man on his way to his daughter's graduation, and a police reservist. Now feminism needed to take a stand here. It did—it stood firmly behind Aileen Wuornos's war of liberation.

One feminist theorist on lesbian violence, whose book is dedicated, "For Aileen Wuornos and for all the women who have been vilified, pathologized, and murdered for defending themselves by whatever means necessary," declared, "Aileen Wuornos's story is quite banal, an all-too-ordinary repetition in a culture of paranoid male fantasies that eroticize their worst nightmares. This time, however, one might say that the fantasy has crossed a certain boundary. The hallucination has been realized."[30]

If serial killers are martyrs for the "patriarchal state" then Aileen Wuornos is a martyr for second-wave feminism. Wuornos's defense for her murder and robbery of seven victims was that each had attempted to rape her. As she stated in her trial, "Everybody has the right to defend themselves. That's what I did. These were very violent, violent rapes, and the other ones I had to beg for my life."

In a television interview with *Dateline*, Wuornos vehemently spat out, "Here's a message for the families: You owe me. Your husband raped me violently, Mallory and Carskaddon. And the other five tried, and I went through a heck of a fight to win. You owe me, not me owe you."

Feminist analysis (and they were not the only ones guilty of it) sometimes misrepresented the scope of serial murder by citing unreliable and inflated victim statistics. Some claimed that there were nearly 5,000 serial murders a year in which most victims were women.[31] That is a ridiculous number, but one that even today is still occasionally cited, and not only by feminists.[32] The *maximum total* of *all* known serial killer victims in a *195-year* period in the U.S. between 1800 and 1995 come to a total of 3,860.[33] We have a long way to go to 5,000 *a year*! Other feminist scholars simply go silent when faced with explaining patently calculated, cynical, and savage murders of innocent men, women, and children by female killers.

None of this, I want to say, is to suggest that the extraordinarily high frequency of murder of women by their intimate male partners is a feminist myth. In the recent period between 1976 and 2004 in the U.S., a total of 30.1 percent of all females murdered were killed by their intimate partners, current or former, compared to 5.3 percent of all male murder victims.[34] The problem is not how feminists portray the male murderer and his victims, but their analysis of the female killer and *her* victims. We were counting on the feminists to explain it to us, for in all those women's studies departments at college they must have thought about it more than the rest of us. No? Apparently not, for they appear to be failing us badly. One would have expected something better than, "The story of women who kill is the story of women."

This cult of the female killer as victim is not without its critics among the current rising new generation of feminists (*postfeminists,* a term recently floated)—the 9/11 postmillennium wave. Some of these wild new voices suggest that when female killers are invariably construed in media, in law, or in feminist discourse as victims, women are actually being denied their freedom to be human. Belinda Morrissey argues:

> If a woman kills her male partner, for example, and can demonstrate his extreme abuse of her, then she might win the right not to be viewed as an active participant in defense of herself, but as her partner's victim. This means that her partner must take responsibility for her acts of violence as well as his own; in other words, he is considered culpable for his own murder . . . Having at last taken some action to defend herself against her attacker and having succeeded in overcoming him, the battered woman is immediately cast as not having acted at all. She effectively loses the very agency and self-determination she tried so hard to gain.[35]

Perhaps this will yet represent a frightening future wave of feminism that will insist, as Morrissey's publisher describes her book's argument, "that by denying the possibility of female agency in crimes of torture, rape, and murder, feminist theorists are, with the best of intentions, actually denying women the full freedom to be human."

Please, a little less freedom and humanity for all of us then!

Generally second-wave feminism tends to either ignore or bluntly reclassify female killers who do not easily fit the profile of a victim. The possibility that Aileen Wuornos is a serial killer, for example, is dismissed out-of-hand by one of her political defenders, who asserts, "The State says she is a serial killer. This charge seems implausible, given that the definition of a serial killer is one who kills for sexual arousal within a specific power imbalance."[36]

Feminist critic Lynda Hart reminds us that Wuornos is on death row "for killing seven middle-aged white men," as if *that* explains everything. According to Hart:

> Wuornos is the masculine imaginary's "dream come true," her actions constituting a transgression of the boundary between the real and the phantasmatic [sic]. Having torn this barrier that preserves the phallocratic symbolic, Wuornos has become the "impossible-real" realized. And for that, I argue, she has been sentenced to death.[37]

DEFINING THE FEMALE SERIAL KILLER

There is absolutely no agreed-upon single definition of a serial killer. Male or female. There are as many definitions as there are experts in the subject, and the definitions include so far:

- Someone who murders at least three persons in more than a thirty-day period.[38]

- At least two fantasy-driven compulsive murders committed at different times and at different locations where there is no relationship between the perpetrator and victim and no material gain, with victims having characteristics in common.[39]

- Two or more separate murders when an individual, acting alone or with another, commits multiple homicides over a period of time, with time breaks between each murder event.[40]

- Premeditated murder of three or more victims committed over time, in separate incidents, in a civilian context, with the murder activity being chosen by the offender.[41]

- [Someone who] over time commits at least ten homicides. The homicides are violent, they are brutal, but they are also ritualistic—they take on their own meaning for the serial murderer.[42]

- Those who murder two or more victims, with an emotional cooling-off period between the homicides.[43]

The notion that male serial killers kill only for sexual purposes and that they kill only strangers is long outdated. Serial killers will also kill for power, profit, belief, and politics and some will kill friends, neighbors, and family members. And female serial killers can kill for the same reasons as males do.

The murder of two or more people on separate occasions *for any reason* is serial homicide and defines a serial killer. This represents the consensus of the most current analysis of serial murder: that it is not *exclusively* sexual and necessarily fantasy-driven nor does it only target strangers. It includes organized-crime contract killers— who for the longest time were excluded from the definition of serial killer because they did not choose their own victims—and genocidal murderers, because it was thought they were driven only by ideology or military discipline. But in the final analysis, the psychopathology of both the contract killer and war criminal is similar to that of some "ordinary" serial killers among us.

Most of the women whose histories this book explores are serial killers by the most recent and simple definition: two victims or more on distinctly separate occasions with "cooling off" periods in between. These are killers who thought about it before they chose to kill again and again.

CLASSIFYING THE FEMALE SERIAL KILLER: THE FBI'S CLASSIC *ORGANIZED/DISORGANIZED*

The classification of serial killers is developing into a highly evolved system today. Female serial killers can frequently fit into the same male serial killer profile system. On the most basic level, serial killers are categorized as *organized, disorganized,* or *mixed.* This is a system that the FBI Behavioral Sciences Unit developed primarily as an investigative tool based on the assessment of a crime scene that the serial killer leaves behind.

Organized killers tend to carefully pick and stalk their victims. They plan the murder, they bring a weapon and restraints to the scene, they often take the victim away to another location, and they carefully dispose of the victim's body and evidence. *Disorganized* serial killers on the other hand, often act spontaneously, *blitz* attacking the victim and leaving behind a disorderly crime scene. They frequently use improvised weapons they find at the location. They often leave the victim unconcealed and leave copious amounts of forensic evidence behind. Clinical mental illness is sometimes diagnosed in the *disorganized* offender's psychopathology.

Each of these two categories of serial killer is associated with certain personality and character traits—*organized* killers might be more intelligent, keep a neat house, and be personable. They will use personal charm to trap victims. They will drive clean and well-maintained automobiles, own property, and be gainfully employed. *Disorganized* killers are less intelligent, less sociable, and sloppy. They will use force to overcome a victim. They drive junk cars and live in messy, filthy apartments and have sporadic educational and employment histories.

Since women serial killers more frequently kill acquaintances or intimates, they are most likely to fit the socialized *organized* profile—those who kill by cunning rather than brute force—but there are some differences, which we will see.

The FBI has a third *mixed* category of those serial killers who do not neatly fit into one of the other two categories—who show characteristics associated with both categories. Some critics describe this category as meaningless and cite it as evidence of the weakness in the FBI's *organized/disorganized* profile system.

Using this system, virtually all female serial killers can be classified in the *mixed* category. As *organized* killers, females carefully plan and choose the moment they will kill their victim, they prepare the weapon in advance, usually poison, and they conceal evidence. Yet at the same time many know their victim and leave the body at the crime scene, a characteristic of a *disorganized* serial killer. Only on rare occasions does the female serial killer move and conceal the body. Unfortunately, the FBI's *mixed* category is the least satisfying in making sense of a serial killer's nature.

NEWER CLASSIFICATION SYSTEMS FOR FEMALE SERIAL KILLERS

Criminologists, less focused on investigative issues, tend to categorize serial killers by motive once it has been established. In this approach, the notion of gratification as motive is grounded in the entire spectrum of serial killer classification. There has been a debate in criminology as to whether serial killings are exclusively sexually motivated. This debate is particularly applicable to female serial killers as they rarely commit crimes characterized by gratuitous mutilation or by the sadistic sexual acts of male serial killers. Within the spectrum of serial killer classification, motive is an issue: Is a mob "contract hit man" a serial killer? Is the genocidal executioner or the terrorist a species of serial killer? According to criminologists Ronald and Stephen Holmes, they *all* are indeed serial killers. The Holmes classification of serial killers is strictly based on the gratification motive—what reward or profit, material or emotional, are the serial killers seeking when they murder?[44]

Serial killers can be classified this way into four principal categories, and three subcategories:

- *Power-control*
- *Visionary*
- *Missionary*
- *Hedonist*
  - *hedonist-lust*
  - *hedonist-comfort*
  - *hedonist-thrill*

In only one of these categories is sex the primary motive for serial murder: for *power-control killers* who derive sexual gratification from the power and control they exert over a victim and who commit purely sexually charged homicides.

Sex is less of a motive but still an important motive in one of the three subcategories of *hedonist* killer—*the hedonist-lust* murderer.

In those cases, the killer finds sexual gratification in mutilating or having sex with corpses, drinking their blood, or cannibalizing them. The killing itself is not the source of gratification, but merely the means to an end. These types of killers do not necessarily desire to kill their victim—they just want the victim's body or to harvest some part of it. Edmund Kemper, who murdered, mutilated, and had sex with the dismembered body parts of eight female victims, including his mother, was typically a hedonist-lust killer. As he explained it, "I'm sorry to sound so cold about this but what I needed to have was a particular experience with a person, and to possess them in the way I wanted to: I had to evict them from their human bodies." Kemper described his murders as "making dolls" out of human beings.[45]

There has been no recorded case of a female hedonist-lust serial killer, with two exceptions: that of the Renaissance-era Transylvanian Countess Elizabeth Báthory (1560–1615) who, it was claimed, bathed in women's blood. The other exception might be a case in Texas in the mid-1980s. Ricky Green, a serial killer of two women and two men, claimed that his wife, Sharon, a preacher's daughter, participated in the rape, stabbing, and bludgeoning with a hammer of the two female victims and that the murders were followed by the couple sensuously smearing and lubricating each other with the victims' warm blood and having sex. Sharon Green pled guilty to murder but claimed she was forced to participate in the rape-murders as a "battered spouse." Ricky was sentenced to death; Sharon received a ten-year probation term and a guest appearance on *The Oprah Winfrey Show* televised on November 12, 1991.[46]

In the case of the Transylvanian Countess Elizabeth Báthory, the motive for her bathing in blood is ambiguous as well, as we shall see further on. She is said to have believed it restored the youthfulness of her skin, rather than deriving any particular sexual pleasure from it.

Thus, when feminist analysts insisted that there were no female serial killers, what they really meant was that there were no female power-control or hedonist-lust type female serial killers. We shall see, however, that much has changed since the 1980s and 1990s when they were making those assertions.

Beyond the two categories of power-control and hedonist-lust killers, there remain several categories and subcategories of serial killers whose motives for killing are not driven by sexual impulses. (Although that does not mean that sexual acts are necessarily absent in the homicides they commit.)

Visionary killers are driven by visions or voices to kill. For the most part they are clinically and legally insane, suffering with organic brain disorders and hallucinations and are usually a highly disorganized type of offender. They are rare and are often quickly apprehended.

Missionary killers have political, moral, ethical, or some other notional motives that drive them to kill. These killers target a particular type of victim who they believe should be destroyed, eliminated from society or punished: homeless people, abortion doctors, senior citizens, homosexuals, or members of a particular race.

Hedonist-thrill killers derive gratification from the transgression inherent in the act of kidnapping, torturing, and killing a victim. Rape is frequently a characteristic of these killings but it is an expression of aggression rather than the sexual drive.

Hedonist-comfort killers murder simply to profit materially from the victim's death. The hedonist-comfort killer is, of course, the category with which we have most frequently in the past associated female serial killers. The stereotypical female serial killer remains one that uses her feminine charm to get close to her male victim, gain control of his property, and then murder him, moving on to the next victim—the Black Widow.

The most recently proposed new classification system comes from Richard Walter, a Michigan State Prison psychologist, and criminologist Dr. Robert Keppel, a veteran of fifty serial murder investigations, including that of Ted Bundy, the Atlanta Child Murders, and the Green River Killings. Their system is focused more on classifying sexual murderers, both single and serial, and is inspired by the FBI's classification of rapists developed in the 1980s by Roy Hazelwood and Dr. Ann Burgess.[47] For investigative purposes, Keppel and Walter propose the following classification of sexual serial killers divided into four categories:

- *Power-assertive*, whose motive is the assertion of a masculine power over a female or male victim

- *Power-reassurance*, who seeks from the victim reassurance that they are "pleasing" them or are "better" than other lovers

- *Anger-retaliatory*, who have a need to avenge, get even with or retaliate against a female, or her substitute, who somehow offended the killer in his perception

- *Anger-excitation*, whose primary motive is to inflict pain and terror on the male or female victim for the sexual gratification of the perpetrator

All these various described profiles, however, are focused on and defined by male psychopathology. There is a range of newer categories, which seek to more specifically address female serial killers:

- *Black Widows*, who traditionally murder their husbands, lovers, or other kin for either financial profit or other motives

- *Angels of death*, who kill patients they nurse or children they babysit for various motives—sometimes profit but most often unexplained

- *Cult disciples*, who are led to kill by a charismatic leader—the Manson Family women are the most high-profile example of this category of female killer

- *Accommodating partners*, who resign themselves to participate in murders initiated by their husbands or lovers

- *Depraved sadistic partners*, who enthusiastically participate in rapes and murders committed by their partner

- *Explosive avengers*, who are driven to murder a particular type of victim reminding them of past abusers in their life—Aileen Wuornos is most likely a candidate for this category

- *Profit-predators*, who kill strangers for material gain—Aileen Wuornos can easily fit into this category as well

- *Missionaries*, who have a political or social agenda that they attempt to achieve or conform with through serial targeting of a particular type of victim—Nazi nurses, for example, who participated in the medical killing of handicapped children and adults

- *Power-seekers*, in which the female offender attempts to attain some form of control or power in politics or in her personal life

- *Munchausen syndrome by proxy* killers—an elusive category in which mothers and caregivers serially murder their children or nurses kill patients in order to focus sympathy and attention on themselves[48]

Another method of classifying female serial killers could be by their personality type. One study identified six behavioral personality types of women who were sentenced for both serial and singular homicide in California:

- *Masochistic* female offenders, who generally appear to be stable, have a good reputation, and might be strictly religious but who tend to become intimately involved with abusive and violent partners whom they end up killing

- *Overtly hostile violent* females are emotionally unstable, impulsive, and violent. They frequently have a history of assaults and while they do not plan to murder, their violent outbursts can result in death unintentionally

- *Covertly hostile* female killers suppress rage and express it secretly, often by targeting their own children or other vulnerable victims in a killing range

- *Inadequate* female killers have few coping skills, limited intelligence, and low self-esteem. Their primary concern is pleasing their partners, which they sometimes do by participating in murders or sexual assaults led by their partner

- *Psychotic* offenders are clinically insane. Similar to *visionary* serial killers, they are driven by voices or hallucinations to kill

- *Amoral* offenders commit premeditated murders with no remorse for personal or material gain. They could be described as *psychopaths* or *sociopaths*—a personality disorder rather than a mental illness. They are aware of the acts they commit but do not care. Most serial killers, female or male, can be diagnosed as *sociopaths*, or as suffering from *Antisocial Personality Disorder (ASPD)*[49]

Yet another study focuses on the victim/offender relationship to categorize female killers as:

- *Alpha* females, who use violence to protect themselves or others from harm. These are cases of self-defense against the victim who is an abuser

- *Beta* females, who are provoked to kill by emotions such as jealousy and hatred or who provoke to some degree their own victimization, resulting in an impulsive murder

- *Omega* females, who use sexuality to deceive their victims and are emotionally detached from them, killing their victims coldly and frequently for personal material gain[50]

All these different categories can exclude each other or overlap. There is no single definition of a serial killer, nor is there a single universal system of categorizing serial killers, male or female. One thing, however, is clearly evident: the wide range of definitions and categories reflects a phenomenon of female serial killers far more extensive and diverse than we customarily thought existed.

GENERAL CHARACTERISTICS OF FEMALE SERIAL KILLERS

Some general observations can be made about the sum total of female serial killers. Statistically speaking, female serial killers are better at it than their male counterparts. While the average male serial killer kills for a period of about four years before being apprehended, the female serial killer kills twice as long before she is stopped: slightly over eight years.[51] Some female serial killers have been known to kill for over thirty years.

This is partly the result of our common reluctance to recognize a female as capable of sustained long-term violence and the fact that females often murder in their home or in hospitals where a death might not be recognized as unnatural and the female's presence at the scene professionally related. Female serial killers rarely leave community-alarming bodies of young women or teenagers by the roadside. Described thus as "quiet killers," their crimes can continue for years before they are even known to have occurred.

Another aspect of female serial killer longevity might be more gender based. Male serial killers, particularly sexually driven ones, appear to burn out and slow down once they are over forty years old.

With female serial killers, however, it is not unusual to find cases of women in their fifties and sixties still active and not even near peaking in their killing careers. Dorothea Puente was 60 years old at the height of her killing when she was charged in 1988 with murdering nine male and female victims. Puente is still going strong in prison: a collection of her recipes has been recently published.

Nancy "Nannie" Doss was 50 years old when she was arrested for poisoning her husband in 1954. In their investigation, police uncovered a twenty-eight-year-long career in which the grandmotherly serial killer apparently murdered four husbands in four different states, her mother, two of her four daughters, a mother-in-law, and other family members, by poisoning them with prunes soaked in rat arsenic.

At this writing, 73-year-old Olga Rutterschmidt and her 75-year-old friend Helen Golay face two counts of murder and two counts of conspiracy to commit murder for financial gain in the deaths of Paul Vados, 73, in November 1999, and Kenneth McDavid, 51, in June 2005. The women, who met decades ago in a health club, are accused of masterminding a $2.3 million insurance-fraud murder scheme in which homeless men were killed by being run over in staged hit-and-run incidents.[52] *Arsenic and Old Lace* is less a cliché than we think.

Approximately 68 percent of female serial killers operate alone, while the other 32 percent kill mostly with a dominant male partner, although there are cases of females dominating their male partners and all-female killing teams. It is in the female-male serial killer partnership that women are found most frequently complicit in rapes and sexual homicides, which are commonly associated only with male serial killers. Female serial killer partners are a whole category unique unto themselves and this book will explore this complex phenomenon in a separate chapter.

In terms of victim selection, we expect that female serial killers predominately kill family members and acquaintances. This has been true until recently, but today strangers are marginally the preferred victim of the female serial killer, followed by family or intimate victims.[53] The problem in clearly defining an offender-victim relationship rate is that, like male serial killers, many females kill a mix of strangers / family or acquaintances / strangers, etc.

* * *

This book explores the different histories of a wide range of categories of female killers who murdered at least twice on separate occasions for a variety of motives. They are indeed all serial killers, for each have contemplated and chosen to kill again having already murdered once.

The motives and psychology of the killers will both vary and yet have common features among the various categories, and we will explore the various psychopathologies attributed to the offenders and their childhood histories when available. Like male serial killers, female killers are most likely both born and made, although the possible genetic and physiological markers in female offenders have not been as extensively studied as those in male serial killers.

The cult and culture of femininity has been central to this analysis in a way it is not for male serial killers. Female serial killers not only challenge our ordinary standards of good and evil but also defy our basic accepted perception of gender role and identity and, ultimately, our overall understanding of humanity. There are no politics invested in the understanding of male serial killers in the way there are in the analysis of female killers. While male serial killers appear to confirm the worst in masculinity, the question is not as clear for women. Do female serial killers defy the feminine or only confirm the worst of it? Is aggression intrinsic to femininity and how? The question of female serial killers should not be approached in a political or gender context alone, but in its entire human scope.

PART ONE

The Psychopathology and Brief History
of the Female Serial Killer

AGRIPPINA THE YOUNGER **VALERIA MESSALINA** ELIZABETH
BÁTHORY **LA TOFANIA** MARIE DE BRINVILLIERS **JANE SCOTT**
ELIZABETH ECCLES **SARAH DAZELY** ELIZA JOYCE **SARAH**
FREEMAN MARY ANN MILNER **SARAH CHESHAM** MARY MAY **MARY**
EMILY CAGE CATHERINE WILSON **MARY ANN COTTON** CATHERINE
FLANNAGAN **MARGARET HIGGINS** KATE BENDER **PATTY CANNON**
LYDIA SHERMAN **SARAH JANE ROBINSON** JANE TOPPAN

1

THE NATURE OF THE FEMININE BEAST

The Psychopathology of Female Monsters

How and why? How do females become serial killers and why do they kill? The why is easy: They can kill for the same reasons that male serial killers do: for power, for control, for sexual lust, for profit, for thrills, for self-esteem, for revenge and madness.

But there are some notable differences. Male serial killers frequently commit kidnapping, confinement, rape, and mutilation to express their rage and desire for control; female serial killers usually throw themselves straight into the kill—no stopping for mutilation or for a bite along the way. No polaroids or masturbation at the scene or sex with the corpse.* The female serial killer is all business . . . and it's murder. In that sense she is infinitely deadlier than the fantasy-driven male predators.

HOW FEMALE SERIAL KILLERS ARE DEADLIER THAN MALES

Male serial killers can sometimes actually overlook killing some of their victims, because murder is not always a central part of their fantasy. Their fantasy could be to dominate their victim through physical and sexual assault without murder necessarily being a part of it. Once their assault is exhausted for the time being, the victim is of no further interest to the offender—dead or alive. If the victim survived the physical assault, the offender might kill to

---

* In an FBI study of male sexual killers, rape had occurred in 42 percent *after* the death of the victim and in 56 percent before. (In the other 2 percent there was no rape despite the sexual nature of the murder.)

avoid having a witness to the assault or rape. The offender may kill the victim out of shame. Or not kill at all. A few might even trip-out on the power of granting mercy.

Richard Cottingham in the late 1970s, for example, left the hor-ribly mutilated and dismembered corpses of street prostitutes in ho-tel and motel rooms after drugging and torturing them for hours; he chopped the heads and hands off some of his victims.[54] How can anyone survive a homicidal maniac like that? But some women did, regaining consciousness by a roadside or on motel room floors, bruised and battered but alive. Why? He did not kill them because they did not die in his attack. Simple as that. He never set out to kill them—only to torture and humiliate them. But once he was done, they did not matter—dead or alive, they were just garbage to him. So he dumped them—some dead, some living. Some died in the pro-cess; they weren't strong enough to take it—skinny street girls all jacked up on nothing but Coke and chips. Those that he mutilated, he did so not for pleasure, but to destroy their identities—severing their heads and hands not as souvenirs, but to impede the investiga-tion. Of the ones he *chose* to kill he did so to coldly eliminate wit-nesses. It was a necessary task and not a pleasure for him.

Occasionally some victims survive the male serialist's post-cathartic flagging interest or vague and sudden remorse. Some-times it could be what the victim says or does that deflects an attacker's intent to kill. When I wrote about male serial killers, I concluded with a chapter on how to improve the chances of surviv-ing a serial killer based on accounts from surviving victims and on explanations offered by killers themselves as to why they let some of their victims live. There will be no such concluding chapter for female serial killers.

Other than those victims who survived by some twist of angel-borne luck, there are almost no accounts from survivors of female serial killers. Women killers do not change their minds once they make the decision to murder and they rarely go through any kind of fantasy torture ritual on the way there—they go straight for the kill. (Although female serial poisoners have been known to prolong the deaths of some of their victims by manipulating dosages of poison, the reasons why have never been conclusively determined.)

Female serial killers rarely, unless accompanied by a male

partner, kidnap and rape their victims. Female serial killers rarely if ever kill to harvest the corpse or some body part of their victim for their own hedonistic lust. They almost never capture, bind, confine, and torture their victims before killing them. The female serial killer's gratification *begins* with the victim's death and often continues for days, weeks, and months afterwards. While for many serial killers death is only a conclusion to their fantasy or a function of it, females kill to kill. It is their mode of expression.

One frequent reason given by male serial killers as to why they did not kill a particular victim is because they learned something about them. This triggers a personalization of the victim in the offender's perception and misdirects their killing desire. This phenomenon reflects the proclivity of male serial killers to target strangers whom they objectify, imposing their own lethal fantasy upon them. Yet if they come to somehow see the victim for who they really are, the fantasy can be interrupted.

According to FBI behaviorists, the best way of surviving a serial killer's attack is to attempt to talk to them and let them get to know you as a person, to deflate the serial killer's fantasy construct of you as their victim.

None of this is going to help the victim of a typical female serial killer. First, it is probable that the female killer is already intimately familiar with her victim: She is working, living, or sleeping with them. She already knows who they really are—there is no victim fantasy.

Second, the victims are unlikely to realize that they are in danger as the female often uses the cover of the established killer-victim relationship within which to kill—nurses kill patients, mothers kill their children, wives kill their husbands, landladies kill their tenants. Thus the attack occurs in accepted social and professional relationships while the means is often surreptitious like poison or a drug overdose or sudden suffocation. The murder is invisible and the body is usually found where it belongs, not dumped by a roadside or in a shallow grave.

Finally, as the female serial killer does not bother with torture or rituals but goes straight to the kill, there is rarely time for the unsuspecting victims to respond if they even realize they are in danger.

Who expects a wife, lover, mother, or daughter might try to kill them? This is what made Aileen Wuornos so different: She was targeting strangers, killing them almost as soon as she met them.

With some female serial killers you might not find out you are being murdered, until you are dead. You just get a little too sick and weak for your age and the next evening suddenly you can't speak or move and when the night comes you die in the dark in your own snot behind a closed door with nothing but the sound of your own congested whimpering to comfort you. It all appears to be of natural causes—nobody will even suspect you were murdered. Two phone calls and three hours later a night shift will lift and wheel your pronounced body away and by morning you will be prepped for embalming. There can be no lonelier way to die than that.

MURDER AS THE FEMALE SIGNATURE

The "signature" is the opposite of the MO—the modus operandi, or method used in committing the crime. Profilers carefully differentiate crime scene characteristics between signature and MO.

The MO is what the serial killer *needs to do* to accomplish the crime—pose as a repairperson, force a window open, offer a hitchhiker a ride, use a weapon to gain control, wear a mask, wash evidence away, perhaps dismember a corpse for ease of disposal, set a fire to destroy evidence. The MO usually changes—it improves as time passes because serial murder is very much a learning process. Over time, serial killers need to improve their tactics because as they repeatedly murder they increasingly raise their risk of apprehension. At the same time, they are also driven by an addiction to narrow the margin between their fantasy and reality—between the intense pleasure of the fantasy and the dissatisfaction they feel with its reality. They can never satisfactorily bridge their act with their desire. They need to try it again, but better. For all these reasons, serial killers are fantasy-driven killing machines fueled on both need and desire—pragmatism and madness.

Serial killing requires a certain kind of studious discipline. And some can show it out of the gate, but four years is usually as far as the males get. Four years can often be equally the odds for successfully sustaining a marriage, business, or partnership—undertakings at least as challenging as serial murder. So the MO needs to change and evolve from murder to murder, increasing the odds of surviving those four years.

Signature is the opposite of the MO in that it is what the offender does *not need to do* to complete the murder. For example, to bind a victim who is not resisting, to torture a victim who is cooperating, to pose the body in some particular way, to dismember the corpse for purposes other than ease of disposal, to take a trophy or souvenir, deliberately leave behind some kind of message or clue. While the MO defines *how* the murder was done, the signature is often the key to *why* and it rarely changes through the years.

The female serial killer, on the other hand, usually leaves the same simple signature—the actual murder. Sometimes the murder itself is misinterpreted as part of the female serial killer's MO leading to categorizations such as Black Widow or Angel of Death. The murder is seen as a *method* to attain other goals—profit usually the most often cited motive. On closer examination, though, murder is often entirely unnecessary for the attainment of the goals. There are easier and safer ways to steal than murdering someone. Why kill then?

That is not a helpful question to ask. Because when we say "easier to steal" without killing we put a different value on human life. For a female serialist a human life is as valuable as a used tissue. It actually *is* easier for them. The hedonistic comfort of material gain outweighs the price of human life.

But many kill because *that* is what they want to do the most.

It's about the pleasure of the kill—the sense of power she gets—the buzz. Taking property is just a warm snack in the feast of control—a little further satisfaction, a tingling in the killer's tummy.

That's how murder happens for cigarettes or pennies.

Many Black Widows actually kill for motives far more complex than simple material profit—rage and need for control often supercede the desire for material gain.

However, none of this is particularly helpful for profiling female serial killers by crime scene analysis because often there is no crime scene to analyze. There is no scene because nobody knows a crime has occured. The female killer rarely surfaces as an "unsub"—an "unknown subject" in FBI profiler parlance—because she is so often already known and somehow related to the victim. That is, if someone realizes that there *is* a victim—because for a long time there's a good chance that nobody will.

SURVEYING SERIAL KILLERS MALE AND FEMALE

Between 1979 and 1983, FBI agents from the Behavioral Science Unit (BSU) conducted intimate and detailed interviews in prisons with thirty-six convicted male sex murderers, of whom twenty-nine were serial killers.[55] They were exhaustively questioned, from their earliest childhood recollections to the most horrifying details of their crimes and motives.

The families, friends, and acquaintances of the killers were also extensively interviewed, as were their surviving victims. The BSU also made a detailed study of the 118 victims who didn't survive: their occupations, their lifestyles, vital statistics, where they encountered their killers, their autopsies, and the conditions in which their bodies were found.

No equivalent study of this type currently exists for female serial killers. The closest thing to it is a similar study attempted by Dr. Deborah Schurman-Kauflin, who approached 26 incarcerated female multiple murderers and secured the cooperation of seven.[56] Not all of the seven were serial killers—at least one, and maybe more, was a mass killer, torturing and murdering five victims on a single night. One major difference between male and female serial killers that can be noted immediately is that females tend not to favor discussing their crimes and lives with researchers, while male serial killers are quite chatty and eager to talk.

The seven offenders in the Schurman-Kauflin survey killed a total of 36 victims—an average of 5.14 victims per killer; a much higher figure than the 3.8 victims on average of the 29 serial murderers in the FBI study. (Assuming that the other 7 offenders in the FBI study killed one victim each.)

A study by Eric Hickey at California State University, Fresno, is probably the most comprehensive statistical study on the subject, analyzing the data on serial killers in the U.S. between 1800–1995. Hickey identified 337 male serial killers with an accumulated range of victims estimated between 2,613 and 3,807: an average of between 7.8 and 11.3 victims per male killer in the low and high estimates.[57] The same study found 62 female serialists attributed with a range of total victims between 417 and 584, with an average of 6.7 and 9.4 victims each.[58] The high-end estimate of average victims for female serial killers exceeds the low-end estimate for males.

But just to illustrate how little we know precisely about female serial killers, another data study of 14 female serial killers identified 62 potential victims: an average of 4.4 per offender.[59] (But the women were actually *convicted of* killing 27 victims. Frequently in serial murder prosecutions, particularly those committed in several jurisdictions, the serial offender is not tried for all the murders they are known to have committed. This further confounds statistical analysis.)

AVERAGE AGE

The average age of the male serial killer when he first murders is 27.5 years.[60] This is consistent with the onset of acute psychopathy in adolescence and its relationship to the offender's isolation and evolution of aggressive sexual fantasies during their adolescence, teens, and early twenties.

In their study of female serialists, B. T. Keeney and K. Heide found that the average killing starting age for women was 32.9 years, with the youngest offender 19 and the oldest 53.[61] Schurman-Kauflin determined a similar average age of 32.5 with an age range of offenders from 17 to 58 years old.[62] Thus females are likely to start killing at a later age and continue killing beyond middle age, with some females killing when they are in their sixties and even seventies. Male serial killers rarely kill once they are over forty, which has been linked to the apparent diminishment of the effects of psychopathy in middle age. It appears that while middle age renders the male killer docile, menopause galvanizes the female into murderous action.

* * *

But just when we think we have the female serial killers pegged in age, along comes an anomaly like eleven-year-old Mary Bell in

England. In May of 1968, little Mary strangled a four-year-old boy after luring him into an abandoned building. The boy's body was discovered the same day but police concluded that his death was accidental. The next day, Mary attempted to strangle an eleven-year-old girl, but was interrupted by the girl's father who ejected her out of the house. It never dawned on the father that Mary was seriously attempting to murder his daughter. Nobody suspected the little girl.

Mary knocked on the door of the house where the little dead boy once lived and asked to see him. When the parents told Mary that the boy was dead, she replied, "Oh, I know he's dead, I wanted to see him in his coffin."

Nine weeks later, accompanied by another girl, Mary strangled a three-year-old boy, stabbed him in the stomach with a pair of broken scissors, and after failing in her attempt to castrate him with them, carved her initial "M" into his abdomen. His body was found between some concrete blocks on a piece of wasteland. When Mary began accusing other children of having committed the murder, suspicion fell on her. After being awakened in the night and taken away for questioning by police, the eleven-year-old boldly refused to answer questions and demanded that the astonished detectives call a lawyer for her before she would say anything further.

Mary Bell was convicted of manslaughter with "diminished responsibility" by the English jury that heard her case. She was sentenced in 1969 to detention for an indeterminate period of time in psychiatric facilities.

Mary Bell's mother had a psychiatric record and was seventeen when she gave birth to Mary. A prostitute, she often abandoned Mary with relatives and once attempted to give her up for adoption. In 1998, in interviews with author Gitta Sereny, the now adult Mary Bell claimed that she was forced by her mother to have oral sex with her clients when she was a child.

Mary was described as highly intelligent and manipulative. She told a policewoman guarding her that she wanted to be a nurse so that she could stick needles into people. "I like hurting people." During her trial, Mary said, "If I was a judge and I had an eleven-year-old who'd done this, I'd give her eighteen months. Murder isn't that bad. We all die sometime anyway."[63]

Mary Bell was released at the age of twenty-three in 1980 and had a daughter in 1984, whom she fought authorities to keep, and apparently raised as a loving mother. She lives today in anonymity enforced by a British high court order in 2003, prohibiting the press from disclosing her or her daughter's current location and identities. She remains the youngest known serial killer in history.

VICTIM SELECTION

Victim selection is different for male and female serial killers. Historically, at least 70 percent of male serial killers murder strangers only, while another 16 percent kill a combination of strangers with acquaintances or family. Some 8 percent of males murder acquaintances only and 3 percent family only.[64]

This contrasts with the 34 percent of female serialists who kill family only and 19 percent who killed acquaintances only. At least one stranger was murdered by 32 percent of female serial killers and strangers only were targeted by 24 percent. At least one family member was killed by 50 percent of all female serial killers and at least one acquaintance by 35 percent.[65] This basically confirms that female serial killers tend to *historically* target victims with whom they are intimate or acquainted.

But the percentage of victims who are strangers to the female serial killer has been increasing since 1975 and strangers are now marginally *the most preferred category* for female serial killers: a total of 24 to 30 percent of victims are strangers compared to 22 and 25 percent of victims who are family followed by 11 and 15 percent who are acquaintances.[66]

In terms of victim-type selection, male serial killers prefer young, unaccompanied females as their first choice for victim in both stranger and acquaintance murders, followed by, in order of preference: male children, female children, travelers, and young unaccompanied males. For female serial killers, historically husbands and their children are first choice as victims, followed by friends, male suitors, in-laws, mothers, patients in hospitals or nursing homes, and tenants.

TABLE 1. Percentage of Offenders Killing *Only* One Type of Victim (1800–1995)

VICTIM	MALE SERIAL KILLERS	FEMALE SERIAL KILLERS
Children	4	19
Teens	6	0
Adults	43	32
Elderly	3	13
Female	40	10
Male	22	18
Both	37	66

TABLE 2. Percentage of Offenders Killing *At Least* One Type of Victim (1800–1995)

VICTIM	MALE SERIAL KILLERS	FEMALE SERIAL KILLERS
Children	21	39
Teens	45	8
Adults	82	60
Elderly	16	29
Female	78	53
Male	58	61

Essentially we see that male serial killers tend to victimize young adult women while females tend to kill both female and male adults, with a marginal preference for males and children. The female serial killer also frequently prefers elderly victims in contrast to the male killer.

MURDER SITE

While only 10 percent of male serial killers are "place specific"— killing between 16 and 19 percent of serial victims at one location to which they would lure the victims or find them there—32 percent of female serial killers are place specific: killing at their home or a health-care facility, for example. The victims went to female serialists either by being lured or by chance and accounted for 42 percent of all their victims. The average number of victims per place-specific female killer was the highest, between 9 and 13.[67]

Local female serial killers, who killed at different locations within the same city or state, accounted for a larger proportion of offenders, 45 percent, but for fewer victims—between 33 and 35 percent of victims. These killers also had a lower average of victims: 6 to 8 victims each. (Local male serial killers represented 55 percent accounting for 45 to 48 percent of victims.)

Migratory or traveling female serial killers represented a lesser total of 23 percent of offenders, killing between 23 and 24 percent of victims but with a higher average kill rate of 7 to 10 victims each. (Migratory males made up 35 percent of male serial killers and killed 36 to 37 percent of all victims.)

WEAPON OF CHOICE

As the most frequent source of prepared meals and drinks, the female serial killer's overwhelming choice of method of death is poison. At least 45 percent of females used poison sometimes, and 35 percent only poison. Some shooting was used by 20 percent of female serial killers; some bludgeoning by 16 percent; some suffocation by 16 percent; some stabbing by 11 percent; and some drowning by 5 percent. *Only* suffocation was used by 11 percent; *only* shooting by 8 percent; and *only* stabbing by 2 percent. Some combination of the above-described methods was used by 33 percent of female serial killers.

Most evident was the contrast between the male's use of force, weapons, ropes, chains, duct tape, and other forms of restraint to incapacitate and render victims helpless compared to the female's preference for victims who are already helpless or unsuspecting—children, the elderly or sick—or for the use of a surreptitious means of murder such as poison, drugs, or suffocation while the victim is asleep or unconscious.

FEMALE SERIAL KILLERS COMPARED TO SINGULAR
FEMALE MURDERERS

There are evident differences between female serial murderers and "ordinary" female singular killers who killed only once.

A study of all incarcerated female murderers found that on average 77 percent were unemployed when they committed their offense, 65 percent were African-American, and 76 percent had children. Their median age was 27.[68] The average female murderer is young, poor, and often kills in a socioeconomic environment where interpersonal violence is more frequent and part of the street culture of respect and intimidation.

The statistics for female serial killers are substantially different: 95 percent were white, their median age was 30, and only 8 percent were known to be unemployed while 10 percent were professionals, 5 percent were skilled workers, 15 percent were semiskilled, 10 percent unskilled, and 11 percent were other, such as self-employed or business proprietors (and 41 percent unknown).[69] Their higher socioeconomic class, where interpersonal violence is less the norm, suggests some kind of psychopathology behind their killing. These frequently middle-class female serial killers contemplated and planned their murders carefully, far from the pressures of the street.

The apparent motives of female serial killers are substantially different from those of the female singular killer. On average, 74 percent of female serial killers in this study appeared to be at least *in part* motivated by personal financial gain, both a sad reflection on the aspirations of the middle-class but also a behavioral artifact of those who desire to control their victim after death by seizing their property.[70]

COMPARING MALE WITH FEMALE SERIAL KILLERS AS CHILDREN

The FBI study found that male sexual and serial killers often came from unstable family backgrounds where infant bonding was likely to be disrupted. Only 57 percent of killers had both parents at birth and 47 percent had their father leave before the age of twelve. A mother as the dominant parent was reported in 66 percent of the cases and 44 percent reported having a negative relationship with their mother. A negative relationship with the father or male parental figure was reported by 72 percent of convicted male sex killers.

Of ten female serial killers for whom childhood data was available in the Keeney-Heide study, 40 percent were adopted by nonrelatives, 40 percent were raised in nontraditional homes composed of some relatives and nonrelatives, and only 20 percent were raised in traditional families by both biological parents until the age of 18.[71]

The history of the parents had also a great role to play in the child's future. A Washington School of Medicine study found that biological children of parents with criminal records are four times as likely to commit criminal acts themselves as adults—even if they have been adopted by law-abiding parents! The FBI study showed that 50 percent of the male offenders came from parents with criminal pasts and 53 percent from families with psychiatric histories.[72]

Schurman-Kauflin's study indicated 71 percent of her female multiple killers came from families with a history of drug and alcohol abuse. However, only 14 percent had parents with a criminal or psychiatric history—but that only represents one out of seven females in the study, so it is impossible to draw reliable percentile conclusions here.

CHILDHOOD TRAUMA

Many male serial killers had truly traumatic childhoods: 42 percent reported physical abuse, 74 percent psychological abuse, while 35 percent reported witnessing sexual violence as children, and 43 percent reported being sexually abused themselves. "Sexually stressful events" were reported by 73 percent of sex killers and 50 percent admitted that their first rape fantasies began between the age of twelve and fourteen.

A full 100 percent (7/7) of female multiple killers in the Keeney-Heide study reported physical, psychological, and sexual abuse in their childhood and 71 percent in their adolescence. Four women (57 percent) identified nonrelatives as their abusers while another two women (29 percent) identified relatives. The study found data for eight female serial killers, five of whom reported sexual abuse (63 percent), which in the case of four women occurred before the age of 18; four reported physical abuse (50 percent), and two reported witnessing sexual abuse or violence in their family (25 percent).

THE MACDONALD TRIAD: CRUELTY TO ANIMALS, ARSON, BED-WETTING

Cruelty to animals, fire setting, and bed-wetting are a behavioral set (called the Macdonald triad) that is most often identified with the childhood histories of serial killers. The appearance of all three behaviors in a child could signal a higher likelihood of a future violent adult. One of the most common childhood attributes of serial killers is the torture and killing of animals. The FBI study indicated that 36 percent of male subjects displayed cruelty to animals in their childhood and 46 percent by the time they were adolescents.

There appears to be no studies of childhood history of the triad per se in female serialists but the Schurman-Kauflin study reports acts of cruelty to animals in her female subjects. Two women reported hanging cats, one drowned them, two strangled them, and one reported eviscerating a cat with a knife. The remaining woman in the study reported killing her mother's small terrier with rocks.

THE NATURE OF AGGRESSION IN GIRLS

One of the reasons that we might not see the manifestation of the classic behavioral triad in women as children and adolescents is that female aggression takes a different form in young girls and continues to do so into adulthood as well. Females often commit aggression through others—by manipulating others to commit a violent act or manipulating the circumstances around an intended victim leading to their exposure to harm.

Newly emerging studies of female violence in various societies, both primitive and modern, reveal that preschool-age girls are as violent as their brothers. They are equally prepared to push and punch and use physical force to achieve their goals. But when they reach the age of ten or eleven it appears that females become less physically aggressive.

This does not mean that females are no longer aggressive at that age, but that their aggression begins to take a different form than it does in males. In the male a public display of aggressive prowess is encouraged, while the female begins to use her newly acquired linguistic and social skills to practice aggression surreptitiously. Females begin to use indirect or "masked" aggression, manipulating others to attack or somehow using the social structure to harm their intended victim.[73] The use of gossiping, exchanging derogatory notes, and excluding a victim from groups, the forming of hate clubs and recently hate websites are common media for adolescent female aggression and sometimes these forms can lead to serious physical repercussions.

Anthropologist Ilsa Glazer observed that in both Zambia and Israel, female leaders tended to scapegoat and gossip about other ambitious subordinate women in an attempt to exclude them from power. In nearby Palestine, where often women are murdered by their fathers or brothers to "defend family honor," Glazer discovered that the killing was actually instigated by women who first insistently spread accusatory gossip, which spurred the men to act.[74] In North American youth gangs, girls sometimes instigate violence by deliberately calculated acts of "bad-mouthing" that compel their boyfriends to commit acts of violence. This kind of evidence points to a longer-standing notion of female "masked criminality" where as an offender the woman is perceived as instigating and inspiring violence rather than partaking in it directly.[75]

OBESITY, LONELINESS, AND FANTASIES IN FEMALE SERIAL KILLERS

Schurman-Kauflin further reports that 100 percent of the female offenders she interviewed reported childhood obesity and 43 percent reported teenaged acne. Today, obesity is all too common but when these women were growing up it could have, along with the acne, contributed more severely to their social isolation.

And social isolation—loneliness—might be arguably the *most* common characteristic of the childhood of serial killers. Male or female. It is in their isolation from playmates and peers that future serial killers begin to dwell upon violent fantasies of revenge and domination so closely linked to their lack of self-esteem. And fantasy appears to be a key factor. The FBI study of male sexual murderers rejected the notion that they murdered as a defensive-reactive response to extremely abusive experiences in their life. What troubled the FBI analysts was the fact that not all the serial killers they were interviewing suffered severe abuse in childhood. The FBI concluded that serial murderers "programmed" or conditioned themselves in childhood to become murderers in a progressively intensifying loop of fantasies. The most common childhood trait of serial killers, which also extends into adolescence and adulthood, is daydreaming and compulsive masturbation. As defined in the study, daydreaming is "any cognitive activity representing a shift of attention away from

a task." Fantasy is defined as an elaborate thought with great preoccupation, sometimes expressed as images, or feelings only, anchored
in the daydreaming process.[76] The study found that 82 percent of offenders reported daydreaming in their childhood. An equal 82 percent reported compulsive masturbation (probably accompanying the
daydreams.)[77] When the offenders reached their adolescence and
then their adulthood, there was only a one percent drop in their daydreaming and compulsive masturbation.

Fantasies serve to relieve anxiety or fear and almost everybody
has them to one degree or another. A child that is abused may un-
derstandably develop aggressive fantasies in which the child develops a power and means by which he or she can destroy the tormentor.
But the trigger of these fantasies does not necessarily need to be an
extraordinarily abusive or violent event—relatively common events
such as parental divorce, family illness, or even rejection by a friend
can all give a child a sense of loss of control, anxiety, and fear, and
may as a result spark aggressive fantasies as a method of coping
with the stress.

It is only at this point that the other factors noted in the serial
killers' childhood take effect. The child that lacks bonding and contact with others will internalize fantasy and cloud the boundary between fantasy and reality. Living in a private world the child begins
to repeat and elaborate on fantasy, finding comfort while continually narrowing the perimeters between fantasy and reality. Of the
killers interviewed in the FBI study, 71 percent reported a sense of
isolation in their childhood. As they grew into adolescence, the
sense of isolation apparently increased to 77 percent of subjects.[78]
Such increased social isolation only encourages a reliance on fantasy as a substitute for human encounters. Schurman-Kauflin reported that 100 percent of her female subjects recalled being isolated
from others in childhood, adolescence, and adulthood and that
their time alone was spent engaging in violent fantasies.

The individual's personality development becomes dependent
on the fantasy life and its themes rather than on social interaction.
The total escape and control that the child has in the fantasy world
becomes addicting, especially if there are continued stresses in the
child's life.

If the particular fantasy involves violence, revenge, or murder, they become part of that addiction and when combined with mas-turbation, a sexual component to the fantasy is developed. This process is a form of deeply rooted conditioning where the repeated pairing of fantasized cues with orgasm results in the acquisition of sexually arousing properties. Violence and the sexual drive be-come merged into a murderous obsession, which often is kept secret. As one unnamed killer in the FBI study said, "Nobody bothered to find out what my problem was, and nobody knew about the fantasy world."

We have scant data on the fantasy life of female serial killers and no or few studies of the relationship between fantasy and mas-turbation in female adolescents. Nonetheless, the seven women in Schurman-Kauflin's study reported homicidal fantasies in their childhood. The study reports that fantasy appears as a critical component of the female killer's childhood and suggests that not only does it result from social isolation, but contributes to it as well. According to Schurman-Kauflin, at least one of her subjects reported being aware of the inappropriateness of her murderous fantasies toward others and as a result further isolated herself from social contact.[79] This, of course, confirms the nondelusional nature of female serial killers: They are highly aware of the charac-ter of their fantasies.

Schurman-Kauflin reports that many of the women reported at first simple and vague fantasies involving the murder of another human being. These fantasies included a specific method of kill-ing. Five reported they fantasized strangling or suffocating their victims, one reported shooting, while the remaining subject re-fused to discuss the specifics of her fantasies. In the early stages of these fantasies, no identifiable individual figured in them. The fan-tasy victims were generically identified: children, men, the elderly, women, etc. But after months of this generic fantasizing, the women reported that they began to fixate on a specific individual, usually somebody they knew.[80]

The closer the women came to killing, the more detailed and elaborate the fantasies became. The fantasy eventually incorporated the actual MO to be used to ensure that the murder would not be detected and that the evidence would be destroyed. The fantasy be-came increasingly violent, detailed, repetitive, and intrusive until it gradually became a plan. When there was nothing further to elaborate on, the offender would proceed to the next stage—the realization of the homicidal fantasies.

Several of the women in the study admitted to careful research in forensic pathology, investigative procedures, and criminal psychology. They reported feeling a rise in self-esteem with the success of their multiple murders: They were doing something nobody else could.

Eventually, in a pattern typical for all serial killers, the problems of their daily life would submerge the euphoria they were experiencing in the wake of their successful murder. They would sink back into depression and isolation and return to their fantasies to seek solace. And the killing cycle would begin again.

Schurman-Kauflin's study is problematic: She only had seven subjects, which skews the percentile figure by a huge 14 percent for each subject. Moreover, not all of her subjects were serial killers—at least one if not more was a mass killer, which involves a totally different psychological dynamic more akin with suicide than with serial murder.

The Keeney-Heide study is also problematic as it relies on records and media reports to collect its data on female offenders. These studies of female serial killers, however, are the best we have, and nothing for females currently approaches the study the FBI conducted when its agents extensively interviewed the twenty-nine male serial killers.

Despite this lack of parity between male and female studies, gender issues should not entirely obscure our understanding of women serial killers. While there are some significant differences, much of the psychopathology of female serial killers is similar to that of male killers—what we know about males can often be applied to understanding female serialists as well.

THE MAKING OF SERIAL KILLERS

We know that an overwhelming majority of serial killers experienced traumatic childhoods usually in the form of physical and sexual abuse. This applies to males as equally as females (with the exception of female partners of males). This observation is not intended to defend the serial killer—lots of children are abused and do not become serial killers. The point is that abused children can develop psychological states that facilitate the emergence of a serial killer—psychopathy in particular, which will be discussed below in more detail.

A history of chaotic and unstable family life is common to a majority of serial killers. Most serial killers come from broken homes with frequent parental histories of drug and alcohol abuse and criminality.

Along with abuse, an early disruption of an infant's physical and emotional attachment to its mother and even father can also result in lifelong behavioral disorders. There are cases of adopted children who are raised in apparently loving and stable families who nonetheless become serial killers. Irreparable damage had already occurred prior to adoption when the child was an infant. But again, none of these factors alone sufficiently explains the mind of a serial killer because there are hundreds of thousands of adopted children who do not become killers.

Brain injuries can cause violent behavioral patterns and many serial killers have a history of head injuries when they were children or recent injuries prior to the onset of killing. But again, this is not the *cause* alone of their murderous behavior—already other behavioral problems are frequently present. Most people who sustain head injuries do not become killers.

Serial killers frequently test positive for abnormal levels of chemicals in their body associated with depression or compulsive behavior, such as monoamine oxidase (MAO) and serotonin. Other biochemical or physiological conditions in serial killers have included cortical underarousal, EEG abnormalities,[81] the presence of an extra Y chromosome* and high levels of kryptopyrrole—"hidden fiery oil" (or bile)—a rare biochemical marker sometimes found in severe mental dysfunctions: a natural human organic metabolite with a chemical structure resembling man-made substances similar to LSD.[82]

There is also evidence suggesting that there might be some type of congenital genetic abnormalities resulting in brain damage common to many serial killers. One study found twenty-three

* The 47×44—(extra-Y disorder).

physical abnormalities common to serial killers, including: bulbous fingertips, fine or electric wire hair that will not comb down, hair whorls, head circumference outside a normal range, malformed ears, curved fifth finger, high-steepled palate, singular transverse palmer crease, third toe is longer than second toe or equal in length to second toe, and abnormalities in teeth and skin texture.[83]

Finally, loneliness, an inability to form attachments with peers, social rejection, and isolation combined with the emergence of violent fantasies also characterize the childhoods of most serial killers. Again, it is a chicken-or-egg type of quandary: What comes first—rejection by peers that leads to behavioral disorders or disorders that lead to rejection by peers? Or a cycle of both? Again, not all lonely children become serial killers, some only end up writing books about them.

The prevailing theory is that there is a delicate balance between a chaotic or abusive childhood, disrupted attachment to parental figures and peers, and biochemical factors that can trigger murderous behavior. Healthy social factors can intervene in a biochemically unstable individual otherwise predisposed to criminal behavior; or on the other hand, healthy biochemistry can protect a person with a turbulent childhood from growing up a killer.

Violent offenders emerge when all or most elements are out of balance. This theory goes a long way to explain why some children with difficult childhoods do not become serial killers or why not everyone with a head injury behaves criminally. It also gives us clues as to the type or profile of serial killers that emerges: It is like the bass and treble adjustment on a sound system. Some serial killers are self-confident and highly organized; others are extremely shy and chaotic. The combinations of degrees of the above-described childhood factors not only can produce a serial killer but also will determine what kind of serial killer he or she will be.

DIAGNOSING SERIAL KILLERS: PSYCHOPATHY AND ASPD

A vast majority of female and male serial killers are psychopaths. Psychopathy is currently called antisocial personality disorder (ASPD) although some argue the two are different disorders. "Psychopath" is a popular and policing term and not an official psychiatric diagnostic term and does not appear in the *DSM-IV*.

The psychopath should not be confused with the psychotic, who is often delusional, paranoid, and suffering from an organic disease in the brain like schizophrenia. Psychotic serial killers are extremely rare because psychosis is not conducive to the long-term maintenance of a serial-killing career. Psychotics are clinically and legally insane, and are more often a danger to themselves than to others. The psychotic is unaware of the reality of their situation or of the acts they are perpetrating and are driven by voices in their head and hallucinations. Sometimes these symptoms can be controlled by medication. The psychotic is rarely able to maintain the so-called "mask of sanity"—an appearance of normality—that is required of the serial killer between murders.

THE PSYCHOPATH

The psychopath is an entirely different creature. Psychopaths are acutely aware of reality. They fully understand the harmful nature of the acts they commit but simply do not care. The closest things to insanity in psychopaths are their fantasies and their inabilities to resist the compulsion to realize their fantasies. But these fantasies are not delusional. Serial killers are perfectly aware of the criminal and homicidal nature of the fantasies they harbor.

Psychopaths are essentially incapable of feeling a normal range of emotions but there is more to it than that: Psychopaths are capable of *simulating*, for various periods of time, those emotions. They display very convincing shows of sympathy, love, attachment, and caring. This is the so-called "mask of sanity." Psychopaths learn to call on a repertoire of simulated emotions for the benefit of others, while themselves feeling either nothing or entirely opposite emotions. This is critical to understanding the female serial killers, as so many of them kill victims they appear to be intimate with. For the female, this intimacy can be entirely simulated.

The unique nature of psychopathy has been identified for at least three centuries now. In France in the late 1700s, the often-called "father of modern psychiatry," Philippe Pinel, noted that some of his patients committed impulsive, destructive acts despite their awareness of the irrationality and harmful nature of the acts. These patients did not appear to have their reasoning abilities impaired and Pinel called the disorder *manie sans delire* (insanity without delirium.)

THE QUESTION OF SANITY

In criminal justice the notion of insanity as a defense goes back to medieval times but was formalized in modern law in England in 1843 with the M'Naghten Rule, named for a mentally ill man, Daniel M'Naghten, who was charged with murder but found not guilty by reason of insanity and confined in a mental asylum instead. It is used in many Western countries today, including the U.S., to define insanity in the courts. The rule states that to establish a successful defense on the grounds of insanity:

> It must be clearly proved that, at the time of the committing of the act, the party accused was laboring under such a defect of reason, from disease of the mind, as not to know the nature and quality of the act he was doing; or, if he did know it, that he did not know he was doing what was wrong.[84]

The M'Naghten Rule does not obviously describe psychopaths who are completely aware of "the nature and quality of the act" they are committing. Nonetheless, courts at one time accepted an insanity plea in the defense of psychopaths based primarily on the argument that they suffered from an "irresistible impulse" to kill. In the 19th century, psychopathy was described as "moral insanity" or "moral imbecility" and was grounds for an insanity plea.

By the 1970s, juries in the U.S., in the face of a rising number of serial killers, began to reject the "irresistible impulse" insanity plea, fearing that the serial killers may eventually be released from their confinement in psychiatric facilities. In 1984, after John Hinckley was acquitted by reason of insanity for his attempt to gun down President Ronald Reagan, Congress passed the Insanity Defense Reform Act. It conclusively excluded "irresistible impulse" as a ground for an insanity plea.

The last major serial murder trial where the plea was made was that of Jeffrey Dahmer in 1992, who was charged with the murder of fifteen men and boys. He kept some of their body parts in his fridge, occasionally eating them. He constructed altars from their skulls while reducing the remains of their corpses in drums of acid stored in his bedroom. He attempted to transform several of his still-living victims into sex zombies by drilling through their skulls and injecting their brains with battery acid. One would think if that were not crazy, then what is? And that is precisely the argument his attorney attempted to present. It did not work.

No modern-day female serial killer to the best of our knowledge has yet come even close to replicating the gruesome behavior of Jeffrey Dahmer. The insanity plea itself has become rare in serial killer cases, male or female, no matter how gruesome or "insane" their acts appear to be. However, some female serial killers have attempted to mitigate their sentences with a plea that they suffered from Battered Woman Syndrome, resulting in temporary insanity.

THE NATURE OF THE PSYCHOPATH

Our modern definition of the psychopath stems from the research of Hervey Cleckley, a professor of psychiatry in Georgia who published his results in 1941 in a book still studied today, *The Mask of Sanity*. Essentially, the psychopath, according to Cleckley, is grandiose, arrogant, callous, superficial, and manipulative. Psychopaths are often short-tempered; get bored easily; are unable to form strong emotional bonds with others; lack empathy, guilt, and remorse; and behave in irresponsible, impulsive ways—often in violation of social and legal norms.

In the earlier editions of his work, Cleckley argued that psychopathy was actually a form of psychosis not technically demonstrable and concealed by an outer surface of intact function—a mask of sanity—and only manifested in behavior. In the 1950s this was challenged because, according to one critic, Richard Jenkins:

A psychosis is a major mental disorder. A psychopathic personality shows not a disorder of personality but rather a defect of personality, together with a set of defenses evolved around that defect. The defect relates to the most central element of the human personality: its social nature. The psychopath is simply a basically asocial or antisocial individual who has never achieved the developed nature of *homo domesticus*.[85]

In 1952, the American Psychiatric Association's diagnostic manual replaced the term psychopath with "sociopathic personality" and the psychopath came to be informally called the *sociopath*. One of the major problems with the definition of *psychopath* and *sociopath* at the time was that it did not account for criminal behavior and the use of the term in the legal system. Under the definitions of these terms, one could easily find not only serial killers and sex offenders but functioning business executives, physicians, judges, politicians, movie stars, and a host of other seemingly "successful" members of society. Cleckley acknowledged this issue:

> It must be remembered that even the most severely and obviously disabled psychopath presents a technical appearance of sanity, often with high intellectual capacities and not infrequently succeeds in business or professional activities for short periods, some for considerable periods. Although they occasionally appear on casual inspection as successful members of the community, as able lawyers, executives or physicians, they do not, it seems, succeed in the sense of finding satisfaction or fulfillment in their own accomplishments. Nor do they, when the full story is known, appear to find this in an ordinary activity. By ordinary activity we do not need to postulate what is considered moral or decent by the average man but may include any type of asocial, or even criminal activity . . . [86]

This lack of consensus of defining the disorder led to the adoption in the 1990s of yet another term: *antisocial personality disorder (ASPD)*. This is currently the "official" psychiatric definition of what we used to call psychopathy as described by the standard *Diagnostic and Statistical Manual of Mental Disorders—Edition IV (DSM-IV)* which defines it by the following symptoms:

A. Pervasive pattern of disregard for and violation of the rights of others, occurring since age 15 as indicated by at least three of the following:

1. Failure to conform to social norms with respect to lawful behavior.

2. Deceitfulness, as indicated by repeated lying, use of aliases, or conning others for personal profit or pleasure.

3. Impulsivity or failure to plan ahead.

4. Irritability and aggressiveness.

5. Reckless disregard for the safety of self or others.

6. Consistent irresponsibility, as indicated by repeated failure to sustain work behavior or honor financial obligations.

7. Lack of remorse, as indicated by indifference to or rationalizing having hurt, mistreated, or stolen from another.

B. Individual is at least 18 years of age.

C. The occurrence of the behavior is not exclusively during the course of a schizophrenic or manic episode.

D. Evidence of conduct disorder onset before age fifteen.[87]

PROBLEMS IN DEFINING PSYCHOPATHY AND ASPD

Some psychiatrists argue that the diagnosis of ASPD is too behaviorally based and neglects persistent personality traits. There is a faction in psychiatry that suggests that ASPD is actually a disorder that *some* psychopaths suffer from—in other words, a symptom of psychopathy—not the disorder itself. In the 1970s and 1980s, Canadian psychologist Robert Hare returned back to Cleckley's *Mask of Sanity* definitions and found that while all psychopaths can be diagnosed with ASPD, not all those diagnosed with ASPD are psychopaths.

Hare developed a different type of diagnostic test for psychopathy to differentiate it from ASPD and it is used extensively in psychiatric testing. Known as the Psychopathy Checklist-Revised (PCL-R) the test relies less on questions requiring the scoring of self-reported symptoms, which—according to Hare—psychopaths can learn the correct responses to and manipulate, and instead relies on a scoring matrix focused on observable factors that a therapist can collect and score without securing the subject's cooperation.

The PCL-R scores the presence of psychopathy based on criteria such as: glibness or superficial charm, grandiose sense of self, pathological lying, conning or manipulative quality, lack of remorse or guilt, shallow affect, callousness or lack of empathy, failure to accept responsibility for one's actions, constant need for stimulation, proneness to boredom, parasitic lifestyle, poor behavioral controls, early behavioral problems, lack of realistic long-term goals, impulsivity, irresponsibility, juvenile delinquency, revocation of probation, promiscuous sexual behavior, many short-term relationships, and criminal versatility. Arrays of factors like those are scored on a 3-point scale (0=does not apply; 1=applies somewhat; 2=definitely applies). A final score of 30 or more identifies a psychopath.

Hare discovered that nearly 50 to 80 percent of criminals can be diagnosed as having ASPD according to criteria of the *DSM-IV* but only 15 percent to 30 percent of those same subjects score as psychopaths on the PCL-R test.[88] The difference between ASPD and psychopathy is not so much in the definition of the disorder as in the diagnoses of the symptoms—the *DSM-IV* definition for ASPD, according to Hare, relies too much on the presence of criminal behavior and inappropriate interpersonal acts as criteria; the PCL-R test, on the other hand, expands the criteria to persistent personality traits rather than focusing so heavily on interpersonal behavior and criminal history. Where all this will lead in the future remains to be seen, but the PCL-R is *the* diagnostic tool for psychopathy today, available in forensic versions specifically for criminal offenders.

WHAT CAUSES A PSYCHOPATHY?

It is believed that the interruption of an infant's physical bonding with its mother or childhood trauma—typically physical or sexual abuse—can trigger a basic animal instinct for "fight or flight." Obviously, the child unable to fight instead stores, redirects, or suppresses the rage necessary to fight and goes into the flight mode by emotionally detaching from or numbing the pain of separation and/or trauma.

The human mind is unable to selectively switch on or off this emotional detachment—it becomes permanently welded to the subject's personality along with a number of other defensive mechanisms ranging from fantasy to other personality traits already described above. The psychopath's mind is permanently rewired—as if certain emotions are amputated like limbs that will never heal and grow back. To this day there is no "cure" for psychopathy. The only thing that happens is that psychopaths in their middle-ages—at least male ones—tend to "act out" fewer behavioral aspects of their disorder.

Nevertheless, females, who more frequently kill in late middle-age, conversely rarely score on ASPD diagnostic tests once over the age of 44. This leaves questions unanswered as to what may be driving them to kill if not their psychopathic state.

The development of psychopathy is linked to attachment theory advanced by developmental psychologist John Bowlby in the 1950s. After observing the effects on children suddenly separated from their primary caregivers in England during World War II, Bowlby became convinced that when dealing with disturbed children psychiatry was overemphasizing their fantasies instead of focusing on the children's real-life experiences. According to Bowlby, "the young child's hunger for his mother's love is as great as his hunger for food."[89] Bowlby argued that a child's healthy development is entirely dependent on its reliance on access to its primary caregiver. If this access is interrupted, the child develops defensive mechanisms that may assist the child in emotionally surviving the separation, but that may cause irreparable damage in the child's ability to bond with others and develop a normal emotional range as an adult.

In the 1970s, experiments were conducted on infants, known as the "Strange Situation," where primary caregivers were separated from the infants and substituted with strangers. The infants' responses were measured and showed three distinctively different patterns of attachment:

1. Secure (63 percent): the infants were distressed by separation, sought comfort on reunion, and stabilized once in their caregiver's presence.

2. Insecure/Avoidant (21 percent): these infants exhibited little or no distress upon separation, did not seek contact on reunion, and focused their attention on toys or other objects and shifted their attention away from their caregivers.

3. Anxious/Ambivalent (16 percent): these infants were distressed prior to separation, and cried more often than others.[90]

It is the insecure/avoidant category of infant that is troubling. These infants do not re-establish attachment to their primary caregiver once reunited, nor do they establish an attachment to anybody else. They focus on objects or on themselves and are only cursorily sociable with others. Some theorize that these infants interpret attachment as a precursor to hostility and develop defensive "preemptive aggression" toward those becoming emotionally close to them.

These infants grow up to become adolescents and adults with no feelings of empathy, no attachment, and no remorse or concern how family, peers, neighbors, school, employers, or society might judge their behavior. Again, this alone cannot be attributed to the making of a serial killer, nor even guarantees the making of a psychopath, but it becomes a significant factor when combined with other circumstances. A child with interrupted parental attachment *plus* physical or sexual abuse *plus* rejection by peers *plus* perhaps a biochemical imbalance *plus* head injury, or a selective combination of the above at different intensities together can spawn a serial-killing monster. (To make matters even more complex, the *DSM-IV* also offers the Reactive Attachment Disorder (RAD), which is characterized by "markedly disturbed and developmentally inappropriate social relatedness in most contexts that [occurs] before the age of 5 years and is associated with grossly pathological care."[91] Yet another step to psychopathy—a kind of childhood psychopathy.)

What we do not know is where the "red line" is located for psychopathy or even serial killers, because again, not all psychopaths are serial killers, and not all children who suffer trauma or detachment become psychopathic. There are many other causes under consideration for the development of psychopathy, including prenatal and postnatal hormones, prenatal alcohol poisoning, neurotransmitter turnover, and head trauma, but none of these theories have been conclusively resolved at this point in time.[92]

So in the end, it is not childhood abuse and trauma alone that create serial killers; they may spawn psychopaths, and *some* psychopaths can act out as serial killers—others we might elect to Congress. The road to making a serial killer is a long and twisted one with many byways, stopovers, and detours to the final destination. Not all psychopaths arrive there, but the ones that do are spectacularly deadly.

THE FEMALE PSYCHOPATH AND ASPD

There are some distinguishing features of the female psychopath. First, ASPD in the U.S. can be diagnosed in approximately 0.5 percent of the population—in one out of every two hundred people.[93] Clearly if they were all serial killers, we would be in serious trouble, although the fact that we might be electing them to office, working for them, hiring them as our attorneys, and watching their movies, listening to their music, or reading their books, might not bode well for our society either.

The rate of ASPD, however, is significantly lower for females: 0.2 percent or one in five hundred. Males have a four times higher rate of prevalence: 0.8 percent or one in one hundred twenty-five. Studies of subjects diagnosed with ASPD in the 1960s showed that females tended to have a later onset of childhood behavioral problems compared to boys, but were more frequently engaged in sexually deviant behavior.[94] Episodes of arson, cruelty to animals, physical aggression, and bullying were more rare among girls than boys. (Although Schurman-Kauflin contradicts that for at least the seven female offenders in her study, who all reported killing animals as children and adolescents.) Again, perception is the problem—aggression in females slips below the radar because they tend to express early aggression through social and verbal forms. Today few would deny that girls commit physical bullying: Schoolgirl bullies are a huge juvenile issue these days. In the past, females tended to first use gossip and social exclusion as a form of aggression among their peers, but today that expression is frequently a prelude to conventional physical violence.

The murder of fourteen-year-old Reena Virk in British Columbia in 1997 by seven girls and one boy is indicative of the nature adolescent female violence can take today. The girls beat their acquaintance, Virk, and burned her with lit cigarettes before attempting to set her hair on fire. Virk survived the first round of beatings after most of the girls lost interest and left, but was then attacked a second time by a boy and girl who remained behind. Without apparently speaking to each other, the two beat her again and then drowned her by holding Virk's head in a creek. All the adolescents swore to a pact of silence and the crime was only revealed when Virk's body was discovered eight days later. The fifteen-year-olds who actually murdered Virk were sentenced to life imprisonment, but the female, Kelly Marie Ellard, was granted a retrial on appeal. While awaiting the new trial, Ellard was charged, along with another female acomplice, in the beating of a 58-year-old woman.[95]

During the retrial, witnesses testified how Ellard had bragged about "finishing off" Virk and had conducted tours of the murder scene for her friends. After a mistrial during the appeal, a third trial finally resulted in Ellard receiving a life sentence in 2005. Two of the girls convicted in the initial beating allege that Virk stole one of the girls' phone book and started calling her friends and spreading vicious rumors about her. That girl stubbed a lit cigarette into Virk's forehead.

Gender stereotyping still plays a major role in the underdiagnosis of females as psychopaths. Women are traditionally perceived as nurturing and passive and to classify them as dangerous repeat offenders contradicts typical conceptualization of the female. Moreover, diagnosing somebody as a psychopath means condemning them to a morally reprehensible category associated with incurable, dangerous, lifelong criminal behavior.

Gender bias often leads to women being diagnosed with another behavioral disorder called Histrionic Personality Disorder (HPD), the diagnosis of which includes five or more of the following symptoms:

a) Uncomfortable in situations in which he or she is not the center of attention.

b) Interaction with others is often characterized by inappropriate sexually seductive or provocative behavior.

c) Displays rapidly shifting and shallow expression of emotions.

d) Consistently uses physical appearance to draw attention to self.

e) Has a style of speech that is excessively impressionistic and lacking in detail.

f) Shows self-dramatization, theatricality, and exaggerated expression of emotion.

g) Is suggestible, i.e., easily influenced by others or circumstances.

h) Considers relationships to be more intimate than they actually are.

In 1978 an experiment was conducted using 175 mental health professionals as subjects. They were given hypothetical case histories with similar mixed symptoms indicative of ASPD and HPD. When the therapists were told that the patient was a female, they tended to diagnose ASPD in 22 percent of the cases and HPD in 76 percent. However, those cases in which the therapists were told the patients were men, the same symptoms were diagnosed as ASPD in 41 percent of the cases, and HPD in 49 percent. (There were six other possible diagnostic options offered to the therapists.)[96]

Clearly mental health professionals were attributing the same set of symptoms to psychopathy in men but to hysteria in women. Feminists argue, with good reason, that mental diagnosis of women is entirely related to socially constructed stereotyping of femininity. (Remember "nymphomania" for example? It no longer exists in the psychiatric catalog of disorders and is instead labeled "sexual addiction" and applied to men and women equally.)

* * *

A study of equal groups of males and females diagnosed with ASPD indicated certain social characteristics in the subjects.[97] Women with ASPD who tended to be married showed a higher incidence of marriage breakdown than the average population—and higher than married men with ASPD. Women with ASPD were four times more likely to be receiving welfare payments than women without. They were more likely to be less educated and unemployed and living in rental housing than females without ASPD. Both males and females with ASPD were more likely not to have been raised by both their parents until the age of fifteen. Yet another study found that in males the lack of contact with the father increased probability of ASPD while in females it was the lack of contact with the mother.[98] Women with ASPD were found to be pervasively troubled with relationship problems, followed by job problems, violence, and lying.[99]

Women (and men) diagnosed with ASPD tended to also have related problems that were not directly linked to ASPD. Both males and females had higher rates of suicide attempts. Women with ASPD were ten times more likely than those without to be alcoholic or drug addicted (compared to men with ASPD who were three times more likely).[100] Unlike males with ASPD, women with it were more likely to be depressed than women without. Women with ASPD were also more likely to have phobias than those without, which contradicts the early notion that psychopaths are less likely to be anxious or fearful because of their emotional numbness—at least in females.[101]

* * *

The relationship between psychopathy and male killers has been extensively studied. Male inmates incarcerated for homicide had higher rates of psychopathic symptoms than those who committed other crimes.[102] There are no major studies in the U.S. of the relationship between psychopathy and homicide by females. The one current study comes out of Finland. When compared to the general female population of Finnish females, the prevalence of ASPD in murderers was 12.6 percent compared to 0.2 percent among the average population there.[103] The author of this Finnish study, however, warned that it applies to countries with relatively low rates of violent crime, and would not be applicable to the United States.

At this point in time we do not know anything conclusively about the relationship between psychopathy and ASPD. Is one a symptom of the other or are they different ways of diagnosing the same thing? In the end consensus in psychiatry is as elusive as string theory in quantum physics.

SUMMING UP

- Serial killing by males or females is most often simply about power. The most common type of gratification that serial killers seek is a sense of power and control over their victims—to the ultimate point of life and death. The sadistic power-control or power-assertive sexual murderer is the largest category of male offenders, found in 38 percent of nearly 2,500 incarcerated sexual killers (singular and serial).[104]

- Sexual satisfaction as you and I imagine it is not the primary motive driving sexual assaults by these types of offenders. Power over a victim is the primary motive. The sexual battery is only one of many means by which the offender humiliates and dominates the victim. This partly explains why sometimes these attackers do not ejaculate during rape (and the reality is probably never as satisfying as the fantasy).

- For some serial killers murder is not a part of their fantasy. Killing becomes collateral to the escalating violence they inflict to primarily control, possess, and humiliate their victim. The murder can sometimes be an afterthought or even entirely forgotten by the attacker, because the power-control individual loses interest in the victim once the assault is over. The attacker could not care less if the victim is dead or alive.

- All this presents a problem in understanding what motivates female serial killers. We are misled if we assume that murder is the paramount fantasy of every serial killer, the way we think sexual desire is for every rapist. It is for some, but not all. Power is the key. We presumed that the motives of female offenders were diametrically different from males because females rarely use sexual assault as a medium of aggression and control. We even hesitated to characterize females as serial killers for that reason. That kind of limited thinking has less of a hold on forensic analysis of serial murder today. We are beginning to understand that female killers can murder for many of the same reasons male serial killers do.

- The more likely scenario is that similar motives can be applied to both female and male, but it is the *mode of expression* that is different. Thus while power-control males may express their fantasies of domination through sexual assault, which may or may not end up in murder, most female offenders bypass the "expressive" sexual component, going directly to murder and theft. The male power-control killer gets his gratification from domination through rape and physical violence; the female offender gets her gratification from the actual death of her victim and seizure of their property. While the male power-control serialist needs to bind, confine, and physically assault the victim, the female is satisfied to kill remotely by poison or by manipulating or paying others to do it. The *result rather than the process* is more gratifying for the female. Uninterested in the process, the female offender tends to leave little apparent signature, other than the murder itself.

2

THE QUEST FOR POWER, PROFIT, AND DESIRE

A Brief History of Female Serial Killers

We mistakenly presumed that serial killers were a symptom of modernity; a product of the newly industrialized urban society with its mass of faceless crowds so inviting to the sick and lost to anonymously act out their most primitive and dark demented homicidal compulsions upon the weak and the expendable; every atrocity salaciously reported by a newborn mass media feeding the voracious imaginations of a rising wave of serial monsters and their victims.

Serial killing actually has been around since the beginning of recorded history in both the cities *and* the countryside and long before the industrial age. It ebbed and waned at different times in different segments of society. When we look back into history for the earliest traces of serial killers, we discover them among the ranks of old-world despots, dictators, emperors, and aristocrats who literally had the power of life and death over their subjects. Many appeared to have killed only because they could. This is precisely the kind of imperial power that so many serial killers today fantasize of wielding over their victims.

Did ordinary people of the past commit serial murder? Average people were extraordinarily busy years ago doing what we take for granted: finding food, building shelter, avoiding plague and disease, paying dues and taxes, and fighting off homicidal enemies, raiders, and slavers. There probably wasn't a lot of leisure time to brood and foster compulsive homicidal sexual fantasies. Only the aristocracy could afford that kind of time.

If there were serial killers among commoners, it was not reported or recorded anywhere. Until very recently history was mostly written by elites for elites about elites—it was all about princes and kingdoms and empires and fortunes. The common people were irrelevant except on harvest and tax days.

Of course commoners committed serial killing and cases of it are surely imprinted on our collective imagination in the form of monsters: werewolves tearing, mutilating, and cannibalizing flesh; vampires biting, draining, and drinking blood from their victims. These are only a few of a horrific range of grisly acts serial killers are capable of perpetrating in reality—true tales of horror. And as unfathomable as these acts were then, even today they are explained in almost the same way: as incomprehensible acts of monsters. The modern serial killer is really our secular monster.

It was in the eighteenth and nineteenth centuries that we began giving our monsters precise names and human identities when we could, and individual monikers when we couldn't. That Jack the Ripper emerges in the London of the 1880s—the newspaper capital of the world—is no coincidence. It is only with the advent of cheap printing, resulting in the rise of popular mass media in the form of novels, pamphlets, broadsides, and eventually newspapers, that monsters began to be identified as real people and not mystical animallike creatures roaming in the dark of the woods.

Jack the Ripper really is the first industrial-age serial killer with lasting fame of any consequence, despite the fact there were so many others before and after him, and mostly females as we will see.[105]

For nearly a century Jack the Ripper framed our popular conception of serial killers until the 1970s, when Ted Bundy brought serial killing into the new age. He was the first postmodern serial killer—the handsome, angelic boy-next-door-with-a-college-degree, somebody who should never have been a serial killer. He was too much like so many of us! (Aileen Wuornos in her diametrically opposite way is our female serial postmodernist. We will see how in the next chapter.)

FEMALE SERIAL KILLERS IN EARLY HISTORY

Inevitably the earliest accounts of female serial killers take us into the ranks of the aristocracy. It is here that some historical record survives.

The names of murderous tyrants are infinitely familiar: Caligula, Ivan the Terrible, Attila the Hun, Vlad the Impaler, Hitler, Stalin, Pol Pot, Pinochet, Saddam Hussein. Less familiar are their female equivalents, who we believed simply did not exist. They could not exist because (remember?) we thought women were only capable of emotionally driven "expressive" violence.

The Bible is the best reflection of the most inner corridors of the Western cultural psyche and there we find Salome—the female murderer who has John the Baptist's head cut off in response to his condemnation of her mother's "adulterous" marriage to King Herod. The figure of Salome is a typical example of the deeply rooted notion in our culture of female expressive violence.[106] John lost his head because Salome got too emotional.

But a closer look at the historical record shows different kinds of killing by women with plenty of examples of carefully planned "constructive" acts of violence. Women were coldly seeking to achieve the same goals their murderous male counterparts yearned for: dominance, power, and wealth. Queens and empresses—how tainted are they with aberrant psychopathology or are they merely products of their times?

If in the Bible we find the psyche of Western civilization, then in the Roman Empire we find its spine. There is no better place to seek out early female serial killers than in Rome.

THE EMPIRE OF DEATH: FEMALE SERIAL KILLING
IN THE ANCIENT WORLD

About two thousand years ago, Roman emperors Caligula and Nero reigned in the years immediately following the death of Christ (circa A.D. 33). Caligula and Nero represent the high madness of Imperial Rome on the path to collapse—the bloodlust of psychopath rulers who married, raped, and murdered family members as readily as strangers for the sake of power and amusement.

If one needed a fertile hothouse in which to raise and grow serial killers then Rome's Imperial court would be perfect. Aside from its traditions of ruthlessness and cruelty in maintaining personal and state political power, Roman culture also celebrated acts of popular recreational serial death performed for paying spectators and guests in nearly two hundred stadiumlike arenas interspersed throughout the huge empire that stretched from Britain all the way down to North Africa. The Coliseum in Rome, the perpetual Super Bowl of slaughter with individually numbered seating for 70,000 drooling spectators, was merely the largest of these facilities, competing with each other to stage the most spectacular and gory shows of death for eager crowds. Professional warriors and slaves—gladiators—fought and killed each other all day, while the half-time noon show amused lunch-munching crowds with brutal torture-executions of helpless condemned prisoners.[107] Christians were victims of these half-time cruelties, where exotic animals were first used to tear at the humans before being killed for the amusement of the crowds.

The presence of women in these games—other than as victims— is mostly confined to a few rare references to the occasional appearance of a female gladiator—the gladiatrix—and the descriptions of the prostitutes who plied their trade under the arches of the Coliseum to customers aroused by the bloodletting. About female spectators we know very little other than that there were many.

But in the corridors of power at the imperial court of the Caesars, the presence of women is more prominent in the historical record. We know their names and stories. Some of their faces we can still view on surviving Roman coins and sculptures.

Agrippina the Younger—the Empress of Poison

No Roman coinage perhaps features a portrait showing a more cruel determination and lust for power than those of the dark and pretty, curly-haired Agrippina the Younger—the "Empress of Poison"—the sister of Caligula, wife of Claudius, and mother of Nero, three Roman emperors in a row.

Agrippina, sometime referred to as the "she-wolf," was born in A.D. 15 or 16 on the Rhine, where her father, a Roman general, was brutally putting down the revolt of barbarian Germanic tribes (as loosely portrayed in the movie *Gladiator*.) Agrippina's lineage included some royal Roman superstars: she was the great-granddaughter of Mark Anthony and granddaughter of Caesar Augustus. She was born into a small incestuous power elite that ruled the Roman Empire and whose individual members were obsessively gnawing and murdering their way to the top through an endless cycle of corruption, conspiracies, and betrayals of each other.

When Agrippina was three years old, her father was murdered by the reigning Emperor Tiberius, for no reason other than his fear of her father's popularity with the Senate and citizenry. In the ensuing years, Agrippina and her sisters and brothers lived in various imperial households, witnessing their mother's plotting attempts to avenge her husband's murder. As a result, by the time Agrippina was seventeen, her mother and her two eldest brothers were put to death for conspiring against Emperor Tiberius. Remarkably, after having killed almost her entire family, Tiberius adopted Agrippina's youngest surviving brother, a very disturbed youth nicknamed Caligula, and eventually anointed him as his succeeding son.

Like his sister, Caligula grew up in Germany in his father's military camp and ran loose among the Roman troops as a child, often dressing up in their armor. This earned him the nickname Caligula, which means "little boots." (His real name was Gaius.) He was adopted by the Roman legionnaires as a sort of good-luck mascot. As a child he witnessed the brutalities of the Roman campaign in Germany against the pagan tribes. He survived being taken hostage in a mutiny and the assassinations of his father, mother, and two brothers. Then, at the court of the ruthless Tiberius—adopted by the very man who had killed his parents and brothers—Caligula let loose with an unbound sexual sadism, obsessively observing the torture and executions of condemned prisoners and disguising himself while raping both male and female victims.

A degenerate gambler and bisexual with vicious mood swings, Caligula eventually turned his sexual aggression onto his three surviving sisters—Julia, Drusilla, and Agrippina. It is unclear whether he forcibly raped them or whether they had their own agenda and voluntarily entered into incestuous relations with their unbalanced but up-and-coming brother. But when these acts of incest were brought to the attention of Emperor Tiberius, the sisters were immediately married off to suppress a scandal. Incest offended even their corrupt Roman sensibilities.

Agrippina was married to an aristocrat twenty-five years her elder and had a son who she promptly named for one of her murdered brothers—Nero. This would be the same Nero who would later become the infamous emperor who "fiddled as Rome burned" according to legend.

In A.D. 37, Tiberius died and was succeeded by crazy Caligula, who quickly installed his favorite sister, Drusilla, at his court as his mistress while at the same time re-established his incestuous relations with Agrippina. To keep up appearances, Drusilla was married to Caligula's political ally and possibly his male lover, Lepidus. All three of Caligula's sisters—Agrippina, Julia, and Drusilla— were elevated to imperial godlike status and in an unprecedented move appeared on Roman coinage during Caligula's reign.

When Drusilla died from fever in A.D. 38, Agrippina attempted to take her place as Caligula's favorite lover, in the hope that her son, Nero, could rise to succeed as emperor. To her dismay, her brother Caligula rebuffed her. It is here, at the age of twenty-two, that the homicidal career of Agrippina begins to ferment. Her motive was, as ascribed by Roman historian Tacitus, *spes dominationis*—"desire for power [hope to dominate]."

Upon being rejected by her brother, Agrippina turned to her widowed brother-in-law, Lepidus, and offered to marry him if he assisted her in assassinating Caligula. (Agrippina's first husband had fallen ill and had died, perhaps with some help from her.) Caligula discovered the plot and executed Lepidus while exiling Agrippina. Agrippina's son, Nero, was taken away and put into the care of her sister-in-law and rival, Domita Lepida. Agrippina remained in exile for eighteen months until Caligula became so erratically homicidal that his fearful courtiers assassinated him in A.D. 41.

The Senate selected Caligula's (and Agrippina's) fifty-year-old uncle Claudius as the new emperor, made famous by Robert Graves's historical novels, *I, Claudius* and *Claudius the God*, and the 1970 BBC-PBS television series. Claudius was mature, intelligent, and easygoing, but because he had a speech impediment he was thought to be an idiot and was ignored (which did much to enhance his survival at the Roman court).

Agrippina and Valeria Messalina—the Teenage Killer

To the frustration of Agrippina—who was released from exile by her kind uncle Claudius—Claudius had married her sister-in-law's daughter, the fifteen-year-old Valeria Messalina, who gave birth the next year to a male child, Britannicus. Despite the good turn in her fortune and return to Rome, with the birth of Britannicus, the chances for Agrippina's son, Nero, of becoming emperor were rapidly fading.

The teenage Messalina was Agrippina's match. Smart, cruel, and manipulative, she was also pathologically jealous of Agrippina and her sister Julia. Agrippina made things worse when she convinced her sister Julia to attempt to seduce Claudius. When Messalina got wind of this plot, she persuaded Claudius to send Julia back into exile and then had her secretly murdered. Some have speculated on Agrippina's motives for persuading Julia to undertake such a dangerous gambit. With Julia dead, Agrippina remained her assassinated father's only surviving child.

The teenage Messalina began a reign of terror as Claudius's imperial wife. When she came to covet the beautiful gardens belonging to a prominent Roman senator, she convinced Claudius that the senator was plotting against him. The senator was forced to commit suicide and his gardens were expropriated and came into Messalina's possession.

Messalina took on a series of lovers, and as she tired of each, she accused them of treason or embezzlement of state funds, not only sending them to their deaths, but also their friends and any other witnesses to her indiscretions with the victims. Completely enchanted with his pretty young bride, Claudius blindly believed in Messalina's accusations. In a seven-year period, between the ages of fifteen and twenty-two, Messalina murdered dozens of imperial courtiers, many of whom had managed to survive the psychopath Caligula, only to randomly perish at the urgings of Messalina, merely because they were friends of one of her illicit lovers or had witnessed some aspect of her misconduct.

When the terrified courtiers conspired to murder both Messalina and Claudius, Messalina struck first, unleashing a murderous purge of the Roman aristocracy, confiscating more of their estates and property. Completely in control of Claudius, she not only had charge of the death lists but also sold imperial favors—citizenship, building contracts, and official appointments—to the highest bidder. Murdering anybody who dared to question her authority, Messalina built a lucrative empire of her own.

In the meantime, Agrippina remarried and bided her time carefully, monitoring Messalina's debauchery and swearing vengeance for the murder of her exiled sister Julia despite her own role in her death. Finally, when Messalina was twenty-two, she went too far. In A.D. 49 she held a mock marriage ceremony with a lover in a roomful of invited guests while Claudius was away. Agrippina quickly rallied Claudius's advisors to convince the Emperor that he could not survive such a humiliation. While the participants at the wedding were put to death, Claudius vacillated as to the final fate of Messalina, until one of his advisors had her executed before the brokenhearted Claudius could commute her sentence.

Now Agrippina made her move. She seduced the widowed Claudius and had her allies among his counselors convince him to marry her. Of course, one of the problems was that Agrippina had recently married again, but that was quickly dealt with when her husband died of a mysterious illness. The other problem was that Claudius was her uncle, but she secured a decree from the Senate authorizing her marriage with him, despite its incestuous nature.

Agrippina was thirty-three when she triumphantly entered Rome in her ceremonial carriage—a daughter of a popular and legendary Roman commander, the sister, wife, and future mother of emperors. Agrippina wielded a cruelly poisonous authority far exceeding Messalina's petty murderous plots. The first to die was Caligula's last wife, who had been a rival for Claudius's hand in marriage in the wake of Messalina's execution. Agrippina accused her of witchcraft and evil designs on the state, and convinced Claudius to have the Senate confiscate her property and exile her where she was secretly forced to commit suicide by Agrippina's agents.

Agrippina then turned on her sister-in-law, Messalina's mother, Domita Lepida, having her and all her trusted servants, aides, and allies executed or secretly murdered. Anybody remotely associated with Lepida was dismissed from the court, if not killed.

Agrippina's objective was to propel her young son, Nero, into power as the next emperor. To consolidate Nero's position in the imperial court, she sought to have him marry Octavia, Claudius's daughter by Messalina. The problem was that the child Octavia was already married, but that did not stop Agrippina. She had Octavia's husband accused of having an incestuous affair with his sister (much like the one Agrippina had with her brother Caligula, ironically), resulting in his exile.

As soon as Nero was engaged to Octavia, she began to urge that Claudius adopt him as his eldest son and therefore likely heir to the throne. This, of course, presented a problem because legally that would make Nero and Octavia brother and sister, again forcing the issue of incest to the surface. Agrippina resolved the issue by having Octavia adopted by another family.

Agrippina amassed a huge pool of wealth and power, frequently riding next to Claudius in his carriage and sitting with him at tribunals. The easygoing Claudius was more concerned about the nuts and bolts of governing the Roman Empire, from the details of taxation to those of the construction of ports and aqueducts. Claudius was content to leave the issues of power, politics, and security at the court to Agrippina, who ruthlessly murdered any potential opposition to herself or the regime.

By A.D. 54 Claudius's natural son, Britannicus, was twelve and approaching adulthood by Roman traditions. Claudius was now 64 years old and in fragile health, and it is believed he was considering naming Britannicus as his appointed heir as soon as Britannicus achieved adulthood. He was also apparently tiring of Agrippina's domination and was considering divorcing her and disinheriting Nero, who by most accounts was a young lout interested only in singing and performing.

Many Roman historians believe that Agrippina at this point killed Claudius by personally preparing his favorite dish of mushrooms and poisoning them with a dose of belladonna alkaloid from hemlock, aconite, or yew. According to the Roman historian Suetonius, Claudius lost his power of speech and then fell into a temporary coma. But then Claudius awoke and vomited the contents of his stomach, whereupon Agrippina either had him fed a poisoned gruel to "revive him" or administered another dose of poison by an enema, ostensibly intended to clean his bowels of the contaminated mushrooms. Whichever it was, it worked, for Claudius died the next morning and shortly afterward Nero was appointed emperor.

One would assume that with her own flesh and blood son as emperor, Agrippina was at the height of her power. Indeed, she was given the title of Augusta—Empress—and her portrait once again appeared on Roman coinage along with Nero's, as it had when her brother Caligula was in power.

One can by now easily imagine the psychology of anyone brought up as a child in these murderous imperial households. Nero was fully the product of Agrippina's psychopathic drive for power. Nero did not first yearn for power, but wanted to be an actor or singer, but failing in that, found a dark side to his urges satisfied through the exercise of his imperial power. He raped both boys and girls and squandered huge amounts of money. Nero's public games reached new levels of cruelty and bloodletting, and Nero targeted a new religious sect appearing in Rome—the Christians. He devised a spectacular nighttime public display of torture by having Christians covered in tar and lit as torches.

At home, Nero displeased Agrippina by having an affair with a former slave girl, which Agrippina felt was a sign of disrespect to her and the marriage she had arranged for her son with Octavia. Then Nero exiled Pallus, a close confidant of Agrippina's, who might have also been her lover at the time. In a classic "I made you and I can unmake you" case of power conflict, Agrippina threatened to have Nero removed and replaced by Claudius's natural son, Britannicus. Coming from Agrippina, this was no idle threat, especially when she suddenly began to shower the hapless fourteen-year-old Britannicus with attention.

Nero struck first. He had Britannicus poisoned and then turned on Agrippina, murdering Pallus, stripping her of all her titles, and banning her from the imperial palace. Agrippina fought back, attempting to organize a coup against Nero but it was quickly discovered. Only her fast talking and previously placed allies managed to rescue her from being exiled or put to death by her own son.

The crazed, unhinged Agrippina now sought an old path to power—incest. She attempted to seduce Nero but was prevented by Nero's close advisors, who warned him that the army would not tolerate such behavior. Nero then resolved to murder his mother.

Nero apparently made three attempts to poison Agrippina, but as she was skilled in that art, he failed. Next Nero invited her for a reconciliation on an island he was vacationing on and sent for her in a boat specially designed to come apart once in open water. Not only did Agrippina survive by swimming back to shore, but she witnessed a woman demanding to be rescued by claiming to be the "mother of the emperor" battered to death with an oar instead. Agrippina decided that the best strategy was to pretend she was not aware of her son's attempts to murder her. She sent back a message to Nero stating that the gods had favored her during the "accidental" sinking of the vessel, and that while she was sure Nero wanted to visit her, he should wait until she recovered from the ordeal.

Instead, as the story goes, Nero dispatched soldiers to murder her, making it look like suicide. The details are unclear, but the monstrous Agrippina died at the age of forty-four at the hands of a monster she herself had borne and raised, leaving a trail of murdered victims in her wake. Nero is reported to have carefully handled his dead mother's corpse, limb by limb, to ensure she was truly dead.

* * *

Certainly the environment and circumstances of their upbringing forged the murderous careers of Agrippina and Messalina. They killed because they could, and because they learned how to by example. Murder satisfied not only their desire for power but their emotional and material needs as well. They committed constructive and expressive violence interchangeably and if they felt any remorse they left no trace in the historical record.

Agrippina and Messalina can be considered paragons for many female rulers in subsequent history.[108] Russia's Catherine the Great and England's Elizabeth the First both ruthlessly put down opposition by torture and murder. "Bloody Mary" Tudor had hundreds of Protestants burned at the stake in her attempt to reintroduce Catholicism into England. Between 1830 and 1860, Madagascar's Queen Ranavalona, in a campaign to rid the island of Christianity, put missionaries and thousands of native converts to death by having them thrown from cliffs, beheaded, burned at the stake, or boiled alive in pits. Madame Mao engineered the detention and murder of hundreds of potential high-ranking opponents to her faction in "re-education camps" in China.

But we often dismiss these imperial serial killers—motivated by political power—as artifacts of a different time. Their crimes lack the sexual dimension we associate with modern serial killers. The first female who classically fits the bill of the modern serial killer is Elizabeth Bathory—the female Dracula.

Elizabeth Báthory—the True Story of the Blood Countess

Everyone by now has heard the story of the seventeenth-century female vampire serial killer in Transylvania—the Blood Countess, the female Dracula—Elizabeth Báthory.

Elizabeth was once said to be the first "real" female serial killer—one who killed for sadistic, sexual, hedonistic lust instead of political or personal power. Her victims were not her rivals but mostly peasant girls employed in her service or daughters from minor, declining aristocratic families. Elizabeth Báthory is special in that she is the only known female sexual sadistic serial killer without a dominant male partner—to this day, four hundred years later. We have never had another quite like her.

It was said that she bathed in the blood of her adolescent servant girls in the belief that it nourished the beauty of her skin. She was accused at one point of having killed as many as 650 girls— many tortured to death in the most savage and cruel manner.

* * *

Portraits of Countess Elizabeth from her youth show a beautiful woman with raven black hair pulled back from a high forehead, smoky, almond-shaped intelligent eyes, and sensual, pouting lips. Yet there is a cruel curve to her mouth and her face exudes a sullen petulance that betrays an underlying rage.

Elizabeth was born in 1560 into the powerful and wealthy Báthory family in the eastern regions of the Holy Roman Empire—a fluid confederation of territories today roughly covering Hungary, Austria, the former Czechoslovakia, Romania, and other Balkan States, and parts of Germany and Poland. This included the region bordering Hungary and Romania called Transylvania (of Dracula fame, and not coincidentally as we shall see) where her branch of the Báthory family had their seat of power.

At the age of eleven, as traditional with the aristocracy there, Elizabeth was engaged to marry when she would have turned fifteen a minor Hungarian count named Ferenc Nadasdy, five years her elder. A year before the marriage, Elizabeth became pregnant while "horse playing" with a peasant boy on her future mother-in-law's estate. After having the child in a remote estate and giving it away to a local family, Elizabeth finally married Count Nadasdy in 1575 as scheduled.

The marriage was a happy match, although Elizabeth's husband was away for years at a time fighting the Turks in the south where he developed a distinguished reputation as a warrior. Together the couple lorded over a vast network of castles, country manor houses, and palaces in Prague, Vienna, and other cities. At their country estates and inside the walls of their castles they had the power of life and death over their servants and peasants. The adolescent Elizabeth developed a reputation for excessive cruelty while disciplining her female servants.

Elizabeth used her power to torture to death in the most horrific and sadistic ways her servants, mostly peasant girls, burning their genitals with a candle; biting them to death; ripping their mouths open with her own hands; burning them with heated metal rods and rivets; beating them with whips, clubs, or iron bars; cutting and stabbing them; throwing them naked into the snow and pouring freezing water over them; pouring boiled water on them and tearing away their skin; hauling them up in suspended barrels spiked inside and rocking and rolling them while showering in their blood below; or closing them in spiked Iron Maidens like garlic in a garlic press.

Perhaps as many as 650 girls and young women were murdered over a thirty-five-year period—and at least between 37 and 51 in the last decade before Elizabeth's arrest in 1610 at the age of fifty, when she started killing not only peasant girls, but girls of noble birth as well. This led to her downfall.

When her castle was raided during the Christmas holidays of 1610, it was said mutilated corpses of girls were found strewn in the courtyard and in the basement of the tower. When the arresting party burst into her chambers, according to legend, she was found sitting on a stool chewing on the mutilated dying body of a girl prostrate before her. The Hungarian authorities ordered that Elizabeth be walled-in for the rest of her life in a castle apartment with only a small open port for food. After four years she died at the age of fifty-four, her legendary cruel beauty still preserved. The true story of Elizabeth Báthory, however, is slightly more complicated, but horrific nonetheless in its details.

Báthory's Place in the History of Serial Murder

There has been no female serial killer like Elizabeth Báthory because—depending upon what you believe about her—she was either a hedonist lust killer harvesting blood in which to bathe or a highly sadistic power-control freak who loved to torture young women. There have been lots of female serial killers like that, especially recently, but almost all with dominant male partners taking the lead. Not Elizabeth. She started on her own with her husband away at war, learned additional battlefield torture techniques from him when he was home visiting and—after his death in 1604— commanded a retinue of servant accomplices comprised of strong old hags and a manservant, who would lure peasant girls into the household service of the countess where they would be killed. Hundreds of girls vanished like that over the years.

Elizabeth also stands on the historical time line as a premodern serial killer. Her predecessor was Gilles de Rais—"Bluebeard"— the aristocrat in France who was executed in 1440 for the torture murder and necrophile rape of hundreds of male children, also lured by his servant accomplices into his household service.[109] Elizabeth stands at the halfway point between the medieval world of aristocrat serial killers and the industrial modernity of Jack the Ripper, who ushered in a new age of serial killers in 1888. Between Gilles de Rais in 1440 and Jack the Ripper in 1888, we have no serial killers of any significant endurance in the public consciousness or imagination—except for Elizabeth Báthory.

The primary difference between Báthory's era and that of Jack the Ripper is significant. Báthory came from an entirely different civilization—the ancient agrarian world where most people were illiterate and lived isolated in the countryside. Jack the Ripper belonged to the Industrial Age, where people lived in urban centers and read cheap, mechanically printed mass media. It is no coincidence that Jack the Ripper grew to fame in London, the newspaper publishing capital of the world at the time. Our knowledge of the existence of serial killers has as much to do with literacy, cheap paper, and high-speed printing technology as it does with any criminological, psychopathological, or social phenomena.

We actually came very close to never having heard of Elizabeth Báthory because her trial was held in secret in a remote Slovakian town in 1611 and her powerful family immediately sealed its records. There were no newspapers, pamphlets, or broadsides to report on it. None of the ruling families wanted the details of the horrendous charges against their relative released to public scrutiny—nor did they want Elizabeth's estates confiscated by the crown or the crown's debts to her family cancelled. Elizabeth was not even allowed to appear at the trial. Instead of a public execution, she was walled-in alive, in a room in one of her remote castles. Her servants and accomplices took her place on the executioner's block while the countess herself survived in anonymity in her bricked-in apartment until the summer of 1615 when she was discovered dead on the floor.

While her family divided Elizabeth's property among themselves after her death, the details of her crimes and trial vanished from the public record. The indictments, trial transcripts, and judgments were hidden away in closed archives. Her name was forgotten. Only legends and folktales of a blood-drinking female vampire circulated in the Transylvanian mountains until they were picked up two centuries later by authors like Bram Stoker and given a new life in the form of *Dracula*—inspired by another Transylvanian despot, Vlad "The Impaler" Tepes or Dracul (to whom Elizabeth was actually remotely related through marriage).

The Blood Bathing

Elizabeth Báthory would have remained merely an anonymous monster had not a Jesuit scholar, Father Laszlo Turoczy, discovered the trial records in 1720, about one hundred years after her death. Turoczy restored the legendary female vampire to human form with a name, identity, history, and detailed description of her crimes in a book published only in Latin.[110]

It 1796, Michael Wagener, in a book entitled *Articles on Philosophical Anthropology,* was the first to publicize the story of Elizabeth's alleged bathing in blood skin-care motive, stating that after a chambermaid noted some hair out of place in Elizabeth's coiffure, the countess struck her so hard that the girl's nose spurted blood into Elizabeth's face. When Elizabeth wiped the blood, according to Wagener, she discovered that her skin seemed rejuvenated. From then on she would bathe her entire body in fresh blood.[111]

These details, however, often differed depending on the source. The most common version states that Elizabeth's handmaiden's blood spurted onto the countess's *hand.* Moreover, the girls had to be virgins or of aristocratic origins before Elizabeth would believe in the renewing power of bathing in their blood. What was the true story?

It was not until the 1970s that Boston College professor and Fulbright scholar Raymond T. McNally, along with his colleague Radu Florescu, established rare access to Hungarian and Romanian archives (then still behind the Iron Curtain) that led to their hugely popular book, *In Search of Dracula*, a history of the Transylvanian Prince Vlad Tepes, nicknamed Dracul ("Devil" or "Dragon")—the historical figure who inspired Bram Stoker's decision to name his fictional vampire "Dracula" and situate him in a Transylvanian castle.

In the wake of the success of *In Search of Dracula*, McNally returned to the archives in Transylvania and discovered an abundance of original documents from the trial of Elizabeth Báthory.[112] It was not until 1983 that we began to get a more accurate glimpse of what crimes the Blood Countess was actually charged with, and the blood bathing became the first myth to fall. Nowhere in the trial record was there any mention of bathing in blood. It was local gossip and folklore picked up by writers in the eighteenth century. But still, the likely explanation for how this myth took root bodes darkly for what Elizabeth was really into: She was thought to have bathed in blood because she was so covered in it after torturing her victims, it appeared as if she had bathed in it.

Her Arrest
The events that precipitated Elizabeth's arrest in 1610 began when a Lutheran reverend named Janos Ponikenusz was assigned to take

charge of a church in the Slovakian village of Cachtice (Cséjthe), where the widowed Elizabeth lorded in a castle overlooking the village below. Reverend Janos was sent to replace the previous pastor who had recently died. On his journey, just like in a horror movie, the closer he came to Cachtice, the more Janos began to hear peasants' mutterings of vampires and mutilations of young women in the town and guarded warnings of evil deeds in the castle.

On his approach into the village, Janos could see the gloomy castle perched on a steep crag overlooking the town below. Janos could feel the tension as he entered the town. The populace seemed sullen and frightened and very few young women were visible on the streets or the fields. Climbing up the steep deserted road to the castle, Janos reported to the Countess Báthory. The countess was fifty years old and recovering from an illness but her legendary beauty was still evident. She was courteous but Janos detected an unusual cowed tension among her servants and saw very little movement or life in the courtyard—parts of the castle appeared to be deserted and locked-down in silence.

As Janos began to put in order the church records and accounts left behind by his predecessor he uncovered cryptic notes about horrors in the castle on the hill. He found unusually long lists of names of young women who had died in the employ of the countess, women his predecessor would inter only at night while making strange references to the unexplained nature of their deaths and his reluctance to bury them. One note indicated that he had recently entombed nine women in a single night in an underground crypt near the castle walls. Armed with the keys to the crypt, Janos proceeded to explore the tomb. No sooner had he unlocked and thrown open the crypt doors than the fetid smell of death rose up to meet him. In the gloomy chamber Janos discovered nine boxes stacked haphazardly in a corner. The lids were not even nailed shut, according to the deposition Janos later gave. Opening one box after another, Janos was shocked by the condition of the young women's corpses. They were all mutilated, some partly burned, and all caked in dry, dark, crusted blood. On several bodies Janos saw to his horror the clear impressions of human bite marks and deep jagged wounds where it looked like their flesh had been bitten away.

Clearly these women did not die of natural causes, disease, or in the clutches of animals or inhuman monsters: The bite marks were clearly human. The victims had been brutally tortured.

Reverend Janos immediately sent a messenger with a report to his ecclesiastical superior in the provincial capital, but his messenger returned shortly afterward with the news that the countess's guards on the road out of the town had read and confiscated his message. Horrified at the news that the countess knew of his report, Janos attempted to flee the village. He was apprehended by her guard on the road leading from the town and ordered to return and remain in his church. Two hundred fifty years later, Bram Stoker introduced in *Dracula* the character of Jonathan Harker, the English realtor who journeys to Transylvania on business and finds himself imprisoned by the vampire in his castle. Reverend Janos was the real Jonathan Harker, held in a church beneath a horror castle wall by a female monster.

As the situation began unraveling and Janos waited for what would happen next, he gathered details from the villagers about what had been transpiring. His predecessor had been secretly burying bodies of young women who were dying of unexplained circumstances for years, until so many deaths had accumulated that he refused to bury any more. Dumped bodies were being found in the region—four mutilated corpses were found in a grain silo, several in a canal behind the castle, others in the cornfields, and woodcutters discovered freshly dug mass graves in the forest. All the bodies were horribly tortured and mutilated. To his dismay, Janos realized that he was not the first to discover the horror unfolding in Elizabeth's castle.

Denunciations and complaints had been filing in to the Royal authorities for several years. Numerous parents who had sent their daughters to work at Elizabeth's castles lodged official complaints that the countess unsatisfactorily explained their daughters' disappearances. While reports of the cruel torture deaths of peasant girls in Elizabeth's employ circulated for decades, nobody was overly concerned. Disciplining one's servants to death was, in the 1600s, perceived as excessively cruel and impolite but nonetheless it remained an aristocrat's prerogative. But reports began to filter in from other aristocratic families about their daughters' disappearances while in the care of Elizabeth Báthory. These could not be ignored.

The year before her arrest, some twenty-five young women from declining minor noble families were invited to stay at Elizabeth's castle. Some of these minor aristocratic families were happy to send their daughters to Elizabeth, hoping somehow to raise the prestige of their family through an association with the countess. But during their stay, several of the girls vanished. When concerned parents began to inquire into the fates of their daughters, the countess reported that one of the other girls had murdered the girls for their jewels before committing suicide. When her family demanded that the body of their daughter be returned, Elizabeth refused, stating a suicide fatality had to be immediately buried unmarked on unconsecrated ground. She explained other multiple deaths as being caused by outbreaks of disease, and cited the fear of an epidemic panic as the reason for secretly burying those victims.

By the time Reverend Janos finally managed to successfully smuggle out a letter to authorities, he was in the depths of traumatic paranoia. In the 1970s, Professor McNally discovered a letter in the Hungarian archives from Janos to his superior describing how Elizabeth had sent six invisible black cats and dogs to attack him in his home in the middle of the night. As he beat back the attack, screaming, "You devils go to hell," none of his servants could observe any of the animals. "As you can see," Janos wrote, "this was the doing of the devil."[113]

While complaints from peasant families were largely ignored, the reports of missing girls of noble birth were investigated by the Hungarian parliament, situated in Bratislava at that time (the capital, Budapest, was under Turkish occupation). Throughout 1610 the parliament's investigators gathered depositions against the countess from numerous witnesses of both noble and common rank. On December 27, 1610, spurred forward by urgent reports smuggled from Reverend Janos and news that four corpses of young women had been dumped over the castle wall in full view of the village, the parliament ordered Elizabeth's superior (and relative through marriage) Prince George Thurzo to ride to Cachtice, raid Elizabeth's castle and manor house, and arrest the countess.

It was the Christmas season and the countess was celebrating the holiday in her manor house in the town when on the evening of December 29 one of her servants, a young girl named Doricza from the Croatian town of Rednek, was discovered stealing a pear. Enraged, Elizabeth ordered that the girl be taken to the laundry room, stripped naked, and tied. Elizabeth and her female servants took turns attempting to beat Doricza to death with a club. Elizabeth was reported to be so soaked in blood that she had to change her clothes. Doricza was a strong girl and did not die in the beating. It was getting late into the night when Elizabeth tired of beating the girl and had one of her female servants finally stab Doricza to death with a pair of scissors. The girl's corpse was dragged out and left by a doorway in the courtyard for disposal the next morning. At almost exactly that same moment, after traveling two days from Bratislava, Prince Thurzo's raiding party arrived at the house and ordered the servants to stand aside. As the party burst into the courtyard they came upon the bloody, battered, and still warm body of the murdered girl. A search of the premises revealed the bodies of two more brutally murdered girls in the manor house. Reportedly, a further search of the castle on the hill revealed numerous decaying bodies hidden at the bottom of the tower, the bodies that Reverend Janos had earlier refused to bury.

Elizabeth Báthory was locked into her castle at Cachtice, but four of her servants—three elderly females and a young manservant—were taken away by Thurzo to his seat of power in the nearby larger Slovakian town of Bytca and there they were questioned and charged for their complicity in the murders. Here the story of Elizabeth Báthory's trial becomes conspiratorial.

Her Trial

Prince Thurzo was related by marriage to Báthory's powerful family, who were all aware of the deliberations taking place in parliament. (As was Elizabeth, who believed she was beyond the reach of the law.) Aside from their reputation, much was at stake for the family if Elizabeth ended up being convicted for murder or witchcraft—which the rumors of blood bathing warranted. Elizabeth's wealth and properties would have been seized by the Hungarian crown if she were put to death under those circumstances.

Moreover, the Hungarian king had borrowed money from Elizabeth's husband when he was still living, and as his widow, the debt was still owed her. If executed, the crown debt would be cancelled instead of being paid out to her surviving family members. Prince Thurzo had the title of Lord Palatine—meaning that he had the king's judicial powers in his regional principality—and Thurzo staged the trials in his own jurisdiction in such a way as to ensure that Elizabeth's property and the debts to her remained payable to all the surviving relatives. There emerged a vast literature in Hungary, particularly in the heady nationalist periods of the twentieth century, suggesting that Elizabeth Báthory was entirely innocent and a victim of a family plot to seize her wealth. Thanks to the discovery of more court transcripts and witness statements, Thurzo's correspondence, and other archival records in the 1970s, the real story of Elizabeth Báthory is now better known.

The news of Elizabeth's arrest and charges did not become widely known. A priest's diary from the period, with detailed descriptions of events, only provides this short matter-of-fact notation: "1610. 29 December. Elizabeth Báthory was put in the tower behind four walls, because in her rage she killed some of her female servants."

The secret trial began within three days of Báthory's arrest, at Thurzo's courts of justice in Bytca on January 2, 1611. All the court officials and jury members owed their allegiance to Prince Thurzo. The plan, apparently, was to quickly sentence the countess to life imprisonment (*in perpetuis carceribus*—"perpetual incarceration") in a fait accompli while the parliament was on holiday to ensure that her properties were not seized or debt to her cancelled.

While the countess was locked away back in Cachtice, four of her servants were questioned at Bytca, including a session under torture to clear away any loose ends. Using the methodology developed by the Inquisition—which is said to be the first in history to use relational databases in investigative procedure—the same questions were put separately to each prisoner, and then their answers carefully cross-indexed and compared. At the end of the interrogations, the servants were charged as Báthory's accomplices despite their pleas that they had no choice but to obey the countess's orders.

The Trial Testimony

The four were put on trial three days later, on January 2, 1611. Their testimony was entered as evidence against Elizabeth. According to the defendants, the countess tortured her female servants for the slightest mistake. With her own hands, she tore apart the mouth of one servant girl who had made an error while sewing. Every day, young servant girls, who had committed some infraction, would be assembled in the basement of the castle for brutal torture. Elizabeth delighted in the torture of the young women and never missed a session. While torture of one's servants in seventeenth-century Hungary was not a crime, it was by then considered "impolite." Thus when traveling and visiting other aristocrats, the first thing the countess would do was to have a private room secured where she could torture her servants in privacy without offending her hosts. It was noted that the girls chosen for "punishment" seemed to be always those with the biggest breasts and they would be stripped naked prior to the torture.

The four accomplices testified:

> The Countess stuck needles into the girls; she pinched the girls in the face and in other places, and pierced them under their fingernails. Then she dragged the tortured girls naked out into the snow and had the old women pour cold water over them. She helped them with that until the water froze on the victim, who then died as a result . . . Her Ladyship beat the girls and murdered them in such a way that her clothes were drenched in blood. She often had to change her shirt . . . she also had the bloodied stone pavement washed . . . She had the girls undress stark naked, thrown to the ground, and she began to beat them so hard that one could scoop up the blood from their beds by the handfuls . . . It also happened that she bit out individual pieces of flesh from the girls with her teeth. She also attacked the girls with knives, and she hit and tortured them generally in many ways . . . Her Ladyship singed the private parts of a girl with a burning candle. One time Her Ladyship lay sick and therefore could not beat anyone herself, so a servant was compelled to bring the victims to the Countess' bed whereupon she would rise up from her pillow and bite pieces of flesh from the girls' necks, shoulders and breasts.

The girls would be beaten so long that the soles of their feet and the surfaces of their hands bristled. They were beaten so long that each one, without interruption, suffered over five hundred blows from the women accomplices. If the folds of the Countess' clothing were not smoothed out, or if the fire had not been brought up, or if the outer garments of the Countess were not pressed, the girls responsible were at once tortured to death. It happened that the noses and lips of the girls were burned with a flat-iron by Her Ladyship herself or by the old women. The Countess also stuck her own fingers into the mouths of the girls and ripped their mouths and tortured them in this way. If the girls had not finished their obligatory sewing chores by ten o'clock at night, they were immediately tortured . . . Her Ladyship with her own hands had keys heated red-hot and then burned the hands of the girls with them.

While at first it was believed that Elizabeth began her killing spree after her husband's death, witnesses testified that the murders began while her husband was still alive and with his knowledge and participation.

At Sarvar during summer His Lordship Count Ferenc Nadasdy had a young girl undressed until stark naked, while His Lordship looked on with his own eyes; the girl was then covered over with honey and made to stand throughout a day and a night. [So that she'd be covered in insect bites. She collapsed into unconsciousness.] His Lordship taught the Countess that in such a case one must place pieces of paper dipped in oil between the toes of the girl and set them on fire; even if she was already half dead, she would jump up.

The accused servants who were in Elizabeth's service for a period ranging from sixteen to five years, testified that they personally witnessed from a total of thirty-six to as many as "fifty-one, perhaps more" girls killed.

The Downfall of the Countess
In 1607 Elizabeth made the mistake of killing girls from privileged minor aristocratic families. It is unclear exactly why she took this

path, but possibly because her reputation had spread by word-of-mouth among the peasants and few dared to go into her domestic service. Indeed, her last victims were girls recruited from distant Croatia where nobody had heard of Elizabeth. With aristocratic families she used a different approach, always selecting victims from minor and impoverished noble families, offering their daughters opportunities to raise the status of their families through Elizabeth's superior status and contacts. But even this theory is cloudy as there was testimony stating that the servants sometimes washed, groomed, and tutored peasant girls to behave as noble ladies when presented to the countess. For some reason Báthory was specifically targeting nobles at that point. That, of course, led to speculation that she believed only the blood of noble girls would serve the purpose of restoring her skin. The problem with that theory is that the bathing in blood story does not appear in any of the affidavits or in the testimony at the trial. It might be entirely the stuff of peasant folklore picked up a hundred years later and reproduced in pamphlets and books dealing with Elizabeth.

Elizabeth became brazen and careless toward the end of her killing career. While staying in Vienna, she ordered a renowned choir singer from the Church of Holy Mary, Ilona Harczy, to perform privately for her at her apartments in the city on Augustinian Street. The girl was never seen again and witnesses claimed Elizabeth killed her when she could not sing for her, either out of fright or shyness.

As was common in those days, the trial lasted only a day. At the end of the trial two female servants were sentenced to have their fingers torn away with hot pincers before being thrown alive into a fire. The male servant, because of his youth, was sentenced to decapitation and his body also thrown on the fire. The fourth defendant was acquitted and vanished from the record. A few months later, another of Báthory's female servants was charged, tried, and sentenced to death.

The case against Elizabeth Báthory herself was reviewed by a higher court five days later, on January 7, and Prince Thurzo himself testified before some twenty judges and jurors. Unlike the January 2nd lower court trial, the records of which were kept in Hungarian, the high court trial was transcribed in Latin. Thurzo and members of his raiding party described finding the still warm battered corpse of Doricza *"ex flagris et torturis miserabiliter extinctam."* Depositions from thirteen witnesses were heard. It is here that a witness identified only as "the maiden Zusanna" testified that a register was discovered in Elizabeth's chest of drawers listing her victims and that it totaled 650 names. Zusanna testified that in the four years she was in Báthory's service, she witnessed the murder of eighty girls. The hearing was presided over by the king's judge, and its purpose was to appear to gather sufficient evidence to sentence the countess to death, confiscate her properties, and cancel the crown's debt to her. Thus the testimony of Zusanna might have been entirely contrived for that purpose. Báthory desperately petitioned the court to make an appearance to defend herself, but her family blocked those attempts. The high court held:

> At the very entrance to the manor house they came upon things pertinent to this case. There was a certain virgin named Doricza who had been miserably extirpated by pain and torture, two other girls were found murdered in similar agonizing ways with that very manor house in the town of Cachtice, which was under the control of the widow Nadasdy. His illustrious Highness [Prince Thurzo], witnessing this evident and ferocious tyranny, having caught the bloody, and godless woman, the widow Nadasdy, *in flagranti* of her crime, placed her under immediate perpetual imprisonment in Castle Cachtice . . .

She remained imprisoned at Cachtice. Despite the crown's attempt to hold a retrial of Báthory and condemn her to death, the agreement between Thurzo and Elizabeth's family prevailed. When she attempted to challenge Thurzo's authority, he condemned her in front of several of her relatives, saying, "You, Elizabeth, are like a wild animal. You are in the last months of your life. You do not deserve to breathe the air on Earth, nor to see the light of the Lord. You shall disappear from this world and shall never reappear in it again. The shadows will envelop you and you will find time to repent your bestial life. I condemn you, Lady of Cachtice, to lifelong imprisonment in your own castle."

Elizabeth Báthory was walled in in her castle apartment. The exterior windows were bricked up and only several small openings for ventilation and food gave her contact with the outside world. On August 21, 1614, one of the jailers observed the countess collapsed on the floor, dead. All mention of her name in Hungary was prohibited for the next one hundred years. The memory of her faded behind the mists of the vampire and monster legends of Transylvania until her identity was rediscovered in 1720.

Unanswered Questions

A number of questions remain—and oddly enough those same kinds of questions haunt several cases of high-profile convicted female serial killers dealt with in this book, including Aileen Wuornos and Nazi concentration camp monster Ilsa Koch, the Bitch of Buchenwald. Were the identities of these women as serial killers constructed from social, political, or propagandistic exigencies? The attempts of the Hungarian Crown to seize Báthory's property were evident. Moreover, Báthory was a Protestant when the Counter-Reformation and restoration of Catholic power became the priority of the Hungarian parliament. Religious sectarian politics exposed the Báthory family to all manner of hostility during that period.

Moreover, Europe was in the throes of a witchcraft crisis, with thousands of women being accused of heretical and satanic crimes and burned at the stake or hung.

Yet at the same time, witchcraft was not one of the charges brought against Báthory. The rumors of her bathing in virgin girls' blood were never introduced in any of the court proceedings simply because there was no evidence nor any testimony attesting to it.

Nonetheless, when we narrow down the charges to the murder of approximately fifty girls, there is a logical consistency to the descriptions of the offenses from many different witnesses. In the 1970s, two new archival sources were discovered in the Hungarian state archives. One source, dating from September 16, 1610— four months prior to Elizabeth's arrest—contained thirty-four affidavits describing Elizabeth Báthory's torture and murder of "many girls and virgins."[114] A second source, dated July 26, 1611, is from the Crown's attempt to retry Elizabeth. In it is a massive collection of testimony from 224 witnesses attesting to the "diabolical impulses" of the countess who murdered "many innocent virgins of noble and non-noble birth."[115]

If, indeed, Elizabeth Báthory was addicted to committing sadistic acts of torture since her adolescent years, then 650 victims over a thirty-five-year period works out roughly to a "mere" 19 victims a year. It is entirely conceivable—with the power of life and death she had over her servants—that she committed that many murders. The descriptions of the alleged tortures she inflicted on her victims pathologically fit a sadistic power-control or sexual lust murderer—particularly in her choice of young female victims and her desire to bite them on the shoulders and breasts. The crimes that Báthory allegedly committed alone or with accomplices under her command are similar to some committed by female serial killers in recent decades—but most of those women are accomplices to dominant males. But not Elizabeth Báthory—in her crimes, she stands alone among female serial killers.

FEMALE SERIAL KILLERS IN THE PREINDUSTRIAL AGE

Between the era of Agrippina and Elizabeth Báthory and the industrial age of Jack the Ripper, there were occasional reports of female serial killers. In Scotland, in the Galloway region, somewhere between 1560 and 1610, Sawney Beane and his family of cave-dwelling cannibals are said to have killed and eaten thousands of travelers over a forty-five-year period. His family, the product of incest consisting of eight sons and six daughters, eighteen grandsons and fourteen granddaughters, fed on human flesh, which was found by soldiers pickled and smoked in the caves. They were all put to death in Leith without standing trial. The historic authenticity of this episode, however, has not been resolved with any finality, as no contemporary documentation for the event has been identified.[116]

In Naples, Italy, between 1670 and 1719, a woman known only as La Tofania is believed to have been complicit in the murder of possibly as many as 600 male victims through her sale of a poison known as "aqua tofania." She distributed the product free of charge to wives wishing to secretly murder their husbands. The vials of poison were labeled "Manna of St. Nicholas of Bari," a name given to a legendary oil said to have dropped from the tomb of St. Nicholas, and had the power of curing many diseases.[117] Tofania's motive was attributed to her hate of men and she is said to have encouraged her clients to use small amounts of her potion in order to prolong the victims' suffering. Tofania was seventy years old when authorities in Naples, overwhelmed with so many deaths of married men, finally traced the vials to her. Warned of her impending arrest, Tofania attempted to take refuge in a convent, but was dragged out by force, much to the consternation of church authorities. She was put to torture, confessed to hundreds of murders, and was strangled in 1723. Her corpse was then thrown back over the wall into the convent where she had sought refuge.

In France between 1664 and 1672, the aristocratic Marie de Brinvilliers was reported to have poisoned fifty or more victims. Prior to murdering her father, who opposed her marriage, and then her two brothers to seize an inheritance, Marie experimented with poisons concocted by her lover in hospital charity wards, where she began volunteering to care for patients. She carefully observed the effects of her poison on the patients, adjusting the doses accordingly. Marie was discovered and became a fugitive until she was captured in 1676 and beheaded in Paris.

THE RISE OF THE MODERN FEMALE SERIAL KILLER

In the two hundred years that followed the life and death of Elizabeth Báthory the world radically changed in a way it had not in all the previous centuries. The decision by landowners to fence in their rural land and the dawn of the Industrial Age in the mid-1700s uprooted millions of people from the countryside. In a period of several decades, they were rapidly forced into cities to seek work.

In the past, the presence of the poor in cities was a seasonal phenomenon—people would migrate to where the work was, often remaining in the countryside during the summer and autumn. But with factories, masses of the impoverished permanently settled in squalid, densely populated industrial city tenements.

In the past, the destitute found help in country parishes from family, church charities, and other small community aid. City churches could not deal with the masses of anonymous poor funnelling in and now trapped in decrepit, overcrowded city quarters cut off from all family or community support. There was no state welfare, soup kitchens, or health or disability insurance. An injury, a small miscalculation in income and expenses, the loss of a job, or an illness could all condemn a person and their dependent family to a precipitous fall into abject destitution and death from starvation or exposure. Making things worse, throughout the 1700s the manufacture and distribution of cheap gin created an epidemic of a crack cocaine–like addiction, destroying lives and families and driving many into deeper degradation.

Women were extra vulnerable in these times. It would not be until the nineteenth century that females began to find opportunities to work as laborers in factories and clothing mills, as clerks in department stores, and eventually in secretarial positions. Before then, women either hawked wares and produce on the street as in medieval times or they found work as domestic servants in the homes of the rapidly swelling middle-class, which was profiting enormously from the process of industrialization.

Domestic female work, however, was strictly disciplined. Young women, often country girls who left their families behind to seek employment in the city, slaved seven days a week as household servants in exchange for meager room and board. The slightest misstep and the girl would find herself thrown out into the street with no references and with no place to go. A pregnancy for a domestic servant was often tantamount to a death sentence for both mother and child: She would be immediately fired for disreputable behavior, expelled from her lodgings with no hope of finding other employment or any place to go for help. Throughout the 1700s and early 1800s, dead babies were routinely found in city streets, alleys, and empty lots. So prevalent was the murder of infants by destitute mothers that in England laws were introduced prohibiting "the concealment of birth" with a penalty of death by hanging if the child died.

Public executions for even the most minor property crimes further brutalized industrial societies through the 1700s and up until the early 1800s. Literally thousands of women found themselves with no means of support except through theft, at the risk of hanging, or through street prostitution, at the risk of murder and disease. It was precisely these desperately destitute lower-class prostitutes that Jack the Ripper would come to victimize in 1888, in the same way today that some serial killers victimize drug-addicted street hookers.

THE BIRTH OF MASS MEDIA AND TRUE-CRIME LITERATURE

In England, the tone for the despair and brutality of these times was set by the expanding new phenomena of mass media in the form of print. Lurid true crime was one of the first popular genres marketed to the growing newly literate masses. In the 1700s, cheap pamphlets and folded broadsides, illustrated with wood-cuts, featured sensationalistic reports of murders and recent executions. The *Police Gazette* in England began publishing in 1772, while in the U.S. the *National Police Gazette* was founded in 1845.

It is estimated that by 1830 probably between two-thirds and three-quarters of the working class could read. This fed a rapid expansion of mechanically printed media dedicated to true crime.[118] The 1840s brought the introduction of the popular Sunday newspaper, and the abolition of the Stamp Act in 1855 and the paper duty in 1861 brought the cost of newspapers down to one penny first, and to a halfpenny by 1868.

This literature was as intricately focused on the lurid details of murder as true-crime literature and TV are today. As the British publication *Punch* pointed out in a tongue-in-cheek manner in 1849:

Upon the apprehension of a criminal, we notoriously spare no pains to furnish the nation with his complete biography; employing literary gentlemen, of elegant education and profound knowledge of human nature, to examine his birthplace and parish register, to visit his parents, brothers, uncles, and aunts, to procure intelligence of his early school days, diseases which he has passed through, infantile (and more mature) traits of character, etc. We employ artists of eminence to sketch his likeness as he appears at the police court, or views of the farm-house or back kitchen where he has perpetrated the atrocious deed. We entertain intelligence within the prison wall with the male and female turnkeys, gaolers, and other authorities, by whose information we are enabled to describe every act and deed of the prisoner, the state of his health, sleep and digestion, the changes in his appearance, his conversation, his dress and linen, the letters he writes and the meals he takes . . .[119]

Although *Punch* uses the masculine pronoun, nineteenth-century true-crime reporting focused on women as often as men—in fact, female criminals were of a particular interest to the public as their crimes represented such a dramatic contradiction of the feminine ideal of the period. When, in 1849, Maria Manning and her husband, Frederick, were put on trial and executed for the murder of Maria's former lover, the trial was reported in special daily printed reports—the *Court TV* of the period. According to Judith Knelman, a historian of nineteenth-century British true-crime press, one publisher's sales of those reports reached a circulation of an astonishing 2.5 million readers—more than ten percent of England's total population at the time.[120]

By the time Jack the Ripper made his appearance in 1888, the press was primed for and experienced in its coverage of horrendous crimes. Jack the Ripper is often celebrated as the "first" serial killer. He is at least the first to become famous as a certain urban predatory type targeting strangers. But the real fear of serial killers in the nineteenth century unfolded several decades before Jack the Ripper and focused on the female killers who were using poison to kill victims.

The press reports of serial murder by women using arsenic were so alarming that the British parliament urgently enacted special laws to deal with what appeared to be a crisis—very much like the "serial killer epidemic" in the U.S. in the early 1980s to which an alleged disappearance of thousands of children every year was attributed.[121]

Accounts of female serial killers begin to crop up in true-crime literature in the early part of the nineteenth century but from the 1840s onward the accounts began to increase in frequency.

Jane Scott

Twenty-one-year-old Jane Scott is probably one of the earliest known nineteenth-century female serial killers. Sentenced to death

in 1828 for the poisoning murder of her mother, she was also accused of having killed her father, her own illegitimate four-year-
old son, and an eighteen-month-old niece out of revenge after a
quarrel with her sister. The motive for murdering her parents was
that she was getting married and wanted their furniture.

Jane Scott probably typifies the early nineteenth-century female
serial killer in that she killed for meager material gain and to relieve herself of the financial burden of her child. The murder of her
niece in revenge is more unusual. Greed and desperation were the
primary motives of female killers at that time. Desperation sometimes led to parents killing one or more of their children to ensure
that enough was available for the remaining children. With no
compulsory schooling, the disappearance of children at the hands
of their own parents was not be particularly noticed nor did it
alarm the community. Single mothers were especially in desperate
straits.

BURIAL INSURANCE AND THE RISE OF FEMALE SERIAL MURDER

With the 1840s, something new began to happen. One way that
the working classes responded to the absence of state welfare,
health or life insurance, was to pay into various private mutual
aid, welfare, and medical insurance associations. Such insurance
schemes also existed for funerals and were called "burial clubs."
Subscribers paid small weekly fees and when they died the burial
club would pay for their funerals. These payouts would be made,
of course, to the nearest surviving relatives. Death from disease
and accidents was common in the nineteenth century and the
scheme was meant to protect families from bearing the cost of a
funeral, which many could not afford. But there was a loophole: If
death occurred soon after enrollment in the club, then the amount
paid out by the club for the funeral would far exceed the amount
paid in dues. Burial clubs charged up to seven pence every three
months and paid out as much as ten pounds on a death, depending
upon the size of a club. The best of working class funeral services
cost only half that amount—a tidy profit to take home.

Mothers began to bet on their sickly children's lives, enrolling
them in burial clubs just in time to benefit from the maximum payout. Sometimes they would enroll them in several burial clubs at

the same time. When children spoiled the gambit by recovering from their illness, some desperate mothers used arsenic to help them along in the opposite direction. Family members enrolled relatives without their knowledge. And since there were no regulations requiring that death certificates be signed by a medical practitioner giving a cause of death, it was easy to disguise a murder. And even if there was a doctor attending to a death, it was easy to miss signs of poisoning among all the other diseases that frequently killed people in those times.

THE GREAT FEMALE SERIAL KILLER EPIDEMIC OF THE HUNGRY '40S

By the 1840s instances of female serial killers increased dramatically: At least nine women were executed in cases of serial murder between 1843 and 1852. This "epidemic" coincided with a severe downturn in Britain's economy, beginning with a decline in the silk, cotton, and woolen industries in 1839. Food became scarce as people's purchasing power collapsed to a fifteen-year low in 1842. The amount of property crime shot up dramatically in those years. While the economy recovered slightly between 1843 and 1845, a poor harvest the next year along with a rise in the price of cotton and the collapse of railway investment shares drove the economy into another depression for the remainder of the decade, which subsequently became known as the "Hungry '40s."

Elizabeth Eccles

The first of the notorious female killers of the Hungry '40s was Elizabeth Eccles, in her late thirties, who in the autumn of 1842 reported the death of her thirteen-year-old stepson—a common enough occurrence. He was employed at a mill at three shillings a week, which he would promptly turn over to her. He was also enrolled in the mill's burial club. Eccles applied to the mill for burial funds and received fifty shillings. She then promptly asked for another fifty to bury her daughter, who apparently died at about the same time. Since the mill did not employ the daughter, the company refused to pay and alerted the authorities. A coroner's inquest detected the presence of arsenic in the two bodies and in the body of another daughter who had died in 1840. She confessed that she killed her stepson when he threatened to tell his father that she had been drinking and killed her daughter for "the love of money." Elizabeth Eccles was hanged in May 1843.

ARSENIC AND ITS EFFECTS

In the 1840s, arsenic was available as a common household material from any corner druggist. It was a common ingredient for rat poison and as a beauty product as well, said to cure pimples and other skin blemishes. It was cheap: An ounce of white arsenic would cost about ten pence. It was colorless, odorless, and soluble in hot water. Two to four grains—a fraction of a teaspoon—was a lethal dose of the substance. (There are 437.5 grains in one ounce.)

Symptoms of arsenic poisoning are horrific and begin within an hour of ingestion: an acrid sensation in the throat and the onset of unbearable nausea followed by uncontrollable vomiting, which continues long after the stomach is empty. The victim begins to vomit a whitish fluid streaked with blood. The mouth becomes parched, the tongue is thickly coated, and the throat is constricted. The victims suffer from an intense thirst but any attempt to drink immediately results in further bouts of vomiting. In the next stage, the victim suffers from uncontrollable bloody diarrhea and intense abdominal pain with more vomiting, accompanied by a severe burning sensation from the mouth all the way down to the anus. The urine is meager and bloody. Symptoms can include cardiac arrhythmias and ventricular fibrillation often leading to the misdiagnosis of a heart attack in the victim. Whitish lines (Mees' lines) that look much like traumatic injuries are found on the fingernails.

In the final stages, the victim goes pale and the skin takes on a bluish hue, accompanied by a sheen of foul-smelling perspiration. Breathing becomes harsh, irregular, and shallow, the hands and feet go very cold and numb, and the heartbeat grows feeble. Finally, the victim's limbs convulse while their legs are seized by painful cramps. Death comes anywhere from six hours to several days after the ingestion of arsenic, depending upon the amount of poison ingested and physique of the victim.

Essentially, arsenic affects how the body's cells function, disabling their ability to absorb and use proteins and chemicals necessary to sustain human life.

The symptoms of arsenic poisoning resemble cholera, a common deadly infectious disease at the time, the cause of which medical science would not understand until the 1880s. (Bacteria in the water supply or on drinking and eating utensils was often found to be the culprit.) The traces of arsenic left no visible evidence during an autopsy. However, it could be detected by chemical tests—and could be sometimes detected in exhumed corpses several years after death. But it would be several years before coroners began to catch on to the series of murders being secretly committed by some women and testing for arsenic became routine in suspicious cases. In 1847 the *Daily News* trumpeted: "The earth no longer covers the dead. The chemical test discovers what the autopsy left hidden." While the British medical journal *The Lancet* pronounced as late as 1862, "The secret poisoning of the Middle Ages was . . . only a secret because the art of chemical analysis was then very imperfect."[122]

Sarah Dazely

In the meantime, the revelations of serial poisoning murders continued. In March 1843, authorities charged Sarah Dazely with murder. Although in her twenties, Dazely had already been married seven times with her last three husbands dying inexplicably. She was about to be married an eighth time when her husband-to-be, upon hearing neighbors referring to his bride as "a female Bluebeard," decided to cancel the wedding and bring his suspicions to the police. The three husbands were disinterred along with an infant who had died in 1840. Chemical tests revealed the presence of lethal doses of arsenic in two of the husbands while the other corpses had decomposed too much for testing to be possible. Financial gain was never identified as a motive in the murders by Sarah Dazely—she seemed to kill almost vacantly, simply to remove impediments her husbands presented in her desire to marry somebody else. On August 5, 1843, she was hanged publicly before an unruly crowd of 10,000 spectators.

Eliza Joyce

In July 1843 an alcoholic Eliza Joyce was tried for the attempted murder in September 1842 of her stepson. She was already suspected in the death of her 18-month-old stepdaughter in October 1841 and in the death of her 3-week-old daughter in January 1842. Chemical testing could not detect any traces of arsenic and Joyce was acquitted. Her family, however, disowned her entirely and after a year of misery with another infant in a workhouse, Joyce broke down and confessed she had used overdoses of laudanum, a popular opium-based drug used for pain relief and as a sedative for ailments ranging from colds to meningitis to cardiac diseases in both adults and children.

On August 2, 1844, she was hanged before a crowd of 5,000.

Sarah Freeman

The case of 29-year-old Sarah Freeman, who was executed in 1845, was reminiscent of twentieth-century female serial killers who continually murdered their family members without any response from authorities. In a thirteen-month period, Freeman murdered her illegitimate 7-year-old son, her husband, her mother, and her brother. Having completed seven years of school, Freeman was relatively well-educated for the times, but apparently had some sort of personality disorder—she was reported to be so violently short-tempered that her parents expelled her from their home.

Sarah supported herself through prostitution and had two illegitimate children. In 1840 she married a laborer named Charles Freeman and then promptly poisoned him and her son for the twenty-pound payout from a burial club she had enrolled them in. She opened a small shop with the money and moved back in with her parents and brothers. Once again, her violent temper forced them to ask her to leave. She then proceeded to murder her mother and then one of her brothers. It was only after the fourth death that the doctor sent Charles's stomach and intestines for chemical analysis and discovered massive amounts of arsenic.

In the press much was made of the fact that, despite the evidence that members of the same family were dying in the same way, no investigation by the coroner was undertaken. The coroner's office was accused of economizing on the conduct of tests at the expense of working-class citizens. Tried only for her last murder, Sarah Freeman apparently cursed out the court and jury when sentenced to death and was executed on April 23, 1845, before a crowd of 10,000 spectators.

Mary Ann Milner

In July 1847 Mary Ann Milner was tried for poisoning her mother-in-law and sister-in-law. She was found guilty in the case of her sister-in-law. She also eventually confessed to murdering her sister-in-law's infant daughter by feeding her cereal laced with arsenic. Her father-in-law, who ate a poison rice pudding served up by Milner, survived but sustained brain damage. Milner appeared to be underdeveloped intellectually and emotionally, barely able to read or write. She apparently "did not get along" with her in-laws. She committed suicide on July 29, a day before her scheduled hanging.

Sarah Chesham

Cases that surfaced in the countryside appeared to be more disturbing in that there were indications that neighbors were not only aware of poisoners but actually used their services. The *Times* would claim in 1851 that in one district, "the use of arsenic became a kind of family secret, a weapon in the hands of the weaker vessel by which an ill-favored husband or a troublesome family might be readily put out of the way." At the center of these accusations was the 35-year-old Sarah Chesham, who was accused of poisoning an illegitimate baby in the village of Clavering at the behest of the father. The mother of the infant claims that Chesham had inexplicably visited her on two occasions and fed the baby "sugar" and that each time the infant became ill afterward. According to the *Times,* the village was aware that Chesham had killed her own children with poison and was someone who

> . . . could put any expensive or disagreeable object out of the way. The village of Clavering seems to have long ago taken it for granted that the prisoner had poisoned her children, and yet they say little more about it than if she had killed her pigs. It is beyond question that an accepted and reputed murderess walked abroad in a village unchallenged and unaccused, and that all the inhabitants had seen her children buried without a remark or outcry . . . [123]

Nothing could be proven in the death of the infant, but police exhumed the bodies of two of her sons who died under suspicious circumstances within days of each other. The doctor attending the death of the first son recalled that Chesham refused to order a coffin for him, explaining that one coffin can easily hold two bodies. Several days later, her second son died and the two sons were buried together in one coffin. Both had been enrolled in a burial club. When the bodies of her sons were tested, massive doses of arsenic were detected. The problem was that the arsenic could not be conclusively traced to Chesham, and she was acquitted. She went back to the village where she offered advice on how to prepare "special" mince pies that would alleviate any financial family burden. (This kind of rural deprivation-driven serial murder was also reported in the Tiszazug region of Hungary in the 1920s, when police arrested a small secret cabal of female killers who prepared potions for those wanting to murder inconvenient relatives. Some forty murders were uncovered.)[124]

Mary May

In the meantime, Mary May, also in her late thirties, was executed in August 1848 for enrolling her half-brother in a burial club without his knowledge and then serving him a drink laced with arsenic. She planned to use the money to buy a horse and cart so that she could peddle her wares village to village. Mary May had sixteen children, fourteen of whom had died. Shortly before her execution, she also confessed to having murdered her husband, but denied killing the children.

The next year, Sarah Chesham was back in the news, now accused of murdering her husband, Richard, when he became ill and died after Chesham insisted on caring for him. The news of her bragging and offering advice on poison pies to her neighbors was the focus of outraged press reports. Chesham was again tried and this time convicted and executed in March 1851.

A panic was fanned by these press reports, which hinted that secret societies of female serial killers exchanged recipes for poisoned dishes that could be served to husbands, children, and other family members to profit from burial club payments or to simply relieve oneself of them. By now Parliament had passed a bill banning insurance payments of more than three pounds on any child under the age of ten. In 1855 this ban would be raised to six pounds for a child under five, and ten pounds for a child between the ages of five and ten. A death certificate from a physician was required before funds could be released to a beneficiary.

THE SALE OF ARSENIC ACT (1851)

As Chesham was awaiting execution, the House of Lords debated a proposed Sale of Arsenic Act, which required that purchasers of arsenic identify themselves and the amount of and purpose for the poison be registered in the vendors' records along with the purchaser's name. Arsenic was then tinted with a warning color and nobody could purchase less than ten pounds of uncolored arsenic without endorsement by a witness and a written explanation why uncolored arsenic was required. As the history of Chesham's role as a possible village human exterminator-for-hire made the rounds of the press, the House of Lords proposed an amendment to the act adding a clause restricting the sale of arsenic to adult males only. Referring to lower-class rural women, one of the Lords proposing the amendment warned, that "there was a degree of mysterious horror attached to the use of poison, which seemed to attract and fascinate a certain class of minds."

Some opposed the proposed restriction. The nineteenth century liberal philosopher John Stuart Mill lobbied against the amendment, arguing that it:

> . . . singles out women for the purpose of degrading them. It established a special restriction, a peculiar disqualification against them alone. It assumes that women are more addicted than men to committing murder! Does the criminal calendar, or the proceedings of the police courts, show a preponderance of women among the most atrocious criminals?
> . . . If the last two or three murderers had been men with red hair, as well might Parliament have rushed to pass an Act restricting all red haired men from buying or possessing deadly weapons.[125]

In fact, the House of Commons had collected extensive statistics on gender and murder from all the judicial districts in the

United Kingdom between 1840 and 1850. Historically, females represented ten to eleven percent of all of convicted murderers, except in the murder of children where the proportion of female killers is higher than males. But when it came to poisoning in the U.K. in that period, females represented 54 percent of the total of 235 defendants tried for murder or attempted murder by poison in England, Wales, Ireland, and Scotland.[126] (A more recent study determined that there were 342 charges of murder by poisoning in England alone between 1750 and 1914. Females represented nearly 62 percent of the murderers charged in those cases—a total of 210 women.)[127] Despite the unfavorable statistics, cool heads prevailed and when the Sale of Arsenic Act was finally adopted.on May 23, 1851, there was no clause excluding women from purchasing arsenic. The only restriction was that the purchaser had to be an adult.

Mary Emily Cage

There was one more case of a female serial killer from the 1840s when Mary Emily Cage was hanged in August 1851 for the poisoning of her husband. Six years earlier, five of her fourteen children had suddenly died in a two-week period in unexplained circumstances, but there was no conclusive evidence that she was responsible.

Not much detail is known about the 1840s generation of female serial killers other than that they were lower-class impoverished women of limited or no education, frequently living in rural areas or small towns, who used poison to kill both male and female victims related to them. The motive was usually to either profit from burial club payments or to simply relieve themselves of their husbands, children, or other family members. Revenge and rage appeared to be the motive in one of the cases (Mary Ann Milner).

Catherine Wilson

The epidemic of female-perpetrated arsenic serial murders appeared to cease as the 1850s unfolded. There were no comparable cases to those of the 1840s but it is debatable whether that was the result of the Sale of Arsenic Act or murders simply went undetected because female killers began to use other methods. The arrest of Catherine Wilson in 1862 revealed an entirely new profile of the female serial killer.

Unlike the downtrodden, uneducated women who killed their impoverished family members for burial money, Catherine Wilson moved effortlessly among the upper-middle classes posing as a servant or nurse. She was intelligent and cunning. She killed family members, acquaintances, and patients for inheritance or simply to steal their possessions. She developed trusting relationships as a nurse and often convinced her patients to include her in their wills. She did not use arsenic to kill, preferring instead to murder her patients with overdoses of medicine or having them drink sulphuric acid. Leaving behind a trail of victims, she moved around Britain from town to town until she settled in London. Her murders were traced as far back as 1854. She was convicted of murdering her landlady and executed before a huge crowd of 20,000 spectators on October 20, 1862.

Mary Ann Cotton

No sooner had Catherine Wilson been executed than Mary Ann Cotton apparently began her killing. An ordinary-looking former Sunday school teacher and one-time nurse in her late thirties, Cotton reputedly murdered between fifteen and twenty victims in an eight-year period from 1864 to 1872. Killing those in her care, she is believed to have murdered eleven of her own children, five stepchildren, three husbands, a sister-in-law, a lodger, and her own mother. Using arsenic, Cotton easily circumvented the Sale of Arsenic Act by extracting it from rat poison, the sale of which was not controlled. Moving from town to town and remarrying, sometimes bigamously, Mary Ann changed names and identities as she left corpses in her wake. She killed almost mindlessly to relieve herself of the burden of her children or for inheritance. Because she changed jurisdictions so frequently, authorities did not notice a pattern of similar deaths around her—most attributed to "gastric fever."

Mary Ann Cotton was only caught because she tried to unload one of her dying victims into a workhouse. When the victim died, the suspicious workhouse doctor detected arsenic poison and Cotton was arrested on July 18, 1872. Because she was pregnant,

her trial was delayed. But after the birth of a daughter in jail, it began on March 5, 1873. Cotton was convicted for one murder and
executed on March 24.

Cotton became legendary with even a children's rhyme celebrating her notoriety:

> *Mary Ann Cotton*
> *She's dead and she's rotton*
> *She lies in her bed*
> *With her eyes wide oppen.* [sic]

After Mary Ann Cotton, burial insurance regulation, improved
testing for poison, and the control of arsenic sales on a retail level
contributed to a decline in what we might call desperate amateur
poisoning. But it did not stop women who were coldly determined
to kill.

Catherine Flannagan and Margaret Higgins

In 1884 in Liverpool, two sisters, 55-year-old Catherine Flannagan and 41-year-old Margaret Higgins, were jointly convicted of
the murder of Thomas Higgins, Margaret's husband. The two
had managed to insure him with five different burial clubs to the
tune of £108. Then they cleverly soaked arsenic flypaper, the sale
of which was not regulated, until they extracted sufficient arsenic
for a lethal dose. Higgins's brother apparently had been aware
that his sister-in-laws had been profiteering from insuring people
in their slum neighborhood who all seemed to have had untimely
but profitable deaths for the two sisters. After his brother's death,
he alerted authorities and the sisters fled, after Flannagan instructed her daughter to remove and destroy a photograph of her
framed in her house. After their capture, investigators charged
that the two sisters had murdered eight people in addition to
Thomas Higgins, including Mary Higgins, Margaret's stepdaughter, John Flannagan, Catherine's husband, and a woman and her
father who had lodged with Flannagan. They were tried and executed, however, only for the death of Thomas.

Another form of serial murder was connected to "baby farming" and "baby sweating." For small fees women informally ac-

cepted and promised to care for babies that mothers could not afford to keep. Numerous cases arose where the baby farmers simply murdered the infants or allowed them to die from starvation and neglect, while still collecting the fees. "Baby sweating" involved the murder of infants with the knowledge of the mother, often arranged for while the mother was still pregnant. The newly born infant would be taken away by the baby sweater and never seen again.

* * *

The next generation of female poisoners differed from their sisters of the Hungry 40s. The 1850s are divided between past and present by the career of the nurse Florence Nightingale, who became the most famous woman in Victorian Britain after Queen Victoria herself. Nightingale shaped the cottage industry of female nursing into a new disciplined and highly respectable profession, especially after her heroic nursing mission during the Crimean War in 1854–57 when she and a staff of 38 volunteer female nurses reduced British casualties significantly.

The nurse became a new identity and profession for independent women in Victorian society, despite the strict rules and regulations of nursing orders. That mantle of respectability and admiration that nurses garnered was also adopted by late nineteenth-century female serial killers, many of whom were either trained as nurses or pretended to be nurses. This new generation of murdering women was not the class of uneducated, peasant, quasi-medieval, downtrodden female casualties of industrialization, but modern women with professional caregiving status. When Catherine Wilson was arrested, Britain's medical journal *Lancet* commented that her crimes were especially troubling because she posed as a nurse as she killed, a shocking perversion of the ethical principles of medical care and nursing. The "angel of death" female serial killer came to us in the wake of Florence Nightingale and has been with us right up into the twenty-first century.

England would soon become obsessed with Jack the Ripper. But in the U.S. the focus would remain on female serial killers. Although in the usual American way, they put a spin to their crimes uniquely their own.

FEMALE SERIAL KILLERS IN THE NINETEENTH-CENTURY U.S.

One social critic observed that the American Western was really about serial killing all along.[128] And indeed, we encounter some of the first female serial killers in the rural frontier society of the U.S. Kate Bender and her murderous family in Kansas are probably the most famous. The Benders consisted of the 60-year-old father, John, his wife, who was about 50, their 25-year old son, John Jr., along with 24-year-old Kate. Nobody knew where the Benders had come from other than they spoke with a German accent. Upon their arrival in the small railway town of Cherryvale, Kansas, in 1871 they erected a crude cabin measuring 20 by 16 feet. One side of the cabin functioned as their living quarters, while the other side, separated by a canvas sheet, functioned as general store, restaurant, and cheap hotel.

The young Kate Bender appeared to be the pivotal member of the family. She was attractive and claimed to be a psychic and healer, traveling around the towns in the area giving public lectures and séances as Professor Miss Katie Bender. Some of her handbills still survive, which claim that she could "heal all sorts of diseases, can cure blindness, fits, deafness and all such diseases, also deaf and dumbness." The father and mother stayed mostly in the background, while John Jr., it was reported, was an imbecile. Between 1871 and 1873, the Benders murdered numerous travelers stopping to eat or stay at their cabin. Kate would sit them with their backs to the canvas sheet and, while distracting them with her charm, one of the Bender men would come from behind the sheet and smash the victim in the head with a sledgehammer. Kate would then throw herself on the unconscious victim and slit his throat. A specially dug pit and chute in the back allowed them to quickly dispose of a body before another traveler would come in.

Things went wrong when they murdered William York in March 9, 1873, who was returning home from visiting his brother nearby and told him before he left that he planned to stop and have lunch at the Benders' cabin. When William failed to return home, his brother and a posse retraced his journey several weeks later. His trail appeared to go cold at the Bender cabin. After the posse visited the cabin and inquired about the missing man, the Benders packed their things, stripped the cabin bare, and vanished on May 5, 1873.

By then all sorts of suspicious stories were circulating about the Benders and how the men would melt away behind the canvas curtain when customers came in to eat. Several reported that Kate was abusive when they declined to sit against the canvas curtain and took their meals at the counter instead. Another recalled a gust of wind blowing Kate's apron open, revealing her gripping a knife beneath it.

Upon receiving news that the Benders had fled, the posse returned to the cabin and searched it. They immediately discovered the pit and detected a powerful smell of blood rising from it. A search of the grounds around the pit revealed ten or twelve bodies, depending upon the account. The bodies were all male except for one woman and a child. It was estimated that the Benders had robbed their victims of somewhere between $5,000 and $10,000.

The fate of the Benders remains a mystery. It is believed that the posse successfully caught up with them and murdered them, splitting the loot among themselves. The wagon in which the Benders had escaped was later found bullet-ridden. Two members of the posse, one in 1909 and another in 1910, made deathbed confessions that they had killed the family and buried their bodies at the bottom of a twenty-foot dried-out well, although despite attempts, the well could not be found.

Another lesser-known frontier-age female serial killer was Patty Cannon, who between 1802 and 1829 murdered at least twenty-five victims in Delaware, many of them slave traders, whose slaves she'd take and resell for a profit.

Lydia Sherman—American Borgia

While the number of female serial killers flagged in frequency in Britain after the introduction of the Sale of Arsenic Act, in the U.S., where no such legislation was enacted, the 1860s bore witness to the phenomenon that had swept the U.K. One of the first cases garnering major notoriety was that of Lydia Sherman in the 1860s. Lydia would become known as the "American Borgia" in reference to Lucrezia Borgia, a Renaissance-era Italian papal aristocrat reputed to have poisoned several victims in her family's struggles for power. (Although it was never definitively determined to what extent she was complicit in the poisonings.)

Lydia was born in Burlington, Vermont, in 1824 and was orphaned at 9. She and her brother were raised by an uncle in a devout Methodist upbringing. When Lydia was 16 the family moved to New Brunswick, New Jersey, where she worked as a seamstress and faithfully attended the local Methodist Church. It was in church that she met 38-year-old Edward Struck, a widower with six children who worked as a carriage blacksmith. Lydia was 19 when she married Struck in 1843.

Despite the age difference, the marriage appeared to work. In the ensuing years, Lydia had seven children of her own in addition to the six that Edward had from his previous marriage. With thirteen children to support, Lydia and Edward did what many do in their search for fortune—they moved to New York City, eventually settling on 125th Street in Harlem, which was, in that period, a white middle-class neighborhood.

In 1857, Edward, then aged 53, managed to enlist in the New York Police Department, a secure job with additional lucrative opportunities if the officer also happened to be corrupt. Edward apparently was not—to the consternation of his corrupt fellow officers at his precinct—and in his six years of service on the NYPD, he remained honest. This could have been the motive behind his sudden dismissal for cowardice in the autumn of 1863 when Edward was accused of not responding to a barroom fight on his beat. Edward had argued that the fight had been over by the time he arrived, but the dismissal stood.[129]

Edward and Lydia had been married for twenty uneventful years. Seven of their children, six of whom were from Edward's previous marriage, were now adults living on their own, but the couple still had six sons and daughters to care for, the youngest of which, an infant boy named William, had just been born a few months earlier.

Edward was devastated and shamed by the charges of cowardice. At the age of 59, after a lifetime of an up-and-down struggle as a carriage blacksmith, Edward had expected the regular work on the NYPD to cushion the late years of his life. There might even have been a municipal pension in the end. But now that it was suddenly torn from him, Edward could not imagine starting over. Over the winter Edward sunk into a deep depression, unable to seek new work or even leave the family's first-floor apartment. At one point he took a pistol and threatened to commit suicide. By the spring of 1864 he had stopped getting out of bed, washing, dressing, or feeding himself.

Lydia, his faithful wife of twenty years, did her best to help her husband. She took in sewing work at home to make ends meet and cared for him and the children. Eventually she went to see Edward's superior at the police department, Precinct Captain Hart, who had opposed Edward's dismissal, hoping to get him to help her to somehow have her husband reinstated on the force. There was not much Hart could do, and when Lydia described Edward's desperate mental state and the burden he had become to her, Hart suggested that Edward be hospitalized. As he put it, according to Lydia's later testimony, Hart advised that Edward be "put out of the way."

Lydia testified that her husband "caused me at this time a great deal of trouble." After twenty years of marriage, or perhaps precisely because of it, Lydia went to a local pharmacy and purchased an ounce of white arsenic for ten cents. The pharmacist never questioned her purchase of the commonly used household substance—it could have been purchased as easily for poisoning rats as for preventing pimples. The next morning, on May 23, 1864, she fixed Edward a bowl of porridge, mixed a thimbleful of arsenic into it, and gently propping up her husband on a pillow, spoon-fed him the arsenic meal. By the afternoon Edward was in the throes of poisoning, vomiting and suffering from agonizing abdominal pain. As the night wore on Edward was soaked in fetid perspiration while Lydia fed him more poisoned gruel and sat by his bedside wiping his brow and watching her husband curled up in pain. As Lydia explained it, it was the most merciful thing she could do for her husband, for he "would never be any good to me or to himself again."

Edward died the next morning. An attending physician decided that he had died of natural causes—of "consumption" (what tuberculosis was known as in those days). This was 1864 and it would not be until the 1880s that medical science would conclusively identify and understand the relationship between bacteria and certain diseases. Now in her forties, the unsuspected Lydia was a widow with six children, the youngest of whom were 9-month-old baby boy William, 4-year-old Edward Jr., and 6-year-old Martha. It took some five weeks for Lydia to grow despondent and conclude that the youngsters "could [do] nothing for me or for themselves." After thinking about it for a day, in July 1864 she murdered her three youngest children one after the other. The 4-year-old Edward, she recalled, "was a beautiful boy, and did not complain during his illness. He was very patient."

All three children died painfully but there was no suspicion in their deaths. All were attributed to "remittent fever" and "bronchitis." In the 1860s children died even more routinely than adults of a host of illnesses, none entirely understood by the medical science of the day.

With three fewer mouths to feed, Lydia felt she could sustain the remaining three children in her family: 14-year-old George and two older girls, 12-year-old Ann and her 18-year-old namesake, Lydia. Moreover, after witnessing the tender care Lydia gave her three dying children, a neighborhood physician hired her as a full-time nurse. (No evidence was found later, however, that Lydia killed any patients during that period of employment.)

Employed as a nurse, with her son George working as a painter's assistant for $2.50 a week and her daughter Lydia clerking at a dry-goods store in Harlem, the family seemed to get along financially. But then George developed what was then known as "painter's cholic"—a disabling disease resulting from lead poisoning from handling paint. Lydia nursed her son for a week, but when he failed to regain his health sufficiently fast enough to go back to work, she recalled that she became "discouraged."

Lydia confessed later, "I thought he would become a burden upon me, so I mixed up some arsenic in his tea. I think he died the next morning."

In the winter, little Ann became frequently sick with chills and fevers, requiring that her sister Lydia remain home from the dry-goods store to care for her while her mother worked as a nurse. Eventually, the sister had to leave her employment at the store and take on the much less-paying home job of sewing hat and bonnet frames. The mother later said, "I thought if I got rid of her that Lydia and myself could make a living."

Lydia went to a drugstore and bought some cold medicine, into which she then mixed arsenic. Ann began to vomit and suffer agonizing stomach pains as her mother attempted to "nurse" her. The physician who employed Lydia diagnosed her daughter as suffering from typhoid fever and gave Lydia time off work to stay at home to "care" for her little girl. It took Ann four days to die her horrific death.

Only the two Lydias remained. Mother and daughter moved into a smaller and cheaper apartment on upper Broadway, but in May the young Lydia came down suddenly with a fever. Despite her mother's efforts to nurse her back to health, young Lydia was buried in a family plot in New York's Trinity graveyard next to her father and five brothers and sisters. Despite the recollections of a pastor who witnessed the daughter's convulsive death, the same physician diagnosed it as typhoid fever again. Lydia herself, while confessing to the other murders, insisted that she had nothing to do with the death of her eldest daughter.

Lydia's adult stepson was suspicious of his father's death and the rapid demise of his stepbrothers and sisters. He urged the New York District Attorney's office to exhume all seven bodies and conduct tests for arsenic. But it was too late. Lydia, totally free of any familial obligations for the first time in twenty-two years, had disappeared.

In his study of American female poisoners, Harold Schechter writes that, "In her own grotesque way, the forty-two-year-old ex-wife and mother was authentically American: a true believer in the possibility of endless self-renewal, of leaving the past behind and reinventing her life."[130] Lydia had left her work as a nurse and moved back downtown, finding employment as a clerk in a sewing machine store on Canal Street. There she met and charmed a customer from Stratford, Connecticut, who was impressed with her lively personality and experience as a nurse, and hired her to take care of his invalid mother for room and board and eight dollars a week. Within weeks of arriving in Stratford, Lydia met a wealthy old farmer, Dennis Hurlburt, whose wife had recently died. Hurlburt was looking for a housekeeper and Lydia leapt at the opportunity. She later stated that she had been there only a few days when the old man wanted to marry her.

Lydia was a relatively attractive woman. Her photograph from the period shows a thin, delicately featured woman with a full mouth and slightly melancholic eyes who looks younger than her 40 years. In addition to her good looks, if she was a psychopath she might also have had the typical psychopath's charismatic personality that mesmerized the physician who employed her, the gentleman who hired her to take care of his mother, and now the widowed farmer who wanted to marry her.

Lydia later confessed that she agreed to marry Hurlburt if he promised, "all that he was worth should be mine." The old man signed a will leaving his entire estate to Lydia. Witnesses later recalled that for more than a year they saw Lydia greeting her husband at the door with kisses, cooking his meals, mending his clothes, and even shaving him when his hands began to tremble too much.

One Sunday morning in 1868 as Hurlburt was preparing to go to church, he felt suddenly dizzy and fell ill. As the day went on, he became progressively weaker. Noting his absence, neighbors dropped by the next day and brought along some freshly dug clams, from which Lydia diligently prepared a chowder laced with arsenic. Throughout that Monday, Hurlburt twisted with abdominal pains and vomiting. On Tuesday, at his insistence, a physician was called, who later recalled that he could immediately see that Hurlburt was at death's door. The physician was touched by how much care Lydia lavished on her dying husband, wiping his brow and attempting to keep his strength up with broth and medicines she carefully prepared herself. Hurlburt died an agonizing death the next day, which the physician certified as "cholera morbus."

The 46-year-old widow inherited $20,000 in property and $10,000 in cash, a substantial amount in those days. She had no financial cares left in her life and no husband or children to cramp her space or cause her concern. Just as Lydia had recalled when her last child died, she now "felt good . . . I had nothing to fret or trouble me."

Within a year Lydia took up with another widower, Horatio N. Sherman, an outgoing, heavy-drinking factory mechanic whose wife had just recently died leaving him with four children, one of whom was a sickly infant child, and a mother-in-law living in his house. It is hard to explain Lydia's motives. Horatio was actually in debt, and Lydia ended up paying the $300 he owed—he was no cash cow. Perhaps by now Lydia was addicted to a surge of power she felt every time she put a victim to death.

Lydia and Horatio Sherman married in September 1870. Two months later, Lydia put arsenic in Horatio's infant son's milk and after a bout of terrible stomach pains the already sickly infant died the same night. The next month, Horatio's 14-year-old daughter, Ada, well known in the town as a pretty and sweet child, became ill during the Christmas holidays. Lydia did her best to nurse Ada back to health, diligently making sure she drank the tea she prepared for her every day. Ada was a strong and healthy girl and for five days suffered from constant vomiting, bloody diarrhea, and excruciatingly painful abdominal spasms until she succumbed on New Year's Eve.

By April 1871, the couple was said to have taken separate bedrooms. Despondent over the death of his infant son and his young daughter, Horatio went on a drinking binge in New Haven. Lydia sent his 17-year-old son to find him and bring him home, which he did. The next day, Horatio went back to work at the factory. When he returned home, Lydia was waiting for him with a delicious cup of hot chocolate. It took Horatio four days to succumb to an agonizing death on May 12, despite the efforts of his physician Dr. Beardsley.

Beardsley was an experienced physician who had treated several cases of accidental arsenic poisoning and who immediately recognized the symptoms. While treating Horatio, Beardsley had asked if he had taken any medicines other than the ones he prescribed. Horatio respond with his last known words, "Only what my wife has given me."

Beardsley secured permission to autopsy Horatio's body and sent specimens to a toxicology expert at Yale. Enough arsenic was found in Horatio's liver to kill several men. A warrant was immediately issued for Lydia Sherman's arrest, but she had already left town, returning to New Brunswick. In the meantime, the bodies of Horatio's two children and Lydia's second husband, Hurlburt, were exhumed and arsenic was also found in their bodies. Soon, police also learned of the seven deaths linked to Lydia in New York.

On June 7, 1871, detectives followed Lydia on a shopping trip from New Brunswick to New York. That evening, when she returned to New Brunswick, she was arrested as she stepped off the commuter train at the station. She was tried in New Haven, Connecticut, in April 1872, in a highly publicized eight-day trial. Nicknamed the "American Borgia" and "Queen Poisoner" Lydia became the subject of numerous books and songs and poems. The American public was fascinated with this serial murderess.

So inexplicable and insane were Lydia Sherman's murders that the authorities could not see their way to charging her with capital murder and instead she was tried for the murder in second-degree of Horatio Sherman. Her murders to relieve herself of the burden of her spouses and children are reminiscent of Susan Smith, the 23-year-old woman who in 1994 in South Carolina let her car roll into a lake with her two children strapped in the backseat. The defense attempted to argue that she had "accidentally" murdered Horatio—or that perhaps he had committed suicide after the death of his children and that there was no conclusive evidence Lydia poisoned anyone.

But in the end a jury convicted Lydia on circumstantial evidence. She was sentenced to life imprisonment. She had only served five years when she became ill and died in prison in May 1878 at the age of 54.

Sarah Jane Robinson

No sooner had Lydia Sherman died than Sarah Jane Robinson made her appearance. While the murders committed by Sherman were inexplicable in their motive, Sarah Robinson was on a hedonistic murder-for-profit campaign. Sarah was born in Ireland around 1837. When her parents died within months of each other in 1850 the 14-year-old Sarah took her 9-year-old younger sister, Annie, and sailed to America to join their older brother in the Boston area. Once in the U.S. the sisters, although remaining close, lived separate lives. Annie McCormick married, but unfortunately her husband was killed in an industrial accident. Several years later, in 1879, she married for a second time, an unskilled laborer named Prince Arthur Freeman. They lived in crushing poverty, Prince making a few dollars a week at a metal foundry while

Annie worked as a seamstress. Shortly after their second child was born, Annie contracted pneumonia in February 1885 and needed bedside care.

Sarah volunteered for the task and settled in the Freeman residence, dismissing the nurse hired by Prince's mother to care for Annie. Sarah, although a seamstress by trade like her sister, claimed to have also had nursing experience. Sarah appeared to be a caring, outgoing, energetic, friendly, and diligent, churchgoing woman, but there was trouble lurking in the shadows. Sarah was married to laborer Moses Robinson and had eight children, three of whom had died. Although she had a reputation as a trustworthy seamstress with private and corporate clients, she was always behind in her rent and bills. She attempted to raise money by renting furniture and then mortgaging it several times over to different companies, but ended up being caught.

It was 1881 when Sarah is thought to have committed her first murder. When her family's landlord, 70-year-old Oliver Sleeper, fell ill, Sarah offered to nurse him. He died of "heart disease" despite Sarah's constant bedside care. Sarah charged his estate fifty dollars for her services but instead received a remission on her rent, which she sold on discount for cash to other tenants. Sleeper was known to have $3,000 cash on hand, but it was never found. It's unknown whether Sarah got her hands on that money.

The next year Sarah husband, Moses, suddenly died. Moses had been insured for $2,000 with the Order of Pilgrim Fathers insurance association. But when Sarah attempted to collect on the insurance it was discovered that an agent had stolen the premium payments Moses had made. The company refused to pay out and Sarah sued. The lawsuit was pending when she was arrested for murder several years later.

By the time Sarah arrived at the Freeman's tenement apartment, her sister's health had significantly improved. But Sarah, who claimed to have psychic powers, insisted that she had dreamt that Annie was going to get only sicker and die. And sure enough, the first night that Sarah nursed Annie, she suddenly developed wrenching stomach pains and started vomiting. As hard as Sarah tried to nurse Annie, making sure Annie took down every medicinal drink she prepared for her, Annie eventually died on February 27, 1885.

The caring and generous Sarah revealed to the family that Annie's last wish was that her husband, Prince, and their two children—1-year-old Elizabeth and 6-year-old Thomas—move in with her. Stunned at the sudden death of his wife and overwhelmed by the warmth of his sister-in-law, Prince and the two children moved into Sarah's home in April.

Three weeks later, tragedy struck again. Elizabeth contracted an intestinal disorder and despite the care that Sarah lavished on the little girl in her attempt to nurse her back to health, the girl died painfully. Sarah sat Prince down for a heart-to-heart talk. Death and disease were rampant among the poor of their class, Sarah explained. Prince had wisely purchased a $2,000 life insurance policy, also from the Pilgrim Fathers, but the beneficiary, Annie, had died. Would it not be wise if she were made the beneficiary, Sarah suggested. Who would care for his little boy, Thomas, should anything happen to him, Sarah argued. On May 31, Prince made Sarah the beneficiary of his $2,000 insurance policy.

Witnesses would later testify that Sarah's kind and caring treatment of Prince immediately vaporized to be replaced by a harsh and critical attitude. She told friends that Prince was "good-for-nothing" and that she wished it had been he who died and not her poor sister. She began to get her psychic visions again with premonitions of death for somebody in the household.

On June 17, 1885, she told Prince that it might be a good idea that he visit his mother because it might be the last chance to see her. Prince, who believed in Sarah's psychic powers, rushed over to his mother's home, but to his relief found her in excellent health.

On the morning of June 22, 1885, Sarah served Prince a bowl of oatmeal and molasses and saw him off to work. On his way to work Prince was overcome with nausea. He managed to get to work but was so wracked with abdominal pains that he was sent home. Two different physicians attended to Prince and they recognized symptoms of poisoning but assumed that he somehow was poisoned accidentally in the workplace. Nobody suspected the caring and gregarious Sarah Jane Robinson. When Prince's sister came to nurse her brother, it appeared that he might still recover, but when his health improved so much that his sister returned home, Sarah took up nursing him again. That same night, on June 27, Prince died.

Sarah collected the $2,000 insurance benefit from the Order of Pilgrim Fathers and set out to pay her debts, move into a larger apartment, buy new clothes and furniture, and take a trip to Wisconsin. With the last of the money she bought an insurance policy on the life of her 25-year-old daughter, Lizzie. Just in time, too, because six months later, in February 1886, Lizzie contracted some kind of stomach ailment and, despite all the nursing done by Sarah, she died an agonizing death.

In the year since his father's death, the now 7-year-old boy Thomas was virtually ignored by Sarah and often treated brutally. When neighbors remarked that the lad appeared to be undernourished, Sarah commented that his health was not all that good to begin with. On July 19, 1886, little Tommy fell ill with some form of gastric infection and died on July 23, curled up in pain.

In the meantime, Sarah's adult son, William, shortly after his sister's death, insured his life with the Order of Pilgrim Fathers, making his mother the beneficiary. A month later he felt nauseous after eating a breakfast prepared for him by Sarah. In the evening, after drinking tea his mother served him, William began to suffer from stomach cramps.

The next morning a physician was sent for to look at William. The doctor was affiliated with the Order of Pilgrim Fathers and was acutely aware of the strange series of deaths dogging this family whose members had bought insurance policies. The doctor secretly took a sample of William's vomit and sent it to a Harvard toxicologist, who discovered massive amounts of arsenic. But it was too late: By the time the test results arrived, William had died. The last words witnesses heard him saying were, "The old lady dosed me."[131]

Sarah Jane Robinson was arrested for the murder of her son while authorities exhumed the bodies of six of her victims: her brother-in-law, Prince; her daughter, Lizzie; her sister, Annie; her nephew, Tommy; her husband, Moses; and her aged landlord. Tests revealed massive traces of arsenic in all the corpses.

Sarah was charged with first-degree murder because of the obvious profit motive, but her defense attorney argued that mere financial profit could not be motive alone for so many murders. Sarah had to be suffering from "uncontrolled depravity," the attorney insisted. She was a monster. "I do not know that the law hangs monsters," Sarah's lawyer argued. The jury thought otherwise and Sarah was convicted for murder and sentenced to death, but the sentence was later commuted to life imprisonment. She died in prison in 1906 at the age of seventy. She insisted on her innocence to the end.

Jane Toppan—American Female Serial Killer Superstar

While the eight murders attributed to Sarah Robinson were clearly committed for profit, the thirty-one or more killings perpetrated by Jane Toppan between 1880–1901 were entirely inexplicable. Unlike the poor lower-class wretched females who murdered for small financial gains, Jane Toppan was a trained nurse who moved effortlessly among the middle and upper-middle classes. While we know very little about the early lives of the female serial killers so far described, we know more about Jane Toppan.

She was born Honora A. Kelly somewhere between 1854 and 1857—sources vary on her age—and was the youngest of four sisters from a desperately poor family of Irish immigrants in Massachusetts. Her mother died when she was a year old and her father, Peter Kelly, a tailor, attempted to raise the girls. Unfortunately, the father was mentally ill and several years later he was confined to a mental institution for the rest of his life. A grandmother attempted to raise the children but soon found herself destitute and unable to keep them. The girls were turned over to the Boston Female Asylum for Destitute Girls and adopted out to different families.

An English protestant family named Toppan, who already had two adult daughters, adopted Honora when she was 5 years old under a type of indentured adoption where if unsatisfied they could send her back to the asylum at anytime up to the age of 18. Her name was changed to Jane Toppan. With thick black hair, olive skin, a prominent nose, and big brown eyes, Jane was passed off as an Italian orphan whose parents had died at sea. To have been Irish in those days was humiliating, and Ann Toppan, Jane's WASP stepmother, whom Jane called "Auntie," reminded her that just because she was born Irish she did not have to behave that way. Jane developed a loathing for her family heritage.

Ann Toppan was a strict disciplinarian and treated Jane as a household servant. Despite the fact Jane carried the Toppan name, she was never accepted on equal terms as a family member. When she turned 18, she was emancipated from her indenture and received a payment of fifty dollars from the Toppans. Although now free, she remained living at home providing housekeeping services in exchange for room and board.

Several years later, when Jane's stepmother died, she left an inheritance to her two daughters, but made no mention of Jane in her will. One of the daughters, Elizabeth, took over the house. Jane remained living in the house, basically performing the same household servant functions for Elizabeth that she had for her mother, but unlike their mother, Elizabeth treated Jane with kindness and respect.

Witnesses who went to school with Jane recalled that she was a gregarious and popular girl but that she told exaggerated lies about herself—that her father had sailed around the world and lived in China, that her brother was personally decorated by Lincoln at Gettysburg, and that her sister was a renowned beauty who had married an English lord. In fact, one of Jane's natural sisters would be confined in an insane asylum when she was in her twenties. Nevertheless, Jane was regarded among her peers as the "life of the party" and attended picnics, skating, and boating parties.

What we can see in Jane's childhood profile are the potential seeds for a psychopath: an early breaking of the bonds between mother and child, possible traumatic childhood events, mental illness in the family, lack of genuine affection and nurturing from her stepparents, a tendency to fantasize and tell lies, a sense of disempowerment and shame. While Jane maintained an outwardly open and friendly personality, internally she was locked down in a defensive posture, even though after her adoption she was not necessarily abused severely. In the territory between her outward personality and her inward psyche, fantasies were at play, possibly focused on empowerment and esteem, which she clearly lacked. The grandiose lies she told hinted at the vast gulf between her desire and her actual life.

Jane's stepsister Elizabeth married a church deacon, Oramel Brigham, who moved into the house. Jane continued to live in the house with the newlywed couple in exchange for her services as a maid. Jane had no inheritance, no social status, no profession or higher education, no husband or family of her own. Despite the fact the Brighams apparently treated Jane kindly, some kind of unarticulated seething hostility eventually led to relations becoming so strained that in 1885 Jane moved out of the home she had lived in for nearly twenty years. Nevertheless, Elizabeth told Jane she was welcome to visit her home anytime and that "there would always be a room waiting for her."

Almost nothing is known about what Jane did for the next two years. Few rewarding opportunities were available for a "respectable" single woman in those days: schoolteacher, seamstress, housemaid, or textile worker. None of these appealed to Jane, who had grandiose ideas of being destined for something better. And so it came to pass that in 1887, at the age of 33, the psychopathic Jane decided on a career in nursing. She was admitted to the Cambridge Hospital nursing school in Boston.

Jolly Jane

In the nineteenth century, going to nursing school was akin to becoming a nun in terms of lifestyle, commitment, and discipline. This is not unusual considering that traditionally church monasteries functioned as the first organized hospitals in the medieval era with nuns serving as nurses and monks as physicians. Florence Nightingale had introduced a new standard of professional disciplined nursing in the 1850s, which demanded strict conformity, obedience, and sacrificial devotion to duty.

In the 1880s nurses in America typically trained for two years in grueling conditions: They worked seven days a week for fifty weeks a year—no Christmas, Easter, or Thanksgiving holidays. Several student nurses would share a small room, sleeping on narrow cots. They would be awakened at 5:30 A.M. and given time to make their beds, dress, and prepare their own breakfasts. They typically worked twelve-to-fourteen-hour shifts with seventy-five-minute breaks for lunch and supper, which were provided for them. The food was so bad that they frequently had to purchase their own provisions. Each nurse would have approximately fifty patients to take care of: prepare food for and feed, bathe, dress, clean their wounds, change their bandages, wash their clothing and bed linen. Student nurses were also expected to take care of their wards by cleaning, dusting, washing the floors and windows, and stoking the stove.

Discipline administrated by head nurses was strict—the smallest infraction such as lateness, failing to clean properly, leaving the ward without permission, or even complaining about the food could be punishable by dismissal or penalizing comments in the student's record. The nurses would sign a contract by which they were bound to serve a period of two years. In exchange they received room and board, a bib apron and nurse's cap, and a salary of seven dollars a week, from which they had to pay for clothes, textbooks, and other expenses.[132] Once a week they were required to attend lectures in the evening on medical theory. At the end of two years the students would be examined on their medical and nursing knowledge by a board of physicians and, if they passed, were issued a diploma certifying them as professional nurses.

Jane Toppan's fellow nursing students remembered her as a gregarious and cheerful person but with a hidden threatening side to her. Jane Toppan tended to spread gossip and rumors about student nurses she did not like and implicated several students in infractions they did not commit but which resulted in their dismissal. Several of her acquaintances would later testify to the glee with which Jane celebrated the innocent students' dismissals from nursing school. If we accept anthropologists' assertions that gossip and slander are early signs of female aggression, then Jane Toppan fits the bill.

Along with the gossip, Jane also spun exaggerated, aggrandizing lies about herself, claiming, for example, that the Tsar of Russia had offered her a nursing position with his family.

Although it was never proven, she apparently committed acts of petty theft against fellow students and from hospital supplies, but evaded detection every time. Many of the students and supervisors came to detest Jane, but senior staff and patients were completely enamored with her happy disposition and daily good cheer. She was nicknamed "Jolly Jane."

Jane Toppan appreciated the admiration that some patients gave her. She liked those patients so much that when there was the possibility that they had sufficiently recovered from their illnesses to be released, Jane would doctor their medical charts to indicate worsening conditions or she would administer small overdoses of medicine causing alarming symptoms that would result in the patients being held longer in the hospital. But for those patients Jane did *not* like, another fate awaited.

Jane's Addiction

After her arrest, investigators found numerous textbooks, many of them showing extra wear on pages dealing with poisons and dangerous drugs—particularly morphine, an opiate used for pain relief, but which in a massive dose can cause death. According to her confession later, Toppan became addicted to the thrill of watching patients die from morphine overdose. She would stand over their beds, looking into their dying eyes and watching their pupils contract, listening to the breath shorten and then cease. She said that these murders became "a habit of her life" and caused her "delirious enjoyment."

Eventually, she began to experiment with combinations of drugs, such as morphine with atropine, which had opposite effects from morphine. Overdoses of atropine would cause the pupils to dilate, the heart rate to increase, and spasms to shake the patient. Often there was delirium and seizures with the patient hallucinating and losing all muscular control. Toppan would first inject morphine and as the patient sank into a coma she would then revive her victim with doses of atropine, which would then cause death. She was sadistically transfixed by her patients' deaths. She would inject alternating doses of morphine and atropine just to watch their opposing effects on the victims' pupil sizes. Like a deranged, mad scientist, she toyed with different combinations of lethal doses of the two drugs, which misled the physicians, who failed to note any kind of recognizable pattern in the symptoms of the dying patients. All this, she confessed, gave her a "voluptuous delight"—a Victorian way of saying "sexual pleasure."

There was only one known survivor of Toppan's murders, who was able to describe what transpired. Thirty-six-year-old Amelia Phinney was hospitalized with a uterine ulcer and was tossing in her bed in pain, unable to sleep. Then Jane Toppan came in, raised her head and put a glass to her lips. She told Phinney to drink the liquid because it "would make her feel better." Phinney recalled feeling her mouth and throat go unusually dry, her body grow numb, and her eyelids feel heavy as she began to slip into unconsciousness. Then a strange thing happened: She felt the blankets pulled back, the bed creak, and the mattress sag as Toppan got into the bed with her. Toppan cuddled with her, stroking her hair and kissing her face. She remembered Toppan then getting up on her knees next to her and peering into her eyes, no doubt observing the state of her pupils. Phinney was convinced she was dreaming, but when Toppan lifted up the glass again to her lips and told her to drink some more, Phinney mustered up all her strength and turned away. The last thing she remembers is Toppan suddenly jumping off the bed and dashing out of the room. Somebody must have been approaching.

Phinney awoke the next morning in an extremely groggy state, but her recollections of the night were so weird that she was not sure whether she had hallucinated them or not. Moreover, they were embarrassing. Phinney did not report her experience until years later when Toppan was arrested.

Although "Jolly Jane" charmed senior staff and particularly physicians—who had sporadic contact with her—her immediate supervisors and fellow students developed an intense dislike for her. Her constant tall tales and her gossiping about others alienated people around her. She was also suspected of thieving hospital supplies and patients' belongings, but nothing could be proven. Nor could anything be proven about the unusually high rate of death among patients in Jane's care. It would have been inconceivable that a student nurse was deliberately murdering them.

Despite this, or precisely because of it, Toppan transferred in 1888 to the Massachusetts General Hospital nursing school. She arrived with a handful of glowing recommendations from Cambridge Hospital physicians. Very soon, however, she alienated her immediate supervisors at Massachusetts General. In the summer of 1890, shortly after having successfully passed her exams, Toppan was reported to have left a ward without permission and was immediately dismissed without a diploma being issued.

Toppan secured employment as a head nurse at another Cambridge hospital using a forged diploma, but she was dismissed a few months later after the forgery was discovered when she was again suspected of stealing patients' property and doctoring patient records.

Toppan then decided to go out on her own as a private nurse. She still had excellent recommendations from physicians and over the next ten years she received so many testimonials and referrals from physicians that she became known as Cambridge's most successful private nurse. She had a host of clients from New England's prominent families and physicians clamoring for her services for their wealthy patients. As a private nurse, she earned twenty-five dollars a week, a fortune compared to the five dollars a week that women on average earned in the U.S. in that era. Despite this success, minor complaints from patients continued to dog Toppan: She borrowed money without repaying it, she fibbed, and she was suspected of small thefts from the patients' homes she visited. These faults, however, were overlooked because of the cheerful and exuberant manner in which Jane Toppan nursed her patients. Jane had developed a dual personality: With clients she was demure, never drank, and was pleasantly well-behaved, but to the friends she socialized with she showed another side, telling obscene jokes, drinking beer, and displaying a seething vindictiveness against those she thought might have crossed her. She took great delight in causing grief for no reason by telling tales, gossiping, and turning people against each other.

Victims

It is unclear how many patients Toppan murdered during her period as a student nurse and later as a private nurse. In the end, Toppan confessed in detail to the murder of thirty-one victims between 1880 and 1901. In her later stage of killing she focused her attentions on individuals other than her patients. After befriending her elderly landlord couple, 77-year-old Israel Dunham and his wife, Lovey, Jane murdered them one by one: first the husband in 1895 and then, two years later, his widow. According to Jane, they had become "feeble and fussy" and "old and cranky." Several witnesses from nursing school and from her period as a private nurse would recall Toppan commenting "there was no use in keeping old people alive."

In December 1889, 70-year-old Mary McLear, while visiting her granddaughter in Cambridge over the Christmas holidays, fell ill. The attending physician sent for "one of his best nurses"—Jane Toppan—to care for the elderly woman. McLear died on December 29 after four days in the care of "Jolly Jane." After the funeral, relatives noticed that some of McLear's best clothing had gone missing and voiced suspicions to the doctor who immediately assured them that nurse Toppan was one of "the finest women and best nurses he knew." The issue was dropped.

Jane Toppan was in demand and well paid. Financial gain could not have been a pressing motive in these murders. The stealing must have been the final exercise of her power over her victims or perhaps a satisfaction of her need for trophies, a characteristic of some serial murders.

A Cold Dish of Vengeance

Eventually, Jane Toppan turned her murderous attention on her older stepsister Elizabeth and her deacon husband, Oramel Brigham. Every once in a while "Jolly Jane" would take Elizabeth up on her offer to visit and stay at the house she was raised in. The tensions of years ago had long been forgotten and soothed by Jane's good-natured cheer. She was sincerely welcomed at the house.

But in the summer of 1899 Elizabeth found herself suddenly unable to shake off a persistent winter melancholy. Jane came to the rescue. She invited her sister for some picnicking on the beach and fresh air at a cottage she was renting on Buzzards Bay in Massachusetts. Giving her fifty dollars for expenses, Oramel saw his wife off on August 25, entrusting her into Jane's care. Two days later, he received an urgent telegram from Jane informing him that Elizabeth had fallen seriously ill. By the time Oramel arrived on the train, Elizabeth was in a deep coma. According to an attending physician, she had had a stroke. She died the next day on August 28.

Broken-hearted, Oramel was packing Elizabeth's things when he noticed that her handbag had only five dollars in it. Forty-five dollars were missing and when he asked Jane about it, she said she knew nothing about it. As Oramel was leaving, Jane told him that

Elizabeth, in her last dying days, had wanted Jane to have her gold watch and chain as a reminder of her. Touched by his wife's tender concern for her younger stepsister, Oramel immediately gave Jane the watch. In later years he was equally touched by Jane's reluctance to carry the watch—she had such fond respect for a precious artifact in Elizabeth's memory. He had no way of knowing that Jane had immediately pawned it. A few years after her arrest, police would find the pawnshop ticket dated shortly after her stepsister's death.

In her confession several years later, Jane admitted to inviting Elizabeth to the cottage specifically to "have my revenge on her." Toppan explained that for decades she had hated her sister; she was the first of her victims that she "actually hated and poisoned with a vindictive purpose." She took years to lull and cheer Elizabeth into a trap. She confessed that she had deliberately prolonged Elizabeth's death to torture her and that she had climbed into Elizabeth's bed and cuddled and groped her as she died: "I held her in my arms and watched with delight as she gasped her life out."

Jane's Downfall

By June 1901, after five summers at the cottage, Jane owed a total of $500 in unpaid summer rentals to the Davis family, the parents and two adult daughters who owned the cottage and who had befriended "Jolly Jane." From June to August she methodically murdered the four members of the family—wiping out the family entirely.

Jane then packed her things and headed to her childhood home where 60-year-old Oramel Brigham lived. Jane was set in her mind to marry Oramel. She later would confess: "Everything seemed favorable for my marrying Mr. Brigham. I had put the three women to death who had stood in the way."

The first woman was, of course, her stepsister Elizabeth. The second was Oramel's longtime housekeeper, a middle-aged widow Jane had killed the year before while on a visit when she was still welcomed by Oramel. Jane later explained, "I was jealous of her . . . I knew she wanted to become Mr. Brigham's wife."

In the wake of the murder of the Davis family, Jane arrived at Oramel's home on August 24, but to her dismay she found his older sister, the 77-year-old Edna Bannister staying there. Despite the fact that Edna had already made plans to leave in a few days and was not a romantic rival, she was dead within three days of Jane's arrival. The same physician who a year earlier had certified the housekeeper's death, certified Edna's death as a result of heart disease. Jane now prepared herself for marriage to Oramel Brigham. She would finally become the mistress of the house she grew up in and slaved in.

Back in Massachusetts, authorities had become suspicious about the four sudden deaths of the Davises and Jane Toppan's proximity to them. At the end of August they decided to exhume the bodies and send samples to Harvard Medical School for analysis.

In the meantime, Jane had encountered a problem. Despite her attempts to impress Oramel Brigham with her housekeeping skills, he made it clear to her that he had no intention of keeping her as a housekeeper or as a wife. Jane then attempted another strategy, as she said, "to win his love." She poisoned him with a dose just enough to make him sick and then nursed him back to health. When this ploy failed to change his mind, she then threatened to ruin his reputation by claiming that he had impregnated her.

Brigham ordered her out of his house on September 29, at which point Jane took an overdose of morphine. It took several days for her to be nursed back to health and then she was moved out of the house into a local hospital. By this time, Jane Toppan was being followed by a Massachusetts state detective who was ordered to watch her pending the results of the autopsy. Upon her release from the hospital, the detective followed Jane to Amherst, New Hampshire, where she went to stay with a middle-aged friend, Sarah Nichols, and her brother George.

The final report on the autopsies was issued near the end of October. Traces of lethal amounts of arsenic in the exhumed bodies had been found. On October 29, 1901, state police and deputy marshals arrested Jane Toppan at the Nicholses' house. She was charged with a single count of murder in the death of the married Davis daughter, Minnie Gibbs.

Toppan's arrest made big news. Nobody could believe it. A torrent of letters poured in from influential and happy former patients, who praised Jane Toppan as a fine, cheerful, respectable, compassionate, highly skilled, and effective nurse. Physicians praised her dedication and professionalism and expressed their trust in her care for their patients. The funeral home came to Jane's defense, pointing out that the embalming process they used with Minnie involved massive amounts of arsenic. It looked like Jane might go free. But then the prosecution dropped a bombshell: Jane did not use arsenic. She killed with combined doses of morphine and atropine, the traces of which had been found in the victim.

"Don't Blame Me, Blame My Nature. I Can't Change What Was Meant to Be, Can I?"

Toppan's motives were equally confounding. At first it was suggested that Jane had become a depraved morphine addict, but no evidence of that surfaced. The idea that she had killed for profit held sway for some time, but as more victims were identified it became patently clear that there was no profit to be had from some of the murders. Was she insane? In the winter of 1902, the prosecution and defense agreed that an impartial committee of "alienists"— what psychiatrists were called in those days—would interview Jane to determine whether she was insane. It is from those interviews that the full extent of Jane's murders and her motives (or lack of) became known.

Jane told the committee, "When I try to picture it, I say to myself, 'I have poisoned Minnie Gibbs, my dear friend. I have poisoned Mrs. Gordon. I have poisoned Mr. and Mrs. Davis.' This does not convey anything to me, and when I try to sense the condition of the children and all the consequences, I cannot realize what an awful thing it is. Why don't I feel sorry and grieve over it? I cannot make sense of it at all."

Jane's description of her lack of empathy with her victims and absence of remorse for the pain she caused could come straight out of a current psychiatric diagnostics manual for psychopathy and antisocial personality disorder. Toppan herself attempted to explain her motives clearly in terms of sexual impulses, as she put it, "the desire to experience sexual excitement by killing people."

The stodgy Boston puritan psychiatrists were skeptical, characterizing her admission in their report as "a shameless recital of a story of sexual excitement occurring in the presence of a dying person . . . [Jane's] representation as to the nature of this impulse and conditions attending it were so at variance with any known form of sexual perversion that feigning was suspected by her interviewers."

Jane herself summed it all up: "I seem to have a sort of paralysis of thought and reason. I have an uncontrollable desire to give poison without regard to consequences. I have no objection against telling my feelings, but I don't know my own mind. I don't know why I do these things." A Boston newspaper quoted Jane as saying, "Don't blame me, blame my nature. I can't change what was meant to be, can I?"

Toppan told the psychiatrists, "Most of the people I killed were old enough to die, anyway, or else had some disease that might cause death. I never killed children. I love them."

Jane was charged with one count of homicide. Her defense attorney admitted that she had committed eleven murders in the recent years. In her psychiatric interviews, Toppan provided the details of thirty-one murders she committed, mostly since nursing school. If one was to include the string of patients she killed as a student nurse, Jane claimed to have killed more than a hundred victims.

At her trial she was found not guilty by reason of insanity, which Jane herself questioned, claiming that she could not be insane because she knew she was doing something wrong. Indeed, had Jane been tried today, the insanity plea would not have held— psychopathic serial killers are not insane by legal definition, which requires that the offender not understand what he or she is doing or understand that it is wrong. Serial killers are acutely aware of the wrong they are committing and go out of their way to evade getting caught for it. The only element of "insanity" with serial killers is the irresistible compulsion buried somewhere in their psyche that drives them in their addiction to killing.

On June 24, 1902, Jane Toppan was committed to a mental hospital at the age of 48. She died at the age of 84 on August 17, 1938, after thirty-six years of confinement. It was reported that she was a quiet patient in her old age but that she would occasionally taunt the hospital nurses by inviting them to "Get some morphine, dearie, and we'll go out in the ward. You and I will have a lot of fun seeing them die."[133]

Jane Toppan might have wrapped up the nineteenth century for female serial killers, but there was much to come in the twentieth.

PART TWO

Selected Case Studies of Female Serial Killers and Accomplices in the Twentieth Century

AILEEN WUORNOS **VELMA BARFIELD** DOROTHEA MONTALVO PUENTE **GENENE JONES** MARYBETH TINNING **MARTHA BECK** MYRA HINDLEY **CAROL BUNDY** CHARLENE GALLEGO **KARLA HOMOLKA** ILSE KOCH **IRMA GRESE** MARY BRUNNER **SUSAN ATKINS** PATRICIA KRENWINKEL **LINDA KASABIAN** LESLIE VAN HOUTEN

3

THE CULT AND PASSION
OF AILEEN WUORNOS

The Postmodern Female Serial Killer

In a previous book, which focused primarily on the history of male serial murderers, I described Ted Bundy as our first postmodern serial killer because unlike "outsider" serial killers of the past, he was more like us—or at least like those of us who believe in a college education and the middle-class values and ambitions that go with it. Bundy was not one of those solitary, backwoods, cellar-dwelling creatures hanging corpses by the heels on hooks in the mudroom or some twitchy, glassy-eyed vagrant trolling for hitchhikers and runaways behind the wheel of a Dumpster car full of crumpled beer cans and dirty rags. Bundy had his own upscale apartment with drawers full of fine linen, glassware, and ski sweaters. He was attractive, charming, well-mannered, and appeared to be ambitious—the quintessential 1970s yuppie. But sometimes Ted would snatch young women from public places, beat them into unconsciousness, and take them away in his cute Volkswagen Beetle to some lonely dark place. Then he'd kill them and have sex with the corpses. He was the real *American Psycho*—a popular dinner guest and date, a handsome law student with political ties to the Republican Party in Washington State. Eventually he could have been a candidate for governor—maybe higher. His smile and hair were styled just right for that.

AILEEN WUORNOS

Aileen Wuornos was everything Ted Bundy was not, and that precisely makes her our postmodern female serial killer. While—until Ted Bundy came along—we thought male serial killers were creepy monsters, our perception of female serial killers was that they were lethal "ladies." We saw them as respectable and sometimes attractive women who harbored homicidal intentions behind a façade of feminine mystique: arsenic and old lace, deadly damsels. They used their very beauty, charm, and genteel manners to lure victims into their homicidal webs (just like Bundy) while maintaining their façade of wife, mother, nurse, babysitter, or widow. Aileen Wuornos would tear that stereotype down.

Between the male Ted Bundy and the female Aileen Wuornos our perceptions of gender differences in serial killers crisscrossed to opposite poles. Ted Bundy normalized the serial killer into one of us while Aileen Wuornos, randomly preying with a handgun on strangers in the night, unleashed the female serial killer from the cult of feminine domesticity. Aileen Wuornos thrived in the very territory where other women feared to go and where so many women were themselves killed—hitchhiking on darkened highways and turning tricks on roadsides. She was like no other female serial killer before her and she might be signaling the shape of things to come—the infinite possibilities of female serial emancipation with its dark burden and price to pay, an opposite predatory polar star to the traditional female as victim.

Just like Ted Bundy, after her apprehension, Aileen became a television courtroom celebrity, a documentary star, and an interview-of-the-week. Long before we heard of her, Aileen claimed that one day somebody would write a book about her and make a movie and she was right. Several books have been written, in fact, since her arrest. But books were just the beginning. *Murder Trail,* a four-part docudrama that looked at the Wuornos phenomenon and other criminals, was produced for the Discovery Channel and was only one in a string of film and television programs about her. Others included A&E's *American Justice* and endless coverage on Court TV. Wuornos made more appearances on *Sixty Minutes* and *Dateline* than some presidential candidates. Then there was the 1992 made-for-TV movie *Overkill: The Aileen Wuornos Story,* starring Jean

Smart of the television sitcom *Designing Women,* and two documentary features by director Nick Broomfield: *Aileen Wuornos: The Selling of a Serial Killer,* followed by the sequel, *Aileen: Life and Death of a Serial Killer.*

There are hundreds of websites devoted to Wuornos, which portray her alternately as victim, heroine, or fiend. Wuornos was even the subject of an opera in San Francisco by Carla Lucero, who explained, "I feel a strong yet reluctant connection to Aileen Wuornos. Her story embodies the darkness in every victim's soul and the fleeting fantasies of every survivor . . . Aileen takes us into an abyss, leaving us to seek our own light. Maybe the light is in the knowledge that we chose another path; that we survived."[134]

A year after Wuornos was executed, she achieved the ultimate cult status with a Hollywood movie, *Monster,* which won an Academy Award for Best Actress for Charlize Theron for her portrayal of Wuornos.

Aileen Wuornos As a Child

In life Aileen Wuornos was as far as one can be from the red carpet of Oscar night. She was born in 1956 and raised in Troy, Michigan, a forlorn suburb fifteen miles north of Detroit. Aileen's mother, Diane, was 16 years old and already separated from the father, a 19-year-old delinquent named Leo Pittman, reportedly a cruel and abusive spouse. Diane believes she was severely beaten by Leo when she was several weeks pregnant with Aileen. In any case, Aileen never met her natural father—he would commit suicide while serving a life sentence for kidnapping and raping a 7-year-old girl. It happens that way with serial killers—sometimes and not infrequently, they are just born into bad blood.

Diane had already given birth to Aileen's older brother, Keith, the year before. She was a single mother with two children, and she attempted to raise them but she did not do a very good job of it. Witnesses later recalled the two children crying and wailing for hours as Diane slept or just went away. One day when Aileen was six, Diane went out to dinner, leaving the children with her roommate. She never returned, and after a week the roommate called Diane's parents, Lauri Wuornos, a Ford factory worker, and his wife, Britta, who came by and picked up their grandchildren.

There was a twisted psychopathology already in play between Diane and her parents. Diane claimed that her mother, Britta, was jealous of her because Lauri was sexually interested in her. Although she stated that her father never actually sexually abused her, he would frequently touch her accidentally and once attempted to passionately kiss her. Aileen would later claim that her grandfather Lauri abused her but never went as far as accusing him of sexual abuse, other than laughingly recounting one similar attempt to French kiss her.

When Aileen was two, Diane returned to reclaim her two children but shortly afterward abandoned them again with the babysitter. If early infant attachment theory has anything to do with mental disorder and psychopathy, then definitely Aileen Wuornos is a candidate. Britta and Lauri, who already had two older children of their own (in addition to Aileen's mother, Diane), finally adopted Aileen and her brother as their own. Like Ted Bundy, who believed his grandfather was his father and his mother was his sister, Aileen believed that Britta and Lauri were her natural parents, and her aunt and uncle were her siblings. And like Ted Bundy, Aileen would be about 11 years old when she learned the truth from other kids about her actual family ties. But here end the similarities with Ted Bundy.

Photographs of schoolgirl Aileen Wuornos reveal a beautiful, fine-haired, blonde, freckled little girl with a beaming, open smile dressed in one those cheap synthetic dresses with a white frilly collar that all smartly dressed little girls wore in the early 1960s. There are family photos of Aileen at the age of 6, preciously seated in the center of her family on a footstool, while her brother, Keith, and her "stepbrother," Barry, and "stepsister," Lori, are lined up in a semicircle standing behind her—everyone smiling. There is Aileen on the deck of a small boat vacationing in the summer with her family at the age of 13, a gangly skinny 'tween with long legs in cutoff jeans all pretty and again smiling. And yet another picture of her on her bike—smiling. Aileen was always smiling in family photographs somebody was proud enough to take—memories apparently worth recording.[135] But things were not as they seemed.

Neighbors recall that the Wuornos home was always dark and curtained, and nobody was ever invited in. Lauri was reportedly a despotic "stepfather," disciplining Aileen with a leather belt, beating her on her naked buttocks and legs according to her own testimony. Moreover, Keith and Aileen were disciplined by Lauri and Britta by stricter standards than their natural children, particularly their youngest child, Aileen's "stepsister," Lori, who was only two and a half years older than Aileen. Later the accounts by Aileen of her "stepparents'" alcoholism and her abuse at their hands came into conflict with the recollections of her "stepsister" and "stepbrother," who denied their own abuse and Aileen's as well.

Parental abuse at such a young age is difficult to interpret. The line between physical and sexual abuse can sometimes be razor thin and memories are often repressed or modulated by children. In the early 1960s, being spanked or even hit with a belt, naked buttocks or not, was not unusual. This kind of punishment also modulated between ritualistic light slaps on the behind with a belt sufficient to frighten any child to actual brutal beatings with a belt—it all depended upon the particular parent. One parent's spanking is another's brutality. Yet Aileen appeared to be singled out for punishment. Lauri did not allow her to receive Christmas presents. Once, when she threw away a baked potato, which she could not finish, Lauri made her take it out of the garbage and eat it. He forced her to watch as he drowned a kitten she was not supposed to keep.

From an early age, Aileen showed a precocious talent for singing and dancing and said she wanted to be a movie star. She craved the center of attention. But about the age of eight, Aileen developed a hair-trigger temper, which isolated her from other children, who became afraid of her. Lori recalls that Aileen desperately attempted to fit in and that she counseled her several times to "be nice" and keep her temper and moodiness in check. It did not work. Lori attempted to include Aileen with her own playmates, but inevitably Aileen would whine and rage, alienating them. Lori was told by her playmates not to come back with Aileen. She didn't. Some thirty years later, after Aileen was charged with seven murders, Lori would tearfully say, "I still cry that we rejected her when she was little. The time she wanted to play and we wouldn't let her."

Lori recalled that Aileen could be very nice, but it seemed somehow forced, as if she was deliberately tailoring her niceness because she knew that was the only way people would accept or tolerate her. But she would easily lose control and fly into rages. Lori felt sorry for her, but she was not going to sacrifice her own friendships and social life for Aileen. Lori recalled that later, when Aileen began to abuse drugs, her temper got worse and on several occasions when enraged she lunged at her or Keith with a knife, threatening to kill them.

At school until about the age of eight, Aileen was clever and received good marks. But from eight onward, with her developing behavioral problems, Aileen had no friends, received low grades, and had conflicts with her teachers. She was also diagnosed with vision and hearing problems. But Britta refused to have Aileen evaluated for these problems, insisting that she simply "did not pay attention." Aileen's verbal IQ was tested at a low 80, but despite her behavioral problems, she did not receive any counseling— probably as a result of Britta's resistance. During her trial, one psychiatrist testified that there was a wide gap between Aileen's verbal IQ and her functional IQ, which apparently was quite high. This gap could have resulted in the uncontrollable behavioral episodes. The psychiatrist described it as "sand in the fuel line" of an otherwise working engine. Her brain sputtered—would stop and start. Sometimes she was emotionally in control, at other times she'd be raging completely out of it.

Cigarette Pig

By the time Aileen was eleven there was something seriously wrong: She was having sex with neighborhood boys in the surrounding woods and ravines in exchange for spare change or cigarettes. This kind of sexualized behavior at so early an age almost inevitably suggests that Aileen had been sexually abused as a child. Although she would occasionally hint at it, in the end she denied it vehemently. If not that, then she might have desperately found sex a key to overcoming the rejection she suffered at the hands of her peers.

Numerous male witnesses later recalled losing their virginity to Aileen when they were 12 to 14 years old. They said it was joyless and mechanical, with Aileen saying very little during these encounters. Sometimes she participated in group sex with six or more boys. With these acts came denigration—she was nicknamed "Cigarette Pig" by the boys in the neighborhood and at school for her propensity to exchange sex for cigarettes. When she attempted to form an attachment to some of the boys she had sex with, she was brutally and publicly rejected.

This just underscores how deceptive the smile of the cute 13-year-old in the photographs might have really been.

It was the 1960s in a Detroit suburb. Aileen quickly fell into a world of available drugs and alcohol, as did many kids her age. She smoked weed and dropped LSD but eventually settled on tranquillizers and alcohol as her drugs of choice. She shoplifted, getting caught in the same K-Mart where Britta was employed. Britta quit in embarrassment. Aileen fought with Lauri and Britta and had sex with her brother, Keith.

When Aileen was fourteen she became pregnant. Wuornos gave different versions of how she became pregnant: In one version it was a family friend and in another it was an Elvis impersonator who kidnapped and raped her. Lauri was unsympathetic. On January 19, 1971, Lauri drove Aileen to Detroit and dumped her into the Florence Crittenton Home for unwed mothers. On March 24, Wuornos gave birth to a boy, whom Lauri insisted be given up for adoption without Wuornos being allowed to see him, despite her pleading. Aileen named the baby Keith in honor of her brother.

After returning home, Wuornos re-entered high school but did not last long there. She ran away from home several more times and got into minor trouble with the law. Eventually, Lauri told her not to return. She ended up bingeing on alcohol and drugs, hooking up with men she'd pick up hitchhiking, or sleeping in abandoned cars or in the woods near their home. Keith, likewise, had gotten into trouble and had left home.

Aileen was 15 years old when the only mother she had really known, Britta, died of cirrhosis of the liver. It came as a shock to most of the children—Britta had effectively concealed her alcoholism from them. Although Aileen had ambivalent feelings toward Britta, she nevertheless was the closest thing she had to a caring mother. When she was in the home for unwed mothers, Lauri had prohibited any visits or phone calls from home, but Britta wrote numerous letters to Aileen. Now she was dead.

Aileen's stepsister, Lori, had to search her out among the abandoned cars on the outskirts of town to tell her of Britta's death. When Aileen went to the funeral home she acted out, dressing inappropriately in jeans, frivolously switching signs between the men's and ladies' washrooms, and blowing cigarette smoke into Britta's face as she lay in her coffin. Wuornos growled, "If I want to blow smoke in the old slob's face, I will!" before she was ejected from the funeral home. With Britta's death, her last connection with any caregiver of consequence had been severed.

Diane, Aileen's natural mother, arrived shortly after the funeral of her mother and was shocked to find her children as hardened and homeless juveniles living on the street. Diane had given birth to two other children since abandoning Keith and Aileen and was raising them in Texas, again as a single mother on social assistance. She claims that social services authorities in Texas would not allow her to bring home an additional two children. "It sounds so cold . . . not being able to take your own children . . . but there's only so much a person can do," Diane says. Completely estranged, Lauri, 15-year-old Aileen, and her 16-year-old brother were cast adrift into their separate ways.

Back then, Aileen did not look anything like she did when she was arrested for murder. She was blond and very attractive in a cute kind of way. But she led a vagrant's life, hitchhiking and hooking along Michigan's roads, sleeping over with men she picked up along the way or prostituting herself from dingy motels, ever increasing her travel circle farther out to Ohio, then Pennsylvania, and eventually south to Georgia and Florida. She habitually stole from clients and from people who befriended her for short periods of time before her sudden rages would put them off.

Keith would pull himself out of drug and alcohol abuse to successfully pass his physical and join the Army in 1974, only to be diagnosed with cancer a month later. While he battled the cancer, the now widowed Lauri committed suicide in 1976 by running his car engine in a closed garage. Neither Aileen nor Keith went to the funeral. Aileen was nowhere to be found and had she been contacted it is unlikely she would have cared much about her hated stepfather/ grandfather's death. Keith's condition by this time was critical with the cancer having spread to his throat, brain, lungs, and bones.

Four months later, Keith died.

In the middle of all this, Aileen got married. One day while hitchhiking in Florida she was picked up by Lewis Gratz Fell, a wealthy retired 69-year-old blueblood Philadelphian. Fell wanted a beautiful young blonde on his arm and Aileen fit the bill. Aileen wanted a secure "sugar daddy" and Fell was exactly what she thought she needed. Fell gave Aileen a large diamond engagement ring and the marriage made the Daytona newspaper social pages along with a wedding photo of the strangely mismatched couple.

Aileen returned for a visit to Troy, proudly showing off her ring and new silver-haired husband, claiming she was blissfully happy. But within days the bride began to get drunk and hang out in her familiar lowlife bars, much to the annoyance of Fell. He quickly returned to Florida without her and filed a restraining order claiming that Aileen had beaten him with his cane. Shortly afterward, he filed for divorce.

Aileen reversed the story and claimed that it was she who was beaten but several witnesses had been told by Aileen that she became fed up with Fell when he doled out money to her "thirty dollars at a time." She said she took his walking cane away from him and beat him. Altogether, the marriage lasted for a month.

Missing Years Adrift

For the next ten years, Aileen drifted across the U.S. living on the fringes of the highway system—hanging out at biker bars, hooking and stealing, occasionally dropping in on people she knew like her mother, Diane, in Texas and Lori, who was now married. The visits never lasted long and were always punctuated with Aileen's raging outbursts.

Aileen had an ingratiating charm about her but it could turn dark and ugly on a dime. One can see it in her interviews in the Broomfield documentaries. Broomfield had developed a relationship with her over the duration of two films made in the years while she stood trial and then awaited her execution. As long as the interviews went her way, she was charming, sweet, and friendly with him, but anytime Broomfield strayed from the agenda her eyes would go cold and dark like a shark's, her nostrils flaring.

Hours away from her execution she angrily dismissed Broomfield from her sight forever when he failed to stick to a closely scripted scenario she had wanted to play out before his camera. Aileen was like one of those friendly and cuddly pit bulls that suddenly turns and lunges for your throat for no apparent reason other than something clicks in their brain.

In the 1970s and 1980s, Aileen Wuornos began to accrue a long list of criminal convictions, albeit under several different pseudonyms: assault and battery, armed robbery, theft, prohibited possession of a firearm, drunk and disorderly, and DUI. At some point she—either accidentally or in a botched suicide attempt—shot herself in the abdomen.

In Daytona in 1981 she finally settled into a comfortable, casual relationship with Jay Watts, a 52-year-old autoworker. She moved in with him and apparently they lived relatively happily together for two months. This, perhaps, was the first relationship that Aileen managed to sustain. But one night they argued, according to Watts over some matter so trivial that he could not even recall what it was. Watts testified that Aileen was always a boisterous, outgoing, friendly woman who was fun to be with, and he had never witnessed her legendary temper. That night was no exception—she seemed a little upset but she was not at all violent.

Aileen remembered it differently. She recalled that she had a lot on her mind that evening and had asked Watts if he'd mind giving her some privacy in the bedroom they shared. According to her, Watts took it the wrong way and said, "You can leave my room and the rest of the house for that matter!"

Waking up the next morning, Aileen was convinced that it was over between the two of them. Taking a six-pack of beer and driving off in a car that Watts had bought and restored for her, she drove down to the beach and got drunk. She then bought more beer and afterward purchased a .22 handgun at a pawnshop. She walked over to a K-Mart and bought some bullets, then to a liquor store where she bought some whisky and mixed it with Librium. She says she was contemplating suicide.

Then, dressed in her bikini, she stumbled into a convenience store, waving her gun as she attempted to rob it. According to her, she wanted to be arrested so that Watts would have to come to rescue her, pay her bail, and take her home. That would prove he still loved her.

Aileen was arrested without any trouble a few miles down the road. She was sentenced to three years in prison. Watts found a lawyer for her and visited her and they corresponded. Watts recalled that Aileen railed against lesbians in the prison, saying that she had to fight them off and that they disgusted her. Watts supported Aileen in prison for about a year before they finally drifted apart. Realizing that Watts was drifting away from her, Aileen placed a personal ad in a biker magazine and received several hundred replies.

Aileen was released in August 1983 and immediately hitched a ride to Washington, D.C., where she showed up at the door of one of her pen pals, Ed, a 47-year-old Maryland engineer. After telling him she was gay and that they would have to keep it platonic, she moved in with him for a tumultuous three months of nonstop drinking, raging, and fantasizing. During the three months she made several trips back and forth to Florida in Ed's car, where she would stay with Jay Watts, stealing things from him on her departures.

Ed would later recall that Wuornos spun fantasies of stomping a biker who had attempted to rape her. She described and acted out how she turned the tables on him, getting him to the ground and kicking and stomping on his head. She would lose her temper at the most trivial provocation and sometimes with no provocation at all.

Aileen initiated sex with Ed once, who was surprised because she had told him she was gay. Aileen replied, "I was just joking! Let's go find out how gay I am." Five minutes after having sex, Aileen got up and returned brandishing a kitchen utensil, threatening to kill Ed. He managed to talk her down, but she was clearly wearing out her welcome.

Both Ed and Jay Watts recall that Aileen also had a fantasy about being like Bonnie and Clyde, admiring the bandits' violent migratory careers. She was fascinated with outlaws and bikers and the violent subculture that enveloped them.

Ed eventually managed to get Aileen out of his apartment when she drank so much that she collapsed and had to be hospitalized. It was a relief to be free of his raging houseguest. Aileen drifted back toward Florida, sometimes hooking along the highways and sometimes stealing things from the cars of clients and people who might have given her a ride. Somewhere along the way she stole a handgun from a car glove compartment.

In the ensuing months, under various aliases, Wuornos built up a lengthy criminal record. She was arrested driving a stolen car. In another incident she tried to drive away from a license checkpoint and was pursued and stopped by police. A search of the vehicle uncovered the stolen handgun and a box of ammunition. Several months later she was again arrested with another handgun in her possession. She was arrested again for forging bad checks totaling $5,595 but she did not show up for sentencing. The only thing that kept Aileen out of prison was her uncanny luck in passing herself off under different aliases and fleeing.

Since her release from prison in 1983, Aileen began claiming to be a lesbian. In a telephone conversation with Lori in 1984, Aileen said, "I'm gay and I know you are not going to like that." Around this time, Aileen had a brief and tumultuous relationship with a woman named Toni.

Tyria "Ty" Moore: Aileen Finds True Love

Sometime in June 1986, Aileen met Tyria "Ty" Moore in a gay bar in Daytona. Their relationship was vividly documented in the movie *Monster,* with Christina Ricci in the role of Ty (although her name would be changed in the movie). This would become the longest sustained relationship Aileen ever had—four and a half years—during which Aileen would come to commit her string of seven known serial murders. Ty was six years younger than the 31-year-old Aileen, who was now using a truncated version of her name: Lee. Ty and Lee became a couple. Ty was mesmerized by the boisterous, hustling, and motor-mouthed Lee, who dominated the younger woman.

Over the next four years the couple drifted from cheap motel rooms and small backroom apartments, mainly in the Daytona area but in other parts of Florida as well. Tyria would work as a chambermaid in the low-end motels that dotted the Florida highway system while Lee would remain in her room getting drunk.

Whenever there was a shortage of money, Lee would hit the high-ways and hitchhike from exit to exit, turning tricks in between. Sometimes she made only $20 but other times she would come back with as much as $300.

Aileen was extremely jealous and possessive of Tyria, preferring that she not work at all and remain in her room while Lee turned tricks to sustain them. Some of the couple's former landlords record that there were sometimes days when the two women would not come out of their rooms other than to purchase beer, cigarettes, and snacks. Housekeeping would remove mountains of empty beer cans and snack wrappers from their room.

Ty, who had no previous criminal record other than a breaking-and-entering charge when she attempted to recover her belongings from the apartment of an ex-lover, began to accrue minor charges and incidents: driving without headlights, disobeying a traffic sign. In July 1987, Ty was treated for scalp lacerations after an altercation in a bar. All minor things compared to Aileen's record.

Lee and Ty lived a shadowy existence on the dark fringes of the Sunshine State. They plodded on foot in a freeway world of out-of-state cars rushing north and south. Lee and Ty inhabited a world of dingy, dirty little bars and stale, low-rent motel rooms and trailer parks, only needing to be within walking distance of a minimart with its supply of beer and cigarettes. It was a cash world where identities were rarely asked for—only that the rent be paid in advance. They were constantly on the move, either because of trouble with the law or because of eviction for noise as Lee and Ty fought frequently and loudly, or for failure to pay rent or damage to the premises.

While Lee kept mostly kept to herself and focused all her attention on Ty, with whom she was madly in love, Ty worked and circulated among other people. Sometimes Tyria invited her fellow workers home to the motel room she shared with Lee. Almost everyone had the same impression of Aileen—she was outwardly friendly but there was something darkly menacing and overcontrolling about her at the same time. She was scary.

In the autumn of 1989 Lee and Ty were living in a room at the Ocean Shores Motel in Ormond Beach, north of Daytona. Ty was working as a housekeeper in the nearby Casa Del Mar Hotel.

On November 23, around the Thanksgiving holiday, Ty brought over a fellow employee, Sandy Russell, a pretty 29-year-old blonde, for a Thanksgiving meal of frozen turkey TV dinners. Russell would later recall that although Aileen was outwardly friendly, she did not partake of the meal she served and instead just sat there watching her eat. Later in the evening, Aileen was drunk and waved a handgun around, describing how she had shot herself in the stomach some years ago. Again, Aileen's incipient menacing behavior overshadowed her overt attempt at maintaining a friendly demeanor toward the guest Ty had brought home.

The First Murder

On November 30, Aileen set out to make some money by hooking on the highways. She was no longer the cute blonde she was when she was twenty. Overweight and cranky, her face and teeth showed the years of neglect and drug and alcohol abuse. Aileen was rough trade, dressed in unflattering cutoff jean shorts and a sleeveless T-shirt, which did little to disguise her flabby beer belly.

Numerous authors remark how Aileen's overweight and rough look must have had a detrimental effect on her earning potential as a prostitute and perhaps that was the motive for her killing—desperate need for cash. Aileen was not a call girl, the kind of refined and pretty prostitute men hire for a "girlfriend experience." She was a roadside ho and the rougher and more haggard she looked the more she attracted a specific clientele desiring some quick and dirty sex with an underclass female with whom they would never imagine being seen in the light of day. They were not looking for a girlfriend substitute; these men wanted a fix of degrading sex. Aileen was for them the roadside Cigarette Pig of her childhood, and no matter how rough and worn she looked she would have suffered no shortage of clients who wanted this kind of sex.

Tyria would later testify that Aileen returned early in the morning the next day smelling of alcohol and with a Cadillac she said she had "borrowed." They had been looking at a small apartment nearby and were planning to move soon, having already packed some of their things in boxes. Lee told Ty that she had made a lot of money the night before and that they could move to the apartment that very day. After having moved their things, Aileen put a bike in the trunk and drove off to "return the car."

That evening as Lee and Ty sat in their new apartment guzzling beer and watching TV, Lee suddenly said, "I killed a guy today." Ty said nothing, glassily watching TV. Aileen continued to pour out details: She shot the man and hid his body in the woods, covering his remains with a carpet. The unfamiliar possessions and clothing that Ty saw Aileen bring to the apartment belonged to the victim. Lee attempted to show Ty a photograph of him, obviously taken from his wallet. Ty looked away. The car, Lee explained, was his and she had gotten rid of it this afternoon.

Ty did not pose a single question, not even why. She just continued watching the TV show like a docile cow. When asked later if Aileen ever told her why she had killed the man, Ty would reply that motive never came up in the conversation.

On December 6, using identification she stole from Ty's former roommate, Lee pawned a camera and radar detector she had taken from the car for thirty dollars. As required by local law, her thumb was inked and a fingerprint pressed into the pawnshop's receipt book next to her signature. The name was fake; the thumbprint was not. With the press of thumb, Aileen had crushed any possibility of getting away unidentified. The stolen identification would later bring police to the roommate, and from the roommate to Ty, then from Ty to Aileen and her thumbprint. That's how eventually Aileen Wuornos would go down, but not for at least a year.

Police on a routine patrol found the abandoned car first, emptied and carefully wiped clean of fingerprints. A check of the VIN number and tags returned the name of 51-year-old Richard Mallory as the owner. In a small depression near the car police found a wallet with several expired credit cards and business cards. Also found half-buried were two plastic tumblers and a bag containing a half-empty bottle of vodka.

The driver's seat was pulled more forward than a distance compatible with the height description of the owner. Ominously, there appeared to be a bloodstain on the backrest of the driver's seat.

Mallory was found later, on December 13, approximately five miles away from the car. His body was discovered by several men scavenging for recyclable debris in a small clearing littered with garbage among palmettos. The body had been almost entirely hidden beneath a large scrap of carpeting. Mallory was lying facedown, fully clothed, his jeans zipped up fastened, and his belt buckled with the buckle slightly off-center. His front pockets were pulled out as if somebody had been searching through them. He was shot four times in the chest with copper-coated hollow-point .22 bullets. One of the bullets appeared to have entered his body while he was still seated in his car. His blood alcohol level was .05, in the lower limits of intoxication.

Mallory was the owner of an appliance repair shop and was known to frequent prostitutes. After her arrest, Aileen would claim that she had shot him because she "realized" he was *going to* rape her.

"The Psychic Abolition of Redemption"—Aileen's Second Murder

Aileen killed for the second time six months later. The victim was 43-year-old David Spears, a large, soft-spoken man who was described as "everyone's idea of a nice guy." He was predictable, hardworking, honest, sweet, and responsible. In many ways he was the opposite of the first victim, Mallory. Spears had three children and although he was divorced from his wife of twenty years, they had continued in a relationship for the last six years and were considering remarrying. David had already bought a new engagement ring. His wife and children lived about a hundred miles away near Orlando, and it was Spears's routine to spend every weekend staying at their house. On Saturday morning, May 19, 1990, he was on his way in his pickup truck for one of those weekend stays. This one was special, too, because one of his daughters was celebrating her twenty-third birthday and college graduation. He was carrying a large sum of cash as a graduation present for his daughter and was due to arrive at around 2:00 P.M. He never showed up and did not call—very unlike him.

David Spears's badly decomposing naked body was found on June 1, in a clearing amidst pine trees and palmettos south of Chassahowitzka off route US 19, about 80 miles beyond his planned destination. The corpse was so badly decomposed and gnawed at by animals that at first it could not be determined if it was a man or a woman. The autopsy found at least nine bullet wounds and recovered six .22 slugs. At least one or two bullets had been fired into Spears's back, while the rest were fired into his torso and abdomen from the front.

Spears's pickup truck had already been found earlier, looted and abandoned. Police found blood on the driver's side inner running board and an empty condom package.

According to Aileen's confession after her arrest, Spears had picked her up hitchhiking near where route 27 intersects with I-4—approximately thirty minutes away from where his wife and children lived and were waiting for him to celebrate. She claimed that without phoning his wife and offering some excuse, the reliable and predictable Spears drove some eighty miles beyond his destination to the Homosassa area where he pulled off the road into a deserted area to have sex with Aileen, at around one or two in the morning—nearly nine hours after he was due to meet his family.

Wuornos claimed they drank a lot of beer, both got naked, and were "screwing around" when Spears invited her into the back of the pickup truck. There Wuornos says she saw a lead pipe just as Spears got violent with her. Wuornos said she leapt from the back and ran to the passenger door, retrieved her bag, and shot Spears as he stood by the opened tailgate of the truck. Wounded, Spears made a desperate dash back to the driver's side and attempted to get in to presumably drive away. Wuornos stated that she then shot him across the cab from the passenger side, shouting, "What the hell you think you're doin', dude . . . I'm gonna kill you, 'cause you were trying to do whatever you could with me!"

Spears staggered back away from the truck, whereby Wuornos slid over to the driver's side and fired a third shot that brought him down to the ground. She did not recall firing at least another four shots into his chest and two in his back. Before she drove off in his truck, she stole about $500 to $700, which she found in his clothes and hidden in the vehicle. She then drove home, unloaded some of the tools she thought she could sell from the back of the truck, and then dumped the pickup by a remote roadside. Ty, who was working the day shift that day, recalled Aileen coming by with a "borrowed" pickup truck but she did not ride in it.

The geography of the murder site, the time line, and Spears's reliably consistent commitment to his family suggests that it is unlikely that thirty minutes before arriving at his appointment with them he would have suddenly changed his mind and spent the next nine hours hanging out with a roadside hooker some eighty miles beyond his original destination. At least not without calling.

Ian Brady, the Moors Murders serial killer, the accomplice of Myra Hindley whose story is told further on, wrote that it is the second murder that is the most important in the evolution of the serial killer. The first murder leaves the killer in a state of confused shock. According to Brady, the killer is

> . . . too immersed in the psychological and legal challenges of the initial homicide, not to mention immediate logistics—the physical labour that the killing and disposal involve. He is therefore not in a condition to form a detached appreciation of the traumatic complexities bombarding his sense.
>
> . . . The second killing will hold all the same disadvantages, distracting elements of the first, but to a lesser degree. This allows a more objective assimilation of the experience. It also fosters an expanding sense of omnipotence, a wide-angle view of the metaphysical chessboard.
>
> In many cases, the element of elevated aestheticism in the second murder will exert a more formative impression than the first and probably of any in the future. It not only represents the rite of confirmation, a revelational leap of lack of faith in humanity, but also the onset of addiction to hedonistic nihilism.
>
> The psychic abolition of redemption.[136]

Serial Murder

There were six months between Aileen's first and second murders. She did not wait that long to commit her third. She was now transformed into a monstrous killing machine. About two weeks later, somewhere near Tampa, Wuornos encountered 40-year-old Charles Carskaddon, a laborer on his way to Florida to pick up his fiancée and drive back with her to Missouri where he had just landed a job as a punch press operator. Aileen shot him dead in the backseat of his Cadillac. According to her testimony, she then searched the car and discovered a .45 handgun. Obviously he was planning to kill her, Aileen explained. She became so enraged after finding the gun, she says, that she reloaded her nine-shot .22 revolver and pumped several more shots into Carskaddon.

As before, Wuornos took her trophy car and loot home to Ty. They target practiced together with Carskaddon's .45. The car was kept for about two days before being abandoned.

Seven days later in a coffee shop near I-95 not far from Bunnell, Wuornos met Peter Siems, a 65-year-old preacher traveling in a Sunbird full of Bibles on his way to join a Christ Is the Answer Crusade caravan. She ended up in his car. According to Wuornos they stripped naked and were going to have sex on a blanket on the ground but then she realized that he was planning to rape her. She shot him dead, abandoned his body, and again looted his car and drove it home. Siems's body has never been found.

Ty remembered a Bible suddenly appearing in their room. This time, Aileen kept the car. She parked it behind the motel they were staying at. When Ty asked about it, Lee told her she had borrowed it but there was a problem returning it.

A month later, Aileen still had the car, chauffeuring Tyria around in it. On July 4, Lee and Ty took the car out for a holiday joyride. They kept stopping along the way and buying beer. It was not unusual for Ty and Aileen to put away up to three cases of beer in one day. Aileen was so drunk that she could not drive any longer. She asked Ty to drive, even though she was as drunk as Aileen. Ty ended up losing control and they crashed the car in a ditch near some houses.

As people came out to help, Aileen and Ty ran away, but not before they were seen. When police recovered the vehicle, they found it was registered in the name of Siems, who had been reported missing by his family. Careful descriptions of the two women seen escaping were taken and sketches were produced based on the witness recollections. A handprint belonging to Wuornos was lifted from the abandoned vehicle.

Interestingly enough, police had already suspected that a female offender might be behind some of these murders, although because of different jurisdictions, the murders were not yet linked together. In the case of Mallory, police suspected that one of the hooker-strippers he had recently hired might be behind his death, while in the case of Spears, the possibility that his ex-wife might somehow be involved crossed their investigative minds. The pattern of the shooting—shots to the torso—was to police indicative of a female shooter. Even when shooting themselves, women rarely aimed at the head, preferring instead a shot to the heart or other parts of the torso, according to police.

Next, 50-year-old Eugene "Troy" Burress, a route driver for a sausage company failed to come home on July 30 nor did he return his delivery truck to the company. The truck was found the next day along his route. Troy would be found on August 4 lying facedown off a small dirt road, shot twice. According to Aileen, he had picked her up along the road, they had agreed to have sex, but instead Troy had thrown a ten-dollar bill at her and said he was going to rape her. She shot him once in the chest. As he lay dying on the ground, she put another shot into his back. Eugene Burress was a married man with children and grandchildren with no history of erratic behavior or vices. His family was devastated by his murder and put a reward out for any information leading to the arrest of the culprit.

On September 11, Aileen murdered her sixth victim, Dick Humphreys, a former Alabama police officer and chief and now employed as a child abuse investigator. When he failed to return home one night without calling, his wife began desperately calling his work and former police partners. The next day some kids bicycling in deserted terrain behind housing developments found Humphreys in a field by a road, slumped over in almost a sitting position. He was fully dressed but his pockets had been turned inside out. He was still wearing his watch and wedding ring. He had been shot seven times. One of the shots was to the back of his head. On his right side there was a small bruise consistent with a mark made by a barrel of a gun being forced hard against his side. A toxicology report showed no traces of marijuana or alcohol in his system. Again, Humphreys had no known kinky history and left behind an adoring and grieving family.

On November 17, 1990, around the Thanksgiving holiday, Aileen murdered 60-year-old Walter Jeno Antonio, a trucker, security guard, and member of the reserve police. According to Aileen, she was picked up by him while hitchhiking and he agreed to "help her make some money" by having sex in the backseat of his car. But when she undressed, Aileen claimed that Antonio flashed a police ID and told her he would arrest her unless she had sex with him for free. They got out of the car and began to argue. When Antonio went to her side of the vehicle, Aileen said she drew her .22 handgun. They struggled but Aileen prevailed, and as Antonio ran for his life she shot him in the back. She shot him three more times, once execution-style to the back of the head the same way she had shot Dick Humphreys. She took a gold and diamond ring from Antonio's finger, a present from his fiancée, whom he was to shortly marry.

Downfall and Arrest

Aileen's mistake was to kill four of her victims in the same county—the pattern of .22-caliber shootings of middle-aged and elderly men dumped by roadsides was too obvious to ignore. Eventually, similar murders in the other counties also hit the radar screen. With the description of two women running from Peter Siems's car and the palm print left behind, police traced Wuornos to one of the aliases she was using—the one when she was arrested for possession of a .22 by coincidence. The thumbprint she left behind when she pawned Mallory's camera and radar detector would lead to Aileen and Ty through the identification presented to the pawnshop, which had been stolen from Ty's roommate. For the longest time, police thought that Aileen and Ty were a team and separate task forces searched for both women.

In the autumn of 1990, things between Ty and Lee were not going well. When police issued a public announcement about their search for two female serial killer suspects, along with a sketch of their faces, Ty finally broke up with Aileen and flew back home to Ohio. Tyria knew about some of the murders—at least three. She had ridden in the cars that Lee brought back and she had seen the loot.

Aileen Wuornos was finally spotted on January 8, 1991, and

put under surveillance. When Aileen crashed a huge drunken all-night party at The Last Resort, a biker bar in Daytona, police, fearing that they would lose her in the rowdy crowd, decided to arrest her in the early morning hours. Aileen was actually so burnt out that she had fallen asleep in a corner of the bar—her last sleep in freedom. A plaque put up by the owners would later mark the spot.

A separate team working in Ohio had already tracked down Ty in Scranton, Pennsylvania, staying with some relatives. They picked her up.

Lovers' Betrayal

After her and Lee's apprehension, Tyria Moore would make a series of incriminating phone calls to Lee in jail while police recorded the conversations. Ty was promised immunity if she could prove that she was not present at the murders and assisted police in convicting Aileen. With police prompting her, Tyria began spinning a web over the phone that would entrap Aileen.

WUORNOS: Hey, Ty?

MOORE: Yeah.

WUORNOS: What are you doin'?

MOORE: Nothin'. What the hell are you doin'?

WUORNOS: Nothing. I'm sitting here in jail.

MOORE: Yeah, that's what I heard.

WUORNOS: How . . . what are you doin' down here?

MOORE: I came down to see what the hell's happenin'.

WUORNOS: Everything's   copasetic.   I'm   in   here   for a . . . a . . . vi . . . uh . . . con . . . carryin' concealed weapon back in '86 . . . and a traffic ticket.

MOORE: Really?

WUORNOS: Uh huh.

MOORE: 'Cause there's been officials up at my parents' house askin' some questions.

WUORNOS: Uh oh.

MOORE: And I'm gettin' scared.

WUORNOS: Hmmm. Well, you know, I don't think there should be anything to worry about.

MOORE: Well, I'm pretty damn worried.

WUORNOS: I'm not gonna let you get in trouble.

MOORE: That's good.

WUORNOS: But I tell you what. I would die for you.

The phone calls continued in this vein for several days, with Tyria weeping over the phone that she was scared she would be charged as an accessory to the murders.

WUORNOS: I . . . listen, you didn't do anything and I'm . . . I will definitely let them know that, okay?

MOORE: You evidently don't love me anymore. You don't trust me or anything. I mean, you're gonna let me get in trouble for somethin' I didn't do.

WUORNOS: Tyria, I said, I'm NOT. Listen. Quit cryin' and listen.

MOORE: I can't help it. I'm scared shitless.

WUORNOS: I love you. I really do. I love you a lot.

MOORE: I don't know whether I should keep on livin' or if I should . . .

WUORNOS: I'm not gonna let you go to jail. Listen, if I have to confess, I will.

MOORE: Lee, why in the hell did you do this?

WUORNOS: I don't know. Listen, did you come down here to talk to some detectives?

MOORE: No. I came down here by myself. Just why in the hell did you do it?

WUORNOS: Ty, listen to me. I don't know what to say, but all I can say is self-defense. Don't worry. They'll find out it was a solo person, and I'll just tell them that, okay?

The hint of Aileen's defense was cropping up in the conversation—"self-defense." No doubt that to some extent Aileen was convinced—not in a delusional kind of way but more as a rationalization—that defending herself is what she was doing when she killed those seven victims. But there were lots of other things mixed into it:

WUORNOS: I probably won't live long, but I don't care. Hey, by the way, I'm gonna go down in history.

MOORE: What a way to go down in history.

WUORNOS: No, I'm just sayin' . . . if I ever write a book, I'm gonna have . . . give you the money. I don't know. I just . . . let me tell you why I did it, alright?

MOORE: Mmm.

WUORNOS: Because I'm so . . . so fuckin' in love with you, that I was so worried about us not havin' an apartment and shit, I was scared that we were gonna lose our place, believin' that we wouldn't be together. I know it sounds crazy, but it's the truth.

And there it probably is. Why Aileen Wuornos killed then and not earlier. The sense one gets of Aileen and Tyria is that Aileen was the husband and Tyria the wife who craved security. In fact, Aileen referred to Tyria as her "wife." But it was Ty who would take on miserable little jobs to guarantee a minimum flow of income while nagging Aileen about her freelancing lifestyle. The constant moves and evictions, the poverty and insecurity tore at Tyria and threatened their relationship—threatened Aileen's status as the "husband"—threatened the only long-term intimate relationship Aileen had ever managed to form in her entire life, the only loving family she felt she had. It is a Greek tragedy of epic proportions: After taking a life of abuse and rejection, it was only when Aileen finally found a loving partner that she became a killing monster.

Aileen killed in rage for love and in the end that same love would betray and kill her. Aileen confessed her way into a death sentence to save Tyria.

"I Killed 'Em All Because They Got Violent with Me and I Decided to Defend Myself."

On January 16, about a week after her arrest and after her conversations with Tyria, Aileen made a videotaped confession. Her first murder, the killing of Richard Mallory, became the crucial one in the series for several reasons. First, Wuornos would be tried separately for each murder and this would be the first case to go before a jury. And second, this would be the crucial testing of her claim of self-defense.

After a long introductory statement explaining that she was alone in committing the killings, and that Tyria was in no way involved or knew the details of her crimes, Aileen made a rambling three-hour-long confession.

She recounted that on the evening of November 30, 1989, she was hitching on the highway between Tampa and Daytona after a busy day of turning tricks. Richard Mallory pulled over and offered her a ride to Daytona where he was going to see a woman with whom he had an on-and-off relationship.

According to Aileen, it started off as a pleasant drive across the state. They conversed pleasantly as Mallory smoked marijuana and drank vodka. She turned down his offer of the marijuana but accepted a mixed drink of orange juice and vodka. Along the way they pulled over at a convenience store and Mallory bought Aileen her drink of choice: a six-pack of beer. They arrived outside of Daytona around midnight, but instead of dropping Aileen off and heading to his destination, Mallory and Aileen pulled over to an isolated area away from the road and continued talking and drinking. At some point Aileen said she had told Mallory that she was a prostitute and asked if he wanted to "help her make some money." After quickly negotiating a price, Mallory agreed.

It was around 5:00 A.M., Wuornos said, when Mallory initiated sex. She took her clothes off and they hugged and kissed a little. But when Aileen suggested that Mallory take his clothes off, he refused, saying that he'd just unzip his pants. That is entirely conceivable. People who knew Mallory reported that he was somewhat paranoid and cautious. In the last three years he had changed his door locks eight times and was convinced that somebody was following him. Moreover, smoking weed can heighten a sense of paranoia.

The evening had gone pleasantly so far, but between Mallory's paranoia and Aileen's hair-trigger rages, something suddenly went very wrong. According to Wuornos, Mallory's refusal to get undressed was proof that he intended to rape her. She opened the door and stood outside the car naked. Aileen confessed that she bent down into the car to get her bag off the floor in which she had a .22 handgun. Mallory was still seated behind the wheel of his car. Aileen recounted that as she picked up her bag, Mallory turned in his seat and grabbed at it, which further confirmed for her his intention to rape her.

Aileen said that she wrenched the bag free of Mallory's grip, drew her handgun, and shot him once through the chest as he still sat in the driver's seat. According to Aileen she shouted, "You sonofabitch! I knew you were going to rape me."

Mallory staggered out of the car, attempting to run away. Aileen stated that she then ran around the front of the car to where he was stumbling away and said, "If you don't stop, man, right now, I'll keep shooting." She then fired a second shot, which brought Mallory down to the ground. Hovering over Mallory now collapsed on the ground, she squeezed off two more shots into his chest.

One of the bullets had passed through Mallory's lung and punched a hole through his chest cavity, causing massive internal bleeding. Mallory apparently lived another ten to twenty minutes before succumbing to the wound. Aileen stood by as he died.

Aileen stated in her confession:

So, I said, "Well, since I've been talkin' to you all night long, I think you seem like a pretty nice guy, you know, so okay, let's . . . let's go have fun. So I started to lay down and he was gonna, you know, unzip his pants. And I said, "Why don't you take your clothes off?" My God, you know, I said, "Well, it will hurt to do it like that." Then he got pissed, callin' me. He said, "Fuck you, baby, I'm gonna screw you right here and now" . . . something like that.

. . . And I said, "No, no, you're not gonna just fuck me. You gotta pay me." And he said, "Oh, bullshit." And that's when he got pissed. Now I'm coming back to recollection. Okay, so then we started fightin' and everything else and I jumped out. He grabbed my bag and I grabbed my bag and the arm busted and I got the bag again and I pulled it out of his hand and that's when I grabbed the pistol out. And when I grabbed the pistol out, I just shot 'im in the front seat.

. . . And then when I shot him the first time, he just backed away. And I thought . . . I thought to myself, Well, hell, should I, you know, try to help this guy or should I just kill him. So I didn't know what to do, so I figured, well, if I help the guy and he lives, he's gonna tell on me and I'm gonna get it for attempted murder, all this jazz. And I thought, Well, the best thing to do is just keep shootin' him. Then I'd get to the point that I thought, Well, I shot him. The stupid bastard woulda killed me so I kept shootin'. You know. In other words, I shot him and then I said to myself, Damn, you know, if I didn't . . . sh . . . shoot him, he woulda shot me because he woulda beat the shit outta me, maybe I would have been unconscious. He woulda found my gun goin' through my stuff, and shot me. Cause he probably woulda gone to get for tryin' to rape me, see? So I shot him and then I thought to myself, Well, hell, I might as well just keep on shootin' 'im. Because I gotta kill the guy 'cause he's goin' to . . . he's gonna . . . you know, go and tell somebody if he lives, or whatever. Then I thought to myself, Well, this dir . . . this dirty bastard deserves to die anyway because of what he was tryin' to do to me.

So those three things went in my mind for every guy I shot . . . I have to say it, that I killed 'em all because they got violent with me and I decided to defend myself. I wasn't gonna let 'em beat the shit outta me or kill me, either. I'm sure if after the fightin' they found I had a weapon, they would've shot me. So I just shot them.[137]

After waiting for Mallory to die, Aileen went through his pockets taking his money and identification and then dragging his corpse away and covering it with a scrap of carpeting and some cardboard. Still naked, she drove Mallory's Cadillac away from the scene to another isolated spot nearby. She then dressed and finished her remaining beer. She kept what she thought was valuable and the rest of the items, like Mallory's extra clothing, she flung into woods along the way and into a Dumpster. As the sun rose, she drove back to the motel where Ty was still asleep.

Explaining Aileen Wuornos

Years later when Aileen was waiting on death row, she would say, "It took me seventeen years to finally kill somebody . . . to have the heart to do it . . . a rapist or anybody. But I finally got really stone-cold and said, you know, enough is enough."

There is a certain melancholy logic in Aileen's confession—a meeting of Mallory's paranoia with Aileen's own long-standing rage. There is a string of accounts going back to her childhood of how Aileen's mood would suddenly shift from friendly to menacing. Although Aileen had not hurt anyone seriously for many years, she had scared a legion of people with her sudden rages—from her own stepsister to friends, lovers, and casual acquaintances. It was only a matter of time before she hurt somebody.

Once she killed, however, she crossed into a whole new cathartic territory—she was in a sense reborn as a monster. However voluntarily she pursued murder in her life, Aileen nonetheless had been used and abused sexually since the age of eleven—that is an indisputable fact. Whatever violent fantasies she might have kept in check during her rages were finally unleashed into reality and there was no going back. She had become a killer and one more or less murder would never change that. Whatever had restrained her from taking life until that point was rendered meaningless.

The morning of the first murder, she made no mention of the attempted rape to Ty when she returned to their motel room nor did Aileen have any marks or bruises on her according to Ty. In fact, Aileen on no occasion ever told Tyria that she had been raped or assaulted when she was roadside hooking. It was only thirteen months later, when she was confessing to police, that she first claimed she shot Mallory because she became afraid he intended to rape her.

In their psychological analysis of Wuornos, Stacey Shipley and Bruce Arrigo argue that she is a perfect case study of attachment disorder–triggered psychopathy. Her rages, parasitical behavior, inability to form attachments, and grandiose narcissisms rise like monsters in the night from her dysfunctional childhood. These behavioral traits lead to further alienation from her peers and abuse, which further deepened and amplified her behavioral disorders. Her sexual behavior as a child exposed her to even more victimization. By the time Aileen was in her midteens she had been thoroughly abused, used, and conceivably raped numerous times—a Cigarette Pig from the age of eleven. The fact that Aileen Wuornos did not kill anyone until she was in her thirties is somewhat of a miracle, actually, and might even argue for some sort of deep inner spark of goodness in the woman.

As Shipley and Arrigo argue:

She was socialized to modulate her own emotions through de-tachment and to control her environment through aggression and violence. In spite of the abuse she endured, Aileen learned to iden-tify with the aggressor. The world was made of two kinds of peo-ple: victims and offenders. She chose the latter category. Her rigid internal working model of herself and the world she inhabited did not allow for anything in between. She no longer would be the victim.[138]

Deborah Schurman-Kauflin writes about the female multiple murderers she surveyed:

Within their lives, they had felt powerless against a parade of hor-rible events, and in order for them to restore a sense of balance (at least in their minds), they used the murders of other people like many people use a cigarette . . . They crave it because it calms them down, for within it, though they know it is bad for them, it serves as an immediate source of pleasure. And to the female mul-tiple murderer, controlling another human being to death serves the same purpose. They are seeking a calm in their lives that they will never have, and deep down, they truly know it will never "fix" their lives.[139]

We will never really know what happened with Richard Mal-lory. Did he actually attempt to rape Aileen? Many will, of course, say yes, that even if she had agreed to have sex with him, was na-ked, and then suddenly refused at the last moment even for a rea-son as trivial as that he did not want to take his pants off, it was rape. No means no.

Others might say that even if that is rape, it is not the kind of rape that would justify killing. Mallory was not making an un-expected unilateral sexual advance. They had agreed to have sex. The issue was not whether they were going to have sex, but *how*— whether Mallory was going to take his pants off or just unzip.

Aileen's Defense—"I Thought I Gotta Fight or I'm Going to Die."
None of this would be an issue, however, by the time Aileen went to trial for the murder of Richard Mallory a year later. Her defense

had changed radically as did her account of her encounter with Mallory.

According to her courtroom testimony on January 25, 1992:

I told him I wouldn't have sex with him. "Yes, you are, bitch. You're going to do everything I tell you. If you don't, I'm going to kill you and have sex with you after you're dead just like the other sluts. It doesn't matter, your body will still be warm." He tied my wrists to the steering wheel, and screwed me in the ass. Afterwards, he got a Visine bottle filled with rubbing alcohol out of the trunk. He said the Visine bottle was one of my surprises. He emptied it into my rectum. It really hurt bad because he tore me up a lot. He got dressed, got a radio, sat on the hood for what seemed like an hour. I was really pissed. I was yelling at him, and struggling to get my hands free.

Finally, he untied me from the steering wheel and put the rope around my neck. He's still saying all kinds of jazz about what he wants to do to me. He told me to turn toward him, lie down, and spread my legs. And I guess he's going to zipper fuck me. He had his clothes on. He was holding the cord around my neck like reins. I thought, I gotta fight or I'm going to die.

I jumped up real fast, and spit in his face. And he said, "You're dead, bitch. You're dead."

I grabbed my bag and whipped my pistol out toward him, and he was coming toward me with his right arm, and I shot immediately. I shot at him. He started coming at me again. I shot. He stopped. I kind of pushed him away from me. He kind of sat up on the driver's seat. I hurriedly opened the passenger door, ran around the driver's side, opened the door real fast, looked at him and he started to come out. And I said, "Don't come near me, I'll shoot you again," or something like that. "Don't make me have to shoot you again," something like that. He just started coming at me and I shot him . . . He fell to the ground.

Despite efforts by the defense to exclude from the evidence Aileen's videotaped confession from the previous year, which was radically different from her claim now, the jury got to see the evolution of Aileen's defense from having shot Mallory because he did not want to take his pants off after her agreeing to have paid sex with him to now his outright anal rape of her after tying her hands and threatening to kill her. Moreover, it wasn't just Mallory—all seven of Aileen's victims were nothing but rapists she had shot in self-defense. Not only was Aileen defending herself, but they deserved to die. This was a particularly reprehensible defense because it instantly reduced all of the victims to the lowest denominator of rapist and raised Aileen to the height of victimhood.

"Everywoman's Most Forbidden Fantasy": Feminist Martians to Aileen's Defense

The case of Aileen Wuornos and her "self-defense from rape" claim attracted a radical fringe of feminists like flies to a turd and there was no bigger fly than Phyllis Chesler, a professor of women's studies and psychology at City University of New York (College of Staten Island), an author and an "expert witness" on battered women who kill their male aggressors. As one reviewer of Chesler's ideas states, "This isn't feminism for cowards."[140] Indeed it isn't.

Chesler offered herself to Aileen's attorney as an "expert witness" in the phenomena of female-perpetrated murder in self-defense against rape and lobbied the media on behalf of Wuornos, writing an opinion piece for the *New York Times* entitled "A Double Standard for Murder?"[141]

When Chesler was smartly turned away by Aileen's lawyers, she bulled ahead anyway and made contact directly with Wuornos, eventually meeting with her and bolstering her assertions with the assurance that she is the victim and that her righteous self-defense against rape has led to her being falsely accused of being a serial killer by the phallocentric heteropatriarchal oppressors of all women.

Chesler published an account of her role in the case in her book *Notes of an Expert Witness*.[142] Chesler tells us that as soon as she had heard, even before Aileen was identified and arrested, that Florida police were seeking two women suspects in a series of highway murders, she thought the story . . .

. . . sounded diabolically whimsical as Orson Welles's 1938 broadcast on the Martian invasion. What was Everywoman's most forbidden fantasy and Everyman's worst nightmare doing on television? Was this some kind of joke? Perhaps these women were *feminist* Martians on a mission to avenge the Green River killings or the Montreal massacre.* If not, did female serial killers really exist on earth?[143]

According to Chesler, women could not be serial killers because, "Serial killers are mainly white male drifters, obsessed with pornography and woman-hatred, who were themselves *paternally* abused children."[144] (Emphasis in the original.)

This, of course, is nonsense. Most serial killers are not drifters (only 35 percent are migratory) and many male serial killers were *maternally* abused, the single greatest contribution to their hatred of women. For example, Edmund Kemper, who would eventually kill eight women, including his mother, was disciplined by her at the age of eight by being forced to sleep in a dark cellar for eight months, his only exit a trap door in the floor on which she would stand a kitchen table.[145] Henry Lee Lucas's prostitute mother, Viola, would insist that both Henry and his legless invalid father watch her having sex with her customers. If they refused, she would beat them with a club. The only thing Lucas loved in his childhood was a pet mule, but when his mother found out about his affection for it, she forced him to watch as she shot it dead. She then beat Lucas for how much it was going to cost to haul the dead animal away.[146] Ottis Toole, who would partner with Lucas and who is suspected to have murdered and decapitated Adam Walsh, the son of John Walsh, the host of *America's Most Wanted*, was dressed as a girl in petticoats and lace by his mother. Eddie Cole, who murdered thirteen victims, was dressed as "Mamma's little girl" by his mother and forced to serve drinks to her guests and lovers. At least seven serial killers when they were boys, including Charles Manson, are known to have been tormented by

---

* On December 6, 1989, in Montreal, 25-year-old Marc Lépine, after being refused admission to an engineering school, entered one of the classrooms with a rifle and, after sending away all the males, murdered fourteen female engineering students and staff while screaming "I hate feminists." He then committed suicide.

their mothers by being dressed as girls. When Jerry Brudos's mom discovered nocturnal seminal stains on his bedsheets, she forced him to wash them by hand and sleep without sheets while they dried on the line for the neighbors to see. Brudos was forced to live in a garden shed, when his mother decided that her favorite older son needed a room all for himself. Joseph Kallinger's mother refused to allow her adopted son to play outside, flogged him with a whip, beat him with a hammer, threatened to cut off his genitals if she caught him having erections, and selected his wife for him. In every serial killer's life, Mom is always there with him.

Chesler proclaims that, "99 percent of mass, sexual, and serial murder" is committed by men.[147] I don't know about mass and sexual murder, but according to the most extensive study on serial homicide in the U.S. between 1800–1995, 83–85 percent of victims had been killed by male serial killers only.[148] That means women are complicit in 15–17 percent of all serial homicides—nearly every sixth serial killing! While men commit a large majority of serial homicides, women's contribution to the death toll is not nearly as insignificant as Chesler claims. So much for Chesler's claimed "expertise."

It is not Chesler's ignorance in the face of her claim to expertise that is so daunting.[149] What makes Chesler so offensive is her blanket denigration of the victims that Wuornos murdered. Chesler is no different from those who devalue the lives of prostitute victims "because they were worthless whores who asked for it by cruising the streets" or those who would claim "that prostitutes deserve to be raped—it is an occupational hazard," when she proclaims that Wuornos was a victim simply because, "The men she killed all fit the profile of johns, those who frequent prostitutes."[150] Tell *that* to the family of the preacher Peter Siems whose body has never been found, the Bibles in his car flung out the window by Wuornos. Or to the widow of former police officer and child abuse investigator Dick Humphreys, who was never late without calling her. Or the daughter of David Spears, whose graduation gift Wuornos spent on beer and cigarettes after murdering her father. What "profile of johns" did these victims have according to Chesler? She never says. That they were all males perhaps?

Yes, preachers and cops sometimes pick up prostitutes. But with the exception of one victim, none of these men had arrests on their records for picking up prostitutes or any other criminal offenses. It is entirely unclear how Aileen got into their cars in the first place. Humphreys, the former police officer, for example, had a mark on his body consistent with that from a barrel of a handgun being pressed hard against his side. Aileen was not dressed provocatively as a prostitute: She wore grungy cutoff jeans and a T-shirt and hitchhiked, propositioning men once inside the car. She could have just as easily been posing as a motorist in distress. In fact, the profile of the preacher, the ex-cop, and the police reservist, was precisely of the type of male who would stop and assist a person by a roadside appearing to be in distress, especially a woman. Chesler should be ashamed of herself. At least Aileen Wuornos was fighting for her life when she slandered her victims. What was Chesler's excuse?

Chesler reserved her contempt for one victim in particular—the first, Richard Mallory. In many ways, Richard Mallory is the Rosetta stone for understanding what might have triggered the one-year killing spree unleashed by Aileen Wuornos. According to Chesler, Mallory's former girlfriend, Jackie Davis, gave a "grim" portrayal to the police of the victim

> Mallory, Ms. Davis recounted, had served ten years in prison for burglary, suffered from severe mood swings, drank too much, was violent to women, enjoyed the strip bars, was "into" pornography, and had undergone therapy for some kind of sexual dysfunction. A search of Mallory's business revealed that he was erratic in business, heavily in debt, in trouble with the IRS, and had received many hostile letters from angry customers.[151]

Chesler says that in a series of meetings with Wuornos's public defender, Trish Jenkins, nearly seven months before the trial, "feminists, myself included, had asked Jenkins and her investigator, Don Sanchez, to look into Mallory's past. They never did."[152]

Moreover, according to Chesler's account, the testimony of Jackie Davis about Mallory's "past violence toward women" was not admitted into evidence by the judge. Chesler also claims that the defense's request "for a continuance to allow the defense to find and question Davis anew" was also denied. Chesler concludes, "In my view, the absence of such corroborating evidence was absolutely damaging to Wuornos's self-defense claim."[153]

Sounds like a conspiracy between a phallocentric judge and an incompetent defense to railroad Wuornos into a death sentence because she dared to defend herself against a member of the patriarchy attempting to rape her. But Chesler does not tell us the full story of Jackie Davis's statement to the police.

In fact, Davis never said that Mallory was abusive or violent with her. She actually stated that he was "kind and gentle but prone to mood swings. Sometimes he was sweet and easygoing, at others, he shrank back into his shell."[154] Chesler's definition of "abusive treatment of women" consisted of Mallory's propensity to hire strippers and prostitutes, two at a time, and watch them having simulated sex with each other.

For radical feminists like Chesler, there are no prostitutes—only "prostituted women." That is almost the only term that Chesler uses in her article, implying that all prostitutes are forced into selling themselves, obviously by men. She consistently refers to Wuornos as a "prostituted woman" despite the fact that nobody forced Wuornos into prostitution, nobody "ran" Wuornos, she never had a pimp (at least not one who could survive her temper). Aileen sadly chose to prostitute herself instead of taking on menial work the way her lover, Tyria, did. Wuornos's reluctance to work was even a source of conflict between her and Tyria.

(Not that Chesler has much respect for what Aileen told her either when they met. After being told by Aileen that she chose to be a prostitute and that some of her johns were her friends, Chesler said, "She's as conventional as most (abused) women."[155] For creatures like Chesler it was never about Aileen anyway.)

Nor did the judge prevent Jackie Davis from testifying. It is true that the defense learned very late about Jackie Davis. But during the trial, Davis was brought into court and deposed by the defense to decide whether to put her on the stand in front of a jury. Her testimony, it turned out, consisted of inadmissible hearsay—gossip she had heard from other people. She personally had *never* been abused by Mallory nor did she herself have any direct knowledge at all of his abusing other women (as we on

Earth understand the term "abuse" and not as Chesler defines it on her feminist Mars).

Not only did Jackie Davis have a date with Mallory the day he disappeared, but after his death she took the responsibility of arranging for his funeral. She was very fond of Mallory and reluctant to testify for the defense. At the end of her questioning, it was the defense lawyer who decided not to call Davis to the stand in front of a jury, not the judge.[156]

But one cannot write off Chesler as some kooky radical feminist that easily. Between the trial in 1992 and the appeals that would be lodged the next year, to her credit Chesler did what Wuornos's defense team did not. She hired a private investigator, an ex-police officer who had initially worked on the Wuornos case, to investigate Mallory's past. He discovered that Mallory had served four years (Chesler says ten) for housebreaking with the intent to commit rape! If Mallory was "abusive" because he liked to hire "prostituted women" then imagine what this made him now!

The only problem is that Mallory had committed this one offense thirty years ago when he was a pimple-faced 19-year-old on the eve of his induction into the army. Mallory broke into a home he was familiar with when he worked as a beverage delivery boy and he advanced on the woman who lived there but ran off the instant she resisted. Mallory did indeed undergo therapy and was confined in a psychiatric wing of a Maryland prison. He confessed that he had irresistible impulses to make sexual advances toward women—not quite the same as rape but still well on the way there. He was released after four years but was registered as a "defective delinquent" until 1968—for ten years. (Probably the source of Chesler's error that he was imprisoned for ten years.)

Mallory was acutely aware of his problem early in his life and attempted to deal with it himself. He had actually quit his job as a delivery boy because he was concerned about his desires to make inappropriate sexual advances toward female customers. In the thirty years subsequent to his release, Mallory did not commit any other offense and seems to have redirected his sexual impulse toward his girlfriends and prostitutes. Mallory frequented prostitutes for over twenty years in the area where he lived and many knew him by name. Not one reported any abusive behavior by him, before or after his murder. Nothing in this makes him an upstanding citizen and decent human being, but neither is it evidence for the credibility of Wuornos's claim of her brutal anal rape at the hands of Mallory.

A judge in Aileen Wuornos's appeal ruled that this information would not have changed the validity of her defense claim of being raped, and would not have been admissible anyway, as Mallory's offense had happened only once and so long ago that it could not have served as evidence for assessing his current conduct.

* * *

As Aileen Wuornos grew more menacing in court, yelling at a jury when convicted, "I hope you get raped. Scumbags of America!" her feminist defenders began to fade and fall by the wayside. In the end, Chesler concluded, "Her bullets shattered the silence about violence against prostituted women, about women fighting back: and about what happens to them when they do."[157] And then Chesler moved on to her next new soapbox.*

"On a Killing Day . . ."—What Triggered Aileen?

Something could have happened halfway between the prosecution's scenario and Wuornos's claim. It did not take much to set Wuornos off and Mallory was known to be paranoid, particularly after he drank. It could have even happened on an animallike level—when the scent of fear can spark aggression. Perhaps Mallory sent a fear signal to Wuornos, which made her afraid that he might attack her and she responded. Perhaps he just said something that triggered Wuornos's legendary temper, like the hundreds of people in the past. Maybe there was a scuffle exactly as Wuornos described in her confession, and in the heat of the moment she shot Mallory dead. Or maybe he actually did rape her

---

* These days Chesler is buzzing around another turd—the Middle-East and terrorism. Her recent book is *The Death of Feminism,* in which, according to *Publisher's Weekly,* Chesler "takes liberal feminists to task for not speaking out against what she sees as the most important threat to Western freedom: Islamic terrorism." We can all sleep better now knowing that Phyllis has joined the war on terrorism.

exactly as she testified a year later in her trial. It is possible. Mallory, at least at some point in his life, had that in him—maybe this was the night it flowered once more. It is possible.

Whether Mallory actually raped Aileen, attempted to, or whether she thought he did or whether both their damaged and twisted personalities came violently together in a lethal cocktail of rage and paranoia, the fact remains that Wuornos went on to murder another six middle-aged men in what appears to have been cold-blooded rage and profit killings. Did they all try to rape her? Rape indeed can seriously be an occupational hazard of a prostitute, but if so, to what extent? Is it conceivable that in a year a roadside prostitute like Aileen could get raped seven times? Nobody can definitively answer that question because there are no objective studies of the issue. One study that is commonly cited by feminists reported that 55 prostitutes in Oregon claimed to be raped an average of 33 times a year, but the study was conducted by the Council for Prostitution Alternatives, which had its own agenda, nor were the claims of the women documented in any way.

Police officers have a different take on it. As one officer explained, cops on a daily basis go out on the street *looking for trouble* yet some spend twenty years on patrol without ever needing to draw their weapon. It's not quite the same thing, but it illustrates that the frequency with which bad things happen on the street is difficult to determine.

It becomes a little easier, if one considers the histories of the men Wuornos murdered. With the exception of one, none of the men Aileen accused of trying to rape her had any criminal records for sexual assault. Could Aileen have met six first-time rapists in the span of a year—six middle-aged and elderly men who, after a lifetime of never having committed (at least as far as we know) a sexual assault, chose so late in their life to do so for the first time with Aileen? Not likely.

Much was made of the fact that Aileen had picked up hundreds of men (she claimed 250,000—you do the math as to how impossible that is) without killing them. Aileen herself pointed out how many rides she had in men's cars without killing them. It was only these seven rapists, she insists. And Chesler grabs on to this argument as well, citing a favorite film, the obscure Dutch *A Question of Silence*, in which, while shopping in a store, three women, each of whom "has had enough of being treated like a 'woman' by men . . . spontaneously stomp to death the 250,001st man who treats them with contempt; and they do so without exchanging a word."[158]

But that is not how serial killers function. Once they start killing, they do not kill everybody they meet whenever they have an opportunity. Serial killers function in a cyclical pattern with peaks and valleys in their desire to kill. There is more to it than just opportunity. Wuornos not killing every man who came into contact with her does not make the ones she did kill rapists.

Many of the men who had come forward to say they had survived an encounter with Aileen Wuornos had some scary stories to tell. One described her akin to a werewolf, her personality suddenly changing to such a dark and menacing tone that he suddenly became so afraid that he had to trick her into getting out of his car and then suddenly drove off before she could get back in.

Most likely, Aileen went into one of her well-documented high rages—and perhaps her rages have always been driven by a history of sexual assault—and once she learned to kill, she would express her rage with the finality of murder and took cathartic satisfaction in the control she exercised over her victim's body and property: murder as a calming cigarette.

Even if Mallory had really attempted to rape her and she really was defending herself, once she had killed she became addicted to it. There might have been a remnant of some moral compass still guiding Aileen; her assertions that she would never kill in cold blood ring true, even though she did precisely that. To overcome that paradox, she needed to convince herself that the men she was killing were really going to rape her and thus deserved to die. It is unlikely that she made up the motive as an afterthought—she was probably deluding herself as she went along—looking hopefully for some sign that the man whose car she had entered harbored some sinister intent and therefore deserved to die.

As Aileen said, "I had a lot of guys, maybe ten to twelve a day. I could have killed all of them, but I didn't want to. I'm really just a nice person. I'm describing a normal day to you here, but a killing day would be just about the same. On a normal day we would just do it by the side of the road if they just wanted oral sex or behind a building or maybe just off the road in the woods if they wanted it all.

"On a killing day, those guys wanted to go way, way back in the woods. Now I know why they did it: They were gonna hurt me."

Maybe that is all it took.

Her relationship with Tyria might have been critical to the killing as well. Not only was she in love with Tyria, but the love was reciprocated. After a lifetime of rejection, beginning with her own mother, mistreatment at the hands of her grandparents, rejection by her peers, by the boys she had sex with from the age of eleven, her infant child being taken away from her, her failed marriage, and all the other brief relationships that came apart, Tyria was the first to stay with Aileen. Tyria was Aileen's first significant relationship that appeared to function on some level. But it might have also been the very "trigger" that finally turned her to serial murder.

Fantasies, facilitators, and triggers are the three pillars of serial murder. Aileen fantasized about revenge against the males who had sexually abused her throughout her life—even in the highly unlikely case that she had *not* been actually raped in the past, she certainly felt she had been. One does not need a psych degree to figure out what kind of fantasies a woman might have who was sexually used from age eleven the way Aileen was. Facilitators are the "lubricants"—pornography, drugs, or alcohol—which enhance the fantasy and lower the inhibitions to realize the fantasy. Aileen was almost always drinking when she killed (although Aileen was almost always drinking when she did anything). Finally, the trigger is usually a series or combination of pressures in daily life that law enforcement call "stressors," which at some point drive the predisposed individual to crack and act upon their fantasy. When investigating a serial murder suspect, police will often attempt to seek out and identify a pattern of "stressors" in the suspect's life—divorce, loss of a job, a death in the family, some kind of failure, a breakup with a girlfriend, parental conflict. In the FBI study of male serial killers, 59 percent reported conflict with a female occurring just prior to their killing for the first time, and sometimes before subsequent murders. Other stressors included: conflict with parents: 53 percent; financial: 48 percent; employment problems: 39 percent; marital problems: 21 percent; legal problems: 28 percent; conflict with a male: 11 percent; physical injury: 11 percent; death of a significant person: 8 percent; and birth of a child: 8 percent.[159]

Aileen's relationship with Tyria could have easily served as the stressor for her murders. Aileen killed her first victim, Richard Mallory, just a few days after Ty brought home for a Thanksgiving meal, Sandy Russell, a pretty 29-year-old blonde. Aileen did not kill again until Tyria's half-sister, Tracy Moore, came to stay with them during the summer and Ty was focusing all her attention on her. During Tracy's stay, Aileen murdered David Spears, Charles Carskaddon, and Peter Siems. Just before Lee murdered Dick Humphreys, Ty had lost a job and was talking about leaving Florida and moving back to Ohio. When Aileen murdered Walter Jeno Antonio, Ty had gone off by herself to Ohio for the Thanksgiving holiday with her family, having told Lee that she needed a break from her. And as Aileen herself blurted out in those taped telephone conversations with Tyria, "Let me tell you why I did it, alright? . . . Because I'm so . . . so fuckin' in love with you, that I was so worried about us not havin' an apartment and shit, I was scared that we were gonna lose our place, believin' that we wouldn't be together."

The Prostituted Serial Killer

Aileen Wuornos might not have been the "prostituted woman" that Chesler wanted her to be, but she was a prostituted serial killer. Everybody made money or mileage from the plight of Aileen Wuornos (including, I suppose, me with this writing). Three police officers and Tyria were negotiating Hollywood deals before Aileen even went to trial. Her attorney was charging the media $10,000 per interview, with Aileen deciding how the money would be dispersed among her hangers-on. (She herself could not retain the money under the Son of Sam Law, which prevents offenders from profiting from their notoriety.)

A born-again Christian legally adopted Aileen so that she could have access to her and then went on to support Aileen in her "no contest" pleas to hasten her execution so that "she could go home to Jesus." Filmmaker Nick Broomfield made two films about Aileen, falling just short of following her with his cameras into the death chamber. And a few years after Aileen was dead, actress-model Charlize Theron put an Oscar statue on her shelf for her portrayal of Aileen in *Monster*. Everybody got a piece of Aileen—from the virgin boys who fucked her for a cigarette to the low-budget filmmakers, true crime hacks, documentary voyeurs, lawyers, TV producers, radical feminists, militant lesbians, born-again Bible thumpers, both pro- and anti-death activists, and the Florida justice system that let her sloppily put herself to death. During her last "no contest" trials, Aileen did not even bother attending, preferring to remain in her cell. She just wanted it all to be over. Her claims of being raped became muted and ambiguous and her final story was that the police deliberately allowed her to commit the series of murders so that they could enhance the value of the movie deal about her case.

Aileen Wuornos finally got her wish when she was executed by lethal injection at the age of 46 on October 9, 2002. She was the tenth woman in the U.S. to be executed since the reintroduction of the death penalty in 1976. Aileen's last words were, "I'd just like to say I'm sailing with the Rock and I'll be back like Independence Day with Jesus, June 6, like the movie, big mothership and all. I'll be back."

She was cremated and her ashes were sent back to Michigan where they were spread around a tree, at Aileen's request, to the sound of Natalie Merchant's song, "Carnival." Aileen had listened to the song repeatedly while on death row.

In the Last Resort Bar in Daytona Beach where Aileen was arrested there is a portrait of her with the inscription: HERE LIED AILEEN "LEE" WUORNOS HER LAST NIGHT OF FREEDOM JANUARY 9, 1991, AT THE LAST RESORT BAR. The adult woman in the portrait is as shining, spirited, and beautiful as the little girl in the family photos of Aileen when she was a 6-year-old schoolgirl. Somebody once brought in an unflattering photo of Aileen clipped from a newspaper and attempted to place it over the face in the portrait because the woman in the painting looked too much better than Aileen really did.[160] The artist objected, saying that she had painted Aileen that way deliberately because everybody deserves a break. If so, then it probably is the only break Aileen ever got in her sad and, as Natalie Merchant said of her, "tortured, torturing life."

4

MURDERING FRIENDS AND INTIMATES

Black Widows and Profit Killers

The Black Widow is the female serial killer we all imagine we know best—the female that charms and seduces males, takes them as lovers, marries them, and then kills them for profit. (Insert your own joke here.) It's not only men that snicker; women, too, but for different reasons. Phyllis Chesler chuckled that female-perpetrated serial murder is, "Everywoman's most forbidden fantasy, and Everyman's worst nightmare" when she asked, "Did female serial killers really exist on earth?"[161]

They do, Phyllis. And not only do female serialists kill men, but they also kill women and children—their own and those of others as well. They kill acquaintances, relatives, siblings, the young and the old, patients and clients, and they can do it for no reason other than profit.

We imagine the Black Widow as a thing of the past, belonging to an entirely different age and different world—a world of crushing poverty, mail-order brides, and handwritten or manually typed index cards instead of digital databanks—a time when people could slip in and out of identities like worn-out shoes. It was as easy to marry and disappear as it was to kill.

We think of Belle Gunness, killing perhaps as many as forty-eight people in Illinois and Indiana from 1900–1906, or Nancy Hazel Doss, who was arrested in 1955 in Tulsa, Oklahoma, and charged with murdering with arsenic in a thirty-three-year period four of her five husbands, and suspected of killing her two sisters, her mother, two of her children, a nephew, and a grandson—a known total of eleven victims between 1921–1954.

We imagine that such creatures no longer exist—not these days . . . But they do, and two cases, one from the 1970s and the other from the 1980s are described in detail in this chapter.

The Black Widow is really a subspecies of profit-motivated female serial killers—the female equivalent of the male *hedonist comfort* serial killer. The term Black Widow really describes her MO—the seduction of males to render them helpless—more than her signature or profile. Black Widows may kill for different reasons, not only for profit, for example, and may target not only male suitors or husbands. Sometimes the motive is vengeance, sometimes control, and sometimes even a manifestation of Munchausen by proxy syndrome (which will be dealt with further below). Because Black Widows are sometimes driven by demons other than profit, the taking of the victim's property can be an expression of the final control over the victim rather than necessarily materialistic desire. Thus we have cases where some Black Widows appear to kill for ridiculously minor sums of money.

Likewise, not all profit-motivated female serial killers are Black Widows. Some come in the guise of Angels of Death, killing their patients for their property. Others escape definition entirely, killing intimates, acquaintances, and strangers for a variety of reasons.

Velma Barfield—the Death Row Granny

In September 1976, Stuart Taylor, a North Carolina farmer in his fifties, was going through marriage difficulties. He and his wife had separated and were considering divorce. That autumn, Taylor went to visit his aunt and uncle, Dollie and Montgomery Edwards. Montgomery was 94 and suffering from advanced diabetes, which had cost him his sight and his legs. His wife, Dollie, was 84 and suffering from intestinal cancer; she had recently undergone a colostomy. Unable any longer to care for her husband, Dollie had hired a local woman to take care of him for seventy-five dollars a week plus room and board. That is how Stuart Taylor met Velma Barfield.

Taylor was immediately attracted to the 45-year-old Velma. She was a widow with two adult children: a son, Ronnie, and a daughter, Kim. Both her children were married and had kids of their own. For a grandmother, Velma was still relatively young and good-looking and Taylor was feeling lonely and abandoned. He and Velma began to date, going out mostly to dinner or fishing trips on weekends. But after about a month, Taylor and his wife decided to reconcile and he stopped taking Velma out. Not that Velma seemed too upset—she understood and wished him well.

In January 1977, Montgomery died and a month later in February, Dollie died, too. Velma went to work for another aged couple, John Henry and Record Lee. The 76-year-old Record had fallen in her carport and broken her leg. Confined in a cast she had difficulty moving around while her 80-year-old husband, John, was not able to give his wife the care she needed. Their daughters, looking for somebody to take care of their aged parents, were given Velma's name by the local church. Velma moved into the Lee's house for fifty dollars a week. But in June, John Henry Lee became sick with a severe case of gastroenteritis and died in the hospital emergency ward when his heart apparently gave out. The Lee daughters were so impressed with the care Velma gave their parents that they continued to employ her to care for their mother.

Suddenly that summer Stuart Taylor reappeared in Velma's life. After an eight-month reconciliation his marriage was definitely over. He and his wife were getting divorced. Would Velma like to go out again? Yes, of course. The couple began dating seriously, sneaking off for sex in motels in the strictly religious Robeson County where they lived. Taylor was a tobacco farmer with two daughters and a son from his first marriage, which ended when his wife died in 1970 from kidney disease. Six months later, Taylor married a woman he knew from childhood and another six months later the marriage ended in divorce. Several years later he married for a third time, but that marriage did not work out, and it was just a matter of time before the divorce was to be finalized.

Stuart Taylor was described as an exuberant man with a love for life—the type that got up every morning singing. He had loved his first wife deeply and her loss had depressed him. The failure of his second marriage further depressed him and Stuart developed a habit of binge drinking, something frowned upon by the Pentecostal and Baptist churches that dotted that part of North Carolina like so many stars in the sky. Stuart was also aware that this might be a problem for Velma, who despite her liberal attitude to unmarried sex, was a pious churchgoing woman who did not tolerate drinking. She would say that a drink of alcohol was a way of letting the devil into a person.

At first he kept his drinking habits from her, but later he learned that others had warned her of his binges. She still seemed interested in him, and this gave Stuart hope. He courted and wooed her. Much to the amusement of his friends, because Stuart was not particularly a religious man, he took her to church and gospel meetings, laughing, "I'm going out with my Christian woman tonight."

In October Velma quit her job taking care of Record Lee, explaining that it was too confining. She moved into a trailer park while taking a job at a local nursing home. Her son, Ronnie, would recall that near the end of October Velma showed him a diamond engagement ring; she and Stuart would be getting married in the springtime when his divorce would be finalized. Ronnie was somewhat taken aback. He remembered growing up in a house torn by bitter and violent argument over drinking between Velma and his father. If she felt so strongly about it, how could she consider marrying Stuart? His mother assured him that Stuart would overcome it.

That was not the only thing that troubled Ronnie. His mother's past had a few skeletons of its own. His mother fell in and out of tranquillizer and painkiller abuse and she had not conclusively kicked the habit. She had overdosed numerous times, with Ronnie and his wife, Kim, and his sister, Kim, and her husband, Dennis, having to take her to the hospital emergency ward. Once they had left her for a brief period at their house only to return to find her passed out overdosed on the floor with her collarbone protruding through her skin. There was also the small matter of Velma's stint in prison—she had attempted to forge a prescription. She received a provisionary suspended sentence if she stayed out of trouble but then was arrested for forging checks. That landed her with an automatic prison sentence of six months. Was Stuart aware of all this? Ronnie wanted to know. Velma told her son to mind his own business. Stuart was aware that she took pills "for her nerves." She told Ronnie that she loved Stuart and was intent on living with him. Later she would confess, "Deep down inside I never really cared for him. I never felt close to him at all. I can't comprehend why I wanted to be with him. Sometimes we're just lonely. Somebody to talk to, you know."[162]

In November, Stuart called at Velma's trailer to pick her up to go out, but she did not respond. When he heard moans coming from inside he tried the door and found it unlocked. Inside he found Velma on her bed in her underwear, gagged and bound with duct tape. After freeing Velma, he called the police.

Velma was visibly upset and crying. She said that she had risen to take a shower that morning but the moment she entered the bathroom, a man had thrown a towel over her head and had forced her back to the bed where he had bound and gagged her. He left her there and departed.

The investigating officer, Lumberton Police Detective Benson Philips was perplexed. The assailant did not say anything. He did not molest her sexually. He did not hit, choke, or hurt her in any way, nor did he take anything. There were no signs of a break-in. How did he get in? Velma suggested maybe he was a past tenant who kept a copy of the key to the trailer. It made no sense and led nowhere.

When Detective Philips heard Stuart tell Velma not to worry, she was not going to spend another night in the trailer but would come live with him in his house, he felt he had gotten a hint of what might have really taken place. He quickly forgot all about Velma and the break-in.

Velma took her belongings and moved into Stuart's house. The arguing began almost immediately. Several times Velma phoned her daughter, Kim, or her husband, Dennis, crying and asking for them to pick her up. Stuart would then come by apologetically and take Velma back home.

One day Velma came back from her shift at the nursing home and found Stuart upset and angry. Velma had made some friends during her time in prison and exchanged letters with them. She had brought some of those letters with her when she moved into

Stuart's house and he had found and read them. They argued bitterly. Stuart accused her of covering up her criminal past; Velma accused him of snooping among her things and reading her letters. He responded that he had the right to know what kind of person he was marrying.

In a book Velma wrote on death row, she claimed that Stuart had taunted her, telling her he would reveal her prison record to people at church, and that whenever they would argue he would always bring it up. Whatever love she felt for him died, she said, and she would never feel comfortable with him again.[163]

Things got worse in December when Stuart discovered Velma had taken one of his checks, forged his signature, and cashed it for one hundred dollars. Velma claims in her book that when Stuart found out he was enraged and had threatened to turn her over to the police. This was a violation of her probation terms and the consequences would have been severe—Velma would be returned to prison. Although apparently Stuart forgave the debt, Velma claimed that he would constantly bring it up and threaten to have her arrested whenever they argued.

Stuart's daughter Alice testified later that after discovering the checks, her father cancelled his plans to marry Velma, but that she continued to live with him and wear the diamond engagement ring. He was not planning to break up with her, he told his daughter, but he was not going to marry her now.

Stuart and Velma raged on in this manner—breaking up and making up—over and over again. Every time they fought, Velma would go to stay with her daughter and wait for Stuart to bring her back home.

The Murder of Stuart Taylor

On Tuesday, January 31, 1978, Stuart drove Velma into town to fill a prescription. Velma was very worried. Unknown to Stuart, she had cashed a second forged check of his and the bank statement would be arriving in the mail soon. According to her recollections, while waiting for the prescription to be filled, Velma went to buy some hairspray. As she walked through the household section of the store, her eyes fell upon a bottle of ant poison. Velma would claim that she only wanted to make Stuart sick long enough to buy time so that she could replace the money in his account. She states:

> That afternoon I knew what I was going to do. But the serious-ness of it didn't get through to me. My thinking was so distorted by years of heavy medication that even though I knew what I was doing, I couldn't connect poisoning him with the suffering he would go through. By that time, the ant and roach poison was my antidote to the unbearable. I knew it would help.[164]

The years of heavy medication might have facilitated Velma's deeds, but her inability to "connect poisoning him with the suffer-ing he would go through" was one of the most predominate symp-toms of APSD—antisocial personality disorder—an inability for empathy, as she says, "even though I knew what I was doing." Stu-art Taylor had brought a psychopath into his home without know-ing it.

Before returning home, the couple turned up at Alice's house for a surprise visit. Alice was home with the flu and would later recall she was sure that her father had broken up with Velma for good and was surprised to see them together again that morning. But she liked the affable, grandmotherly Velma and welcomed her into her house. Alice had just had a baby and they were looking at snapshots when Velma asked to see the "dead" photo of Stuart that she had heard about. This was a joke photo that Alice had snapped of her father as he lay sleeping on the couch with his hands crossed. It became a family joke when Stuart said he always wanted to know what he might look like when he was dead. Alice brought the photo out and they all laughed about it.

That evening Stuart had promised to drive Velma into Fayette-ville to see TV evangelist Rex Humbard, who was passing through with his crusade. Around five Stuart had put on his good clothes and sat down for a dinner Velma had prepared. He had a beer with his meal but she did not object. They drove the twenty miles to Fayetteville and entered the Cumberland County Civic Center where Humbard was preaching. Almost as soon as the service be-gan, Stuart doubled over with severe stomach pain. He told Velma to stay while he would go lie down in his truck in the parking lot.

Again, Velma recalls thinking that she was in a religious meeting yet she had just poisoned a man. *Oh my God, what have I done?* But it didn't change anything. She didn't suddenly rush Stuart to a hospital. She sat and sang and prayed with Rex.

Emerging from the service, Velma found Stuart prostrate in the truck. He was in so much pain that Velma had to drive them home. Along the way, she stopped so Stuart could vomit by the side of the road. According to Velma, she urged Stuart to allow her to drive him to a hospital but he refused. Velma called Alice in the middle of the night to tell her that her father was very ill but that she was looking after him. It looked like the same flu that Alice was suffering from.

Stuart's friend and neighbor Sonny Johnson came by the next morning. On Monday they had gone out together to check their tobacco beds. Sonny knew Stuart for nearly forty years and knew that he was in robust health. He was surprised to see how weak and terrible Stuart looked. He offered to take care of Stuart's pigs until he got over the flu. Alice kept calling. Velma told her there was no improvement but not to worry, she was taking care of Stuart. Alice, herself bedridden from her flu, was relieved to hear that.

On Thursday, Velma brought Stuart into the emergency ward of a hospital in Lumberton. He had pains in his chest, stomach, and arms, was severely dehydrated, and his blood pressure was low. When asked for Stuart's medical history, Velma reported that he was healthy except for his drinking binges. The doctor diagnosed Stuart's condition as gastritis triggered by excessive drinking, even though Stuart had denied drinking recently. He prescribed Mylanta and lots of fluids and told Velma she could take Stuart home. He seemed to be improving.

Velma would later claim that the medicine the doctor prescribed made Stuart worse after she took him home. He got so ill the next day on Friday evening that she had to take him back to the emergency ward by ambulance, where he promptly died. Witnesses would recount a different story. Sonny Johnson came by to see Stuart the day before, when Velma brought him to the emergency ward, and remembers seeing Stuart sitting up on the edge of his bed smoking a cigarette.

According to Alice, on Friday Velma had told her that Stuart was doing much better. He was sitting up and able to go to the bathroom by himself. In fact, he was doing so well that Velma said he had asked her to make him his favorite dish—oyster stew—and that she was going to run into Lumberton to buy some. Alice was relieved. If her father was asking for his favorite dish he must be feeling much better.[165]

Yet on Friday night Velma called another neighbor, John McPherson, and told him that Stuart needed an ambulance urgently. McPherson was over to the house within five minutes and found Stuart on his bed, the sheets covered in feces. He was moaning and flailing in pain, and when asked where he was hurting, Stuart was unable to respond. Velma had put kitchen chairs around the bed so he would not roll off.

Stuart Taylor was pronounced dead an hour after arriving in the hospital that Friday night. He was 56 years old and in good health. His children had gathered at the hospital and were stunned to hear about their father's sudden death. The doctor suggested an autopsy and the family included Velma in their decision. She agreed that it would be a good idea.

"Gentlemen, I Think We Have a Serial Killer on Our Hands."

That weekend Lumberton Police Detective Benson Philips received a call at 5:30 A.M. at his home. The caller was a woman, who sounded drunk and hysterical. She claimed that a murder had occurred the night before and that "somebody must stop her." The woman was making no sense. Philips tried to persuade her that if there had been a murder he would have been called out, but he suggested that she call back later that morning at his office when she was more calm and could give him more details. After getting into work and assuring himself that no murder had indeed occurred, Philips was convinced that the caller was some drunken crank and he would not hear from her again. He was surprised when the caller phoned him at his office.

This time she sounded more collected and sober. After some prodding she told him that Stuart Taylor had been murdered by his girlfriend, Velma Barfield. Not only that, but Velma had also murdered her own mother the same way. When Philips pressed the caller for evidence, she had nothing to offer. Exasperated, Philips then asked how she knew and was surprised to hear her tell him that she was Velma's sister.

There was not much that Philips could do other than call the hospital and ensure that indeed a Stuart Taylor had died there on Friday night and that an autopsy would be conducted. He was assured that there would be an autopsy as the family had asked for one. This was outside his jurisdiction, but Philips made a note to follow up on the information. It would be weeks before Philips made a connection between Velma Barfield and the strange break-in and assault he had investigated in a trailer park three months earlier.

* * *

The results from the autopsy would take weeks. In the meantime, Velma and Stuart's children drew together in their loss. They were touched by the care that Velma had shown their father and by her obvious grief. On the day of the funeral they took Velma to Stuart's house to get her belongings and asked if Velma wanted anything of his. With tears in her eyes, Velma only asked for the wedding ring that Stuart had bought along with the engagement ring. The family embraced Velma and gave her four hundred dollars as a token of their affection and gratitude for the care she had shown for Stuart.

The autopsy had initially only revealed a case of gastroenteritis— a severe inflammation of the stomach and intestines that would not be enough to kill a person as healthy as Stuart at his age. It was indeed puzzling and the doctor could not let the mystery rest. He cut away some of the internal organs and kept them while releasing the body for the funeral. The next day he began to examine them and discovered abnormalities in the liver tissue. He sent them to Page Hudson, the chief medical examiner in North Carolina, for further tests.

Page Hudson immediately detected what appeared to be traces of arsenic poisoning in the liver samples. A few days of testing confirmed massive doses of arsenic in Stuart Taylor's tissue samples. North Carolina should have been the worst place for Velma to use arsenic, because it had the highest rate of arsenic deaths by homicide and suicide in the U.S. Since 1971, when the state began keeping records, there had been sixteen arsenic deaths, mostly murders.[166] In one year there was a total of six. Because of North Carolina's extensive agricultural activity, arsenic was readily available in the form of pesticides, many of which were sold in retail stores over the counter.

One in particular was problematic. Singletary's Rat Poison came in the form of an odorless, tasteless, clear liquid. The North Carolina Pesticide Control Board attempted to ban it in 1976 but only succeeded in introducing a diluted version of Britain's Sale of Arsenic Act which had been passed one hundred and thirty years before. Buyers in North Carolina were subsequently required to sign for their purchase of Singletary's, but they did not have to show any identification when signing. Many of the proprietors of the country stores where Singletary's was sold were not even aware of the new regulation when it took effect in 1977. Moreover, there were many arsenic products other than Singletary's that were likewise odorless, tasteless, and clear in appearance, like, for example, Terro ant poison, which was sold in almost every drug and hardware store and was not covered by the regulation. This was the product Velma had plunked down sixty cents for in the drugstore while she waited for her prescription on January 31.

* * *

By March the family had still not been informed of the autopsy results. Instead the information went to Robeson County District Attorney Joe Freeman Britt. Joe Britt got a crash course on arsenic poison, from Page Hudson, who reported that it was his experience that arsenic poisoners frequently had already committed the crime and had gone undetected.

Joe Britt gathered together his homicide investigators from the Robeson County Sheriff's office. One of the investigators had already heard from Benson Philips, who had told him about his 5:30 A.M. phone call naming Velma Barfield as not only the murderer of Stuart Taylor but also of her own mother, Lillie Bullard. As it often is in rural counties, everybody knew each other.

One of the investigators knew both Velma and her family, including her mother, and Velma's first husband, Thomas. He knew Stuart Taylor as well, although he did not know that Velma had been having a relationship with Stuart. He recalled that Velma's first husband had died in a fire and that she had then married somebody in Fayetteville, but he did not know what had happened to him.

He had run across Velma in another case. An elderly man by the name of John Henry Lee, shortly before dying the summer before, had called to report that one of his blank checks had somehow been stolen and fraudulently cashed. The investigator visited his home and was surprised to find Velma there working as a caregiver. His inclination was to suspect Velma but both John and his wife, Record, insisted that Velma was a pious, churchgoing Christian and it was inconceivable that she would have stolen the check. There were no further leads.

Another investigator knew the son of Montgomery and Dollie Edwards, the elderly couple who had died within a month of each other. Velma had been employed as a caregiver in their household he told them. Once they pulled on those threads, it all started to quickly unravel.

Within days the investigators had assembled the death certificates of Stuart Taylor, Lillie Bullard, Dollie and Montgomery Edwards, and John Henry Lee. "We spread them out across the desk," Britt later said, "and it was just like a damn suit of cards: gastroenteritis, gastroenteritis, gastroenteritis . . ."[167] Later Velma's second husband, Jennings Barfield, would be added to the suspected victim list.

"Gentlemen, I think we have a serial killer on our hands," Britt said.

Velma's Childhood

Margie Velma Barfield was a local girl—born and bred in the counties between Fayetteville and Lumberton in North Carolina's cotton and tobacco belt. She was a child of the Great Depression, born on October 29, 1932. Velma was the second child of 21-year-old cotton and tobacco farmer Murphy Bullard and his 22-year-old wife, Lillie. Her brother, Olive, was born two years earlier. They lived in a world without electricity and running water. Water was drawn from a well dug just behind the kitchen and butter and milk were kept in buckets suspended in the cool waters of the well in the hot summer months. There was no outhouse—they would go out into the woods to relieve themselves. Bathing and washing clothing was done in huge galvanized tubs that hung from the wall when not in use. It was the Beverly Hillbillies before Jed found the oil and without the laugh track. But it was not unusual. Power lines did not arrive in that part of Cumberland County until after World War Two.

Murphy owned his own land and for a while he was able to support his children and aging parents despite the Depression, but eventually cotton prices crashed and Murphy, like so many rural men, had to find industrial work in the city. He got a job in the Fayetteville textile mills repairing looms. He would commute daily to the mill, come home and sleep a little, get up at dawn to farm, and then head back out to the mill. Over the decade Velma's family grew. Lillie gave birth to seven more children over the next fifteen years: five sons and two daughters in addition to Velma and Olive.

Murphy was known as a good neighbor, friendly and ready to give a helping hand whenever it was needed. If somebody was sick and could not get their crop in, Murphy was there to do it. If farm equipment was needed, Murphy would readily loan his.

The family, however, saw a different version of the man. At home Murphy was tyrannical and full of violent, uncontrollable rage. If anything was out of place or not done the way he wanted it, he would unleash a violent beating, sometimes onto the nearest available target. He whipped his children, usually with a strap, but was known to use anything else that fell into his hand. Murphy did not drink often, but when he did his temper and violence would get only worse.

As the oldest son, Olive often took the brunt of the beatings, and Lillie often did her best to protect Olive, sometimes taking the blame for some error or infraction Olive might have committed. This was a cause of deep resentment in Velma, who felt that her mother favored Olive and sometimes protected him at Velma's expense. Her resentment of her mother also deepened because of her meekness in not openly intervening in the beatings. Velma and Olive, despite the beatings, still talked back to their father. With every beating she received, Velma resented her mother more and more instead of her father.

Velma shared her parents' bedroom and sometimes would be awakened by the moans of pain from Lillie to see her father twisting her mother's arm or bending her fingers. But Velma writes, "Daddy didn't hit her."

"Mom never fought back," Velma said. She summed up her childhood in four words, "I was always afraid."[168]

Yet there were many good times. On Sundays Murphy would organize baseball games in the field out back and the kids would play until dark. Sometimes he would take the family on picnics and outings to swim in a nearby pond. He taught them all how to swim.

Velma said that her father was not always bad tempered and she craved his affection when she was 10 or 11 years old. He would call her "sugar" and "honey." She recalled how sometimes he would sit her on his lap and hug her, and how much she loved that closeness and warmth. She said of her death row reminiscences of her father that this was the first time she was expressing how much that meant to her.

The happiest memory of her life, Velma recalls, was when her father spontaneously bought her a pink dress she was admiring in a store window. She recalls how she looked forward to showing the dress to her mother when they got home, but Lillie spoiled the mood by complaining that it would be difficult to iron.

Velma had started school when she was 7 and was taunted by other children who were better off than she. Other kids ate sandwiches on store-bought bread and store-bought cookies for dessert. Velma had chunky dark homemade bread or biscuits and a slice of meat or sausage. She began to eat her lunch alone. Her clothes were shabby. She only received a new pair of shoes at the beginning of the year, which were always practical and ugly. Velma began stealing coins from her father's pants and buying candy and eating it in front of the kids to taunt them back. Then Velma stole eighty dollars from an old man's cabin near where she was visiting some relatives: It was an enormous amount of money in those days. Velma was found with some of the money and insisted that the man had given it to her for safekeeping. Murphy whipped her with a belt and Velma either suspended her thieving or made sure she was never caught again.

Teachers complained that Velma was boisterous and short-tempered. She was easily offended when things did not go her way. Velma had hoped that school would give her refuge from her problems at home, but instead it only created new problems. But home was worse. Every Wednesday, Murphy would fetch Velma from school at noon so that she could do the family laundry. She would have to do it by hand until evening.

When Velma was in high school she showed a talent for basketball and was offered a place on the team, but that would have meant staying after school for practice. Her mother refused permission for Velma to join the team, insisting that she needed her at home to help with the kids. This deepened Velma's resentment of her mother even more.

When Velma turned 13 the family moved to a larger property in Robeson County, which would, some forty years later, put her to death. It was around that time that Velma says her father raped her. She was home from school in bed not feeling well and her mother was working outside in the yard. Her father walked into the room and raped her without saying a word. Velma says he also fondled her several times when the family went swimming.

It took Velma a long time to reveal this episode. After her arrest, she told her psychiatric examiner that her father had once climbed naked into her bed but that somebody came into the house and he quickly left without completing the assault. She could not bring herself to talk about it until near the end of her life. She said that it made her resent her mother even more. Velma stated, "I did feel angry at her. I couldn't understand why she could not protect us. As a child I could not understand that."

Velma wrote that when she came down for supper that evening she felt "dirty and awful" and that she then hated her father as much as she loved him. "My feelings were so mixed up, and I was ashamed of how I felt. I couldn't tell my brothers and sisters—how could I admit that I deeply loved a father who did the kind of things he did to me?"[169]

* * *

Almost every serial killer's story begins with some awful, tragic childhood. Velma's childhood is typical of serial killers—a history of rape and physical abuse. Her psyche's defense system displaced her anger away from her father toward Lillie, who she felt was passive in the face of Murphy's abuse. It also disconnected her emotional network, displacing the anger and hate she felt for her father with a false love and affection she felt she *should* have had for her father. For the rest of her life until her father died, she appeared to have a normal and loving relationship with him, visiting with him and taking her own children to their grandfather—the same man who had brutalized and raped her. She directed her own rage and anger elsewhere.

Velma's First Marriage

Velma was seventeen and in grade eleven when she escaped her house by marrying her high school boyfriend and neighbor, Thomas Burke, in December 1949. They married in secret after driving to South Carolina, and revealed the marriage only later to Murphy and Lillie. There was some hell to pay at first, but they got used to the idea. Both Velma and Thomas dropped out of high school and eventually moved in with Olive, who had recently married. Thomas took a job driving a soft drink delivery truck.

Two years later in 1951, Velma gave birth to her first child, a son she named Ronald Thomas, who would be called Ronnie. She was 19 years old. Two years after that she gave birth to a daughter, Kim. By all accounts Velma was a passionately loving mother who ensured that her children's lives would be nothing like her own childhood. There would be no beatings or yelling. The children were smothered in love and affection. Velma read to them every night. She and Thomas joined the Baptist Church and Velma devoutly attended, never missing a service, ensuring that her children always attended with her.

Some might say that Velma might have been too attached to her children. Once, when Thomas and Velma went away for a few days' vacation leaving the children with Thomas's parents, Velma practically hyperventilated with anxiety by the end of the second day. She forced Thomas to pack up and the next day drive back late into the night, waking up the parents and taking the children home in the middle of the night. Only once Velma was reunited with her children did she relax.

When Ronnie was in third grade, Thomas was making sufficient money to move the family into a new large house with plenty of space for the kids to play, in the small town of Parkton. The house was just down the street from a Baptist church and the family's religious activities escalated. Velma taught Sunday school and Bible classes while Thomas served as an usher.

The family did everything together. Went to the movies, the beach, bowled, and played miniature golf. Velma played basketball with her kids and they would spend the summer weekends visiting country fairs or driving out to the beaches on the coast.

Ronnie was deeply attached to his mother. On his first day of school Velma spent the entire day with him to get him used to being without her. She always volunteered to help with class trips and picnics. Ronnie would later say, "I wouldn't say I was a mama's boy, but I was close to it. I really loved my mamma to death, a real adoring-type love."

Kim was more attached to her father, following him around everywhere. Thomas gladly took her with him on errands. She sat on his lap as they watched her favorite TV shows and she adored her cheerful father who always had a joke to make her laugh.

It was a perfect marriage and a perfect family with no hidden shadows or dark demons scratching at the back door. But for all four of them, those days would become nothing but a distant misty memory of better things past.

In 1962 when Velma was thirty and Ronnie was twelve and Kim was ten, fibroid tumors were discovered on Velma's uterus. Velma and Thomas had planned on only two children so they went ahead with what the doctors recommended—a hysterectomy, the most common nonpregnancy-related surgery performed among American women. A hysterectomy is instant menopause and nobody had accounted for how the hormonal changes would impact on Velma's personality. Velma and Thomas were apparently unaware of the possible negative emotional toll that was more prevalent among women of Velma's age having hysterectomies than in older women.

Velma became irritable and nervous, snapping angrily at the kids and at Thomas. She was depressed and felt that she was becoming overweight. She began taking diet pills. She went on spending sprees, occasionally writing checks knowing there was not enough money in the account to cover them. When they bounced she somehow managed to cover the amounts with the stores before charges were accrued. She kept this secret from her family.

In 1964 she developed back pains and was prescribed painkillers to which she quickly became addicted.

Thomas, in the meantime, began to drink heavily. Velma writes that she thinks he began around 1965 and escalated the next year after his father died. He had also joined the Jaycees and often after meetings would drink and socialize with other members. Velma abhorred drinking. For her there was no such thing as a social drink. She saw the effects that alcohol had on her father and the one thing she had admired most about Thomas when she met him was that—unlike the other boys—he did not drink. But he was getting dead rolling drunk, coming home and passing out on the couch.

Velma began to rage at Thomas, perhaps in the way she thought her mother should have with her father. Thomas was charged with drunken driving. He lost his job and had to take another. It got so bad that at one point Velma had Thomas committed to a mental hospital. Thomas signed himself out several days later but he would rarely show his face in town again: He was too ashamed. The marriage began to spin out of control into some dark and violent vortex. Velma and Thomas fought bitterly and violently.

After inexplicably collapsing one day in 1968, Velma was prescribed the highly addictive tranquillizer Valium. She later said that whenever she would take the pills they would soften the anger and rage that was tearing her up. Eventually Velma would become addicted to a combination of painkillers and tranquillizers, which included Elavil, Sinequan, Tranxene, Tylenol III, and Valium. She juggled as many as five doctors simultaneously: all were writing the same prescriptions for her in ignorance of each other's existence.

Neither Ronnie nor Kim could understand what had happened, but the happy, sunny, carefree days they all used to pass together as a family were gone forever.

The Death of Thomas

On the morning of April 19, 1969, Thomas came home from the night shift at a textile mill where he had found work. According to Velma, Thomas nodded off while sitting in his chair smoking.

The cigarette fell out of his mouth and rolled onto his shirt, and he would have caught fire, Velma said, if she had not snatched up the cigarette. She recalled, "As I picked up the burning cigarette and put it out, I screamed, 'I don't care! I don't care anymore! Burn yourself up if you want to!' "[170]

Velma claimed that Thomas then managed to make his way to the bed and collapsed into it still dressed. In the meantime, she drove off with the weekly wash to the Laundromat in town. When she returned she says she smelt smoke in the house. Entering the bedroom she found the smoke so thick she could not see anything. She called the fire department. It was too late. Thomas had died from smoke inhalation.

Later that day when Ronnie came back from school he walked through the smoke-damaged house. What caught his attention was that the firemen had had to chop through the kitchen door with their axes. Strange, Ronnie thought. Had his mother locked the door when she left? If Velma had entered the house as far as the smoke-filled bedroom, why had the firemen needed to chop through the kitchen door?

Velma denied almost to the end that she had murdered Thomas. Yet her account of removing a burning cigarette from his shirt as he slept on the very same morning that he would then light another and carelessly set the mattress on fire is a strange coincidence. In the last days before her execution, Ronnie asked Velma if she had killed his father. She replied that she "probably" had but could not remember the details other than leaving either a burning cigarette or a lit match on the mattress as he slept and then closing the door as she left the room.

Velma Remarries

The death of Thomas did not bring peace to the house. In the next two and a half years, Velma's house would catch fire two more times and be burglarized once. Velma made insurance claims for losses in all the incidents. She had become heavily addicted to tranquillizers, going to different doctors to get multiple prescriptions. She also began to weigh heavily on Ronnie in his last year of high school, obsessing about him. When Ronnie graduated from high school it was tradition that graduates would go to Carolina Beach for a weekend of partying. But as his friends waited in the car out-side, Velma wept that he had grown up and she was losing him. Consoling his mother, Ronnie told his friends to go without him: He was going to remain with his mother that weekend.

Velma was working in a department store. In September 1969, about five months after the death of Thomas, one of Velma's coworkers, Pauline Barfield, died. Velma knew Pauline's husband, Jennings, quite well. He often dropped in to pick up Pauline and would chat with Velma while he waited. Jennings was 54, a re-tired civil service worker collecting a disability pension because of diabetes, emphysema, and heart troubles. He had six adult chil-dren and lived in a house in Fayetteville with his 16-year-old daughter. After Pauline's death the lonely widow and widower be-gan to date.

In July 1970, a little over a year after Thomas's death, Velma announced that she and Jennings were getting married, much to the surprise and concern of Ronnie and Kim. Jennings was not very healthy, they felt, and Velma had her own drug problems. Nevertheless, on August 23, 1970, the couple was married in the church wedding that Velma had never had when she eloped with Thomas. Velma wore a pink suit, pink pillbox hat, and pink shoes, reminiscent of the pink dress her father had bought her when she was a child. Even the flowers and the cake icing at the reception were pink. Ronnie's mother was now Velma Barfield, the name she would take with her to death row.

Velma moved into Jennings's home. Her old house had been re-paired with insurance money after the second fire and she rented it out. Kim still had another year of high school to complete and she moved in with her grandparents, Lillie and Murphy, so she could finish her final year in the same school. Ronnie stayed there, too. The drunken and violent Murphy had long ago changed his ways. After a horrendous car accident while he was drinking, he stopped. His temper mellowed and he and Lillie were stereotypical loving grandparents as their nine children married and had kids of their own.

Ronnie, in the meantime, had a decision to make. He had good grades but could not afford to go to college. Scholarships were rare in those days in that part of North Carolina. Shortly before her wedding, Velma had urged Ronnie to apply to college, assuring him that Jennings would pay for at least one semester. Ronnie applied and was immediately accepted at the University of South Carolina. But when it came time to pay for tuition, Jennings did not come forth with any money. It was some kind of misunderstanding. Ronnie returned to Lillie and Murphy.

The problem for Ronnie was that in 1970 the U.S. was at war in Vietnam and Ronnie was 19—exactly the preferred age for the draft. If he was in college, his draft would be deferred, but if not he was fair game to be drafted to fight in the jungle for a tour of twelve months. Lots of 19-year-olds were coming back from Vietnam in body bags. Poor white trash and black ghetto kids who could not afford to get into college or did not make the grade were the backbone of America's fighting forces in a war that by 1970 everyone knew had gone badly wrong.

There was an alternative to the draft—to voluntarily enlist. The downside was an enlistment lasted three years instead of the twelve-month combat tour of duty, but the upside was you chose which service, branch, and specialty to join. It did not guarantee that you did not end up in Vietnam, but it did guarantee that if you did, as an enlisted specialist you were not going to be stuck as an ordinary infantryman in some rotting jungle hole—a grunt in the mud on the front line of enemy fire. And so Ronnie enlisted in the army in December to be trained as a security specialist. His enlistment was scheduled to begin in spring of 1971.

In this same period both Velma and Jennings were realizing the mistake they had made. About a month after their wedding, after Ronnie was turned away from college, Velma overdosed on painkillers for the first time. Jennings took her to the hospital, but when he learned she had overdosed he drove her to her parents' house and dropped her off, telling Lillie he could not deal with Velma. He was too sick himself.

Ronnie counseled his mother to get her addiction to pills under control if she wanted her new marriage to work. A few days later Jennings came by and took Velma home. But it was not long before Jennings's doctor called to tell him that Velma was refilling his prescriptions and taking the pills herself.

In November Velma was taken to the hospital after a second

overdose. Jennings's daughter Nancy told Ronnie that Velma appeared to be drugged-up all the time, staggering around the house, falling and sometimes unable to speak. They tried hiding pills from her, but she was stashing them everywhere. Nancy was worried for the health of her father. Jennings was the sick one and Velma should be looking after *him* instead of the other way around.

In February 1971 Velma was hospitalized after a third overdose. When Ronnie visited her in hospital, she told him that her marriage was a mistake. Jennings was not watching his diet despite his diabetes and taking care of an invalid husband was not something she had planned on.

Jennings likewise felt that he could not continue. On Friday, March 19, he drove over to his son's house and telephoned his lawyer to plan out divorce proceedings. They made an appointment to meet on Monday.

The Murder of Jennings Barfield

Velma would state that her life with Jennings was getting worse by the day. She claimed that she had to take care of him and that he stubbornly refused doctor's instructions for his diet. The more obstinate he became, the more drugs Velma took, she claimed. She said she began to wonder why she had married him in the first place. She wrote:

> Each day got worse. *I can't bear up under all of this. I've got to get away from this pressure. I can't stand it much longer.* I bought a bottle of ant and roach poison.[171]

Velma insisted that her intention was only to make him sick. "Then he'll be sorry he's caused me so much trouble, and he won't do it again," she claimed.

Jennings did not make the Monday appointment with his lawyer. He died Sunday morning after Velma took him to the hospital with severe stomach pains and vomiting. In her book Velma reveals that she convinced herself that Jennings did not die of the poison she gave him but that his lungs gave out because he was already weak and ill. If Jennings is indeed the first victim she killed, there is nothing in her account that gives us any insight into what was going through her mind as she crossed the line to commit her first murder. It is as if her entire persona had been already programmed and set to kill. She went from "I can't stand it much longer" to "I bought a bottle of ant and roach poison." There is nothing in between, no contemplation of her act, no comment on the last seconds when she held in her hand the poisoned dish or drink she was about to serve him—when she still could have spilled it on the floor or even knocked it out of his hands as he brought it up to his mouth before it was too late

Nothing.

"I bought a bottle of ant and roach poison" is all she had inside of her to reveal to us. And that, of course, is what makes her a psychopath and the rest of us, hopefully, not.

The Disintegration of Velma

After the funeral, which Velma did not attend because she was too drugged out, she moved into her parents' house where Ronnie and Kim were living. Ronnie was scheduled to leave for army basic training at Fort Jackson, near Columbia, South Carolina. Velma took to her bed and begged Ronnie not to go. He went, of course, and during basic training Velma would visit him every weekend— the only recruit in Ronnie's unit to get such visits.

In mid-June, Velma and Kim moved back into their twice burned-out home. Ronnie had completed basic training and was scheduled to begin training at the Army Security Agency School at Ford Devens, Massachusetts, in July. While home for a visit Velma seemed to have improved, but as soon as he left her condition immediately worsened.

Velma wanted Ronnie to secure a hardship discharge. Her doctor wrote to the army describing Velma's medical condition due to her husband's death and the induction into the army of her son. He requested that the army discharge Ronnie so that he could return home to take care of his mother and sister. The army refused.

Velma had returned to work in the department store she had worked in before her marriage to Jennings. She frequently would not go into work, however. Her medical and drug bills grew. She borrowed eight hundred dollars from a bank to pay for them and then the next month reported a burglary at her house. The thieves, she reported, had made off with the cash she had borrowed along with some of Ronnie's shoes and clothes. Velma made an insurance claim for the loss. Her behavior at work became erratic. She frequently was so hostile to customers that she was removed from dealing with them and assigned to the stockroom, marking prices.

On October 14, 1971, Velma asked Kim to take her into town so that she could apply for work at some other businesses. She seemed to linger longer than planned. When Kim and Velma returned home, their house was surrounded with fire trucks. A third fire had burned in their house. Ronnie got emergency leave from the army and rushed home to his mother.

Velma and Kim moved back in with Lillie and Murphy. While home, Ronnie promised his mother he would press vigorously for a hardship discharge and began collecting the necessary medical certificates and other paperwork. Velma, in the meantime, was fired from work. She had become too unreliable, even in the stockroom. Ronnie was also concerned. Two fires and a break-in—was somebody perhaps targeting his mother?

During his visit home, Ronnie met a girl—Kim, a cousin of one of his high school buddies. They began to date and things got serious very quickly. When he left to return to Fort Devens, Kim had promised to write. Ronnie's sister, Kim, in the meantime, moved in with her uncle Jimmy, who offered her work tending a vending machine route. Both children would regularly send money back to support Velma.

More bad news arrived that autumn. Ronnie was being assigned to Vietnam in January. Velma was now almost hysterical. While Ronnie's commanding officer had approved Ronnie's request for a hardship discharge, the army still needed to confirm it.

When Ronnie visited home during Christmas, things were bleak, not only for Velma, but also for his grandfather. Murphy had been sick with some kind of respiratory illness that the doctors could not diagnose and he appeared to be wasting away. Lillie now had to care for an ailing husband and for Velma, who sometimes was so full of drugs that she could not get out of bed for days. The only ray of light for Ronnie during his visit home was seeing his girlfriend, Kim.

After Ronnie returned to duty, Velma's condition worsened. She overdosed on pills again and was taken to the emergency room. She told hospital psychiatrists that she wanted to commit suicide because she could not face seeing her son killed in Vietnam.

Ronnie's assignment to Vietnam was put on hold until the discharge application was reviewed. In March, Ronnie got his answer. His application was turned down, but he would not be sent to Vietnam. He was assigned to duty at the Army Security Agency at Fort Bragg, just outside of Fayetteville. He would be close to home.

Other news was not good. Murphy was diagnosed with lung cancer, and his condition deteriorated so fast that on April 15, 1972, he died. Velma appeared to be deeply upset at her father's death. She said years later, "I had learned to love him as much as I had hated him. He was good to my kids. I think he tried to do with my kids like he wished he had done to us."

That spring Velma also lost her house. She had not made the mortgage payments in months and the bank foreclosed on the house and auctioned it off. Velma took a job at a textile mill but soon lost it after she overdosed on pills again and was hospitalized for three weeks.

Stationed at Fort Bragg, Ronnie was now seeing Kim regularly. In the summer of 1972, they decided to get married. They would not tell Velma of their plans until November, however. When she heard, Velma was devastated. This was a betrayal. Velma cried and told Ronnie, "I've always been the most important woman in your life."

Velma and Her Mother

But unknown to Ronnie, Velma had been in a relationship with a 69-year-old man she had met in hospital during one of her overdoses. Al Smith was a former construction worker who was in for severe alcohol abuse. Velma and Al began to date and eventually moved in together. Just like Jennings, in the past, and Stuart, in the future, Velma had Al attending church services and gospel meetings in her attempt to wean him off his alcohol addiction. But the relationship was volatile. They argued and fought. When Ronnie finally found out about Al he was surprised by his mother's choice of partner and did not approve. It seemed as self-destructive as her pill habit.

In December 1972, Ronnie had bad news for Velma. He thought his assignment to Fort Bragg was permanent, but he learned he was going to be reassigned to Germany in March. He and Kim would be quickly married in February and Kim, who was studying at college to become an elementary school teacher, would join him in Germany in the spring, where she would continue her studies through an extension program with the University of Maryland.

Velma's reaction was predictable: She overdosed herself into a coma. When Ronnie arrived at her bedside, she was on a respirator, and there were doubts whether she would make it through the night. But she survived. When Ronnie married Kim in February 1973, Velma was at the wedding, clean and sober at least for that day. That same month, Velma moved home with her widowed mother.

Ronnie appealed the army's refusal for a hardship discharge and updated his request with more medical letters on Velma's worsening condition. His move to Germany was postponed in March pending a decision.

No sooner had Ronnie gotten that good news than more bad news arrived from Velma. She was in jail, arrested for attempting to pass a forged prescription. On April 3, Velma pled guilty and was sentenced to six months, suspended for three years if she did not get into further trouble.

On April 6, Ronnie received the good news that his discharge was finally approved. He was free to come home from the army. If he thought his life had been hell since he was twelve, it is only because he had no idea what was still to come: Ronnie was going home to Mother.

* * *

In the autumn of 1973, Ronnie and his wife were enrolled at Pembroke State University. His sister, Kim, met Dennis Norton and they were engaged to be married the next autumn. Velma was living with her mother and still seeing Al Smith on and off. Velma bounced between jobs at textile mills, none of which she could hold longer than three months. In November 1973, Velma was arrested again, this time for passing a bad check in the amount of $115. Luck was with her this time as the prosecutor failed to check her record and nobody found out she was under a suspended sentence. Otherwise she would have gone automatically into jail to serve the six months for her previous conviction.

Velma was desperate. Unable to pay for her prescriptions, she began to steal blank checks from Lillie and cashing them. It was not long before Lillie discovered this. She told her son Tyrone about it and showed him the cancelled checks. But Lillie decided not to confront Velma directly. She told Tyrone that her relationship with Velma had become very strained and she did not want to make it any worse. Instead she and Tyrone drove to the bank and made sure that from then on the bank confirmed the authenticity of Lillie's signature on the checks from her account. From then on Lillie kept her checkbook hidden in a locked drawer.

Early in 1974, Kim found her mother overdosed again in convulsions. Again she was taken to a hospital by ambulance. When Velma came home, she showed no interest in going back to work. She seemed in a vegetative state, concerned only with getting her prescriptions filled.

In August, Velma went to meet with Al at a motel near Fayetteville. Late that night, Al attempted to cross the highway to get some beer at a convenience store and was run down and killed by a truck in the dark. Velma was a beneficiary in Al's life insurance for the amount of $5,000.

Kim and Dennis married on November 23 and moved into a trailer park in Lumberton. Velma again was sober and functioning the day of the wedding.

Since Velma had moved in with Lillie, everybody had noticed that there was a brittle tension between Velma and her mother. That Christmas in 1974, the family had gathered for a traditional dinner that Lillie had prepared. Velma rushed around helping her mother in the kitchen—just as she did when she was a little girl. Everybody, including Velma, seemed to have a good time.

On December 28, 1974, the Saturday after Christmas, Tyrone dropped by with his family to visit his mother. Lillie discreetly took him aside to show him something strange. It was a notice from a finance company advising her that her payment for a thousand-dollar loan was overdue, and if it was not made promptly, her car would be repossessed. But she had not taken out any loan. Tyrone told her not to worry about it. It was probably a mistake. If another notice arrived, he would look into it for her.

By then everybody noticed that things were very volatile between Velma and her mother. One day when visiting, Ronnie saw his mother explode in rage when Lillie told her she needed to do the laundry. Velma threw the clothes across the room and cursed her mother. Years later, Ronnie would comment, "I think there was more anger in my mom then than I had ever seen. And it was a different type than I'd seen before, all directed at my grandmother. She just seemed to have a lot of resentment. She resented having to depend on her mother."

Ronnie got the anger part right, but he did not understand the real source of Velma's rage.

Velma Murders Her Mother

According to Velma's death row account, she resented being treated by her mother as she had been when she was a child. Velma felt she was ordered around and treated like a slave. Being told to do the laundry only reminded her of being taken out of school every Wednesday afternoon to scrub the family laundry all day.

Velma said that her aging mother liked to talk about the past and how great it had been. "Almost every day she started on the same things again. I heard it over and over until I couldn't stand it anymore," Velma said.

"But they were such good times. The best days I ever had in my life," her mother would insist.

"They weren't *my* best days," Velma would reply to her mother. But her mother would never listen or ask her why—she would just prattle on about how wonderful all their lives were back then.

"I never could scream, 'Shut up!'" Velma said.

According to Velma, by the autumn of 1974 she was running out of money for her prescriptions, bills were piling up, and with Kim's upcoming wedding, as the mother of the bride, Velma needed to cover the expenses. Velma said she went down to a loan company and got a one-thousand-dollar loan in her mother's name using her house as collateral. She told them her mother was too sick to come in and took the papers home for her signature, which she forged. Velma makes no mention of the five-thousand-dollar insurance payment she received after Al's accidental death, but she does say she paid back the first loan she took—presumably from that payment. "Maybe that's why I didn't think too much about it when I took out a second loan for another thousand dollars," recounted Velma.

Velma said that her mother showed her the first notices of due loan payments, but that she did not seem to be troubled about them, assuming it was a mistake. Velma, however, was in a panic. Every time the phone rang or there was a knock on the door, fear and anxiety would grip her. She knew she had to find work quickly and start paying down on the loan, but she felt paralyzed with anxiety and guilt and rage. She said, "All different kinds of feelings struggled inside of me—panic and anger and worry about not having any more medication."

According to Velma, about a week after Lillie got the notice of overdue payments, she went into town to pick up some medications. She wrote:

> While I waited for my prescription in the drugstore, I walked around and looked at things. I saw some ant and roach poison in a clear plastic bottle. I don't remember thinking about what I would do next. But somewhere inside me, I must have already conceived of the plan. I had done it once, even though I had blotted that from my conscious memory.[172]

Again, Velma insisted that she only wanted to make her mother sick while she paid off the loan before Lillie discovered her deception. She served her mother lunch and a soft drink laced with the arsenic. A few hours later, she gave her a second arsenic soft drink.

Velma said once again the doctors misdiagnosed her victim's condition, this time attributing it to stomach flu. She stated:

> While waiting, I kept thinking of what the doctor had said. *The poison hadn't done this to her. It's something that's going around, like the doctor said. A lot of people are going through*

the same thing, not just Mama. That's how I worked it out in my head.[173]

The medicine the doctors prescribed only made her mother worse, according to Velma, just as when she had poisoned Jennings. Velma's revelations in her death row memoir, both sincere and insincere, give us a frightening insight into the thought process of a homicidal psychopath. How does a wife kill her husband, a daughter her mother, a mother her children? What in the world were they thinking? What did they think they were doing? It is unimaginable to us, but only if we impose our own emotional matrix and thought process on these kinds of acts. Psychopaths like Velma think in different ways—they feel and think in different dimensions that we cannot perceive or comprehend with our ordinary minds. In the world of criminal psychology, theories on the mind of a serial killer are the equivalent of quantum physics' black holes and string theory: Aside from corpses, it's anybody's guess what lies on the other side.

We do not know what happened that weekend after Christmas when Tyrone had visited his mother and Lillie had shown him the loan company letters. Did Lillie confront Velma about the loan company notices? Would she not shut up about past good times? Did she ask Velma to do the laundry again? Did Velma feel Ronnie was not paying enough attention to her or visiting her frequently enough? All we know is that on Monday after lunch, Lillie began to suffer severe stomach pains; she vomited blood and had diarrhea. That afternoon she was taken to the hospital and by the late evening she was dead. As the family gathered at the hospital and questioned Velma about what had happened, she would only repeat, "I did everything I could for her. Everything I could."

Velma Is Arrested for Forgery

Broke, unemployed, and addicted to tranquillizers and painkillers, Velma had no place to go after her mother's funeral. Tyrone settled Lillie's affairs, including the outstanding loans that Velma had taken in her mother's name. He did not bring up the subject with his sister.

Even though Kim and Dennis had married only weeks earlier, they took Velma in to live with them in their trailer. Kim and Dennis did their best to monitor Velma's drug addiction, but she always managed to get more prescriptions behind their backs and kept hidden stashes of drugs. They returned one day from work to find Velma on the floor, unconscious after yet another overdose. Again she was hospitalized and again she returned home with prescriptions for the same drugs.

A week after she returned home from the hospital, Velma paid a visit to Ronnie's home. Ronnie and Kim were on their way out to play golf and they invited her to wait for them inside their house. When they returned, they found Velma unconscious on the floor with her collarbone broken, protruding through her skin.

Several weeks earlier, Velma had begged Ronnie to give her money to make good on bad checks she had recently written. Ronnie was surprised—Velma had gotten five thousand dollars from the life insurance benefit on Al. Where had all the money gone? Remembering that his mother had given him seven hundred dollars, he took out a bank loan and gave her the money back. As Velma was in the hospital recovering from her latest overdose, police arrived at Kim's trailer looking for Velma. She had written more bad checks. If she did not pay them off, she would be charged and arrested—and her suspended sentence would probably be revoked. In her memoir, Velma justified passing bad checks by pointing out that Kim and Ronnie were constantly finding and flushing down the toilet her secret stashes of drugs. She would think to herself, Don't they realize how much those pills cost? It was their fault she had to resort to passing bad checks—another typical psychopathic thought process that lays blame everywhere but on themselves.

Kim had just discovered she was pregnant. Ronnie was exhausted. Together they decided that perhaps forcing Velma to face the consequences of her actions might serve as a wake-up call for her. They could not even afford to help Velma if they had wanted to. Together they decided to let Velma be arrested. Velma had managed to smuggle her pills into jail, and she overdosed there. After a brief stay in hospital, she was sent back to jail after her cell was carefully searched.

On March 21, Velma appeared before a judge who reinstated her six-month prison sentence for forging a prescription. She began serving it at the North Carolina Correctional Center for Women in Raleigh. Velma was 42 years old. Kim could not visit her mother in Raleigh because she was pregnant and feeling sick every day. Ronnie was busy with his new job.

After serving four months, Velma was released on probation. She moved back in with Kim and Dennis. Eleven days after her release, she was in hospital with an overdose again. Velma had apparently stashed a number of prescription refills before she went to prison. That was the only thing on her mind as she served her sentence. She paid for the pills by writing checks on an old bank account she no longer had.

When police arrived with the checks there would be new charges pending—forgery this time. Unlike Velma's previous charges for bad checks, forgery was a felony. Velma wept and begged Kim and Ronnie to help her; she promised to change her ways and kick her habit. Her son and daughter gave in and paid off the checks. No charges were pressed.

In October 1975, Kim gave birth to a daughter. Velma was in attendance at the hospital and the birth of her granddaughter appeared to have contributed to a change for the better. She also learned that Ronnie's wife was also pregnant. She doted on her grandchild, which reminded her of when Ronnie was an infant. Kim and Dennis moved into a house with their newborn baby. Velma, who appeared to be off the drugs for the first time, told them that she would remain living in the trailer. She had found a new line of work—caring for elderly sick people.

Velma Becomes a Home-Care Worker

Velma's first client was an elderly woman who lived in the same trailer park. Eventually the woman was put into a nursing home, but the nurse who cared for her recommended Velma to an elderly couple—94-year-old Montgomery Edwards, who was suffering from the effects of diabetes, and his 84-year-old wife, Dollie, who could no longer care for him by herself.

During this period, Velma seemed to be improving, although there would be occasional lapses. Once Dollie had Velma taken to

Kim's house because Velma appeared intoxicated. Kim and Ronnie had another talk with Velma, who promised not to relapse into her drug habits. She became a regular member of a local Pentecostal church and was regularly attending their services. Ronnie's wife gave birth to a baby boy and now Velma had two grandchildren with which she would regularly visit. Sometimes she would even babysit them. While it did appear that Velma was greatly improving, in reality she had only mastered new ways of concealing her drug addiction.

Velma Barfield worked for Montgomery and Dollie Edwards for nearly a year without any major incident. During this period, she met Dollie's nephew Stuart Taylor and briefly went out with him until he reconciled with his wife. The only thing wrong was that Dollie was getting on Velma's nerves. According to Velma, Dollie was bossy and stingy, constantly telling her how and when to do things. She watched everything Velma did, nagging her that she was using too much talcum powder or baby oil on Montgomery. He frequently soiled himself in bed, but Dollie insisted that Velma not run the washing machine more than once a week and instead spread rubber sheeting over the mattress.

Velma Murders Again

Eventually Montgomery succumbed to his illness and died in hospital on January 29, 1977. Dollie decided to retain Velma to help her around the house. That lasted about thirty days. Velma said she began to have flashbacks of being home again. Dollie was acting like her mother, always telling her what to do and never being pleased by the way Velma did things. Velma said she began to hate her. She wanted to scream at her, but she never did. Then one day, while grocery shopping:

> I saw the same brand of ant and roach poison that I had bought before. I bought a bottle and took it home with me. That evening I poisoned her. The next day she went through a terrible period of pain, but I had so medicated myself I felt divorced from her suffering . . . I made no connection between giving her the poison and seeing her reaction. *She is elderly and must not be well.*[174]

Velma is somewhat deceptive in claiming that she made no connection between the poison and Dollie's suffering. She might not have *felt* any connection, but she made it. When she later confessed to the murders, she told police that she concealed the evidence by throwing the empty bottle of poison into the fields behind the house. Police found an empty bottle of Singletary's Rat Poison when they searched the field.

She was cross-examined during her trial and accused of murdering Dollie: "You made Mrs. Edwards sick with Singletary's rat poison, did you not?"

Velma arrogantly snapped back, "No, I thought it was roach and ant poison." Velma stubbornly insisted on getting the last word.

It took several days to kill Dollie. Velma began on February 26, and by Sunday night Dollie was in so much pain she was brought by ambulance to the hospital. They treated her and then sent her home back to Velma. Then Velma did her thing again on Monday. On Tuesday morning, March 1, 1977, an ambulance took Dollie back to the hospital. She died that night of what doctors diagnosed as gastroenteritis.

"It's the Saddest Thing, but It Seems Like Everybody My Mother Ever Gets Close to Dies."

Velma attended Dollie's funeral and wept. Kim and Ronnie were at first worried that Velma might relapse into her old habits, but within ten days Velma found new employment. On the recommendation of her church, she was hired to care for 76-year-old Record Lee, who had fallen and broken her leg. Her 80-year-old husband, John Henry Lee, was not able to give his wife the care she needed and so their children retained Velma to care for them both.

According to Velma's memoir, the couple drove her crazy with their constant bickering. She said she wanted to shout, "Why don't both of you shut up!" Their bickering increased the pressure on her to take more drugs, Velma claimed. She wanted to leave but could not because she needed the money to support her pill habit. This made her feel resentful and angry. Finally she cracked. Velma recalls, "I decided that the only way to get out of that place would be to poison Mr. Lee. *He hired me, and he is the one who pays me. She is not important.*"[175]

Velma stated that she stole one of John Lee's blank checks and cashed it. She then says that she planned to make him sick so that she could leave, get a different job, and replace the money. John had already called the police when he noticed a cashed check for fifty dollars that he did not write. The investigator had immediately suspected Velma, but the Lees dismissed the idea. They insisted that Velma was a deeply religious woman—a good Christian who had been recommended by their church. The idea that she would steal from them was inconceivable.

Through some kooky logic maybe Velma is telling the truth, because it took her a long time to kill John Lee. About two weeks after the forged check was discovered, on April 27, John began to experience abdominal pains and severe vomiting. He ignored the condition for nearly two days, until he became so ill that an ambulance was called. The medics could not even get a readable blood pressure. John spent four days in intensive care with the doctors puzzled by his ailment. On May 2, he was sent home. His daughters came by to visit him, and as they sat and talked with their father Velma served John ice cream and Coke. The doctors had instructed that John keep to a diet of soft food and drink lots of liquids.

Throughout the entire month of May, John would recover his health and then suddenly fall sick again with stomach cramps, diarrhea, and vomiting. His daughters were grateful for the sweet care and attention Velma gave her father. But on June 3, 1977, John's condition became so bad that he was again taken away by ambulance to the hospital. He died that night of what appeared to be heart failure.

Again, Velma said that in her mind the poison did not kill John. It only made him sick. It was his heart condition that killed him, she convinced herself.

Velma attended John's funeral and sent a huge wreath. At the funeral, the Lee daughters gave Velma a bonus for the care she had given their father while he was sick. They told her they hoped that she would remain to take care of their mother. Velma agreed.

Shortly after the funeral, Stuart Taylor reappeared in Velma's life. He would be her last victim—at least her last to die.

Velma said that after two months of taking care of Record Lee, she left the job because it reminded her of what she had done to John and that she was tired of living with other people. She was feeling "the pressure" again. In early September, Record Lee was taken to the hospital emergency ward, ill with vomiting and stomach cramps, but Velma would always deny poisoning her. In any case, by the time Record returned from the hospital, Velma gave notice and moved into a rented trailer by herself. She got a job on the night shift in a nursing home as a nurse's aid. Every night, as everyone slept, Velma padded about the halls of the nursing home virtually unsupervised. It probably would have been just a matter of time before the predictable would have happened, but for now, Velma focused her attention on Stuart, with whom she was engaged.

In November the incident with Velma being bound and gagged in her trailer park occurred and Velma then moved in with Stuart. He was dead by the beginning of February. It was only one doctor's curiosity to understand precisely why his patient died that led to the discovery of arsenic in Stuart's body, and a distraught sister's phone call to the police that led them quickly to Velma—relatively quickly. Velma would not be arrested until the middle of March. During their investigation, police found a three-hundred-dollar check payable to Velma on Stuart's account written on January 31, the day he fell ill, and cashed on February 2, the day before his death. The writing and signature on the check did not belong to Stuart.

After the funeral of Stuart, Ronnie could only sadly shake his head and say, "You know, it's the saddest thing, but it seems like everybody my mother ever gets close to dies."

In the weeks between Stuart's death and her arrest, Velma began writing bad checks again and the police paid her a visit. When Ronnie confronted her about this she assured him that she had planned to cover the checks by her next payday at the nursing home, but Ronnie knew better than that by then.

Velma's Last Victims

Velma struck one more time before her arrest. After Stuart's death, she moved back in with her daughter and Dennis and their little girl. They noticed that Velma was back into her drug habit again, taking pills in great quantities. One afternoon, when they returned from work, Velma asked if she could use the car.

Velma had wrecked several cars while driving under the influence of pills, and Kim was reluctant to lend her the car. Moreover, she knew that Velma's wanting the car probably had something to do with getting prescriptions filled for more pills. Kim offered to drive her mother wherever she needed to go. Velma went into a rage, insisting that she did not need to be taken anywhere. She sulked the rest of the evening.

That night Kim and Dennis woke up with severe abdominal pains and vomiting. By morning, they were so sick that they went to the hospital emergency ward. They were diagnosed with flu, but Kim later would recall that she never had flu like this. It felt like she was dying. They were so sick that they stayed off work for three days. When they got home, Velma showed concern. It had to be the flu, she told them. The next day, while they were still sick at home, Velma told them she had found a new place to live and, taking her things, she moved out.

It was only after Velma's arrest, as the details of her murders began to leak, that Kim and Dennis remembered the evening they got sick. Velma had made dinner that evening and served them ice tea that had a slightly strange aftertaste. They had even commented on it, and Velma responded that it was saccharine because they had run out of sugar. It had to be the tea, Kim and Dennis concluded, because their daughter drank milk that night and did not get sick. And that is how serial murders like Velma's unfold invisibly, camouflaged by the transparent routine of normal daily life. Nobody thought twice of the tea Velma had served or the "flu" that made them sick that night, until Velma's human, grandmotherly mask was torn away revealing the monster that lurked beneath. It is truly mind-boggling when one thinks what Velma might have gone on to do had she not been exposed.

The Trial and Sentencing of Velma

Velma Barfield's bad luck was to have committed her crimes in Robeson County, which until 1974 was among the counties with the highest murder rate per capita in the U.S. Her bad luck was compounded by District Attorney Joe Freeman Britt, who was convinced that the death penalty was the solution for the problem. He would be listed in the *Guinness Book of World Records* as the world's deadliest prosecutor, having won twenty-two death sentence prosecutions. Velma would be one of them.

Britt, who claimed that the Christian grandma serial killer was his toughest case, chose to prosecute Velma Barfield on only one murder charge—that of Stuart Taylor. If something went wrong, he could have brought additional charges on the other cases.

Velma's defense was that she did not intend to kill Taylor, but only to make him sick. If the jury had accepted that argument she would have been convicted of second-degree murder and would not have faced the death penalty. The defense attorney thought it might be a good idea to put the sweet, pious grandmother on the stand. She testified to her addiction to painkillers and tranquillizers, and how muddled she was at her age. She admitted poisoning Taylor, but only to make him sick.

But when the prosecution cross-examined Velma, she quickly lost her temper, snapping and growling at the prosecutor with steely eyes and visible anger. Velma even challenged him on the type of poison she had used on some of her victims, whose murders the judge allowed into evidence. The courtroom was shocked by the nasty edge that emerged from the sweet, grandmotherly defendant. It was a disaster.

In December 1978, Velma Barfield was convicted of first-degree murder and sentenced to death. There would be appeals, campaigns for commutation, publicized visits from her grandchildren, and a spectacular born-again experience, although it is hard to discern the difference between Velma's Christian piety during the period in which she murdered and the period in which she sat on death row. She wrote a book with a pastor describing her crimes and her death row born-again experience. In it, she admitted to the poisoning, but insisted that she wanted to make her victims temporarily sick and that she was under the influence of drugs and irrational rage.

On November 2, 1984, the 52-year-old grandmother's time ran out. Barfield was the first woman to be executed in the U.S. since the restoration of the death penalty. She died by lethal ejection, and unlike her victims, she went quietly and painlessly in a state of serene unconsciousness, fully convinced that Jesus had forgiven her and paradise was waiting. She left letters to Ronnie and Kim, telling them she would be waiting for them in heaven and reminding them, "Jesus was the answer."

Velma Barfield was buried next to her husband Thomas, whom she had murdered. The grave stands literally yards away from the house where Ronnie and Kim lived their early lives in familial happiness. Ronnie and Kim wanted it that way.

* * *

It is difficult to assess Velma Barfield's history. In the first thirty years of her life, she went from a suffering daughter to a loving mother of two happy children. It all appeared to change so drastically after her hysterectomy. The raging seeds to her madness, however, were planted long before the hysterectomy, way back in her difficult childhood. The drugs became the facilitators of her aberrant, homicidal behavior.

Velma typifies the problem of categorizing female serial killers. Her motives are a complex, intertwined matrix. On the surface, she appears to be a Black Widow in the sense that she financially exploited most of her victims, even though the sums were ridiculously small. At the same time, her rage was so strong that she could be categorized as a vengeance killer—similar to Aileen Wuornos. In Velma's obsessive fixation on her son, Ronnie, and her need for his presence in the wake of her "troubles," there are elements also of Munchausen by proxy syndrome, associated with a category of female serial killers who murder their children or other intimates to gain sympathy from others around them. Or maybe she was just plain, ordinary evil, hiding behind a Bible and a grandmotherly sweetness with arsenic in her hand.

* * *

The next case study is much less ambiguous in its profit motive. What is compelling is how long it took before this offender began to kill—unless there were some earlier murders she succeeded in concealing.

Dorothea Puente Montalvo—Making Crime Pay

It was around the Thanksgiving holiday in 1988 on one of those bright, clear, and relatively cool Los Angeles November mid-afternoons on 3rd Street near Highland Avenue, when Charlie Willgues, a retired carpenter, decided on his way home that he would stop in for a beer at the Monte Carlo, a small, dingy, local bar. It was a Wednesday and Charlie had just bought a glass cutter—essentially the weekly highlight of his lonely, nothing-to-do life. Not that Charlie minded anymore. After a lifetime of work and obligations, misfortune, loss, and broken hearts, Charlie now lived alone contently in an apartment two blocks away in the depressed, low-lying area of small stores and low-rent housing. It was one of those faded, nondescript L.A. neighborhoods one never goes to but only passes through on the way to somewhere else.

Charlie was an old man in his late sixties who suffered from arthritis and emphysema, and had had two strokes. He got by with the help of a monthly Social Security check. Nobody was expecting him, nobody was waiting for him, and nobody was going to say anything if, in the middle of the afternoon, Charlie had a beer or two. Especially since, although Charlie was set in his daily loneliness, on some days—his birthday, Christmas, Thanksgiving, and a handful of other special days he once shared with others—the loneliness would come up on him. And this Thanksgiving he felt it.

It took Charlie a few minutes before his eyes adjusted from the sunny, bright afternoon light outside to the murky dark of the bar's interior. It was a typical, low-end, horseshoe-shaped bar where Charlie was a regular and knew most of the other raggedy-assed loners, pensioners, and disability jockeys who, like him, had nothing else to do at this time of day. So when the door came open and she came into the bar with a momentary flash of bright afternoon light and a shower of reflected sunny sparkles from passing traffic in the street outside, Charlie looked up.

It wasn't that she looked good—she did—dressed in a fashionable, bright red overcoat and sexy purple pumps, but that she was so poised and ladylike as she settled onto a bar stool across from Charlie. She was younger than he, clearly in her late fifties, early sixties. With carefully coiffured gray hair, she was a bit grandmotherly, yes, but still there was a sexy edge to her as she threw off her elegant coat. Sometimes it's just a gesture that gets you going, and when she crossed her legs, for a split second dangling one of those purple pumps, Charlie felt something move in him. Still good to go, Charlie thought, not sure if he meant himself, the woman, or them both.

A female patron sitting a few stools down later recalled, "She looked really cute. She had her hair real pretty and her makeup real nice."[176]

She ordered a vodka and orange, and when her eyes met with Charlie's, her face lit up with a warm and giving smile. Charlie was pretty sure of himself and his loneliness when he politely said to her, "The fan over there blows right at your back, so why don't you move on down here out of the draft."[177]

She smiled sweetly, thanked him, picked up her drink and purse, and moved to a bar stool closer to Charlie. She moved so nicely— so gracefully. It wasn't all sex—it was more that Charlie immediately liked her and fell into a comfortable conversation with her. She said her name was Donna Johansson and that she was staying at the Royal Viking Motel, an L.A. landmark about a mile and half east on 3rd Street near MacArthur Park and Alvarado.

Charlie found her bright intelligence and sophisticated air attractive, but what really moved him deep down was this woman's hint of vulnerability, perhaps even naïveté—she was beautiful in an older, angelic kind of way, and her story was sad. Her husband had died a month ago in Sacramento. She had just arrived in Los Angeles with plans and hopes to start a new life.

Her vulnerability really came through when she described how the taxi driver, who took her to the motel, drove off with all her luggage. She was left with only her small overnight bag and the clothes on her back. She daintily extended a slim leg and pointed out the damage on one of her shoes. She had worn them down walking all this way from her motel in search of a place to live. Charlie gallantly offered to take her shoes to a local shoe repair shop he knew. She thanked him for his kindness, giving him three dollars for the repair. She sat quietly drinking at the bar while Charlie ran her shoes over to the shop.

When Charlie returned, she gratefully slipped her pumps back on and the two strangers fell into an easy flowing conversation. Charlie ordered another beer while Donna had yet another screwdriver. "If you are retired, how do you support yourself?" she asked.

Charlie told her about his sickness and his monthly Social Security check of $576. Donna told him she had lots of experience with social service programs back in Sacramento and that he could easily get $680. She could help him with the paperwork to file a request for an increase. The two settled into a friendly hour-and-a-half conversation. She seemed so intelligent, competent, and sweet, but it was her vulnerability that touched Charlie the most. When she offered to go over to Charlie's apartment the next day and cook a big Thanksgiving dinner, Charlie had no problem agreeing. She claimed to be a terrific cook.

The only thing that slightly put Charlie off was that near the end of their conversation she suggested that they move in together—think of how much money they could save sharing a place, she argued. Charlie was not comfortable with the idea. They had only met ninety minutes ago and besides, he had been living alone for years now and was quite used to it. He actually liked it. But he did not find it unusual, because people in the neighborhood looked for all sorts of ways to cut down on expenses. "It may have seemed weird, but it's normal around here," he later said. Charlie told her he had to think about it, but he would call her later that evening to confirm the Thanksgiving dinner date for tomorrow.

Charlie urged Donna not to walk back to her motel but take a cab instead. Her shoes had just been fixed, why wear them down again? While she waited for the cab, Charlie bought her two takeout chicken dinners with money she had given him. She wanted the second dinner so she would not need to go out from her motel room later that night. She was too scared and nervous of the street after dark, she said. Charlie understood. He put her in the cab, opening and closing the door for her, and promised to call her later that night about the next day's dinner.

As Charlie watched the cab head out east on 3rd Street past all the little shops, low-rise apartments, and fast food joints, he felt a sense of exhilaration. It was nice to somehow suddenly "click" with somebody in this sea of derelict, low-cost loneliness. And somebody who seemed decent, respectable, and intelligent—a higher-class person than the broken-down, poor retirees among whom Charlie lived. Despite the differences between them, there was something almost familiar about the woman from the moment they met, Charlie felt.

What Charlie did not know was that Donna had indeed walked a mile and a half along 3rd Street wearing down her shoes—not looking for an affordable apartment but for somebody exactly like Charlie. Donna should have been familiar to Charlie, but under a different name, Dorothea Puente. He had actually seen her on TV news on the weekend.

Puente had been running a boarding home in Sacramento for alcoholic and disabled Social Security recipients, but one of her boarders had mysteriously vanished while his Social Security checks kept getting cashed. By some bizarre twist of fate, somebody in the social services office actually became concerned enough to look into the disappearance. After weeks of unsatisfactory responses from Puente, the police were finally called in. When they began to dig up bodies from under the flower beds in her garden, one corpse after another, including one without a head, Puente fled.

Dorothea's Bone Garden

It took some time before the social workers called the police, because Dorothea Puente was well known in the Sacramento charity and social services community. She had a reputation for generosity and kindness toward orphans and the elderly at the end of their rope. She had taken in some hardcase alcoholics that social services could place nowhere else, and turned some of them to sobriety and health so effectively that they moved out of her boardinghouse to independent lives of their own—or so social services thought.

She leased a huge Victorian house with numerous bedrooms on 1426 F Street in the heart of downtown Sacramento—blocks away from the Governor's Mansion and some of the city's historic sites. It was well kept and Dorothea planted and groomed a beautiful garden of flowers with lawn sculptures on the grounds surrounding the home. Unlike many of the dark, dingy residences where so many dead-end social services recipients ended up being housed, Puente's boardinghouse was a paradise—more of a beautiful bed-and-breakfast, where Puente's home-cooked meals were legendary.

But when the police were contacted, they knew a little more about Puente than the social workers. She had a criminal record for fraud connected to Social Security payment recipients going back some eight years and there were some suspicions about a death she was connected to. Nothing conclusive, but it was enough for police to take a second look at Puente. Besides, running a boarding home for Social Security recipients was a violation of her probation. Several days of investigation and interviews finally led police to digging up Puente's garden on Friday, November 11.

Almost immediately police found a body, but not of the missing man—of a woman who was buried much earlier than the date of the disappearance. Police interviewed Puente that evening, but she denied any knowledge of the body. She had been cooperative with police and had no objections to their digging in her garden as long as they did not harm the flower beds. This was not easy for police— they did not know the identity of the woman nor did they have at that moment any evidence linking her to the victim. It was entirely possible the body was already there when she moved into the house. She was not arrested. She was allowed to return to her house that evening.

Early the next morning, on Saturday, as crowds began to form outside Puente's house as news of the discovery of a body came out, police began an intensive dig in her garden. Puente was looking visibly upset and worn down. She asked the senior investigator on the scene, Detective John Cabrera, if she was under arrest. Not yet, she was told. Putting on her most grandmotherly and fragile persona, her purple pumps, a pink dress, and red overcoat, Puente asked if she could get away from the noise and chaos for a few minutes and go down the block to the Clarion Hotel for a cup of coffee. If Cabrera had any doubts about the petite, frail, older lady's intentions to flee, they were dissipated by her request that he escort her to the hotel through the crowd of press cameras and gawkers outside. As Cabrera guided Puente through the crowds, TV news crews filmed their departure. This would be the footage that Charlie would later see that weekend on TV in Los Angeles— but he did not link the woman he had met on Wednesday with the woman on TV, despite the same red coat.

Cabrera watched Puente meet with some friends at the Clarion Hotel and felt the little old lady—even if she ran—would not shuffle very far anyway. Satisfied that Puente was not going anywhere,

Cabrera returned to the dig at the house. He had no way of knowing that in her purse Dorothea Puente was carrying three thousand dollars in cash. No more than twenty minutes passed before police exposed a second body in a shallow grave. By the time Cabrera ran back to the Clarion Hotel, Dorothea was long gone. The more bodies police dug up that day—there would be seven in total eventually—the farther away Puente got.

As soon as Cabrera had left Puente at the Clarion, she had taken a cab to Stockton, a city about forty miles away. It cost her seventy dollars. She had the cab take her to the Greyhound bus station at 1:00 P.M. While police were still looking for her in Sacramento, Dorothea was already on a bus from Stockton to Los Angeles. She arrived in L.A. late that night, stayed at a hotel near the bus terminal, and the next morning, on Sunday, she checked into the Royal Viking Motel—an elderly, anonymous lady nobody paid attention to. She stayed locked in her room, watching herself on TV, just emerging long enough to stroll down to the fast-food joints on 3rd Street for takeout meals.

As she sat in her room for the next three days and followed the news reports, she began to realize that she needed to quickly find a place to hide and a source of income before her money ran out. On Wednesday afternoon, Dorothea put on her red coat and purple pumps and began slowly walking along 3rd Street, poking her head into stores and bars along the way, looking for an opportunity. Nobody in their right mind would have thought the grandmotherly woman strolling down the street in her bright red coat and purple shoes was a serial-killing predator on the prowl.

When, after several hours of trolling, she walked into the Monte Carlo and saw a tired, sickly-looking old man, sitting alone, drinking in a shit-hole bar, on a weekday in the middle of the afternoon, she instantly knew that she had found exactly what she was looking for. She sat down directly in Charlie Willgues's line of sight and went to work.

When Dorothea returned to her room at the Royal Viking that late afternoon, she felt energized and refreshed. The alcohol she had drunk with Charlie sharpened her appetite and she ate one of the chicken meals that she had had him fetch for her. She was almost euphoric from the scent of the hunt—still focused in an animallike predatory state. She was pleased with herself. Los Angeles was not entirely familiar ground for her, but she had, within several hours of venturing out into the streets, quickly found herself a potential source of income she knew how to easily exploit—a lonely, sick old man on Social Security benefits with apparently nobody to notice him missing. Dorothea still had a buzz on from her performance when her phone rang later that evening. Only one person had that number—it was Charlie, confirming their dinner date at his apartment the next evening. Every fiber of her body must have been buzzing with the apparent success of her hunt so far. The next day she would take complete control and spring the trap shut. Dorothea popped a cold beer and contently ate the second takeout dinner.

Dorothea Puente's Youth

Dorothea Puente was born Dorothea Helen Gray on January 9, 1929, in Redlands, a small city in San Bernardino County in California. Born on the eve of the Great Depression, she was the sixth of seven children. Her father was Jesse James Gray from Missouri, a suicidal World War One veteran, disabled and mentally ill as a result of mustard gas injury. Her mother, Trudy Mae Gates from Oklahoma, was a dysfunctional drunk who frequently left the family for days or weeks at a time before returning again. Dorothea was essentially raised by her older brothers and sisters. The family was *Grapes of Wrath* dirt-poor, surviving as migrant laborers on local farms, picking fruit and vegetables. With their mother disappearing or being put in jail, and their father in and out of hospitals, the the family was eventually split up between relatives and neighbors.

When Dorothea was seven, what remained of the family began to migrate first to Los Angeles and then to nearby San Dimas, seeking work continually. Along the way, on March 29, 1937, when Dorothea was eight, her father died. Her mother sank deeper into drinking and in 1938 she lost custody of her children. Dorothea was put into an orphanage run by the Church of Christ in Ontario, California. Several months later, her mother was killed while riding drunk on the back of a motorcycle.

Certainly Dorothea's childhood history immediately snaps into
the typical pattern of disrupted attachment between mother and
child that many believe is the seed of psychopathy. Teachers recall
that Dorothea as a child told outrageous lies and grandiose stories
about herself, yet another predictable sign of trouble ahead. As
Dorothea's older sister wisely commented in 1988 after her arrest,
"Sometimes when people have a hard childhood, their own world
is so hard, they make up a pretend one."[178]

Until the age of sixteen, Dorothea lived a nomadic existence,
shuffled between foster homes, relatives, and her older sisters. She
grew up to be a slim, beautiful young woman and she knew it. She
learned to use the combination of her beauty and lies to get people
to do what she wanted. She was a clever and stone-hard sixteen-
year-old. She also decided to reinvent herself.

Heading out to Olympia, Washington, in 1945, and giving herself the name Sheri, Dorothea began working as a prostitute. She
also had a heavy drinking habit. It is unlikely that Dorothea became a prostitute at the age of sixteen as a virgin, and so she must
have had an earlier sexual history that, again, is typical of psychopathic females—but nothing is known conclusively.

Dorothea's own accounts of her past are fabricated and unreliable. She claimed after an early incarceration, "When I was three
years old, I had to start picking cotton, potatoes, cucumbers, chil-
ies, then fruits. I finally married when I was thirteen; he died after
a few years." That was not true.

Dorothea Marries

In November 1945, Dorothea was married, at the age of 16, to
Fred McFaul, a 22-year-old soldier just returned from the Pacific.
They moved to the small, desolate town of Gardnerville, Nevada.
Dorothea had two daughters between 1946 and 1948, but she rejected them both, sending one to relatives in Sacramento and giving up the other for adoption. For a while, Dorothea separated
from Fred and lived in Los Angeles, but they reconciled a few
months later. Dorothea became pregnant again but miscarried. In
late 1948, McFaul became fed up and left her. Humiliated at being
abandoned, Dorothea would lie that he had died within days of
their marriage.

When he was interviewed in 1988, the still very much living Fred McFaul was aging and his memory faded, but he remembered two things about Dorothea—that she was exceptionally beautiful and told all sorts of tall tales about her past: about being a former movie star, being related to royalty, coming from a wealthy family that lost its money in the Depression, etc. She had an amazing ability to pull people in to do whatever she wanted through a combination of her tales, charm, and beauty.

After her divorce, Dorothea moved to San Bernardino and in 1948 was charged with a criminal offense for the first time when she attempted to pass a bad check. She plea-bargained into a reduced sentence and served four months before being released on probation. She immediately vanished. Although an arrest warrant was issued for her, she was such a minor offender that nobody was too concerned about searching her out.

In 1952, Dorothea married her second husband, Axel Johansson, whose last name she used when she introduced herself to Charlie Willgues in 1988. Throughout the 1950s and 1960s, Dorothea continued to drink heavily and spin fantasies and lies. Her marriage with Johansson resembled that of her mother's. She frequently quarreled and left on her own for weeks and months, eventually always returning to Johansson. She returned to prostitution, but when she felt her looks were fading, she established her own brothel in Sacramento. She became quite successful at it, eventually leasing a building for a "bookkeeping" service and staffing it with call girls. Police caught up with her, and after an elaborate investigation, in April of 1960, Dorothea was charged with running a house of ill repute but managed to plea down to a "found in" misdemeanor, serving only three months in jail.

In 1966, when Dorothea was 37, Johansson finally had enough and sued for divorce. Her second marriage was over, she was almost forty, her looks had long faded, she had ballooned in weight, she had a drinking problem, and pimping prostitutes did not seem to her all that secure an activity. If they have not been apprehended by then, most serial killers at this age begin to slow down and even cease in their killing activities. They still occasionally fantasize, sometimes relive their past murders through trophies and souvenirs they kept from the murders, they may occasionally even rise to a kill here and there, but their long-cultivated, fantasy-driven, constant obsession for murder has loosened its grip on their imaginations. But not Dorothea—it would still be another fifteen years, as far as we know, before she would actually begin killing.

Dorothea Goes into the Good Samaritan Business

Sometime in 1968, Dorothea turned her attention to the sick, elderly, and alcoholic. It could be that she saw they had come from the same place she had and might be harbingers of what she herself could end up being if she did not do something. She leased a small building and began making the rounds of Sacramento social services offices, introducing herself as the proprietor of "The Samaritans"—a board-and-care center for alcoholics. When social workers inspected her facility they were impressed with the firm but loving care Puente doled out to the residents assigned to her home. She was kind and loving with the ill and alcoholic boarders, but would not hesitate to swear or physically push them if they resisted taking their medication or bent the house rules slightly.

Sacramento social workers were happy to refer their difficult-to-place alcoholic clients to Dorothea's home, even on her strict condition that their Social Security payments be transferred directly to her. She would deduct the cost of room and board and make sure that the residents spent their remaining money on necessary healthy things and not booze, she insisted. Since Dorothea did not offer any health services or psychological therapy, her facility did not need a license, and inspections were lax. To supplement her income, she hired herself out as a home-care worker and "nurse" for the elderly and disabled.

In her private life, Dorothea was unraveling. She now carried a weight of 200 pounds on her five-foot-eight frame and was drinking steadily throughout the day and heavily in the evening, despite the fact that if any of the residents in her facility appeared drunk she would lash out and berate them viciously. Dorothea also began to take on the identity of a Hispanic, claiming that her family came from Mexico. She had grown up among Mexican fieldworkers in the 1930s, spoke some Spanish, and was familiar with the culture, so it was not a difficult act.

At the age of 39, Dorothea married a 21-year-old Hispanic, Roberto Jose Puente. The marriage ceremony was held in Reno, Nevada. The marriage fell apart within two weeks, leaving behind only the name "Puente," under which she would become famous as a serial killer. In 1969, Dorothea divorced Roberto and declared "The Samaritans" bankrupt with a debt of ten thousand dollars.

Very quickly she set up a new residence in a large, sixteen-bedroom Victorian house on 2100 F Street near 21st. She picked up her business where she had left it off, but now even better organized and under her new married name of Puente.

Every several weeks Dorothea hosted a banquet for social workers and alcoholic residents where the quality of her food and care was put on display. The dinner table would always be carefully set with spotless tableware. Inspectors were always offered a choice slice of pie or lunch in the immaculately kept kitchen. This was not a show—the boarders themselves confirmed they ate well even when nobody from social services was around. Puente hired two cooks and she carefully supervised their performance in the kitchen.

Dorothea ruled over her facility from the third floor of the house where she set up her own apartments. On the first and second floors she housed the more affluent, federally assisted clients in neat little bedrooms, each with a closet and television, just like in a hotel. The poorer, county-assistance recipients she stacked in the basement in little cubicles separated only by curtains. But they all ate well.

* * *

The only thing that was slightly off about Dorothea as far as social services were concerned was that she had a tendency to exaggerate her past. She claimed acquaintance with celebrities and said she had been not only in the Bataan Death March* but had been in Hiroshima when the atom bomb was dropped.

What slipped by the social workers was that Dorothea was increasingly posing as a doctor, hanging fake medical diplomas on

---

* A weeklong forced march of 70,000 U.S. POWs in the Philippines, captured by the Japanese in 1942. Approximately 10,000 American prisoners died along its route, many murdered by the Japanese.

the walls of a small office in the basement, and buying medical equipment like syringes and blood pressure cuffs. A social services physician, who was assigned to monthly visits to Dorothea's house, recalled how she would sit herself down with him during the checkups of the residents. She claimed that she, too, was a doctor and would review with him the pharmacological aspects of the medicines he might prescribe. But everyone was too impressed with the smooth running of her home to begrudge the woman her "eccentricity." In the mostly Hispanic neighborhood, Dorothea began presenting herself as "La Doctora" and offered medical advice and "vitamin" injections to locals.

By 1975, Dorothea Puente had reinvented herself once again, now as a major social figure in Sacramento's Hispanic community. She sponsored numerous charity events and donated money frequently. She dropped her seductive, former hooker persona and now cultivated a much older persona than her 45 years—that of an elderly, gray-haired, wealthy matron. She claimed she owned numerous properties around the world. She sponsored Hispanic performers, assisting them in getting entry into the United States and secured them plays through her contacts with Spanish-speaking radio and television.

In 1976, Dorothea married for the fourth time, again in Reno. Her husband once more was a Mexican ten years younger than she, Pedro "Angel" Montalvo, a laborer she had employed at her boardinghouse. People who worked around Dorothea recalled that he seemed to be mentally disturbed, full of some kind of strange, chatty, unfocused energy. The marriage lasted a few weeks before it was annulled, but it gave Dorothea yet another available alias—Montalvo.

By 1977, Dorothea had become a major contributor to political candidates from both the Democratic and Republican parties. She purchased entire banquet tables at fundraisers, appearing grandly at the events. She chatted intimately with congressmen and state and county officials. At one event, California Governor Jerry Brown approached the regal Dorothea, hugged and kissed her, and then danced with her among the powerful and wealthy contributors at the event. Impeccably dressed and groomed, charming and generous, the socialite Dorothea was a welcomed guest at the pinnacle of California's political establishment.

Puente paid particular attention to young Hispanic girls from troubled families, "adopting" them, sponsoring their schooling and sometimes sheltering them. Puente had her lawyer handle all sorts of legal problems for the girls and their families. She often introduced the girls to visitors as her "daughters," although she never legally adopted them. It was not all bullshit. Perhaps she saw herself in those girls—perhaps she knew exactly what they needed in their lives and it was easy for her. After her arrest for serial murder, several young Hispanic women came forward, claiming that regardless of her guilt, Dorothea had saved their lives. One said, "I just hate to think about where I would be today if this woman had not touched my life."

If Dorothea Puente's story here is familiar, then it should be. It has echoes of another case of a place-specific serial killer, John Wayne Gacy, a successful construction contractor and a respected figure in his community in Chicago. He led the annual Polish Constitution Day Parade and in his spare time he volunteered to entertain sick children at local hospitals, dressed as Pogo the Clown. He was a Democratic Party precinct captain and when the U.S. President's wife, Rosalynn Carter, was in Chicago on a visit, he was one of her escorts. In his house, buried in a basement crawl space, police found the trussed-up corpses of twenty-eight boys and young men, whom he had invited into his home office and then brutally tortured, raped, and murdered.

In 1977, Dorothea checked into a hospital for a weight-reduction procedure involving an intestinal bypass (jejunal-ileal). This procedure has since been discontinued because of the severe effects on the liver and other organs. Before and after the surgery, Dorothea told everyone she was suffering from heart disease and cancer, and on the eve of her surgery she made out a will leaving millions of dollars to her "stepdaughters" and to various foundations and trusts that would be established. It was a will worthy of the wealthy dowager she presented herself as, even if there was no money to back it had she actually died.

This generous and lavish lifestyle—the clothes, the shoes, the hair, the donations and sponsorships, gifts, the intestinal bypass and other cosmetic procedures Dorothea would later have—was all paid for by money that she looted from the Social Security payments of her boarders and from thefts from people she visited at their homes as a "home-care nurse."

Disgraced

Dorothea's whole house of cards came tumbling down in 1978, when a former resident of her house was jailed, but while serving his term his Social Security checks kept getting cashed by Dorothea. The Treasury Department began to probe Social Security payments related to residents placed with Dorothea and when they totaled four thousand dollars in stolen funds, they figured they had enough for a felony charge and stopped investigating further.

With a long list of recent civic accomplishments and her fragile granny persona, no judge had the heart to sentence the little old lady to prison. She received five-years' probation and was ordered into psychiatric counseling. She was also ordered to give up the house on 2100 F Street.

The former "socialite" was snubbed and stripped of her center, her staff, and all the people she had sponsored. Dorothea quietly skulked out of Sacramento and went south to Stockton, where she took on menial odd jobs as a cook, cleaner, or dishwasher. She was now 50 years old and most who experience the kind of rise and fall she did would have by now rolled over and stopped living. Not Dorothea. Psychopathy can work both ways: It can alleviate fear and empathy when victimizing, but it can also buffer against shame and guilt that would make anyone else, after being exposed in the way Dorothea was, reluctant to show her face. Psychopathy in Dorothea did what it was meant to do—it outfitted her with formidable survival tools, and in the end, a deadly predatory talent.

As for Dorothea's psychiatric counseling, she was diagnosed as "a schizophrenic, chronic undifferentiated type."[179] This is an entirely meaningless term, a diagnosis often attributed to other budding serial killers in the 1970s. Schizophrenia is an organic mental disorder characterized by hallucinations, grossly disorganized or catatonic behavior, delusions, and incoherent, delusional speech. There was nothing hallucinatory or incoherent about Dorothea Puente, but in the 1970s, as psychologists debated the exact nature of psychopathy and what to even call it, the term "chronic undifferentiated schizophrenic" became a convenient catchall phrase that encompassed all manner of unexplained behavioral problems.

"I've Got a Psychiatric Condition. I Sometimes Forget My Actions."

In 1979, Dorothea returned to Sacramento and threw herself back into the same business, albeit on a smaller scale. She decided that a smaller operation run personally by her, without the need to sustain a socialite's life, would suit her just fine. Presenting herself now as Dorothea Montalvo, she rented the second floor of another Victorian house on 1426 F Street, down the road from where she had her previous place. To make money, she passed herself off to private nursing businesses as a trained, live-in caretaker for the sick and elderly. She even got herself bonded under her new name and was sent out to feed and care for elderly shut-ins.

In early 1980, a female patient for whom Dorothea was caring was brought into hospital with shallow breathing and an irregular heart rate. No sooner would her condition be stabilized and she be sent home than she would be back at the emergency ward with a relapse. The patient's social worker noticed the hovering presence of Dorothea Montalvo during all these episodes. There were disturbing rumors: Montalvo might be using other names and might have poisoned several husbands. While the first was true, the second was entirely false, but ironically would become a premonition of the nature of Dorothea's future.

The social worker assigned to the elderly female met with the victim's doctor and convinced him to run a toxicology test, which revealed traces of two powerful drugs: phenobarbital and digoxin, neither of which he had prescribed for the patient. In the meantime, the social worker learned that Dorothea was calling the patient's family and telling them that they needed to increase her home-care expenses as she had been diagnosed with cancer. This was entirely untrue. The doctor convinced the patient to fire Dorothea. Afterward the patient had no more relapses, but died in a nursing home nonetheless.

In one of those typical stories, nobody bothered to call the police, have the County Welfare office bar Dorothea from caring for patients or inform the nursing agencies that had contracted her. Not enough evidence was the common excuse. And nobody could quite bring themselves to believe that the sweet, little, gray-haired granny, home-care worker was harboring some kind of lethal intentions. It seemed impossible.

Dorothea was running amok. The same doctor who treated the first patient received another in similar circumstances. On a hunch, when he asked who the home-care worker assigned to the patient was, Dorothea's name came back. By then the Sacramento Police and district attorney's office were paying attention. Yet despite the fact that Dorothea was on everybody's radar, nothing was done. Some social workers and doctors, aware of the problem, steered their clients and patients away from Dorothea, but officially absolutely nothing was done.

It was only in 1982 that Dorothea finally went too far. She picked up a man in his seventies in a bar and convinced him to take her back to his apartment. At some point that evening she drugged him with a substance that paralyzed him, but did not make him lose consciousness. As he sat on his couch unable to move, he watched Dorothea go through his apartment, taking valuables, cash, checks, and his precious coin collection, dumping it all into an empty suitcase she had found. Finally, she took his hand, pulled off a ring he was wearing, and then left. The victim sat there in a paralyzed condition for about an hour before he could move again. He immediately called the police. Dorothea was quickly arrested and found with the victim's checks, which she claimed he had willingly given her.

Around the same time, posing as a county nurse, Dorothea had also shown up at a nursing home where an 82-year-old female was living. They had met earlier at a hairdresser. Dorothea "diagnosed" blood pressure problems and gave the woman some medication. Hours later, when she regained consciousness, she discovered the "nurse" gone and her diamond ring and all her medication missing. The police were able to identify and charge Dorothea through the hairdresser's shop. The victim's ring was never found.

Two more separate cases that year involved elderly women who discovered property from their homes missing and checks cashed in their names after Dorothea was sent to their homes by a nursing agency as a caregiver. And police then found another case from the year before, where an 84-year-old woman reported three thousand five hundred dollars in gold rings and jewelry missing after hiring Dorothea as a home-care attendant.

In all the cases, the victims recalled how solicitous, caring, and friendly Dorothea was. In some cases the victims were even reluctant to fire Dorothea, unable to believe that the warm and gracious caregiver who had attended so conscientiously to their needs harbored any kind of criminal intent.

By the spring of 1982, Dorothea had been arrested four times but released on bail every time. Although she was 54 years old, Dorothea claimed to be in her seventies and presented such a fragile and helpless granny aura that no judge had the heart to detain her in jail. Dorothea argued that the victims had willingly presented her with checks and gifts, but just in case, she reminded them, "I've got a psychiatric condition. I sometimes forget my actions."

Nevertheless, by April 1982, Dorothea faced the prospect of felony convictions for grand theft, robbery, and forgery. In the middle of the preliminary hearing on those charges, police re-arrested Dorothea on additional check forgery charges from yet another victim. Nobody could understand why the fragile little granny was handcuffed and led away to jail once more. But once again, her lawyer argued she was old, had ties to the community, had made all her court appearances and bail payments, and cases against her were being dismissed. Dorothea was again released from jail.

Dorothea Commits Her First Murder

It was at this moment, as she was in the middle of dealing with all her legal problems and a prospect of prison time—according to William P. Wood, the district attorney assigned to her case at the time—that Dorothea committed her first planned murder.[180] That April, Dorothea entered into a business partnership with Ruth Munroe, a retiree whose recent marriage was falling apart as her husband was suddenly diagnosed with a terminal illness. Entirely unaware of Dorothea's legal problems, Munroe agreed to go into the catering business with her. Ruth transferred several thousand dollars of her savings into a joint business account. Dorothea's cooking skills were well known, she appeared as an efficient administrator, and besides, the two women had quickly developed a friendship. Not only that, to further save on expenses Dorothea invited Ruth to come live with her at the house on F Street. On April 11, Ruth's sons helped her move into 1426 F Street. Seventeen days later, Ruth was dead.

Soon after moving in with Dorothea, Ruth had a "nervous episode" over her marriage and needed to be sedated by doctors, according to Dorothea. On April 27, Ruth's son visited 1426 F and was told by Dorothea that the doctor had just left, having given his mother another shot for her nerves. Despite being urged by Dorothea not to disturb Ruth, the son went up to see his mother. He later testified that he found her on her side facing the wall with her eyes open but entirely immobile, as if paralyzed. She appeared not to be aware of his presence. Assuming that was the effect of the drug, he recalled his last words to his mother were, "Don't worry, Mom, everything's going to be all right. Dorothea will take care of you."

He recalled that a tear trickled down from his mother's eye, but otherwise she remained immobile. She was trying to scream for help, but couldn't, paralyzed by a drug administered by Puente.

The next morning, on April 28, Ruth Munroe was dead, dying in her sleep according to Dorothea. Police and paramedics arrived at the scene, as did Ruth's family. As there was no physician present at the scene, an autopsy was conducted and high doses of codeine were found in her system. When the circumstances of Ruth's collapsing marriage were revealed, her death was ruled by "undetermined cause," but believed to have been a suicide. Nobody suspected the visibly upset and fragile, elderly Dorothea.

The district attorney's office in the meantime, while pursuing the conviction of Dorothea on the other charges, was entirely unaware of Ruth Munroe's death and her connection with Dorothea. Nobody in the family realized that Ruth had made a large withdrawal from her bank account or that she had a joint account with Dorothea that had been recently emptied.

At the same time, while awaiting her trial, Dorothea decided to flee Sacramento. On May 16, she phoned a former patient she was friendly with and invited herself over for a drink. By the time the victim regained consciousness, Dorothea had taken her credit cards and some blank checks. She then went out and purchased an airline ticket to Mexico, but was arrested by police before she could leave the country. This time Dorothea's bail was revoked.

The Sacramento press had by now picked up the story of Dorothea Puente, but it was all a big joke: the "quintessential granny" who seduced and drugged a man in his seventies. Ho-ho-ho. She continued to cultivate the persona of a harmless, helpless, fragile, little old lady much older than her actual age. During her presentencing interview in jail, a probation officer noted that when he was speaking with Dorothea she appeared distraught and tearful, but suddenly demanded an explanation for a word he wrote in his notebook. She was reading his notes upside down as she sat on the opposite side of the interview booth.[181]

On August 19, 1982, Dorothea was sentenced to five years in prison. The next day, Ruth Munroe's family called the district attorney to report their suspicions that Dorothea had murdered their mother. Content with having taken Dorothea off the street, the D.A.'s office decided there was not enough evidence to pursue the complaint: It looked too much like suicide.

Dorothea's Last Run

Three years later, in August 1985, Everson Gillmouth, a retired widower in his seventies, was packing his things in preparation for a new life. He had been living in a trailer hitched to his red Ford pickup truck parked on his sister's farm in Oregon, but now he was getting married. Everson was pretty excited, because he knew that at his age this was probably his last chance at marital bliss and an escape from the loneliness that had enveloped him since the death of his wife. He had never met his new bride in person—they had been writing each other through a pen pal exchange for female prison inmates for over a year, and his correspondent, Dorothea Puente, wrote she was ready to settle down and straighten out her life with somebody she loved.

Puente was being released in August after serving three years of a five-year sentence. She invited Everson to pick her up in Fresno, where she'd been in a halfway house, and together they'd drive to Sacramento and move into an apartment she had in a house on 1426 F Street. (Puente had completely charmed the owner of the house, becoming a godmother to his children and a patron of his family. He continued to rent to her a floor in the house while she was in prison, and eventually the entire house after she was released.)

When Everson's sister had not heard from her brother by mid-September, she called Sacramento Police, who dropped by the house on F Street and talked to Everson. Later that night, he called his sister, annoyed at her interference. This would be the last time she would speak with her brother. Then, to her surprise, in November she received a telegram from her brother stating that things did not work out with Dorothea and he was heading south—that she was not to stop him. She thought it strange that instead of telephoning or writing a telegram was sent, but there was not much she could do about it.

In April 1986, the sister received a postcard from a woman claiming to be her brother's new love. The postcard claimed he had a small stroke in January but was all right and living with her somewhere in a desert community. There was no return address.

Everson was actually last seen at the F Street house in mid-December, looking a little ill as Dorothea attempted to help him with medications she prepared for him. Dorothea had already sold his trailer, which she claimed Everson had given her as a gift. After that, Everson was never seen again. In late December, Dorothea hired Ismael Florez, a man she met in a bar, to do some carpentry around the house she lived in. When he was done with the job, she also asked him to build a large storage box for her, about six feet by three. In exchange for the work, she offered him a red Ford pickup truck.

Near the end of December, Dorothea asked Florez to help her load the box into the pickup truck and drive it to a storage unit outside of Sacramento. After they left town and approached the Sacramento River, Dorothea told Florez that she had changed her mind: There was no point in storing the junk she had in the box. She asked him to dump the box by the river. Putting it on a dolly,

Florez and Dorothea maneuvered the box down to the riverbank and abandoned it, assuming the high water in the spring would sweep the box away.

But on New Year's Day, a local resident walking along the river discovered the box. When he opened it, he found a body wrapped in plastic and packed in mothballs and deodorant sticks. The autopsy revealed no wounds or injuries on the body, and advanced decomposition prevented the determination of cause of death. It appeared that the victim had been dead for approximately two weeks. There was no identification and the sheriff filed the case as a John Doe.

In the meantime, Everson's monthly pension checks continued to arrive at 1426 F Street. When there was a mixup in February 1986 over the payments, somebody wrote a letter to the pension fund complaining and the payments were quickly resumed.

In the next two years, Dorothea murdered at least seven more people, whose bodies she buried in the garden of 1426 F Street, despite the fact that the yard was visible from the street and from neighboring houses. She hired individuals to dig shallow ditches in the yard in search of "sewer lines." The next day, the ditches would be found filled in and covered with a birdbath, bench, or planted flowers.

During those years, Dorothea took over the entire house, and once again set up an informal, unlicensed boarding home for derelict, ill, and alcoholic Social Security recipients. Social services were, as usual, overworked and understaffed with a high turnover of employees. In the three years that Dorothea Puente was in prison, several new generations of social workers had taken the places of those who had known her. And Dorothea was using a different surname. Once again, social services people were impressed with Dorothea's nurselike professionalism and friendly and caring demeanor with difficult clients, particularly Hispanics.

All this was completely in violation of her terms of probation, which prohibited her from taking in boarders or cashing assigned Social Security checks. Since her release, Dorothea had had thirty-five contacts with Federal probation officers, fourteen of them at her residence at 1426 F Street.[182] Despite that people were in and out of the house, and neighbors were aware of all sorts of activity there, on none of those fourteen visits did the probation officers detect that there were boarders living at F Street or that Dorothea was supplementing her own Social Security income in any way. As far as they were concerned, Dorothea was a polite, friendly, fragile, little old lady living out the golden years of her life after having made some desperate mistakes.

Only in November 1988 was Puente exposed, when obstinate social workers could not trace the whereabouts of Bert Montoya, a mentally handicapped 50-year-old client who had been boarded with her. Dorothea kept insisting that Bert had left to go live in Mexico, but the social workers who knew him and his mental capacity well did not accept the story. Dorothea then recruited an unidentified accomplice to phone the social services office and claim to be Bert's brother, explaining that Bert was now living with him in Colorado. However, Bert was not known to have any family in Colorado, nor could the caller put Bert on the phone.

When Sacramento Police were finally called, they pulled the file on Dorothea Puente Montalvo and saw what they were dealing with. On November 11, two detectives and Dorothea's parole officer called at the house on F Street. By then the detectives had picked up all sorts of strange rumors in the dark world of alcoholic roomers and Social Security disability boarders. The house on F Street was a place you could get a good meal, but the lady that ran it was brutal. Disobedience was punished with heavy verbal abuse and even a slap and a push. And those who did not fit in were being buried in the garden.

The detectives took the yard story with a grain of salt. The yard was clearly visible from the sidewalk and exposed to the neighboring houses. Just the derelict ranting of aged alcoholics, the detectives thought. Nevertheless, they asked Dorothea if she would mind if they poked around a little in her yard. As long as they did not disturb the freshly planted flowers, Dorothea told them, she had no objections. "You won't find anything," she said.

It was not long before detectives dug up the remains of a corpse buried in a shallow grave near a flower bed. Police took Dorothea in for questioning, but as the corpse was clearly there much longer than the absence of the missing man everybody was searching for, she was released to go home that evening.

The next morning, as police descended on F Street to fully exca-
vate the garden, Dorothea asked one of the detectives to escort her
through the crowd so she could have a cup of coffee away from the
chaotic scene. By the time the second body was uncovered and the
detective had rushed back to take Dorothea into custody, she was
in the cab on her way to Stockton. By the end of the weekend, she
was hiding out in the Royal Viking Motel in Los Angeles, watching the television reports of the seven bodies uncovered in the yard
at F Street.

Among the seven bodies, wrapped and taped in bedspreads and
plastic like mummies, was the body of Bert Montoya, the missing
mentally handicapped man the social workers were so adamant to
find. Also unearthed were:

- Dorothy Miller, an alcoholic 64-year-old Native American
  woman, was discovered with her arms duct-taped to her chest.
  She was last seen, by her social worker, sitting on Puente's
  front porch smoking a cigarette;

- Benjamin Fink, a 55-year-old man with a drinking problem,
  was last seen by a witness in April 1988 when Puente took
  him upstairs to "quiet him down" after he became argumen-
  tative. He was found buried in his stripped boxer shorts;

- Betty Palmer, a 78-year-old victim who was found buried minus her head, hands, and feet, beneath a statue of St. Francis
  of Assisi just a few steps from the sidewalk;

- James Gallop, a 62-year-old who had survived a heart attack
  and brain tumor surgery, but not the care that Dorothea ac-
  corded him at F Street;

- Vera Faye Martin, 64, whose wristwatch was still ticking
  when she was unearthed and who investigators believed, judging by the patterns of the earth around her body, might have
  been buried alive and attempted to claw her way out of her
  shallow grave;

- Leona Carpenter, 78, who had been discharged from a hospital into Puente's care and subsequently vanished.[183]

Dorothea Puente was stealing approximately five thousand dollars a month from her victims. Shortly before police raided her home, she had cosmetic surgery. In her bedroom, police found expensive Giorgio perfume, stylish shoes and clothing, and stacks of paperback Westerns.

Endgame

After Charlie Willgues called about the Thanksgiving dinner she had offered to cook for him, Puente must have breathed a sigh of relief. If only she could somehow get into his apartment and kill him, she'd be safe. For the first time since police had descended on her house, Puente was feeling back in control. Soon she peacefully dozed off.

Until the LAPD began hammering on her motel room door an hour later, Puente had no way of knowing that when Charlie had called her, sitting next to him was a local Los Angeles TV reporter. A few hours after their barroom encounter, Charlie had realized where he had seen the woman before and he had called KCBS-TV. After they had interviewed him, they had decided it was best to call the police. Puente was arrested that night and transported the next day to Sacramento. She would never be free again.

* * *

Dorothea Puente Montalvo was charged with nine counts of murder—for the seven bodies found buried in her yard, for the murder of Everson Gillmouth once his remains found in the box by the river had been identified, and for the murder of Ruth Munroe back in April 1982, while Puente was standing trial for robbery and forgery.

Despite the fact that seven of the bodies were dug up from beneath Dorothea's bedroom window and that she was connected to every victim, it was not an easy case to prove. The advanced state of decomposition of the corpses made it difficult to precisely determine the cause of each death and it was difficult to separate the drug content in the corpses from drugs normally prescribed to the victims. The victims' propensities for alcohol also made drug interaction with alcohol an issue. Were these natural deaths and did Puente conceal the bodies because she was worried her parole might be revoked for taking in boarders? The defense argued that, at most, Puente was guilty of concealing deaths.

In the end, Dorothea was convicted in three of the murder counts and sentenced to life imprisonment on December 10, 1993. Puente was almost 65 years old; she would surely die in prison. But just like some horror movie, Puente came back to life in 2004 at the age of 76 with a cookbook, *Cooking With a Serial Killer*, which featured fifty of her delicious recipes she was so famed for among her derelict victims, an interview with her, and samples of her art. There will be no stopping Dorothea Puente until she stops for good.

5

LOVING US TO DEATH

Serial Killer Moms, Angels of Death,
and Other Murdering Caregivers

The first person we all meet on Earth is our mother. From then on, most of us—the lucky ones—perceive women automatically as sources of love, care, and nourishment. Our mothers' care, we learn as we grow up, is supplemented by the professional care of babysitters, nurses, and teachers. Nurses, in particular, we see as professionals dedicated to healing and easing pain. Yet some women use these very identities to disguise their repeated, raging, homicidal acts.

Genene Jones—the Baby-Killing Nurse

You never know when or where you'll meet your serial killer. United States Army Sergeant First Class Gabriel Garcia, a crew chief with 507th Medical Company, would later testify how he met his serial killer in the back of a UH-1 "Dustoff" Medevac Huey Bell helicopter cruising at 125 mph at 4,000 feet on a civilian air ambulance mission into San Antonio, Texas.

Garcia served in an army MAST unit—Military Assistance to Safety and Traffic, a highly specialized branch that supplied medical air evacuation services for both military personnel and civilian communities near their bases. On August 30, 1982, at 12:32 P.M., his unit got a call with a request to transport to San Antonio two gravely ill children from a hospital in the town of Kerrville, about sixty miles away. Garcia and his platoon leader, Sergeant David

Maywhort, were highly trained and experienced elite emergency medics who had flown many similar missions together. Piloted by David Butler, the helicopter scrambled and landed at Kerrville about forty minutes later, a mile from the hospital. A waiting ambulance took Maywhort and Garcia into town to pick up the two patients.

MAST crews had a lot of discretion whether to accept civilian patients for an air transport. It would be their call whether they felt a patient was stable enough to endure the noisy and bumpy forty-minute helicopter flight back to San Antonio. Upon their arrival at the hospital in Kerrville, Maywhort and Garcia went in to see the two patients for themselves. They were met by Dr. Kathleen Holland, a recently graduated doctor who had just opened a pediatric clinic of her own a week ago in the town. She showed them the first patient, Christopher Parker, a 6-month-old baby boy whose mother had brought him in when his breathing became raspy. Dr. Holland had checked his air passages and found them constricted. She felt the infant should be transported to a San Antonio hospital for observation. The child was stable and calm.

The second child was a 7-year-old boy, Jimmy Pearson, suffering from a host of chronic conditions. The child was severely retarded, unable to speak, and had skeletal deformities that twisted his tiny, twenty-two-pound body into a misshapen contortion. That morning, his family brought him into the hospital when Jimmy began to experience continuous, uncontrollable seizures. Kathleen stabilized his seizures with an injection of drugs through his intravenous line and then attached a breathing apparatus to the boy's face, which blew a steady stream of oxygen into his lungs. Jimmy also appeared to be stable, calm, and sleeping.

Maywhort and Garcia accepted the patients for the flight. Dr. Holland introduced Garcia to her clinic nurse, Genene Jones, who would accompany the two patients on the flight to San Antonio. Jones was a chunky, big-boned, mousy-haired woman in her thirties with a determined jaw, a large, hooked nose, and a frown-set mouth with intensely clever hazel-colored eyes set in a doughy face—the smart, ugly, bossy girl in school, who at the end of the day never failed to remind the teacher that she forgot to assign homework. She exuded uncompromising competence.

When Garcia began to brief Genene on helicopter ambulance procedure, he did not get very far. He later testified:

> I didn't go into a lot of detail, because my impression was that she was an experienced nurse—in every way she presented herself as a highly competent, flight-practiced RN [registered nurse] . . . I also told her exactly what we'd expect from her if there was some kind of emergency, be it aircraft failure or medical problems. I reminded her about how the headset worked once connected, and about how she shouldn't interrupt the pilots unless absolutely necessary. It was just a quick briefing. She gave me the impression that she knew all about it already.[184]

Sergeant Garcia saw that Jones had a paper bag with her. Wanting to know what other supplies would be available to him in case of an emergency, he asked if he could have a look at what she had in it. In the bag he found a laryngoscope—an instrument inserted through a patient's mouth and used to examine a person's air passage, usually prior to inserting breathing tubes—some sterile breathing tubes, a bagging mask for ventilating a patient's air passage, and a preloaded 3-cc syringe, which Genene told him contained Neo-Synephrine, a vascular constrictor, and a container of lidocaine, a local anesthetic used to combat irregular heartbeat.

Garcia recalled that Genene smiled at him gravely and said, "I think we may have some trouble with the Pearson boy. I think he may go sour."

Satisfied that the two boys were secured into berths fixed perpendicularly inside the helicopter's cabin, the 6-month-old baby Christopher Parker on the bottom and the handicapped boy Jimmy Pearson on top, the pilot began to prepare for takeoff. Nurse Jones and Sergeant Garcia strapped into a bench seat facing the patients, inches away from their knees, and put on their communication headsets. Sergeant Maywhort got in on the other side of the stretchers into the gunner's port, from where he would assist in keeping his eye on the patients and on air traffic to the sides of the helicopter.

As the helicopter took off and attained a cruising speed at a 4,000-foot altitude, Maywhort looked back into the cabin to ensure the patients were still calm and stable. The infant, who was hooked up to a heart-monitoring system built into the helicopter, appeared to be sleeping calmly. Maywhort decided to switch the system over to Jimmy Pearson instead, and asked Garcia to do it. Garcia deftly hooked up the boy to the heart monitor, probably without Nurse Jones realizing it. He checked the readout on the screen—Pearson's heartbeat was normal and stable.

Approximately five minutes later, Maywhort threw a glance back into the cabin and saw that Genene was leaning over the Pearson boy, listening intently to his heart through her stethoscope. While Maywhort could observe her from the gun port, Garcia—on the other side of the stretchers—could only see the nurse with her back turned to him. Maywhort signaled Garcia to lean forward and find out what was wrong.

Garcia unstrapped, got up next to Genene, and observed her with the stethoscope pressed against the boy's chest. He asked her what was she doing. He was taken a little aback when she only threw him a contemptuous look of exasperation—like "Mind your own business, I know what I'm doing."

As Garcia looked at her listening intently with her stethoscope, a wave of apprehension swept over him. He recalled, "I was sort of stunned, really. I looked at her trying to use her stethoscope on this poor kid, and it was just absurd."

It was absurd because the patients lie on berths directly connected to the helicopter's airframe and the powerful engine transferred noise and vibration right through the stretcher into a patient's body. Through a stethoscope one would hear nothing but the gut-heaving, heavy *thump-thump-thump-thump* of the helicopter rotors and engine noise, racket and vibration.

Garcia said, "You can't do that."

Genene, thinking he was challenging her authority, barked back, "Of course I can."

Garcia explained, "But you can't hear anything through that."

Genene replied, "I can hear fine," and then began to gesture dramatically and yelled, "He's going bad. He's in trouble. He's having another seizure. Look at him, he's turning black. He's going to arrest just like I said he would."

Maywhort later stated that Jones looked agitated. "Not upset or anything, just agitated. Kind of excited, like something important or, well, *exciting* was going on."

Garcia and Maywhort looked at the heart-monitor screen— Pearson's heart rate appeared to be normal. The boy appeared calm and stable, breathing normally. Genene was still up over the patient, appearing to listen intently through her stethoscope. Maywhort and Garcia exchanged glances—this woman was crazy! As Maywhort looked back into the cabin, he saw Genene bring up a syringe and tap the air out of it.

Reacting instantly, Maywhort shouted to Garcia, "Stop her!"

But it was too late. Genene injected the contents of the syringe into the boy's IV line. Knowing something was wrong, Maywhort alerted the pilot, "Mark time," letting him know something significant had happened in the cabin and that he should note the time. Genene yelled to Maywhort that it was "no big deal" and that she had just injected him with something to dry his mucus and help him breath easier. She threw the used syringe into her paper bag.

Maywhort and Garcia did not know what to think. The Pearson boy was clearly not convulsing or having problems breathing. He had appeared so far quite calm and stable. He did not need any additional medication. But what freaked the two veteran medics out the most was that the nurse was clearly pretending to hear the boy's heartbeat through her stethoscope. They knew that was impossible. What the hell was going on?

Several minutes passed in anxious silence when Garcia began noticing a change in the boy. His chest movement became erratic and his skin began to mottle and turn blue as his respiration grew shallow and increased in pace. Genene flew out of her seat shouting, "He's having a seizure!"

Observing the monitor, Garcia saw that in fact the boy was having a heart attack. He ordered a "Mayday"—an immediate landing of the helicopter so that they had the freedom of movement inside the cabin to assist the arresting child. As they went down toward a farm pasture for an emergency landing, Garcia punched a button on the heart-monitoring system, which printed out a record of the scope's readings. By now Jimmy Pearson had stopped breathing and the monitor registered a fading heartbeat.

Genene Jones pushed Garcia aside and attempted to place a re-

Agrippina the Younger (C.E. 15–59) "The Empress of Poison" The "she-wolf" of the Roman empire of death. She was the sister and incestuous lover of Caligula, the wife of Claudius, and the mother of Nero—three Roman Emperors in a row. She perpetrated numerous "constructive" serial murders in the pursuit of power for her son, Nero, and herself.
Criminal History Archive

Elizabeth Báthory (1560–1614) "The Female Dracula" A Renaissance-era Transylvanian countess alleged to have bathed in the blood of young women to enhance the beauty of her skin. If true, she would be one of the rare cases of female offenders who could be categorized as a "hedonist lust"–type serial killer: those who harvest body parts or fluids for their own hedonistic pleasure, a characteristic predominately associated with only male serialists.
Criminal History Archive

Lydia Sherman (1824–1878) "American Borgia" After twenty years of an uneventful marriage, the attractive forty-year-old wife of a New York City police officer and mother of six children fatally poisoned her husband after he lost his job. She then proceeded to kill her three sons and three daughters one by one over a period of a year. Afterward she assumed a new identity and married twice more—killing not only her husbands, but children from their previous marriages as well. She might be classified as a "hedonist comfort"–type serial killer—those that kill for material gain, profit, and security. This is a category most often associated with so-called "Black Widow"–type female serial killers. *Criminal History Archive*

Mary Ann Cotton (1832–1873) Typical of the mid-Victorian female arsenic killers in Britain, she murdered eleven of her own children, five stepchildren, three husbands, a sister-in-law, a lodger, and her own mother. Long before "Jack the Ripper" appeared in London in 1880s, Britain was so terrorized by an epidemic of female serial killers, who poisoned both family and strangers for meager profits and burial insurance payments, that it was proposed to enact laws banning the sale of arsenic products to women.
Criminal History Archive

Irma Grese (1923–1945) "The Beast of Belsen" A former nursing assistant and teenage Nazi SS Auxiliary female guard in Auschwitz and Belsen concentration camps, Grese had movie star good looks and a dark, sadistic compulsion to torture and kill inmates in her charge. Grese and Ilse Koch, "The Bitch of Buchenwald," would become the inspiration for the 1974 cult movie *Ilsa, She Wolf of the SS.*
LTC Gerald Draper—private collection
(courtesy of Dan Brown)

Irma Grese War Crimes Tribunal booking photo, 1945. Educated under the Nazi system, Irma was trained to function as a state serial killer, but in the end began to kill for her own hedonistic needs. Grese became so excessively homicidal that even male SS guards began to complain. On December 13, 1945, she became the youngest woman hung by the British in the twentieth century. *Criminal History Archive*

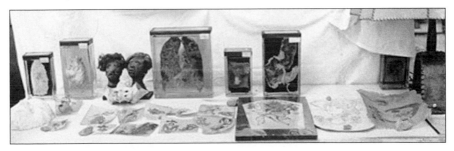

Ilse Koch Cured tattooed human skin, shrunken heads, assorted preserved body parts and a lamp shade alleged to have been made from human skin, were all found in Buchenwald concentration camp when it was liberated in 1945. Surviving inmates accused the former commandant's wife, Ilse Koch—"The Bitch of Buchenwald"—of selecting inmates with the most interesting tattoos and having them murdered for her collection of human body part trophies. If true, then this would make Koch only the second known female "hedonist lust"–type serial killer in history. Recent scholarship suggests that, while Ilse Koch was guilty of other crimes, the human body parts were collected by medical officers at the camp. *Criminal History Archive*

Karla Homolka and Paul Bernardo "The Ken and Barbie Serial Killers" The couple on their wedding day in 1991, two weeks after they had kidnapped, raped, and murdered a teenage girl, their second known victim, recording the assault on video. Homolka had already participated in the videotaping of the rape and death of her fifteen-year-old younger sister as a "wedding gift" to Bernardo. The following year she would lure into a car a third teenage victim whom the couple again videotaped while they raped and brutalized her—before killing her.
Criminal History Archive

Karla Homolka The original *mean girl*. Her nickname in high school—with no irony intended—was "The Princess." All she wanted was to be popular, have a dog, children, a big house, and a perfect husband. She claimed that Bernardo had battered her to participate in the rapes and murders, until videotapes were discovered showing her eager participation in the crimes. But by then she had already struck a deal with the prosecution to testify as a battered wife against her husband. During the bouts of raping and videotaping of one of the teenage girls, Karla would sit reading the Bret Easton Ellis novel, *American Psycho*. When, in cross-examination, she was asked how she could do such a thing, Karla incredulously replied that she was capable of "doing two things at once." While Bernardo is serving a life sentence, Karla was released from prison in 2005 after serving twelve years, and according to press reports recently remarried, acquired a dog and gave birth to a child. *Criminal History Archive*

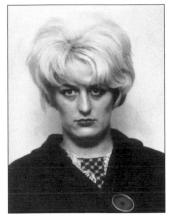

Myra Hindley "The Moor Murderess" While in her early twenties, the otherwise harmless and completely ordinary Myra assisted her boyfriend, Ian Brady, in the rape and murder of perhaps as many as ten male and female children and adolescents, taking photographs of some of them and audio taping their cries as Brady assaulted them. Myra posed on the grave of a twelve-year-old boy the couple had strangled, wearing the silk scarf with which he had been killed. Ian Brady was an admirer of the Nazi female guards and Myra obligingly wore "neo-Nazi chic" black boots and leather skirts in the Ilse style. *Criminal History Archive*

Charlene Gallego and Gerald Gallego A husband and wife team of serial killers who raped, tortured and murdered at least ten teenage female victims in Nevada and California 1978–1980. A college grad, Charlene once nearly shot her husband when he began raping a kidnapped victim "without waiting for her" and chewed away a nipple from another female victim. After testifying for the prosecution against her husband, Charlene was released from prison in 1997 and lives in California, while her husband died of cancer awaiting execution on death row. While solo, female serial killers rarely torture or rape their victims, preferring to proceed directly to murder, but when coupled with a male perpetrator, female accomplices often sadistically abuse and torture their victims. *Criminal History Archive*

Carol Bundy She watched from the backseat of a car as her boyfriend picked up and murdered a Hollywood Boulevard prostitute. When on another occasion he brought home the severed head of a victim, Carol set the hair and applied fresh makeup to the head before her boyfriend had sex with it. Eventually she decapitated a former lover in the back of a van and set his torso on fire to impress her serial-killer boyfriend. *Criminal History Archive*

Martha Beck and Raymond Fernandez "The Honeymoon Killers" After meeting through a Lonely Hearts advertisement in a romance magazine in the 1940s, Beck and Fernandez went on a serial-killing spree. With Martha Beck posing as his sister, Fernandez seduced lonely women and murdered them for their property. Beck and Fernandez are known to have killed at least four victims, but might have murdered as many as twenty. They were both executed the same day in the electric chair at Sing Sing in 1951. Beck, believed to be the dominant of the pair, went to the chair last. *Criminal History Archive*

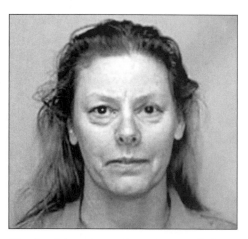

Aileen Wuornos Her booking photo. Sometimes called America's "first female serial killer," Wuornos worked alone, robbing and killing male strangers with a handgun and dumping their bodies along the Florida highway system. Wuornos, a roadside prostitute, claimed that each of her seven victims had attempted to rape her and that she killed them in self-defense. Her case became a cause for some factions in the feminist movement who came to her defense. *Criminal History Archive*

Dorothea Puente She appeared to be the respectable grandmotherly proprietor of a California halfway house for aging alcoholics on social assistance. Police found seven bodies wrapped and taped in plastic and bed sheets buried in the garden of her Victorian home, all former residents of her facility collecting social assistance. Another victim she had placed in a box and dumped in a river outside of Sacramento. She seemed so matronly and harmless, that even after police began excavating bodies from her garden, a senior detective allowed her to leave her house unescorted and escape. *Criminal History Archive*

Genene Jones "The Angel of Death" Remembered by classmates as a bossy and obnoxious "know-it-all," Jones is believed to have murdered as many as forty hospital patients in Texas. Transferring through several hospitals, Jones, although a junior nurse, dominated hospital and clinic pediatric units, leaving a trail of dead children behind while staff praised her for her uncanny ability to recognize infants on the brink of cardiac crisis several hours in advance. Nobody suspected a thing, until it was too late.
Criminal History Archive

Velma Barfield "Death Row Granny" Velma was a grandmother and the first woman executed in the USA since the death penalty resumed in 1977. Using arsenic-based ant and roach poison, she murdered husbands, elderly employees who hired her as a home-care worker and even her own elderly mother—the grandmother of her children. She was executed in North Carolina by lethal injection in 1984. *Criminal History Archive*

Susan Atkins, Patricia Krenwinkel, Leslie Van Houten The Manson Girls
in their 1969 booking photos. *Criminal History Archive*

Susan Atkins, Patricia Krenwinkel, Leslie Van Houten The Manson Girls
thirty years later in their California Department of Corrections ID
photos. *Criminal History Archive*

suscitation mask on Jimmy's face, but because of his deformities she could not get a tight fit. Maywhort stood up on his seat in the gunner's port and leaned over the boy's stretcher. He began to give him mouth-to-mouth resuscitation as the helicopter dropped to the ground.

Once they landed, the medics whisked Pearson out of the berth and laid him down on the cabin floor. Genene pulled out the endo-tracheal breathing tube from her paper bag and attempted to pass it into the boy's breathing passage. She was clumsy and could not do it, so Garcia had to take the tube from her hand and properly insert it, attaching it to an air pump with which he would ventilate the boy's lungs.

With Maywhort and Garcia in the cabin both working on the boy, the helicopter lifted off. Garcia ordered the pilot to fly to the nearest hospital in San Antonio as he gave Jimmy cardiac compression while Maywhort concentrated on the ABC—airway, breathing, and circulation. As the helicopter cruised toward the hospital, Garcia testified to observing that Genene seemed to be in a state of excitation:

She seemed a little pale and appeared to be going through some kind of hyperventilation syndrome. It looked like she was, well, it's hard to describe. Sure, it was a frightening experience, and any-body might pant, but she looked more, well, you know, *excited*.

Jimmy's mother, who was already in San Antonio, had arrived at the hospital before the helicopter landed. She saw her child rushed into Emergency by the medics. Genene Jones walked over to her when she saw her.

The mother would testify:

What I remember most vividly is her appearance. She was trem-bling. She was pale. She had an unusual—I can't explain the look she had in her eyes. It was something I've never seen before. She was "up."

The mother said Genene told her Jimmy was fine and that she had given him some Valium for his seizures. She also said that later in the flight he had stopped breathing; they had had to go down in a cow pasture to revive him. She continued:

> Then I remember she made a sort of joke about the cows not pro-
> ducing milk for the next twenty years because of Jimmy and the
> helicopter. And then—I'll never forget—she looked at me and
> said, "It was one of the most exciting afternoons of my life."

* * *

None of the events of the trip ended up being reported. Garcia remembers the printout from the heart monitor being put into the paper bag that Genene had, but cannot recall who had the bag—it was never seen again. Dr. Holland never got a followup report on the flight emergency because Jimmy Pearson was not her regular patient. Jimmy would die seven weeks later, shortly after his eighth birthday, from an infection and complications caused by his previous illnesses. But throughout the eight years of his grave medical history, he suffered a respiratory or cardiac arrest only once—on the day he flew with nurse Genene Jones. Jimmy Pearson did not live long after his encounter with Genene, but he survived her at least. Investigators would later suspect that as many as forty-seven other sick children were not that lucky.

Dr. Kathleen Holland, for whom Genene worked, had a some-what unconventional career history of her own by the time she opened her pediatric clinic on August 22, 1982, in the small town of Kerrville, an hour's drive from San Antonio. Dr. Holland already had a failed marriage behind her and was preparing to be a Ph.D. medical researcher when a conflict with her advisor forced her to rethink her options. She decided to become a practicing physician. She was older and more mature than the average medical resident and used to doing things her way. She had successfully completed her three-year pediatrics residency in June at San Antonio's Bexar County Hospital, affiliated with the University of Texas's Health Science Center medical school and research facility. Having previously carefully researched the availability of pediatric care in Texas, she picked the town of Kerrville to open her own private clinic. She had wanted to hire an RN for her clinic, but realized she could not afford the salary rate. A less trained LVN—a Licensed Vocational Nurse—was all her startup budget allowed.

Residents were moved around a hospital every few weeks to different shifts and departments, but Dr. Holland recalled working with an LVN in the Pediatric Intensive Care Unit (PICU) by the name of Genene Jones a few times—a super nurse who she recalled was as take-charge and as competent as the RNs. She was a little bossy and outspoken, sometimes even ordering doctors around, it was said, and there were rumors of personality clashes in the PICU and a lot of strange gossip about Genene. Apparently, Genene had become so fed up with what she said was jealous backstabbing that she had quit. This made the slightly rebellious and unconventional Dr. Kathleen Holland even more interested in hiring Genene for her clinic. She wanted somebody who would be passionate about the practice she intended to build in Kerrville. In the spring of 1982, Kathleen contacted the personnel office at the hospital where Genene had worked and informed them she was considering hiring her—was there anything she should know about Nurse Jones's past employment record at the hospital? Any problems or sanctions to report?

Genene's Childhood and Youth

Genene Ann Jones was born on July 13, 1950, in San Antonio and was immediately given up for adoption. She was taken into a family of three other children adopted by Dick and Gladys Jones. Her father, Dick, made a fortune running the Kit Kat Club, a shady San Antonio nightclub with illegal gambling in the backrooms. The family lived just outside the city limits in a huge hilltop mansion with landscaped gardens, swimming pool, private tennis courts, and stables for horses. From their hilltop, the Jones family could see downtown San Antonio ten miles away. Genene's mother and father lived an extravagant lifestyle—they took time to travel and both had acquired pilot licenses.

By the time Genene was 13 years old, Dick Jones was having trouble with his business. The Kit Kat Club was failing, despite his attempts to turn it into a family-oriented restaurant. Jones converted part of the acreage at their house into a trailer park, but nothing could turn his declining fortunes. In the end, Dick Jones

sold off the Kit Kat Club property and went into a new business—
billboards. He sited, built, and maintained a string of billboards in
the San Antonio area.

The adopted children were paired by age: Genene's older brother
Wiley and older sister, Lisa, were respectively four and seven years
older than Genene, while her brother Travis, with whom she was
very close, was two years younger. Travis had a learning disability.
Genene doted on him and was deeply attached to him.

Genene reportedly was the cleverest of all the children and very
assertive, often insisting on dominating conversations. She was
skilled in sewing, crochet, and baking, and was a talented piano
player. She liked to tell stories and be the center of attention. But
Genene was very sensitive—the slightest criticism would send her
to tears. She resented her older sister, Lisa, convinced that her parents favored her. There was constant conflict between the two sisters until Lisa married and moved away. After that, Genene battled
her strong-willed mother. Home life was never tranquil, and Genene would later recall that her happiest moments were riding
around with her father in the countryside as he maintained the
billboards he had put up.

Genene Jones entered high school in 1965. As a teenager she
was no more attractive than she would be when she became an
adult. At five foot four inches she was thirty pounds overweight
and clumsy as a hippo. She did not walk anywhere, it was said, she
rushed. Her lack of looks was only surpassed by her obnoxious
and bossy personality. She worked a number of menial part-time
jobs around the school and berated her fellow workers if she
thought they were not doing their jobs correctly.

Some classmates recall her claiming that she was ostracized because her father was a former gambler. She complained that her
parents favored her older sister. Her lack of popularity bothered
her. She was desperate for recognition and craved esteem.

She told outlandish lies, claiming that she was related to Mickey
Dolenz from the super pop group The Monkees, and that she
would frequently chat with him on the telephone. She claimed that
her parents never loved her enough to adopt her legally, unlike her
other three siblings. She lied about anything and everything. "To
her, lying was just like talking," one classmate recalled.[185]

To compensate for her lack of popularity, Genene developed a reputation for reckless driving, often challenging boys to drag race from behind the wheel of her father's El Camino. She was reckless enough to often win the races.

When Genene was sixteen, tragedy struck their home. Her younger brother was toying with a homemade pipe bomb when it detonated, sending metal shards into his head. He died later that day in hospital. Genene bought a flower wreath of her own for the funeral and shrieked, wept, and collapsed at the service. But her classmates recall that immediately after the morning burial service, Genene had returned to school and milked the sympathy and attention of her friends.

In 1968, when Genene was seventeen, her father died from cancer. Genene would later claim that the day he died "her world went dark," but, in fact, she was planning to get married about six weeks after her father's death. Genene had met the one boy who paid attention to her—a high school dropout named Jimmy DeLany—and she was intent on marrying him. Her mother intensely disliked the dropout Jimmy and withheld her permission—required for the minor Genene—until Genene had graduated, hoping that by then Genene would think better of it.

In June 1968, Genene graduated with a mediocre 78.61 percent—197th in a class of 274. Fourteen days later, almost as if to challenge her mother, Genene married the hapless Jimmy. Her mother paid for the wedding and the couple's honeymoon. Her hated sister, Lisa, was the matron of honor. After the honeymoon, the couple moved into a guesthouse on the family estate.

Jimmy was only interested in cars and partying. He sporadically worked at gas stations, enough to only earn gas and beer money. Genene and Jimmy argued and squabbled. Jimmy was upset to learn that Genene raced his cars while he was away at work. After seven months of partying, drinking beer, and racing cars, the marriage began to stall. Jimmy enlisted in the navy. While Jimmy was away in basic training, Genene found a new route to popularity: She had a string of sexual liaisons with other men. One was the recently married husband of Genene's friend from high school.[186]

Genene's widowed mother sold off the estate on which Genene lived and moved into a house of her own. Genene was forced to find an apartment for herself, but her mother continued to pay her rent and support her. Nonetheless, she urged Genene to find herself some sort of employment. Genene enrolled in a beauty college to train as a beautician.

Before long, Jimmy returned home after he was given an early discharge from his enlistment. He returned to live with Genene, working as a mechanic while she found work as a beautician. In January 1972, Genene gave birth to her first child, a son. Six months later she filed for divorce, but two months after that changed her mind and reconciled with Jimmy. In February 1974, she filed for divorce again and this time it was finalized in June 1974. Genene was 23 and a single mother. She returned to the use of her family name.

Genene Goes to Nursing School

In 1976, Genene became pregnant again. She never clearly identified the father, but it might have been her ex-husband, Jimmy. Genene's older brother, in the meantime, contracted testicular cancer and died. Genene became obsessed with the fear of developing cancer and submitted herself to tests every time she had a rash or a cough. Genene was working in a beauty shop in a hospital in San Antonio when she decided that medicine might be the career for her. When she developed a skin rash that she claimed was caused by beauty products she handled at work, she convinced her mother to pay her way through nursing school. Genene decided to take an LVN's training program. LVNs were not paid as much as RNs, but the training was half as long and Genene wanted to go to work as soon as possible.

Genene had a natural aptitude for nursing, scoring grades in the nineties. Unlike her experience in high school, Genene was popular in nursing school, often cutting and styling her classmates' hair. But students recall she was not very serious. She did not study during her breaks, she made jokes with the instructors during lectures, and in anatomy class she drew caricatures of male genitalia. Nevertheless, Genene graduated in May 1977, one of sixteen students out of fifty-eight to earn honors with her diploma. She was seven months pregnant. In July she gave birth to her second child, a daughter.

When Genene wrote her licensing exam, she scored 559—more than two hundred points bove the minimum passing grade. Genene's mother did everything possible to help launch her youngest daughter's career in nursing—helped her financially and took care of her kids.

"Genene Could Start an IV in a Friggin' Fly."

In September 1977, Genene Jones sufficiently recovered from the birth of her daughter to go to work in her first nursing job. She was hired at the Methodist hospital in San Antonio and assigned to the cardiac intensive care unit. She would last only seven months before being fired. At first Genene impressed her supervisors with her enthusiasm, her energy, and willingness to work additional shifts. But a five-month review warned, "Ms. Jones tends to make judgments that she has neither the experience nor authority to make."

In April 26, 1978, Genene was fired. A cardiac patient had complained that Genene treated her rudely and roughly. When informed of this, Genene asked the supervisor if she could speak with the patient. The supervisor told her absolutely not, but Genene immediately went and confronted the patient, making a scene that resulted in the heart patient requiring sedatives. Genene was dismissed for "improper or unprofessional conduct on duty."

With a desperate nationwide shortage of nurses, Genene Jones had no problems immediately finding another nursing position in the smaller, private Community Hospital on May 15. She lasted there until October 16, when without having accumulated sick leave she had to resign to take time off to have elective surgery. Genene had her tubes tied—she would not be able to have children from then on.

Two weeks later, Genene found her third hospital job in thirteen months after answering an ad calling for nurses at the huge, recently rebuilt—and amalgamated with the University of Texas Medical School—Bexar County Hospital. It has been speculated that the shortage of nurses was so acute that, despite her lack of experience and spotty employment record, she was hired. Genene was assigned to one of the most sensitive areas in the hospital—the PICU. This was a small unit, specially fitted with emergency equipment and drugs, where the most gravely ill children were put in cubicles with glass windows where they could be observed around the clock by a team of nurses and doctors.

Nurses in the PICU are a particular breed. The work requires a high degree of concentration through hours of focused monitoring and care of patients combined with a decisive, steely cool when a patient "codes"—when they go into a respiratory or cardiac arrest and a Code Blue is called on the hospital communications system. Nurses and doctors rush to the patient, wheeling a "crash cart" with emergency medicine and equipment in a desperate bid to revive them. The most experienced PICU nurses have an uncanny ability to spot an oncoming problem in a patient and intervene before they code. They are the SWAT teams of nursing, proud and aggressive.

Immediately upon her arrival at the PICU, Genene became a source of concern. One of the RNs who gave Genene her orientation was disturbed by her behavior from the very beginning. Genene was put in charge very briefly of a 6-day-old infant with a fatal intestinal disease. He died very quickly after his arrival in the PICU. Genene had hardly any contact with the infant, but the nurse recalls that Genene "went berserk" at his death. She broke into deep, dramatic sobs, moved a stool into the dead baby's cubicle, and sat weeping over the baby for hours. This was not normal.

Despite the misgivings, Genene impressed her supervisors. Assigned to the 3–11 P.M. shift—the busiest—she impressed the RNs, who normally looked down at the LVNs, with her enthusiasm, knowledge, and technical skills. She knew a lot more about anatomy and physiology than the average LVN, and if she did not understand something, she would be seen looking it up in medical textbooks.

What distinguished Genene the most was her extraordinary talent for putting in intravenous lines. Never an easy task with an adult patient with veins that move and shift under a person's skin, it was even harder with children and infants—their veins as thin as a thread, some nurses never managed to master inserting an IV line. Genene was a master, never missing a vein, and soon was called by other nurses to help them start an IV with their patients. The saying went around the PICU that "Genene could start an IV in a friggin' fly."

Genene had her champions, among them the chief nurse at the hospital and the doctor in charge of the PICU. Impressed by Genene's technical skills and knowledge, they both encouraged Genene to go back to nursing school and become an RN. The only problem with Genene, the chief nurse noted in her evaluation, was that she needed to maintain "better control of her emotionalism."

One thing that doctors did not like about Genene was that she constantly called them to attend to patients with problems she thought they were having. She had a tendency to page weary doctors four times more often than the other nurses. This was particularly irritating to interns, who often worked straight thirty-hour shifts and would try to catch a few minutes of sleep between calls. Not when Genene was on duty.

But as time went by, Genene developed a reputation for that uncanny ability to recognize a patient about to code. When Genene told you that a patient was on the brink of a seizure or arrest, even if they appeared to be calmly sleeping, she was frequently correct. Strangely enough, despite this developing skill, Genene began to accumulate an increasing collection of serious errors in her record—eight in the first year. She failed to obey a doctor's order to give a child a drug. She did not notice a malfunctioning IV on one of her patients. She set an IV solution at an improperly high rate on another. She overdosed another patient by ten times the normal dosage. When Genene was called into "informal guidance" to discuss these errors, she denied she had made them or submitted elaborate explanations for her error. After her fourth medication error in twelve months, Genene was ordered to repeat a special class on drug administration. She twice failed to show up to the class.

Genene began attaching herself to certain patients and staying with them beyond her shift. She was told with one patient, a ten-month girl with heart trouble, to go home at the end of her shift, but refused. A higher-level nursing administrator was called to the ward to order her to go home, but Genene argued that the patient *needed* her. She wrote in her response to the complaint, "I felt that seeing her through this crisis, her biggest, was very important, not only to me but for her." She was placed on notice that a similar failure to obey orders would result in her suspension and probable dismissal.

Two months later, after completing her previous shift, Genene showed up at 5:00 A.M. in the PICU unexpectedly and went to the bedside of another child patient she was assigned to on her own shift, fetched a syringe, and began to tinker with the child's IV line. Smelling alcohol on her breath, doctors and nurses on the floor ordered Genene out. Genene was cited for "very poor judgment," but allowed to return to work.

In her personnel file, along with the reports of errors and misconduct, were commendations for "meritorious contributions." According to the report, "Over the last four months when the PICU was going through a severe staffing shortage, Ms. Jones worked in excess of twelve extra shifts to help cover the unit; these extra shifts often involved sacrificing days off . . . Ms. Jones is to be commended for her support and dedication to the PICU."

"It Was Like She Knew What Was Going to Happen."

The PICU became divided over Genene Jones. She had her champions and supporters and she had her detractors. She maintained a close rapport with the patient's parents and often was there to console them when their children died. Among fellow staff she was crude and coarse, often telling dirty jokes or cursing loudly. She was free with her opinions of other doctors and nurses.

As in high school, Genene liked to be in the center of attention and told exaggerated stories about herself—that she had been in a coma after a car accident; that she had shot her brother-in-law in the groin after he had beaten her sister.

It is remarkable how similar the personalities of Genene Jones and Jane Toppan are over the gulf of one hundred years—the exaggerated stories, the hostility, and the division of opinion between those who supervised her and those who had to work with her all day.

She became very bossy of the staff. If one doctor rejected her advice, she would call another. She questioned medication, dosages, and treatments. When her recommendations were ignored, she predicted disaster, telling one doctor, "This kid is going to die if you don't do this."

On shift changes, nurses would gather to report on the conditions of their patients. During these meetings, Genene would issue dire pronouncements on certain patients, forewarning that they may die that night. As one RN recalled, "It wasn't like she was predicting it. It was like she *knew* what was going to happen."

All throughout this, Genene Jones was herself a frequent patient. During her first twenty-seven months at Bexar County Hospital, she made thirty visits to the outpatient clinic or the emergency ward where she complained of an extraordinarily diverse catalog of problems: diarrhea and cramps, vomiting, acute gastroenteritis, indigestion, belching, and "burning up" constipation. She experienced shooting chest pains and dizziness. Her thumb had been cut, her hands itched. Excessive menstrual bleeding and lack of menstrual bleeding. Sore throat, allergic reaction to medication. Neck pain, knee pain, abdominal pain, lower back pain.

Early in 1981, Genene began asking to be assigned to only the sickest children. She actually demanded it, refusing to care for patients who she thought had only routine illnesses. Genene had come to dominate the PICU, breaking rules with no consequences. She would choose her own patients, coming in early and penciling in her name to the charts of patients she was interested in. Her choice of patients ensured that she was involved in more frequent Code Blue calls, the excitement of which she thrived on. Genene would later say of these emergencies, "It's an incredible experience. Oh, shit, it's frightening. You're aware of everything, but you only tune in to two or three different people . . . you really have to control your physical abilities, because you really get keyed up."[187]

When her patients died, Genene would break down and weep. Nurses have been known to cry over patients with whom they had developed relationships, but Genene wept over every patient who died—and there were increasingly many. She would ask the doctor to wait before informing the parents, all the while rocking the infant's body. Nurses would normally wheel the dead on stretchers to the morgue in the basement, but Genene, with tears streaming down her face, carried them down in her arms, resembling a grieving mother.

At home, Genene was mostly ignoring her own two children, leaving them to her mother to care for. Her oldest child, the boy, was roaming the streets of his neighborhood alone, showing up at neighbor's houses and suspected by them of stealing things.

Gotten Rid of but "Eligible for Re-Employment"

The number of patients in her care that Genene prognosed would die and did so began to accumulate beyond a reasonable number. Doctors, mostly residents who rotated in and out of the PICU, did not detect any unusual patterns—only the nurses did. When nurses began to voice their concerns to a supervisor, she dismissed them, championing Genene. She accused them of jealousy and threatened to discipline any nurse who dared to raise the issue again without providing solid evidence. One of the nurses did so, collecting statistical data on the death rate in the PICU and whose patients they were. Despite the skewed figure, the chief nurse continued to defend Genene, reminding everybody that Genene was volunteering for the most critically ill patients—of course her death rate would be higher. But in the end, the numbers proved to go way beyond that explanation.

When the statistics were gathered, they revealed that there were a total of forty-three deaths in the PICU between January 1, 1981, and March 17, 1982. Fifteen different nurses were assigned to those patients, including Genene Jones. Her patients accounted for a staggering twenty-two out of the forty-three deaths—about 50 percent. Moreover, Genene was present at the deaths of an additional seven patients, having volunteered her services. This could not be ignored. Finally, three months after nurses began to formally voice their concerns over the deaths of patients in Genene's care, an internal hospital investigation was launched.

The investigation concluded that either Genene Jones was grossly incompetent or she was deliberately killing the patients but could not find any specific evidence. "Either way, the biggest problem facing the hospital, the investigative team was advised by the hospital's attorney, was the possibility of being sued by Genene if they could not come up with sufficient evidence for their suspicions." Things had to be quietly resolved and hushed up.

The problem was what to do with Genene Jones. Judging by her reactions to past complaints entered into her record, Genene was not going to quietly allow herself to be fired nor did she appear to be predisposed to resigning. Cleverly, the investigative board suggested a ploy: upgrade the qualifications for nurses in the PICU to RNs and thus remove the LVN Genene Jones from the unit. When the time came to reassign the former PICU LVNs to new wards, only Genene and the nurse who pursued the complaints against her could not be found new positions. Genene was sent packing in March 1982 with no grounds for complaint, although she did so anyway and is suspected of sending threatening notes to some of the hospital staff. In her hospital employment records, Genene was designated as "eligible for re-employment" and supplied with letters of recommendation.

So when in the spring of 1982, Dr. Kathleen Holland contacted the hospital administration to confirm Genene Jones's status for employment in her own clinic when it opened in August, she was told Genene was classified "eligible for re-employment." Although other doctors from the hospital privately warned Holland that there were problems with Genene, they never got into any detail beyond the gossip and her tendency to be bossy. Dr. Kathleen Holland went ahead and hired Genene. Not only did she do that, but she also rented a house with Genene: They would be living together along with Genene's two children.

* * *

Again the similarity between Genene Jones in the 1980s and Jane Toppan in the 1880s is haunting. Just like Genene, Toppan was shuffled off with letters of recommendation to other hospitals as a student despite the inexplicably high death rate among the patients she cared for. Toppan was finally gotten rid of by her nursing certificate being withheld in ambiguous circumstances, allegedly after her dismissal for leaving a ward without permission—even though she had passed her exams already.

"I Figured It Would Be Okay to Let Her Take Chelsea for a Few Minutes."

After freelancing for a few months while waiting for the clinic to open, Genene began work in Dr. Holland's clinic on Monday, August 23, 1982. That day the clinic had only one patient. The next day they would have their second patient.

Petti and Reid McClellan, both 27 years old, lived fifteen miles outside of Kerrville. They were exactly the type of people that Dr. Holland had hoped her clinic would serve. In June of the previous year, Petti had given birth to a girl four weeks premature, whom they named Chelsea. The baby suffered from respiratory problems typical of premature infants with underdeveloped lungs and she needed to be hospitalized in San Antonio. After twenty-one days, her condition improved. Her weight climbed and the McClellans took Chelsea home. In May 1982, when Chelsea was ten months old, her parents rushed her to the emergency ward in San Antonio when she was having problems breathing. The baby was diagnosed with pneumonia, treated for several days, and sent home with her parents, who were cautioned to observe her breathing carefully. Otherwise, she was a normal and healthy baby.

Petti and Reid were overjoyed when they heard that Kerrville was going to have its own pediatric clinic. San Antonio was sixty miles away and the local hospital did not have any specialized pediatricians. So when Chelsea, who was 14 months old, appeared to have a case of "the sniffles" Petti decided to take advantage of the clinic that had just opened in town the day before. At about 1:00 P.M. on Tuesday, August 24, she brought Chelsea in to see Dr. Holland.

As Holland interviewed Petti in her office about Chelsea's medical history, the baby wiggled out of her mother's arms and began grabbing at things on Holland's desk. Petti recalled that a smiling woman stuck her head into the office through the open door and said, "Mrs. McClellan, why don't you let me take Chelsea while you and Dr. Holland finish talking."

"It was the office nurse," Petti would later recall. "I'd never met her before that, but I figured it would be okay to let her take Chelsea for a few minutes."

Genene Jones carried the giggling girl away, cooing to her, "Come on you, let's go play."

Petti was recounting to Dr. Holland her daughter's medical history and was sort of embarrassed about bringing in Chelsea with minor sniffles, but better safe than sorry. Dr. Holland assured her she did the right thing. She would later testify that then she heard something from the examination room down the hall that would break her concentration—she could no longer focus on what Petti was saying, but only on Genene's voice, which she had heard say in the other room, "Don't go to sleep, baby. Wake up. Wake up, Chelsea. Don't go to sleep."

It was freaky, because five minutes earlier Chelsea had been twisting and giggling in her office. Holland attempted to ignore the growing wave of anxiety rising up in her and refocused on Petti, who was still talking. Then Holland heard Genene call her, "Dr. Holland, could you come out here now, please." There was clearly a cold sense of urgency in her voice.

Chelsea was draped over the examining room table unconscious and Genene was holding an oxygen mask over her face. "She had a seizure," Genene said. "She stopped breathing."

Kathleen began performing an emergency intubation of Chelsea, with Genene smoothly finding and opening the sterile packages of breathing tubes and handing them to Kathleen. As she performed the procedure, Kathleen congratulated herself on her choice of clinic nurse. Genene was performing like a crack surgical nurse, cool and efficient under pressure. Genene started up an IV on the child as ordered by Kathleen, injecting into Chelsea a drug to counteract acidity building up in her failing circulatory system. Paramedics were called and Chelsea was rushed off to the emergency ward at the local Sid Peterson Memorial Hospital in Kerrville where she was admitted at 1:35.

Two and a half hours later, Chelsea was sitting up in her bed and smiling, leaving everybody perplexed. For the next ten days, almost every conceivable test was run on the 14-month-old girl but nothing could be diagnosed. Chelsea was finally sent home. Petti was grateful for the quick response of Dr. Holland and her nurse, Genene Jones. She praised the clinic, telling all the parents she knew that they should take their kids there.

* * *

On Friday, August 27, 18-year-old Nelda Benites brought in her 3-month-old daughter, Brandy, who was suffering from dark and bloody diarrhea. After examining the infant, Dr. Holland decided she should be transferred to Sid Peterson Memorial Hospital for observation. She put an oxygen mask on Brandy and told Genene to start up an IV to prepare her for a routine transfer to the hospital, about a five-minute drive away. Running an IV was a procedure that Kathleen Holland decided would be routine on any transfer of her patients to Sid Peterson. She wanted her patients to arrive there already prepped, with samples of their blood drawn, and on an IV, so there would be no delays at the small hospital.

She then left the child alone with Genene to call the hospital and arrange for the baby's transfer.

When Kathleen returned five minutes later, she was alarmed to see that Brandy appeared to be in worse condition: her face had turned ashen, her finger and toes were turning blue, and her breathing was slowing. Emergency procedures were immediately invoked and the run to the local hospital became an urgent one.

At Sid Peterson, Kathleen Holland stabilized Brandy, but could not explain the cause of the respiratory arrest. She decided to transfer the baby to a pediatric unit in San Antonio. Still breathing on her own, Brandy was put on an IV line, intubated, attached to a cardiac machine, and loaded into an ambulance for the trip to San Antonio. Genene Jones, paramedic Phillip Kneese, and RN Sarah Mauldin from the hospital rode in the back of the ambulance with Brandy. Because Dr. Holland suffered from motion sickness, she followed behind the ambulance in her own car. As they departed the hospital parking lot, RN Mauldin recalled that Brandy was breathing normally.

In the middle of the trip, Brandy suddenly had a cardiac arrest. The ambulance pulled over to the side of the road and Dr. Holland got on board. She gave Brandy CPR, restarting the child's heartbeat. She then returned to her car and they continued on their run into San Antonio. On board the ambulance, despite the fact that Sarah Mauldin was the more qualified RN, Genene Jones took charge. She started up a second IV into Brandy's foot.

The ambulance paramedic later testified: "Since the ambulance didn't carry any IV sets, she had to have brought it with her . . . It's hard to explain, but she was aggressive in the sense that at all times she gave the impression that she knew exactly what she was doing. I just figure the kid needed it for some reason which I wasn't aware of."

Sarah testified that Genene turned to her and looked her in the eyes, and "with a kind of breathy excitement, said: 'The kid's gone bad. Bag like crazy.' And I did."

"Bagging" meant manually pumping a balloonlike bag with oxygen running through it attached to the tubes running into a patient's airway. Brandy barely survived her trip to San Antonio.

Dr. Holland's clinic had had two cardiopulmonary arrests

occur in its first four days. Kathleen Holland was a new and inexperienced doctor. Her experience to date had been in a big-city hospital with gravely ill patients—she had no way of knowing just how statistically exceptional these events were in a small-town clinic like hers. She did not know that Kerrville's oldest doctor had only one pediatric respiratory arrest occur in his practice in a span of forty years.

The next Tuesday, on August 30, Genene went on the MAST helicopter ambulance run, where a third patient suffered a cardiac arrest.

On Friday, September 3, 19-year-old Kay Reichenau brought her 21-month-old daughter, Misty, to the clinic complaining of mouth sores and a high fever. Dr. Holland examined the child with Genene assisting her. Genene pointed out that the child appeared to have a stiff neck and Dr. Holland agreed. This and the other symptoms could have been early signals of meningitis, and Dr. Holland decided to transfer Misty to the hospital for routine observation. She left the child alone with Genene to prepare an IV line for her transfer and take her blood samples. It was not long before the child suffered a respiratory arrest, with all the ensuing emergency treatment in the examining room before the baby was rushed off to the emergency ward at Sid Peterson Hospital. Again, despite a battery of tests, the cause of the arrest could not be diagnosed.

On Saturday, September 11, Nurse Mary Morris, who worked at the Sid Peterson Hospital, heard they were getting a patient in by the name of Genene Jones. She had gone to LVN school with Genene and wondered if it was the same person. It was. Genene was in complaining of a painful ulcer.

Mary and Genene chatted and she was surprised to learn that Genene was employed right there in Kerrville as the nurse in Kathleen Holland's newly opened clinic. Genene then said something strange—that she was also in Kerrville because she was going to help the hospital start up a PICU and she would be put in charge of it.

Mary thought it was a ridiculous notion. First, Genene was only an LVN and not likely to be put in charge of a PICU, and second, Kerrville hardly had enough sick children to justify a PICU. She said to Genene that she had worked in Kerrville for two years and "sure, we have sick children, but I don't know if there are enough sick children here in the area to constitute a need for a PICU."

Genene responded, "Oh, they're out there. All you have to do is go out and find them."

But sometimes, they were just brought straight into Genene's hands.

* * *

On Friday, September 17, Petti had brought back Chelsea for her second visit to Dr. Holland's clinic, along with her brother Cameron. It was a routine appointment and Chelsea was scheduled to receive her immunization shots. Chelsea had recovered well from the last month's episode and was bouncy and alert that morning.

After examining Chelsea and seeing everything was normal, Dr. Holland told Genene to go ahead and give the girl the two routine infant immunizations: a diphtheria/tetanus and an MMR.

Genene said to Petti, "Why don't you wait outside, Mrs. McClellan. I know most mothers don't like to see their babies get shots."

Petti recalled that she told Genene it did not bother her at all and she would come in with them. Petti later testified that Genene did not seem to be at all happy about this and that, "she got sort of huffy."

Cradling Chelsea in her arms, Petti followed Genene into the examination room. She saw that there were two filled syringes already prepared. Petti recalled that Chelsea reacted within seconds after the first injection. "My God, I thought, what's happening. It seemed to me she wasn't breathing right, and her eyes were looking at me funny. She was sort of whimpering—it was as if she was trying to say, 'Help me,' but couldn't."

Petti immediately told Genene that something was wrong, but Genene dismissed her, saying "She's just mad about having to get the shots. It's nothing. She's reacting to the pain."

Petti protested, "No, stop. She's not acting right. She's having another seizure!"

But Genene would not stop. Mumbling something like, "I have to give her this other shot," she stuck the child with the second syringe and plunged its contents into the girl.

Petti said that Chelsea stopped breathing and began to turn blue. She testified in court:

> I looked at her and I could see she was trying to say "Mama." I thought, Oh God, she wants to say "Mama."
>
> Chelsea then went limp; just like a rag doll, just like Raggedy Ann—that's exactly what she looked like, just limp. She was still looking at me, but it didn't look like she could see me. Her eyes were all strange looking and they weren't like they were supposed to be. They weren't like they were supposed to be.

Again there were emergency procedures in the examination room; the ambulance run to Sid Peterson Hospital. In the emergency room Chelsea's color, breathing, and heart rate began to return to normal. Kathleen Holland decided to transfer Chelsea to San Antonio and called the MAST unit. They were busy, so instead she scheduled her transfer in an ambulance by ground rather than wait for the MAST helicopter to become available. As before, Genene would go along in the ambulance while Kathleen Holland would follow in the car. While Dr. Holland was phoning the hospital in San Antonio, one of the nurses at the hospital drove Petti back to the clinic where she had left Cameron and her car. Genene asked for a ride back with them to the clinic to get her and Dr. Holland's purses, she said.

As Petti explained to Cameron that his grandmother was going to pick him up while she went to San Antonio, she saw Genene rushing about the clinic packing medical supplies into her bag. Genene returned to the hospital and boarded the ambulance transporting Chelsea to San Antonio. Holland followed in her car, and Petti, who was by now joined by her husband, Reid, brought up the rear in their vehicle.

In the back of the ambulance, paramedic Tommy James pumped the respiratory bag to assist Chelsea with her breathing, while Genene monitored the child's blood pressure and heartbeat through an electronic monitor. Ten minutes into the drive, the monitor began to give an alarm—Chelsea was having a heart attack.

The ambulance stopped and Holland rushed into the cabin to find the paramedic bagging Chelsea while Genene was performing

CPR. "She's flatlined!" Genene shouted, meaning that the cardio-monitor was showing a flat green line on the scope—no heartbeat.

Dr. Holland stopped everyone for a minute and listened for a heartbeat. There wasn't any. She ordered Genene to begin emergency drug injections. Genene pulled out a number of syringes from her bag and injected Chelsea with epinephrine, calcium chloride, and sodium bicarbonate. There was no response in Chelsea.

Holland ordered the ambulance to proceed to the nearest available hospital. This was Comfort Community Hospital about ten minutes away. The ambulance radioed for them to prepare for a Code Blue arrival. They arrived at 1:05 and quickly wheeled Chelsea into the emergency room. There Kathleen Holland and the hospital doctor, assisted by the paramedic, Genene, and the hospital nurses, attempted to revive Chelsea with rounds of injections of various cardiotonic drugs. The only thing left to do was to attempt to give her an electric shock, but the paddles were too large for the size of the child's body. At 1:20 P.M., Chelsea was pronounced dead.

Although Kathleen Holland said she was in a state of shock and did not remember this, others recall that Genene Jones emerged with the dead child wrapped in a blanket and handed her to Petti, who broke down weeping.

Later, Genene took Chelsea's corpse into her own arms, and cradling the dead child to her breast, rode sobbing in the ambulance all the way back to the hospital in Kerrville, where she logged the body into the morgue.

When Genene returned to the clinic that afternoon, she wrote in big, bold letters in the office log:

. . . CPR DISCONTINUED. PARENTS INFORMED OF DEATH BY DR. HOLLAND. BABY TRANSPORTED FROM COMFORT TO SID PETERSON HOSPITAL BY EMS AND MYSELF, AND TAKEN TO MORGUE. I WOULD HAVE GIVEN MY LIFE FOR HER. GOOD-BYE, CHELSEA

Genene then turned to 19-year-old Lydia Evans, who was sitting in the waiting room with her 5-month-old son Jacob. She had scheduled an appointment earlier for Dr. Holland to have a look at her baby, who had been cranky and irritable all week. The appointment was cancelled when Dr. Holland left on the emergency run to San Antonio with Chelsea, but when she died and Holland was scheduled to return to the clinic, the receptionist phoned Lydia and told her the appointment was "uncancelled." She could come in if she still wanted to. Dr. Holland would be arriving shortly, she was told.

Lydia said she arrived at the clinic with her mother, father, and Jacob between 3:15 and 3:30 P.M. She testified that the receptionist told her Dr. Holland still had not returned, but the clinic nurse would see them for now.

Lydia testified, "Ms. Jones came out from the back of the office then and introduced herself, and said that we could go ahead and do the preliminary work on Jacob. Dr. Holland was due back any moment."

The examination appeared to be routine, with Genene weighing and measuring the baby and asking Lydia about the infant's history. Except for one thing, recalled Lydia, in her courtroom testimony

> I remember that she kept coming back to his eyes—looking into his eyes—and feeling his head, she did that a lot. She seemed concerned and mentioned something about his left eye not responding to light properly, that the pupil was sluggish, or something like that, though the right eye, she said, seemed to been all right. I'd never noticed any problems with Jacob's eyes, and I really didn't see any problem then either—but I wasn't really "double-checking" her.

Genene told Lydia and her mother that she detected a type of eye movement that was symptomatic of seizurelike activity and that she thought it would be best to transfer Jacob to the hospital in Kerrville to run some tests. She left the room for a few minutes and then returned and told the family that Dr. Holland had authorized her to take some blood samples and put Jacob on an IV line in preparation for the transfer.

As soon as Lydia heard that Jacob was going to be put on an IV she became concerned: Why? Is this serious?

Genene assured her it was routine, but "with the kinds of tests they'll be running, you can't always be sure how a baby will react."

Lydia began to have second thoughts about the "tests"—maybe they should wait and think about it. Genene reassured her that Jacob would be fine and began ushering both Lydia and her mother out of the examining room, saying, "Now, ladies, I need to get him ready for the hospital. I'm a mother, too, and I know how it is to watch your child when he's unhappy. I think it'd be better if you waited out in the lobby."

Lydia's mother spoke up and said that Lydia could leave but she'd be glad to stay and help with Jacob. Genene was insistent that it was against the rules to have a relative in the room when performing a "delicate procedure."

As Lydia and her parents sat in the waiting room, they heard Jacob screaming in a way they had never heard before. "It was not the normal crying of a baby," his grandmother would testify. "It was a scream. It was a terrified cry. He screamed several times, and then, in mid-scream—as though it were just cut off—there was nothing, just dead silence."

Kathleen Holland was at Sid Peterson doing paperwork connected with Chelsea's death when she heard from her secretary that Lydia Evans would be coming in to the clinic. Exhausted and drained by Chelsea's death, she told her to tell Genene to immediately send the family to the hospital—she would examine the infant there. She completed the paperwork and was preparing for the presumed arrival of Lydia with her infant son, when the hospital operator stopped her and told her there was an emergency at her clinic—she was needed there immediately.

By the time Holland arrived at her office, an ambulance was parked at the door and Jacob had already been loaded in. The doctor next-door had performed emergency procedures on the child, who had had respiratory arrest. Holland got into the ambulance with Genene and asked her what had happened.

Genene explained, "He had a seizure. I had to call the doctor and nurse from next-door. He ordered 180 milligrams of Dilantin." Genene then coughed and rolled her eyes, according to Holland, and said, "I knew that was too much, so I only gave him 80."

Jacob was stabilized at the hospital and after six days of examinations, they still could not determine what caused the respiratory arrest.

"You've Got a Baby Killer on Your Hands."

Unlike the San Antonio hospitals, Sid Peterson was a small facility in which everybody knew each other and everything that went on in the town of Kerrville. Five emergency seizures in a month at the newly opened clinic did not go unnoticed. One of the doctors commented, "There was just too much smoke. I've been in practice forty-three years and never had one. To the best of my knowledge, we've never had one in Kerrville. Something had to be wrong."

Disturbing also was the fact that the patients would recover within an hour or so after their crisis—unless Genene accompanied them for transfer to San Antonio, where inevitably on the way there they would have another seizure.

On Wednesday, September 22, the medical management team at the hospital decided to schedule an interview with Dr. Holland for the next day to discuss the issue. It was decided also that the next time there was an emergency case brought in from Holland's clinic, the hospital doctors would attend and observe carefully what was going on. They did not have long to wait.

The next day, Thursday, September 23, Clarabelle Ruff brought in her 5-month-old baby girl, Rolinda, to the clinic, suffering from diarrhea and dehydration. After examining the child, Dr. Holland told her she wanted to check her into the hospital for observation. She ran the IV line herself, but asked Genene to prepare the medicine she was going to inject into the line. When she was ready, she asked Genene to hand her the syringe and injected its contents into the IV line. Soon the baby went into respiratory arrest and an ambulance was called to take her over to Sid Peterson.

When the word got out that yet another Code Blue patient was on the way from Kathleen Holland's clinic, almost the entire staff of doctors from the hospital crowded into the room to observe.

As before, the child appeared to be recovering from the respiratory arrest. As the baby convulsed and fought the incubation tube being forced down her breathing passage, one of the doctors, an anesthesiologist immediately recognized what was happening: The child was recovering from the effects of a particular type of anesthetic. Anectine—succinylcholine, or "succs" in medical slang—was a synthetic curare used as a muscle relaxant in delicate surgery. While not affecting consciousness, it paralyzes every muscle in the body, including the diaphragm, and if given in a larger dose, the heart.

The day was not over yet. When Ruff had brought in her girl to the clinic, another mother was in the waiting room with her child—Mary Ann Parker, whose baby boy Chris three weeks earlier had been the other infant on the medevac helicopter and had escaped Genene's attention during that flight. Chris, who had since returned home from the hospital, was now suffering from diarrhea and an ear infection and Parker brought her son back to the clinic. As Holland and Genene rushed off to the hospital with the Ruff child, Genene told Parker to take her child to the hospital emergency room and that Dr. Holland would see her there. Less than an hour later, Genene Jones entered the hospital waiting room and took Mary Parker's son away to an emergency examining room. She placed the child on a bed that was being prepared for an emergency cardiac patient coming in by ambulance. When an emergency room nurse asked that Genene move the child, who was there for a routine examination to free the bed for the incoming emergency, Genene snapped at her, "Well, I hope to hell this baby doesn't go into cardiac arrest."

A few minutes later, Genene called a Code Blue for Chris Parker, who had stopped breathing. The ER doctors quickly responded, stabilizing the child, and soon Kathleen Holland arrived. Remarkably, Holland found a half-filled syringe lying in Chris Parker's bed. Asking Genene and the nurses what it was, nobody knew. According to court testimony, Holland squirted the syringe empty onto the floor and told the nurses to get rid of it.

At the end of the day, as the exhausted Kathleen Holland and Genene walked out of the hospital's intensive care unit and paused before the commemorative plaque at the entrance, Genene wistfully said, "Maybe someday this will be the Chelsea Ann McClellan Memorial Pediatric Intensive Care Unit."

* * *

That same day the hospital doctors were meeting to discuss what they had observed in the emergency room and the suspicions the anesthesiologist had about the presence of succinylcholine. The medical community is a tight one and the doctors decided to call their various colleagues at Bexar County Hospital in San Antonio to find out all they could about Dr. Kathleen Holland, the recently graduated pediatrics resident. One of the doctors talking with a resident he knew at Bexar County was told by him that indeed there was a problem in the PICU in San Antonio—an unusually high death rate that nobody could explain and that the common denominator was a PICU nurse. The resident could not remember her name.

Was it Genene Jones?

The resident said he would check and call back shortly.

Five minutes later the phone rang. The resident said, "You've got a baby killer on your hands."

* * *

On Friday, September 24, Kathleen Holland was called into a meeting at the hospital. There were eleven doctors seated at a board table, one of them a psychiatrist. They began to quietly pose questions to Holland, carefully listening to her responses and observing her body language. A lot of children seemed to be getting sick in her clinic. Why did she think this was happening?

Kathleen explained that every child was a separate medical situation with its own explanation. She had reviewed each case. She appeared to the doctors to be tense but professional and sincere. They asked her a battery of questions about her methods, techniques, instruments, medications, and her approach to pediatrics.

At one point they asked if she used succinylcholine at the clinic. Kathleen told her she had some but had never used it.

They questioned her about Genene Jones. According to their testimony, Kathleen defended her, saying that Genene had actually taught her a thing or two about resuscitating children. She had been an LVN in the PICU in San Antonio, but was moved out after the unit upgraded the nursing staff to RNs. All had been offered jobs elsewhere in the hospital and she had been graded "eligible for re-employment."

The meeting ended when Kathleen's beeper went off. Jimmy

Pearson, the boy who arrested on the MAST flight to San Antonio and who had been returned to Sid Peterson, was arresting and Code Blue was called. It was not a good omen.

After Holland left, the doctors decided to call the Texas Board of Vocational Nurses and explained their concerns to an investigator there, Ferris Aldridge. After hearing out the doctors, Aldridge told them this was not a board matter, but that he would put the proper authorities onto the problem. This was how the Texas Rangers at the Department of Public Safety got involved, the first time in two years of death and suspicion that anybody got law enforcement authorities involved. This was the beginning of the end of Genene Jones's killing career.

When Kathleen Holland returned to the clinic she told Genene about the meeting and what had been asked. She mentioned that they had asked if they had used succinylcholine on any of the patients in the clinic. She also told Genene that they expressed their concern over her aggressiveness and asked her if she had trusted her clinic staff.

"At that point, she became upset," Holland later testified. "She said, 'Somebody's starting rumors,' or something to that effect."

Over the weekend, Kathleen Holland went away, but returned to the house she shared with Genene on Sunday evening. During idle conversation, just before retiring for the night, Genene suddenly said to her, in an offhanded manner, "Oh, by the way, I found that missing vial of succs."

This was news to Holland: "What missing succs?"

Genene went on to remind her of the day she had told her about the missing vial of succinylcholine. The only problem was that Kathleen could not remember having any such conversation with her.

"So where was it found?" Holland asked.

"In the lower drawer of the crash room's table, under the paper lining," replied Genene.

Holland became uneasy. Strange that the very medication that was brought up in the meeting on Friday was now the one that apparently Genene was claiming was lost at the clinic. Holland recalled that Genene suddenly began to volunteer other information. As she spoke, Genene could not look at her but kept staring down at the table.

"There is one problem," Genene continued, "the cap has been popped."

Holland's heart froze.

Genene could not explain how that had happened, other than to say they had a lot of people in and out of the office. That did not satisfy Holland. She remembered once hearing that when people begin to volunteer all sorts of unsolicited information, it usually means something.

The next thing to come out of Genene's mouth, was "Oh, yeah, I checked, and there are no holes in the stopper. I checked it against the replacement vial and all 10 cc's are there. If somebody wants to draw it up, they can draw it up. It's all there."

Kathleen had a hard time sleeping that night. She could hear Genene moving about in her part of the house. The next morning, after doing her rounds at the hospital, she returned to her clinic about the time Genene was going out to lunch. Dr. Holland went straight to the refrigerator where the drugs were kept. She pulled out the two vials of succinylcholine and held them up to the light. She immediately noticed that there was a very slight, subtle difference in the meniscus—the dip in the fluid—in one of the vials. She tipped the vials and looked at their tops. One was still sealed with a cap, but the other vial was missing its cap, and Kathleen could distinctly make out two needle puncture holes in its red rubber stopper.

When Genene returned from lunch she was in good spirits and told Dr. Holland that she had just visited Chelsea. Petti would later testify that she saw Genene that day at her daughter's graveside, rocking back and forth and sobbing, calling out Chelsea's name over and over.

Kathleen called the office staff together and attempted to find out how the two puncture marks could have occurred in the succinylcholine vial stopper. Nobody could come up with a satisfactory answer. Genene kept saying that there were a lot of people coming into the clinic.

After the meeting, with only Genene remaining, as Kathleen put the vials into the fridge, she said, "How am I going to explain those holes, Genene?"

To her surprise, Genene replied, in what Holland later characterized as a coolly defensive tone, "I don't think you should explain them at all. I think you should just throw it out. Tell them we lost it. We won't be lying if we say we lost it. We *did* lose it. I know we found it again, but they don't have to know we found it. Just throw it away."

Holland was horrified. She told Genene that she could not do that ethically or legally. The conversation was interrupted by the arrival of a mother and her child for an appointment.

About an hour later, Genene walked up to Holland and said, "I did a stupid thing at lunch. I took a bunch of doxepin."

Doxepin was a powerful anti-anxiety drug. Looking for the first time that day into Genene's face, Holland saw that her eyes were glazed and her eyelids were drooping. After checking among Genene's belongings, she found an empty bottle of the drug. The label showed it contained as many as thirty pills.

Dr. Holland rushed over to the doctor next-door and told him that her nurse had just overdosed on doxepin and that, "Number one, I am not an adult doctor, and number two, I wash my hands of this woman."

While an ambulance took Genene away to the hospital, Holland called the chairman of the committee at the hospital and told him that she had just fired Genene Jones because she had attempted to commit suicide at the clinic. She asked him to come over. When he arrived with some of his colleagues, Holland told them everything she had learned and turned over the vials of succinylcholine to them. Together, while going through the drug requisition forms, they also discovered that, in fact, three vials had been ordered, not two, and one was still missing. Two of the deliveries were signed for by Genene.

Trial

On October 12, 1982, a grand jury in Kerr County began looking into the death of Chelsea McClellan and the eight other cardiac or pulmonary arrests that children suffered at the clinic and hospital. Chelsea's body was exhumed and the presence of succinylcholine was confirmed. But it was not going to be easy. Nobody had seen Genene actually inject the child with the drug.

In the meantime, in San Antonio, a grand jury there began investigating an extraordinary total of forty-seven suspicious deaths linked to Genene Jones's four-year employment at the three hospitals in that city.

Genene first went on trial on January 15, 1984, for the murder of Chelsea McClellan and injury to the other children. On February 15, 1984, Jones was convicted of murder after the jury deliberated for only three hours. She was given the maximum sentence of ninety-nine years. Later that year, in October, she went on trial in San Antonio and was found guilty on one count of injuring a patient there by an injection of heparin. The two sentences totaled 159 years, but with the possibility of parole.

Although Genene Jones was suspected in the deaths of forty-seven other children, the *New York Times* reported that the administration of Bexar County Medical Center and University of Texas Medical School shredded nine thousand pounds of pharmaceutical records from the period when Jones was employed there, thus destroying potential evidence that was under the grand jury's subpoena. Despite the hospital's protestations that the destruction was "routine" and "a coincidence," the district attorney, acting on a tip from an informant, intervened on the eve of a further attempt to destroy an additional fifty thousand pounds of hospital documents, salvaging forty boxes of material that could have been relevant. The dean of the medical school at Bexar was cited for contempt of court when it was discovered that versions of the hospital's reports from the investigation of Genene Jones while she was employed there were withheld from the grand jury.[187]

Jones became eligible for parole after serving ten years, but Chelsea's family recently lobbied to keep Jones in prison. She comes up for her next hearing in 2009.

MUNCHAUSEN SYNDROME BY PROXY (MSP OR MSBP)

What was going on in Genene Jones's head? Just about the time Genene was committing her acts, her condition was being given its name: Munchausen syndrome by proxy (MSP or MSBP).

Karl Friedrich Hieronymous von Münchhausen was an eighteenth-century German baron and mercenary officer in the Russian cavalry. On his return from the Russo-Turkish wars, the baron entertained friends and neighbors with stories of his many exploits. Over time, his stories grew more and more expansive, and finally quite outlandish. Münchhausen became somewhat famous after a collection of his tales was published.

Almost a century later, an unusual behavior pattern among young men gained recognition in the writings of nineteenth-century pioneering neurologist Jean Martin Charcot. In 1877, he described adults who, through self-inflicted injuries or bogus medical documents, attempted to gain hospitalization and treatment. Charcot called this condition *mania operativa passiva*.

Seventy-four years later, in 1951, psychiatrist Richard Asher described a similar pattern of self-abuse, where individuals fabricated histories of illness. These fabrications invariably led to complex medical investigations, hospitalizations, and at times, needless surgery. Remembering Baron von Münchhausen and his apocryphal tales, Asher named this condition Munchausen syndrome.[189]

The term *Munchausen syndrome by proxy* was coined by British pediatrician Roy Meadow in 1977, just around the time that Genene was graduating from nursing school. Meadow described the mothers of two children in his practice who were engaging in deception that put their children in the role of patients of their own illnesses; they were using the children as proxies.[190] Subsequently, Meadow collected data on a number of similar cases, noting that often doctors responding to the mothers' convincing complaints harmed the child as a result of unnecessary tests and treatments.

Originally, Meadow identified the mother as a perpetrator and the child as a simple victim, arguing in 1982 that only children up to age six were used as proxies because a child older than that would likely reveal the deception.[191] After two more years of study, however, he discovered cases where an older child could act as an accomplice in its own victimization, feigning the requisite symptoms, with the two involved in a sort of *folie à deux*.[192] Meadow warned that this was a pattern that might be perpetuated even after the child reached adulthood. He described the case of a 22-year-old victim confined to a wheelchair because he was brought up to believe he had spinal bifida and could not walk, despite the fact that medical examinations showed his back and legs to be completely normal.

Meadow found that often the mothers appeared normal on psychological tests, with no disorder apparent to the psychiatrist. He added that the psychiatrists frequently reported that they did not believe the mother could have been practicing the kinds of deception that had been discovered. It is often difficult for professionals to reconcile the incongruity between how caring the MSP mother appears to be and what she is really doing: for example, scratching the child's skin to induce a rash, overdosing the child on medications, or suffocating the child to induce seizures, etc.

Kathryn A. Hanon, an investigator with the Orlando Police Department and a specialist in Munchausen syndrome by proxy abuse cases, writes: "[MSP] offenders are uncharacteristically calm in view of the victims' baffling medical symptoms, and they welcome medical tests that are painful to the children. They also maintain a high degree of involvement in the care of their children during treatment and will excessively praise the medical staff. They seem very knowledgeable of the victims' illnesses, which may indicate some medical study or training. They may also have a history of the same illnesses being exhibited by their victims."[193]

The motivations for MSP appear to be varied. Meadow identified various individual "reinforcers," such as increased social status, improved family relationships, and direct or indirect financial benefit. Another study focused on the acting out of sadistic impulses in MSP, while another motivation frequently found is the attention and sympathy the adult caretaker gains by presenting their child in the "victim" role. Additionally, the adult's dependency needs may be met through the symbiotic bond with the child that is reinforced by the production of fictitious symptoms.[194]

Frequently, the mother blurs the boundary between her and the child by "donating" her own symptoms to the child. The mother may borrow from her own medical history and insist that her child has the same condition. The mother may even reenact her symptoms through the child. A case was reported where a bulimic mother induced vomiting and failure to thrive in her infant through illicit doses of ipecac, apparently administered to make the child conform to her ideals of thinness.[195]

In cases of MSP the mother is inevitably in an enmeshed, symbiotic, mutually anxious, and overprotective relationship with her victimized child. The mother relies on the child to meet her needs, and typical of the role reversal noted in other forms of child abuse, the child serves the purpose for the parent to deal with their own psychological or medical obsessions. A case is described where a mother was so depressed by her deteriorating marriage that she needed to express her sense of being "sick" by making her child sick. Her own depression lifted as a result.[196]

MSP is not necessarily confined to mothers. Everyone has heard of firefighters who committed arson and heroically responded to the fire long before the term MSP came into being. It is not a new story. Nurses like Genene Jones can be susceptible to the same complex.

Prosecutors argued that Genene Jones suffered from a hero complex, basking in the acclaim she received every time she successfully predicted a child was going to have a crisis or every time she brought a child back to life. Or it might have been a simple matter of excitement, being the center of attention—getting the doctor's attention by making her patients sick: classic Munchausen syndrome by proxy symptoms. There might have been some kind of symbiotic transfer of Genene's own fears for her health to that of her patients. Genene was constantly going to clinics and emergency wards with a litany of apparently imagined complaints that were never successfully diagnosed.

But as always with female serial killers, motive is never clear-cut. Genene Jones might simply have been punishing those doctors and nurses she did not like. Doctors who did not follow Genene's advice often found that their patients would code. When the nurse in Kerrville told Genene to move her patient from a bed being prepared for an incoming cardiac patient, the nurse shortly found herself dealing with an arrested child—just as Genene had warned: "Well, I hope to hell this baby doesn't go into cardiac arrest."

Marybeth Tinning—the Killer Mom

In an extreme case of MSP, Marybeth Tinning, a housewife and former school bus driver in Schenectady, New York, is believed to have murdered nine of her own children, including one adopted child, one by one in a period between 1972 and 1985.

Marybeth Roe was born in the small town of Duanesburg, New

York, just outside of Schenectady on September 11, 1942. Very little is known about her childhood. In the early years of her life, her father was away fighting in World War Two while her mother was working. Marybeth was shunted around to her relatives, one of whom tactlessly told her that she was an unplanned baby. When her baby brother later became old enough to understand, Marybeth used to tell him, "You were the one they wanted, not me."

Marybeth was said to have had a tendency to throw tantrums. Her father would chase her up to her room with a flyswatter or a ruler and order her to remain there until she got over her "crying spell." Is this abuse? Marybeth refuted it, saying that he had to use a flyswatter because his hands were becoming arthritic, and was, overall, defensive about her father during her trial. Again, the disciplinary culture of the times makes it hard to judge precisely the degree of physical abuse Marybeth experienced as a child.

Her former schoolmates remember her as a lonely, tiresome child, constantly clamoring for attention. Once, when she was appointed school bus monitor, she handled the authority very poorly, screaming abusively at the little children and attempting to boss around those much older than she. She alienated every child on the bus.

As a teenager, almost nobody can remember her. One former schoolteacher said after her arrest, "I cannot recall anything good or bad about her. So far as I am concerned, she was almost a nonentity."[197]

She was remembered as a plain girl who dressed plainly. A member of no clique who caused no trouble. Not despised and not popular. Ignored. A few students recalled that she was moody and tended to lie and tell exaggerated stories to make herself look more important. She was an average student who graduated high school in 1961 with only one comment next to her name: "Temper."

She had wanted to go to college, but her marks were too mediocre. She ended up doing a series of menial jobs, ending up working as a nurse's aide in a hospital in Schenectady. She married Joe Tinning, a worker in the General Electric plant in Schenectady, just like her father.

In the first five years of her marriage, the couple had two children, Barbara and Joseph. Witnesses recalled that they lived in a duplex house near the plant and that while they struggled to make ends meet, they appeared to be a happy family. Despite the fact that she was described as inexplicably "strange" by her friends and neighbors, most felt that Marybeth "cherished" the children. They were always clean and well-dressed and appeared to have the content demeanor of children who felt loved and secure.

In 1971, Marybeth was expecting her third child. When she was in her seventh month, her father died of a sudden heart attack while at work in the GE plant. Marybeth took the death of her father very badly, weeping uncontrollably at the funeral. Ten weeks later, her third child was born, on December 26, a daughter the couple named Jennifer. The child died a week later from meningitis. Nurses recall Marybeth's reaction as "bizarre." Still in bed, Marybeth cradled the child while pulling a sheet over the two of them. Her entire demeanor was passive. Although the nurses noted that she was behaving in a highly disturbed way, no therapy was routinely given in those times as it would have been today. At the funeral, Marybeth looked dazed and did not cry.

It is believed that the outpouring of sympathy and support for Marybeth was so addicting to her that she then began to kill off her other children. Fifteen days after the baby's death, Marybeth Tinning brought her 2-year-old son, Joseph, to a hospital, stating that he had stopped breathing during a "seizure" of some sort. Suspecting a viral infection, the hospital kept the boy for ten days before sending him home. The same day he went home, Tinning rushed back to the hospital with the boy, claiming she had found him tangled in his sheets, his body blue. This time he was dead. Death was certified as "cause unknown," but cardio-respiratory arrest was suspected.

In March 1973, Tinning took her 4-year-old daughter to the hospital, claiming that she was having convulsions. The doctors wanted to keep the child overnight, but Tinning insisted on taking her home. She returned several hours later with the child, who was unconscious. Her daughter died several hours later. Death was believed to have been from sudden infant death syndrome (SIDS), although the doctors could not definitively certify it as such.

Despite the fact that three of her children had died in a very short span of time, in November 1973, Tinning gave birth to a

fourth child, a baby boy. Three weeks later he was returned to the
hospital dead. Marybeth claimed she had found him lifeless in his
crib. The doctors could not find anything wrong with the child
and certified the death as SIDS.

In March 1975, Tinning gave birth to a baby boy, her fifth
child, who three weeks later was brought into the hospital by Marybeth, with breathing difficulties and severe bleeding from the
mouth and nose. Pneumonia was diagnosed, and a month later the
infant was returned to the Tinnings. On September 2, Marybeth
showed up in the emergency ward with the lifeless child in her
arms. She said she had been driving with the child in the front seat
when she noticed he had stopped breathing. The cause of death
was declared acute pulmonary edema.

By then the emergency room hospital staff was divided. Half of
them deeply sympathized with Marybeth and grieved for her extraordinary, tragic loss of five children in so short a span of time;
the other half hated her and dreaded her every appearance at the
hospital. Why didn't she just stop having children, for God's sake?

* * *

Marybeth began theorizing, some say bragging, that there was a
genetic defect that was causing the death of her children. In her latest pregnancies, her fellow workers began to grumble, "Marybeth's
pregnant, and she's going to kill another baby!"

The Tinnings applied to an adoption agency, which sympathized with Marybeth's "genetic" history and hurried through an
adoption of a baby boy—Michael—whom they received in August
1978. But by then Marybeth had already been pregnant for seven
months.

In October 1978, a girl was born. They named her Mary Frances, and in January 1979 she survived her first "medical emergency." A month later, on February 20, Marybeth went into the
hospital with the dead infant cradled in her arms, claiming she had
found her unresponsive in her crib. Cause of death was declared as
SIDS.

Marybeth lost no time getting pregnant again. On November
19, 1979, she gave birth to a boy, Jonathan. In March 1980, she
brought him into the hospital because he had "breathing problems." The doctors could not find anything wrong with him and

sent him home. A few days later, she brought the child back, this time unconscious. The child was found to have no brain function and died on March 24.

Marybeth responded to all these deaths with a round of dramatic funeral announcements and a gathering of all her friends and relatives. Both her birth and death announcements put her in the center of attention. One relative said, "Every funeral was a party for her, with hardly a tear shed."

On March 2, 1981, Marybeth showed up at her pediatrician's office with her adopted son, Michael, wrapped in a blanket. He was dead. Marybeth explained that she had found him unconscious that morning. The death of the adopted child broke the "genetic" explanation and began to make people think the unthinkable: Could this mother actually be murdering her own children?

In August of 1985, Marybeth, at the age of 42, gave birth to another girl, her ninth child, Tami Lynne. On the morning of December 20, the girl was found dead in her crib. Again, SIDS was certified as cause of death.

A neighbor visited the Tinning home the next morning to see if she could be of any comfort to Marybeth, who she assumed would be grieving over the death of her newborn daughter. When she entered the house, she found Joe and Marybeth in the kitchen, nonchalantly eating breakfast as if nothing had happened

Later, after Tami Lynne's funeral, Marybeth had people over her house for a brunch. Her demeanor had changed noticeably. "She was smiling. She was eating, conversing with everyone there," the neighbor testified, "and didn't appear to be upset."

Sandy Roe, Marybeth's sister-in-law, testified that when she met with Marybeth after Tami Lynne's death, she did not seem upset. "We spoke about Christmas," Roe stated, "She never really talked about the death of the baby. It didn't seem to bother her."

Nine deaths were now too many and authorities ordered an autopsy. It revealed that the child had been suffocated.

Marybeth Tinning confessed to the murder of the infant and to the death of two other children, but not the others. She also confessed that she was attempting to poison her husband. In 1987, Tinning was sentenced to twenty years to life and is up for a parole hearing in March 2007.

Christine Falling—the Killer Babysitter

The case of Christine Falling is another extreme example of Munchausen syndrome by proxy. Christine Laverne Slaughter Falling was born in abject poverty in northern Florida. Even though Christine's mother was 16 years old, Christine was already her second child. Her father was 65 years old. Christine was shuffled around to various relatives and foster parents and grew up to be a grossly obese, dull-witted child suffering with epilepsy. Her friends remember her killing cats to "see if they really have nine lives." Despite this, Christine professed a great love for cats.

Christine was adopted into a religious family, but after several years she became so uncontrollable that at the age of nine she was sent away to a juvenile center. There she was reported to be a compulsive liar and thief. When Christine was old enough to go to high school, she went into a special program of half-days, allowing her to work the other half.

When Christine was 14 she married a man in his early twenties. The marriage lasted six weeks, during which Christine launched a twenty-pound stereo at her husband in an outburst of bad temper. In the two years following the breakup of her marriage, Christine made at least fifty visits to the local hospital emergency room, complaining of troubles such as snakebites, red spots, bleeding tonsils, dislocated bones, falls, burns from hot grease, and vaginal bleeding.

Around the time Christine was 16, she was living with her mother. She was too dull to find work as a store clerk and could only earn a living babysitting for others in her poverty-stricken, tar-paper shack neighborhood.

On February 25, 1980, while babysitting 2-year-old Muffin Johnson, Christine says the girl stopped breathing. Falling rushed the child to the hospital, where her death was declared a result of encephalitis. The hospital emergency staff praised Christine for how well she had handled the emergency, wrapping the child up in a blanket and attempting mouth-to-mouth resuscitation on the way to the hospital.

A year later, Christine was babysitting 4-year-old Jeffrey Davis, a distant relative. After Jeffrey was found dead, Christine stated that she had laid him down for his nap and had not noticed that he had ceased breathing. Death was certified as myocarditis—heart inflammation.

Three days later, Christine was babysitting her 2-year-old cousin, Joseph, while his parents were at Jeffrey's funeral. Joseph also failed to wake up from his nap. Again, death was diagnosed as myocarditis as a result of a virus.

There was some speculation that Christine might carry some type of virus deadly to children, like Coxsackie A8, which is passed from person to person through contact with fecal matter. Doctors found no traces of any virus.

When suspicions were voiced that Christine might be murdering the infants, her relatives and neighbors quickly came to her defense, stating how much Christine liked children and how gentle and caring she was with her charges. Journalists pointed out that infant death was not unusual among Florida's poor, where bad hygienic conditions were common.

Christine Falling next found a job as a housekeeper for 77-year-old William Swindle, who lived in a small cottage. The first day she arrived at work, Swindle was found dead on the floor of his kitchen. Death was presumed to be of natural causes.

Christine stated in an interview, "The way I look at it, there's some reason God is letting me go through this. If God hadn't wanted me to go through this, He wouldn't have let it happen." Christine went back into the babysitting business.

On July 14, 1981, Christine was helping her stepsister take care of her 8-month-old daughter, Jennifer. The two women drove to a government health center where the baby was given an immunization injection. The baby was crying when Christine carried her out of the health center. The two women then drove to a supermarket, where the mother went inside to buy some diapers. Christine was left alone in the car with the crying infant. When the mother returned to the car, the infant was silent. As they were driving home, Christine suddenly told her stepsister that Jennifer was not breathing. They rushed to a hospital, where the infant was pronounced dead.

At the baby's funeral, Christine fainted when the organist played "Precious Memories." Later, she told people that the child had died of "a 'yemonia' sickness."

A year later, on July 2, 1982, a 17-year-old mother dropped her 10-week-old baby off with Christine to babysit for a day and a night. Christine stated that at 4:00 A.M. she had fed the child his formula and that he was well. In the morning, however, she found the baby dead in the crib.

Christine was again submitted to a battery of tests. Thinking that perhaps somehow her epilepsy medicine might have gotten into the food of the infant, a careful autopsy was performed. What it revealed was that the child had been smothered. Christine was charged with three counts of murder.

She confessed, "I love young 'uns. I don't know why I done what I done . . . The way I done it, I seen it done on TV shows. I had my own way though. Simple and easy. No one would hear them scream. I did like, you know, simple, but it weren't simple. I pulled a blanket over the face. Pulled it back. Then again I did the blanket pulling over the face . . . just the right amount for the little one. A voice would say to me, 'Kill the baby,' over and over . . . very slow, and then I would come to and realize what happened."

Christine Falling is serving a life sentence, but she became eligible for parole in December 2006.

6

SEX, DEATH, AND VIDEOTAPE

The Female As Serial Killer Accomplice

There are no histories of female serial killers committing acts as brutal and as depraved as those they commit when they act as accomplices of male serial killers. Over a period of three years, Charlene Williams Gallego and her husband, Gerald Gallego, lured and kidnapped ten teenage girls from shopping malls, parking lots, and roadsides, taking them away in their van. Together they both raped and tortured the girls in a mutual, sadistic, sex slave fantasy, and when they were finished, as Charlene watched or waited in the van, Gerald would murder the girls and dump their bodies in remote fields and desert flats.

Karla Homolka drugged her 15-year-old younger sister and offered her as a "Christmas present" to her fiancé Paul Bernardo while her parents slept upstairs on Christmas Eve. She videotaped Bernardo as he raped her sister. She died during the assault from the effects of the sedatives Karla had slipped into her drink. Karla later videotaped and participated in the kidnappings, rapes, and murders of two more adolescent girls.

In her early twenties, Myra Hindley assisted her boyfriend, Ian Brady, in the rape and murder of perhaps as many as ten male and female children and adolescents, taking photographs of them and audiotaping their cries as Brady assaulted them. Rosemary and Fred West, Judith and Alvin Neelley, Carol Bundy and Doug Clark, Catherine and David Birnie, Cynthia Coffman and James Marlow, Martha Beck and Raymond Fernandez, were all

couples who together kidnapped, raped, and murdered numerous victims.

FEMALES AS ACCOMPLICES IN SEXUALLY SADISTIC SERIAL MURDERS

Of the sixty-two known female serial killers in the U.S. between
1800 and 1995, a third (33 percent) were acting as part of a team
or a couple.[198] In most cases, the female was only technically a
killer by definition of law—she did not physically commit the actual murder, but participated in the crime by luring victims or assisting in their captivity, torturing, sexual assaulting, disposing of
their bodies, or destroying evidence. In the majority of cases, the
female serial killer's accomplice was a male, who ostensibly dominated the female, although there are exceptions to this, as we shall
see. There are also cases of exclusively female teams or lesbian
couples and family teams or cult groups—three or more killers op-
erating together, in which, often, the male once again figures as the
dominant element.[199] The Charles Manson "family" is probably
the most notorious of modern-day killer cults to which young females belonged.

Female-male couples overall remain the most common serial-
killing teams in the United States. It is in these teams that females
approach most closely the stereotypical role of the sadistic, predatory, male sexual serial killer. Until most recently, female accomplices were almost exclusively treated as battered victims of their
male partners and sentencing has often reflected this perception.
While convicted male partners are sentenced to death or life imprisonment, their female accomplices are sometimes released after
serving relatively shorter sentences—the cases of Charlene Gallego
and Karla Homolka are perhaps the most notorious examples of
female killers successfully defending themselves by claiming to be
submissive victims battered by their spouses into participating in
horrendous crimes.

The focus on male dominance in this type of killing team is un-
derscored by the fact that the male is almost always older than the
female partner. He often has an extensive history as a solo sexual
predator before he met the female. The female is, on average,
younger (20 years old at the first murder) than typically solo female serial killers (average age 30).[200] While the male accomplice

might have accumulated a substantial criminal history prior to meeting the female, she often has no history of any substantial criminal activities prior to encountering the male. In fact, in the cases of Charlene Gallego and Karla Homolka, both women had what might be described as a "normal" middle-class upbringing with no signs of any abuse, delinquency, or mental disorders in their histories.

Female-male team killers are usually highly organized, carefully planning their crimes and selecting their victims. Interestingly enough, their joint killing careers are often much shorter than the average for solo females: one year for couples compared to the four-year average for single female serial killers. Frequently, the apprehension of the couple can be attributed to disorganization or loss of control by the male partner. The male partner frequently "imprints" a typical sexual predatory profile on the crime—highly visible victims, public disposal of bodies, the use of knives and guns, rape and mutilation. This is not the typical pattern of the solo female serial killer, who kills "quietly" with poison or suffocation and whose victims frequently are not even recognized by authorities as having been murdered. What is frighteningly striking, however, is the extent and capacity of the female accomplice to journey into the male killing pattern.

Wives and Girlfriends of Sexual Sadists

How does an apparently normal female become a homicidal accomplice? There are few reliable studies on that question. In 2002, Janet Warren and veteran FBI profiler Ron Hazelwood published the results of interviews with twenty former wives and girlfriends of sexual sadists, seven of whom participated in the killing of a total of nineteen victims.[201] Four of the women involved with murderers were actually present at the murder and were charged as accomplices and two can be easily identified as Charlene Gallego and Karla Homolka, even thought the study does not identify the participants by their actual names.

Seventeen (85 percent) of the women in the survey were raised in an intact family and had no previous arrest histories prior to meeting their mates. The other three were arrested for minor charges: stealing a tube of lipstick at the age of fourteen, a typewriter from work, a check from work. Seventy-five percent of the women had graduated high school or had some college education and 50 percent were in either a skilled or professional labor category. Twenty percent were students at the time they met their partner. Only four of the women reported alcohol or drug abuse, suicide attempts, or mental health issues prior to their relationship with the sadist. The researchers concluded that the majority of these women "lived rather conventional, stable, and noncriminal lives, before the initiation of the relationship that culminated in rather radical changes in their behavior."[202]

This is diametrically opposite to what we know of solo female serial killers, who tend to have unstable family histories, relatively poor academic performances, juvenile criminal records, and psychiatric histories.

Other aspects of their childhood histories, however, more closely resembled those of solo female serialists and male serial killers as well. Thirty-five percent of the women reported abusive family discipline, and nearly half (45 percent) reported continual sexual abuse in their childhood; 30 percent identified their father as the abuser when they were between the age of 4 and 8. The sexual abusers included fathers, brothers, a grandmother, an aunt, a sister, and other acquaintances. There were no cases of sexual assault by strangers reported.

When asked why they became involved in abusive and sadistic relationships, 75 percent of the women replied that it was out of love and desire to please the man. Two women described themselves as extremely naïve, two indicated that they wanted to get away from home, and one could offer no explanation.

The majority of women (85 percent) stated that the men were gentle and caring when they first met them, gave them surprise gifts (65 percent), took them on trips (40 percent), and had a "great deal of money to spend on them" (85 percent). When asked why they remained in the relationship, only three of the twenty women attributed it to love; eight said they were either naïve or stupid and hoped their partner's behavior would improve; one for financial dependency and one for emotional dependency. Only seven women reported they remained out of fear of their partner. Asked why they left the relationship, eight said out of fear for their lives; three out of fear for their children's lives; three because their partners were arrested; five for other reasons; and one was left by her partner. Fear appeared to be almost equally (35–40 percent) the motive in a large minority of cases why the women either remained or left the relationships.

The authors of the study characterized these women as "compliant." They concluded that while all the women "express a willingness to exchange their compliance in return for the attention and affection of the sadistic male, there also appears to be a more subtle dynamic operative in which some of the women became assimilated into the sexual aggression of their partner." They believed that all of the women who engaged in this type of behavior did so only after meeting their partner, and in those cases where the women participated in murder, they would not have done so on their own, independent of the men. Alternatively, the authors felt the males would have murdered even if they had not met their female partner—at least in those seven cases out of the twenty.

Finally, the study concluded:

> It is also our opinion that these men and their behaviors do not reflect the more extreme end of the continuum of behavior associated with "wife batterers." Although some men who batter their wives may also be sexual sadists, it is our impression that the majority of them are not.[203]

High-Dominance Women

During the mid-1930s, American psychologist Abraham Maslow undertook a number of studies of sexual behavior related to dominance. He noted that in captivity, the most dominant monkeys engaged in almost constant sex, and that the nature of that sex was often "abnormal"—male monkeys mounting other males and even instances of dominant females mounting males. Maslow concluded that sex in those circumstances was often an expression of dominance, rather than the primates' sex drive. He also noted that when a new monkey was introduced into the group, the lower-dominance monkeys would act extremely violent toward it. Maslow linked these attacks to low-esteem violence of the type seen in human beings.

Maslow then turned his attention to young college girls, whom he interviewed at great length. In 1939, Maslow concluded that female sexuality is also linked to dominance. He found that people fall into one of three categories: high-dominance, medium-dominance, and low-dominance.

High-dominance women were more promiscuous, sexually adventurous, and uninhibited. Medium-dominance women tended to also be very sexual, but would usually relate to one male partner at a time. Low-dominance women had a very low opinion of sex, engaged in it infrequently, and felt its only purpose was for reproduction. Maslow noted that the sexual characteristics of each category had nothing to do with sexual desire—while the sex drive was equal in each type, the amount of sex that the women actually engaged in would differ.

Maslow also discovered that women preferred males who were slightly more dominant than themselves but within the same dominance group. High dominance women rejected most males because of their lower dominance. One woman, who claimed that she could orgasm by simply looking at an attractive male, explained to Maslow that she couldn't orgasm when having sex with some males because they were too weak and she could not imagine herself "giving in to them."

Medium-dominance women found high-dominance men too frightening, while low-dominance women found the medium-dominance man intimidating. Each would mate with slightly more dominant men, but from within their dominance class. For Maslow, this was the normal course of male-female relationships. It is often applicable to homosexual relationships as well.

In certain situations, however, partners from different dominance groups mate, and a very severe dynamic emerges in the relationship. The reason that such mating occurs is usually some type of emotional disorder that leads an individual to seek a mate from a different dominance class. High-dominance individuals with personality disorders, needing to sadistically dominate their mate, may seek out partners in lower-dominance categories. While lower-dominance individuals, also suffering with personality disorders, compelled perhaps to act out an abusive scenario, may seek out higher-category mates. Often the result is a slavelike, almost hypnotic relationship between the two parties, where one partner totally dominates the other, yet both are desperately dependent upon each other. Sometimes, the one vital element that a dominant partner lacks in order to unleash homicidal fantasies is provided by the submissive partner.

Martha Beck and Raymond Fernandez— the Honeymoon Killers

Ironically, the first case study offered here of a serial killer male-female couple defies the norms described above to some extent as it appears that the female in this team might have been the dominant figure in a relationship in which the male thought *he* was the dominant.

Martha Beck and Raymond Fernandez, the so-called "Lonely Hearts Killers" of the late 1940s, became the subject of a 1970 cult film, *The Honeymoon Killers,* written and directed by American composer, pianist, film writer, and director Leonard Kastle. Just completed at this writing is a new movie about them, *Lonely Hearts,* starring Salma Hayek, John Travolta, and James Gandolfini.

Martha Beck was born as Martha Julie Seabrook in Milton, Florida, in 1919. Her father was the editor of a local newspaper, but he abandoned the family when Martha was an infant. Martha suffered from a childhood glandular disorder, which caused her to mature so rapidly that by the age of ten she had an adult's body and sexual drive. Along with that came a weight problem, typical in the childhoods of so many female serial killers.

During her murder trial in 1951, Martha stated that she had been raped when she was 13 years old. When she told her mother about the rape, her mother beat her and subsequently kept a close watch on her, chasing away any boys that came close to her. At school, the overweight girl was ridiculed and scorned. She had no friends and withdrew into her own reclusive world of fantasy and romance, and perhaps darker fantasies as well.

Martha was a clever girl, and at the age of 23 she graduated first in her class from a nursing school in Pensacola in 1942. Despite her academic credentials, her excessive weight made it impossible for her to find employment as a nurse. The only work her nursing credentials got her on graduation was working in a funeral home preparing female bodies for burial. At her trial, she would later say of that period, "In a bizarre fashion, I was learning something about disconnecting through my observation of death."

Lonely Hearts

With the war, however, Martha managed to find work as a nurse in a military hospital in California. There she led a lonely, sexually promiscuous life, picking up soldiers and sailors on leave for casual sex. In 1944, she became pregnant. When Martha approached the father of her child about marrying her, he instead committed suicide.

The pregnant Martha returned to Milton, claiming that she had married a naval officer. She even had a ring to prove it. But shortly before the birth of the child, Martha sent herself a telegram announcing that her husband had been killed in action in the Pacific. The small town mourned for her loss and her story was featured in the local press.

Soon Martha was pregnant again by a Pensacola bus driver named Alfred Beck. He married her, but they were divorced after six months. Weighing 250 pounds at this time, a single mother with two children, Martha settled into a lonely life fed by the true romance and confession magazines of the period. She was employed as a pediatric nurse at a Pensacola hospital, where her excellent performance eventually led her to a series of promotions, culminating with her appointment as the hospital's Chief of Nurses.

In 1947, as a cruel joke, some members of the staff who worked under Martha's supervision sent her an ad to join a lonely hearts club—Mother Dinene's Family Club for Lonely Hearts. Before the age of Internet dating, hundreds of agencies provided services for lonely single people to correspond with each other by mail in search of marriage, love, or companionship. Unperturbed by the joke, Martha placed an ad with the club. She made no mention of her weight or the existence of her two children.

In the weeks that followed, Martha did not get a single response to her ad. She had almost forgotten about it when suddenly, just before Christmas, she received a response from a club member, 33-year-old Raymond Martinez Fernandez. Raymond wrote that he was a successful businessman of Spanish origins in the import-export business and that he lived in New York City on West 139th Street "here in this apartment much too large for a bachelor but I hope someday to share it with a wife." Fernandez wrote that he chose to correspond with Martha because she was a nurse and he knew that she would have "a full heart with a great capacity for comfort and love."

For several weeks, Martha and Raymond carried on a passionate correspondence. Martha sent Raymond pictures of herself in group photographs where the bulk of her body was hidden behind other nurses. She purchased expensive stationery and sprayed her correspondence with perfume; she carried her letters from Fernandez with her everywhere she went. The letters Fernandez wrote in a fine handwriting were refined and romantic, full of literary references. Finally, Fernandez made the most romantic request that Martha could imagine: Would she send him a lock of her hair? The starry-eyed Martha obliged.

Martha, unfortunately, had no way of knowing that Fernandez did not want her hair for a romantic keepsake, but as part of an occult voodoo ritual, which he believed would enslave her in a bondage of love. Fernandez was a full-fledged nut job!

Raymond Martinez Fernandez—the Voodoo Spy

Born on December 17, 1914, in Hawaii, Raymond Martinez Fernandez was indeed of Spanish descent. When he was 3, his family moved to Bridgeport, Connecticut, where Fernandez grew up. He was a frail and gentle child, but he grew to be a well-built and handsome young man. When he was 18 he went to live with his uncle in Spain and there he married a local woman and they had a son. During the Second World War he served in the Spanish merchant fleet and spied for British intelligence.

After the war, in late 1945, Fernandez decided to return to the U.S. to seek work and then send for his wife and two children. He secured work on a freighter bound for the Dutch West Indies. But during the voyage he had a horrific accident—a heavy steel hatch smashed shut on his head with such force that it caused an indentation in his skull and irreversible brain damage. Fernandez was hospitalized from December 1945 until March 1946.

When Fernandez emerged from the hospital, his personality had been completely altered. He was distant and moody and quick to anger. He also lost his hair around the region of his injury, where there was an indented scar on his head. He soon took to wearing a wig to cover it. On his journey to the U.S., Fernandez inexplicably stole a quantity of clothing and items from the ship's storeroom. They were discovered by customs upon his arrival and Fernandez ended up serving a one-year prison sentence in Tallahassee Florida. He cellmate was a practitioner of a fringe type of voodoo and introduced Fernandez to the practice.

Fernandez became convinced that voodoo rituals would give him power over women. Plagued by headaches and violent mood swings, Fernandez began corresponding with women through lonely hearts clubs, always asking for a lock of their hair with which he would conduct a ritual. He would seduce dozens of women, gain their trust, and steal their money, jewelry, and anything else he could lay his hands on. The victims were too embarrassed or ashamed to complain.

The apartment in New York belonged to one of Fernandez's victims—one that had ended up dead. Jane Lucilla Thompson was a wealthy divorcee who began corresponding with Fernandez in 1947. The two met and had a whirlwind romance. In October 1947, Thompson purchased tickets for them to go on a cruise to Spain. In Spain, Fernandez introduced Thompson to his Spanish wife and the three were seen frequently dining together in the town, although what they knew about each other is unknown. On October 7, 1947, some kind of argument occurred in their hotel room, and Thompson was found dead in her room the next morning, apparently from a drug overdose.

Fernandez, in the meantime, returned to New York with a forged will and took possession of Thompson's apartment, ejecting her widowed mother from the premises. Within weeks, he had established correspondence with dozens of lonely-hearts club women, including Martha Beck.

Having performed his voodoo ritual with Martha's lock of hair, Fernandez took the train down to Pensacola on December 28 to meet his intended next victim. Fernandez had assumed that Martha, as a chief nurse, would have money to steal.

If Fernandez was surprised by Martha's appearance upon meeting her at the train station, he did not show it. Martha was pleased with Fernandez's good looks. She took him home and introduced him to her two children. She made dinner that night. After the kids were put to bed, convinced of his voodoo power over Martha, Fernandez made sexual advances toward her. Who really seduced whom is debatable, but for the next day and night they stayed together. At some point, Fernandez must have realized that Martha had nothing of worth to steal; he announced that he needed to return to New York.

Martha had other plans. She professed her undying love to Fernandez and hysterically demanded that he remain in Florida to marry her. Fernandez, no doubt convinced of his own frightening voodoo power, barely managed to extricate himself from Martha's grip by promising to return for her or send her money so she could join him in New York. Martha took this as a proposal of marriage.

While Fernandez was hightailing it back to New York City, Martha was telling everybody in town she was engaged to be married. She even threw herself a bridal shower. Fernandez attempted to break things off with Martha, but she threatened suicide. Fernandez relented and allowed her to visit him in New York for two weeks. Upon her return from her visit, Martha was fired from the hospital—probably because she left her job without permission. There was nothing holding her in Florida.

On January 18, 1948, Martha returned to New York, but this time with her two children and her suitcases. She showed up unannounced at Fernandez's door. Fernandez appreciated Martha's slavish attention to all his needs, from feeding to sex, but he told her he wanted her to get rid of her kids. Without much hesitation, Martha abandoned her children at a Salvation Army hostel on January 25, 1948. She never gave them another thought.

"In the History of the World, How Many Crimes Have Been Attributed to Love?"

Raymond confessed his lonely hearts cons to Martha, who had no objection. She saw it as "her duty" to assist him, and together they read through all the lonely hearts mail to pick a suitable victim for Fernandez. On February 28, 1948, Fernandez married a retired schoolteacher from Pennsylvania he had been corresponding with and brought her back to the apartment in New York. Martha posed as Raymond's sister-in-law from a previous marriage. The schoolteacher eventually heard rumors about the death of Fernandez's "wife" in Spain, and after Fernandez began to berate her for failing to sign over to him her teacher's pension and insurance policies, she returned home, minus her car and a large sum of cash Fernandez appropriated from her.

On August 14, 1948, after marrying and robbing several other women, Fernandez married Myrtle Young from Arkansas, a woman who was younger and more active than the previous victims. This time, Martha posed as Fernandez's sister, but she was so jealous at the possibility of Raymond having sex with his latest lonely hearts bride that she insisted on sleeping in the same bed with the newlywed couple—between them! After a few days of this wackiness, Myrtle began to protest, at which point Martha insisted that he render her unconscious with some sedatives. They then carried the unconscious Myrtle to the bus station and sent her back to Arkansas asleep on the bus, after relieving her of four thousand dollars in cash. Unfortunately, they miscalculated the dosage, and Myrtle died upon her arrival in Little Rock.

Martha and Raymond continued with their scam, but failed for a long time to find any suitable victims. Martha would veto any victim she thought was still young enough to have sex with Fernandez. The couple's money had almost run out when they finally hit upon Janet Fay, a 66-year-old widow in Albany, New York.

Janet Fay was a wealthy woman with a large apartment in the center of Albany and money in the bank. She was a pious Catholic so Fernandez took care to make lots of religious references in his correspondence. On December 30, 1948, Martha and Raymond arrived in Albany. Fernandez introduced Martha as his sister and soon Janet allowed the two of them to stay with her in the apartments. It took Fernandez approximately five days to convince Janet to marry him, clear out her account of six thousand dollars in cash, and agree to go to live with him and Martha in an apartment they had already rented in Long Island. By January 4, 1949, they had arrived by car at the apartment.

What happened after dinner that night is unclear. Apparently Martha walked into the bedroom and saw Janet naked with her arms around Fernandez. She flew into a rage. Janet challenged Martha's right to walk in on them in that matter and began to yell. According to Martha, Fernandez told her, "Keep this woman quiet. I don't care what you do! Just keep her quiet!"

Janet was bludgeoned into unconsciousness with a ball-peen hammer and then strangled using a scarf. According to Martha's testimony, she blacked out and does not recall who did what. Martha and Fernandez then wrapped Janet's body in towels and sheets, stuffed it into a closet, and went to sleep.

The next day they bought a trunk and dumped the body inside, storing it at Fernandez's sister's home. They rented a house, then retrieved the trunk and buried it under a layer of cement in the basement of the home. They cashed Janet's checks and typed letters to her family, declaring her happiness and announcing plans to go to Florida. The only problem was that Janet Fay did not type or own a typewriter, and suspicious relatives notified police.

But Beck and Fernandez were already on the move, having lined up their next victim in Grand Rapids, Michigan. Fernandez was corresponding with a 48-year-old widow named Delphine Downing, who had a 2-year-old daughter, Rainelle. When Raymond wrote to her near the end of January that he was going to be passing through Grand Rapids on business with his sister, Delphine responded that she was looking forward to meeting them both in person.

Delphine was so impressed with Fernandez's courteous ways and considerate manner with her daughter that before the month was out she was having sex with him. Martha, in the meantime observing all this, was seething in a jealous rage. But one morning, Delphine accidentally walked into the bathroom to discover Fernandez without his wig, exposing his baldness and horrific scar. She became hysterical and accused Raymond of deceiving her. To calm her down, Martha convinced her to take some sedatives. But while she was unconscious, her daughter, Rainelle, began to cry. Martha grabbed the child and choked her into silence, leaving her throat badly bruised.

Fernandez was upset, fearing that when Delphine woke up she'd find the bruises on her daughter's throat and call the police. Apparently, Martha ordered Fernandez to "do something."

Fernandez took Delphine's former husband's handgun and after wrapping it in a blanket to muffle the sound, he shot Delphine once in the head as her daughter looked on. Martha and Raymond then wrapped her body in some sheets and buried her in the cellar of her home. Later they covered the hole with a layer of cement.

For two days they prepared for their escape, cashing Delphine's checks and looting her house of property as the 2-year-old Rainelle cried for her mother nonstop. When Martha could no longer stand the girl's crying, she drowned her in a tub of dirty water in the basement. Raymond dug another hole for the child.

After the murder of Rainelle, instead of leaving town Martha and Raymond went to the movies. Shortly after they returned to the house that evening, police showed up at the door, having been called by suspicious neighbors. They were arrested on February 28, 1949, and quickly confessed to their crimes because they were convinced that, since Michigan had no death penalty, if they confessed they would serve a maximum of six years.

To their shock, in March 1949 they were extradited to New York State, which had a death penalty. They stood trial there. Martha and Raymond were tried together in July 1949. Each attempted to defend the other loyally in a manner rarely seen when serial killer couples go to trial. After forty days of sensational and salacious testimony, the couple was convicted and sentenced to death. Interestingly enough, their bond of loyalty was only broken when they were on death row and Fernandez heard rumors that Martha was having an affair with a jail guard. Each began to give interviews to the press accusing the other of being a cold-blooded killer.

Martha Beck and Raymond Fernandez were executed by electric chair at Sing Sing on March 8, 1951, along with two other convicts. It was tradition in Sing Sing that in cases of multiple executions, the weakest convict goes first. Martha was the last to die. Martha Beck's last words to the press before she was taken away to the death chamber were, "What does it matter who is to blame? My story is a love story, but only those tortured with love can understand what I mean. I was pictured as a fat, unfeeling woman . . . I am not unfeeling, stupid or moronic . . . In the history of the world how many crimes have been attributed to love?"

Myra Hindley and Ian Brady—the Moors Murderers

In England, between 1963 and 1965, the young couple Ian Brady and Myra Hindley murdered five victims, children and adolescents, and are suspected of killing as many as possibly ten. While Martha Beck and Raymond Fernandez could be considered profit-motivated serial killers, Brady and Hindley were ushering in the phenomena of male-female, serial sex killer couples. Their kind of depraved, sexual predatory killing had been largely unheard of before in a male and female serial-killing team.

Ian Brady, born in 1938, was the illegitimate son of a cocktail waitress from Glasgow. She led a promiscuous, disordered, alcoholic's life and her custody of Ian was sporadic. Childhood acquaintances recall Brady bullying other children in foster homes, burying cats alive, breaking the hind legs of dogs, and once setting his foster parents' dog on fire. Once he was accused of chopping off the heads of four rabbits at school. Brady was said to have felt superior to his peers and was not known to have friends. Indeed he possessed and possesses today a superior intelligence. (He is a prison author of a recent book, *The Gates of Janus,* an analysis of serial murder.)

Brady did not get in trouble with the law until the age of 11, when he began to engage in petty crimes. He served a four-year probation for burglary, followed by the commission of another burglary, then a year's sentence in a reformatory when he was 15. When he got into trouble again at 17, it was decided that his foster parents could not control him, and he was sent by the courts to Manchester to live with his recently married mother. Brady hated his mother and resented this new arrangement.

Although Brady was a disciplinary problem student, he was very bright and could be charming and manipulative. He took to reading on his own. When he was 19, Brady became fascinated with Nazis. He devoured a pulp genre of semipornographic paperback accounts of Nazi atrocities popular in the early 1960s—lurid stories that focused on forced brothels, naked gypsy women herded into gas chambers, and sadistic female camp guards. Feeling out of step with his fellow British victors over Nazism, Brady taught himself German. He discovered the literary pretensions of Marquis de Sade. Brady concluded that society was corrupt and that priests, in order to subjugate the poor, conceived the idea of God.

At 23 years old he found himself going nowhere while working in a position beneath his capacity, as stock clerk at Millwards, an industrial chemical supply house. It is there he would meet a typist—18-year-old Myra Hindley.

Myra As a Child

Myra has been described as a perfectly "normal" girl who loved animals and children and brightly colored lipstick. Born in the industrial district of Manchester in 1942, to a Catholic father and a Protestant mother, according to reports, Myra was sent to live with her grandmother at the age of 4 when her younger sister was born and her mother decided the house was now "too overcrowded." Rejection by their mothers in childhood would appear to be the common denominator between not only Myra and Ian but with many other serial killers—the storing up of fatal childhood resentment. But the story is not as simple as that. Myra's grandmother apparently lived down the same street as Myra's mother, and Myra moved effortlessly between the two homes.

If anything, Myra was spoiled by her grandmother, who essentially let the little girl have the run of the house. Although somewhat self-centered, Myra lived a conventional childhood, playing in the playgrounds and going to school. She was an adequate student. Adequate and average. Her marks only suffered because her grandmother allowed her to stay at home whenever she claimed she was not feeling well. Everything in her life was adequate and average and normal, until Myra turned 15.

Myra became attached to an underdeveloped 13-year-old neighborhood boy in the role of a big sister or mother. She spent all her spare time and energy taking the boy on walks, playing with him, defending him against bullies, buying him candy. One hot afternoon the boy came by and asked Myra to accompany him to an abandoned reservoir where local kids gathered to play and swim.

Myra was feeling lazy that day and declined. The boy went off without her and drowned that afternoon.

Myra was devastated. For days she walked about as if in a trance and did not sleep. Her only activity was to go door-to-door collecting money for a wreath for the boy's coffin. Some of the women who opened the door recall that there was a strange, aggressive edge to the stony-faced girl at the door. One said:

> She wasn't like a little girl needin' sympathy, she made you feel sort o' guilty, like as if it was your fault [he'd] gone drowned and you better fork out for them flowers or she'd go an' tell on you.[204]

* * *

Myra mourned for the boy for months until her mother came by and forcibly took her black clothing away. Her morbid mourning became a self-centered focus of everything in her life. She could not understand how the rest of the world and everybody else in it could go on with their lives while she suffered her loss. How *dare* they? She behaved like a mother whose child had perished and who will never be able to have another and nobody cared. *Somebody* had to be blamed.

As one of Hindley's biographers writes, "Where a girl of normal sensibilities would have thought—and gone on thinking—as much of the dead boy's tragic cutting-off and of his parents' loss as of her own grief . . . this girl's heart stayed exactly where it was: broken perhaps but immovable, right in the center of Myra Hindley."[205]

Again, perhaps it is grasping at straws in a sea of normality, but death of a childhood friend or sibling is sometimes a reoccurring theme in serial killers' childhood histories: the death of Jerry Brudos's "girlfriend" when he was five (he would go on to murder four women so he could dismember their feet);[206] the death of Genene Jones's adopted sibling and her subsequent morbidity. Yes, it's tenuous, but what else do we have here? Myra was just *so* normal.

Aside from a fervent adoption of the Catholic faith, Myra appeared to overcome her obsession with the boy's death over the next few years. She left school, hardly saying good-bye to any of her friends, and began working as a secretary, moving from company to company in search of better wages and opportunities. She dated but "kept herself for marriage." She went to dances and movies, attended church, did not drink, became engaged, but then called it off.

"Out with Ian!"

In January 1961, she went to work as a typist in the secretarial pool at the Millwards industrial chemical supply company. There she would take dictation from stock clerk Ian Brady. Although the two did not date for a year, Hindley's diary would reveal that she was obsessed with Brady, who appeared to be domineering and arrogant, so unlike all the other boys she had known. He would arrive at work on his motorcycle in a leather jacket, goggles, and helmet and peel off the gear at his desk to reveal his business suit beneath. He was mysterious—nobody knew anything about him. For the first seven months, Myra didn't even speak with Ian Brady.

In her diary on July 23, Myra wrote: "Wonder if Ian is courting. Still feel the same." July 25: "Haven't spoke to him yet." July 27: "Spoken to him. He smiles as though embarrassed. I'm going to change, you'll notice that in the way I write."

August 1: "Ian's taking sly looks at me at work." August 2: "Not sure if he likes me. They say he gambles on horses." August 8: "Gone off Ian a bit." August 11: "Been to the Friendship Pub but not with Ian." August 14: "I love Ian all over again. He has a cold and would love to mother him." August 24: "I am in a bad mood because he hasn't spoken to me today." August 29: "I hope he loves me and will marry me some day."

September 9: "Ian is wearing a black shirt today." October 18: "Ian still ignores me. Fed up. I still love him." November 1: "Months now since Ian and I spoke." November 28: "I've given up on Ian. He goes out of his way to annoy me, he insults me and deliberately walks in front of me. I have seen the other side of him and that convinces me he is not good." December 2: "I hate Ian, he has killed all the love I had for him . . ." December 15: "I am in love with Ian all over again."

December 22: "Out with Ian!"

On New Year's Eve, Ian went over to Myra's house to celebrate with her parents and younger sister. He brought a bottle of German wine and a bottle of whisky, a luxury in those days. The whisky was Myra's first taste of alcohol. In her diary, Myra would write, "Dad and Ian spoke as if they'd known each other for years. Ian is so gentle he makes me want to cry."

January 1, 1962: "I have been at Millwards for twelve months and only just gone with him. I hope Ian and I love each other all our lives and get married and are happy ever after."

There are a few more innocuous entries, but Myra's diary stops as abruptly as it begins. She would have little time left from now on to make diary entries or to contemplate her life. Ian would be keeping her busy.

On their first date, they went out to the movies—*Judgment at Nuremberg,* a Spencer Tracy film about the war crimes trial of former Nazi judges who ordered forced sterilization.

Myra had been obsessed with Ian for nearly a year. In her own mind, she was his long before he even knew it. In real life, Myra lost her virginity to Brady and became his slavish girlfriend. Her recent adoption of Catholicism vaporized as Myra was soon convinced by Brady of the nonexistence of God. She was completely enthralled with the older and "sophisticated" Brady, who read intellectual books, sported black shirts, drank German wine, and was learning the language.

Myra later would say, "Within months he had convinced me there was no God at all: He could have told me that the earth was flat, the moon was made of green cheese, and the sun rose in the west, I would have believed him, such was his power of persuasion, his softly convincing means of speech which fascinated me, because I could never fully comprehend, only browse at the odd sentence here and there, believing it to be gospel truth."[207]

Myra testified that after being seduced by Brady he took little further interest in her sexually. He preferred to have her masturbate him while he inserted a candle in his anus. He also wanted her to have anal intercourse with him, which she complained was painful. She also posed for pornographic pictures that Brady would take, using a timer, of the two of them having sex while wearing hoods. Soon Myra began dressing in neo-Nazi-chic—Ilsa black leather skirts and knee-high boots. She colored her hair platinum blonde.

The Killings

Brady, Myra testified, was fascinated by one particular book—*Compulsion* by Meyer Levin. The book was a historical account of Nathan Leopold and Richard Loeb, two university students from wealthy families who, in 1924, in Chicago, killed a 14-year-old boy. Their motive: To prove themselves superior *supermen*, they decided to commit the "perfect crime." The two supermen were quickly arrested after Leopold dropped a unique pair of eyeglasses at the scene of the crime. During the trial it was revealed that the two were homosexual lovers and that Leopold adored Loeb and slavishly did anything the other proposed.

According to Myra Hindley, about a year and a half into their relationship, in July of 1963, Brady began to talk to her of committing a perfect murder as proof of their superiority. On July 12, Myra and Brady set out to commit their perfect murder. Myra drove a van while Brady followed her on his motorcycle. It was Myra's job to pick up a female hitchhiker. She offered a ride to 16-year-old Pauline Reade, who was on her way to a dance in her bright pink party dress.

Myra told Pauline that she was on her way to the moors—a bleak, windy, grassy expanse of wasteland outside of Manchester. She had lost a glove there, Myra said, and if Pauline would help her find it, she would give her some music records as a reward. Pauline agreed, and the two set out to the deserted moors, followed discreetly by Brady on his motorbike.

At the moors, Brady attacked Pauline, raped her, and cut her throat. Although Myra claims that she was in the van when the rape and murder took place, in an open letter from prison in 1990, Brady stated that Myra also committed sexual acts on Pauline. Afterward, using a spade that they had brought with them in the van for the occasion, Myra and Brady buried Pauline's body on the moor. It was only in July 1987 that her body was found by police and identified by the pink party dress she was buried in.

On November 23, 1963, using the same ruse, they murdered a 12-year-old boy, John Kilbride. Myra stated that Brady raped the boy and strangled him because the knife was too dull to cut his throat. Police were later able to find Kilbride's grave by identifying prominent land features in a photograph of Myra posing on the grave with her dog. Later, when Myra was under arrest and was told that her dog had died in police custody, she remarked, "They're nothing but bloody murderers."

On June 16, 1964, they murdered another 12-year-old boy, Keith Bennett, using the same methods again. After being raped and strangled, he was buried on the moor. His body, despite numerous efforts, including some with the help of Myra and Brady, has never been found.

It would be a year and a half before the couple would kill again. On December 26, 1965, they kidnapped 10-year-old Lesley Ann Downey and took her back to their house. Once there, Brady set up a light and camera and forced the girl to pose for pornographic photographs. Then, turning on a tape recorder to record the child's screams, Brady raped her. According to Brady's 1990 letter, Myra "insisted upon killing Lesley Ann Downey with her own hands, using a two-foot length of silk cord, which she later used to enjoy toying with in public, in the secret knowledge of what it had been used for."

In October 1965, Brady decided he wanted to form a gang, and began to talk with Myra's unemployed brother-in-law, David Smith, about committing a holdup. On the evening of October 6th, Smith dropped by the house and complained of having no money. Brady suggested: "We'll have to roll a queer." He went out and came back later with 17-year-old Edward Evans. Brady struck Evans with an ax and strangled him. He made Smith hold the ax so that his fingerprints would be on the weapon and then the two of them wrapped the corpse in plastic and cleaned up the blood. Myra and Brady then went to bed while Smith wandered off home in a state of shock. At home, he told his wife what had occurred and they immediately called the police.

The next morning the police raided Brady's house and found the corpse in a spare bedroom still wrapped in plastic. In the spine of a prayer book, the police found a key to a train station locker where they discovered the pictures and tape recording of Leslie Ann Downey screaming for mercy as she was being killed. The tapes were played in court during Ian Brady and Myra Hindley's joint trial.

"Instead of the Requisite Lady Macbeth, I Got Messalina."

They were both sentenced to life imprisonment in May 1966 on three charges of murder. Ian and Myra would not confess to the murders of Pauline Reade and Keith Bennett until twenty years later, in 1986. They were brought to the moors to assist police in searching for the bodies, but the body of Keith Bennett was never found.

After their sentencing, Myra and Ian continued to correspond with each other for seven years and even asked permission to be married. In 1972, she seduced a prison guard and attempted to escape. Eventually, Myra began to distance herself from Ian and as she began appealing for probation she began to portray herself as a victim. Ian had beaten and drugged her into submission, she claimed. He threatened to kill her if she did not participate in the murders, she said. Claiming to be reformed, Myra began a vigorous campaign to be released in the 1990s after she had served the minimum time of thirty years before becoming eligible for parole.

The crimes of Brady and Hindley touched so raw a nerve in Britain that even in 1997 their crimes remained a sensitive issue. When in September, British Royal Academy of Arts held an exhibition of young artists' works that included a thirteen-foot portrait of Myra Hindley by painter Marcus Harvey, objections were raised. The family of one of Hindley's victims appealed to the Academy to exclude the work. On the opening day of the show, the portrait was splashed with paint, ink, and eggs and had to be withdrawn for a week for restoration.

At the height of her campaign for freedom, when it looked very likely that she would be successful on a technicality, Myra Hindley died on November 15, 2002, of complications related to a heart attack. She was 60 years old.

Ian Brady, from the beginning, confessed to his crimes and insisted that he and Myra should never be released. He recently wrote a study of serial murder without referring to his own crimes, which was released in the United States by the alternative publisher Feral House, much to the indignation of the British.

When Myra was appealing for her release, Brady wrote a letter to the British Home Secretary Jack Straw in 1990, who was responsible for justice policy, arguing that Hindley should not be released. In it he said:

First accept the determinant. Myra Hindley and I once loved each other. We were a unified force, not two conflicting entities. The relationship was not based on the delusional concept of *folie à deux*, but on a conscious/subconscious emotional and psychological affinity.

Folie à deux is a psychiatric disorder sometimes offered as an explanation for why some women might commit horrific murders in the company of their lover or husband. In the *Diagnostic and Statistical Manual of Mental Disorders (DSM-IV)* it is called "Shared Psychotic Disorder." It is induced by a stronger personality upon a weaker one (the *folie impossée*), but delusions can also occur simultaneously in associated predisposed individuals (*folie simultanée.*)

Brady concluded:

She regarded periodic homicides as rituals of reciprocal innervation, marriage ceremonies theoretically binding us ever closer. As the records show, before we met my criminal activities had been primarily mercenary. Afterwards, a duality of motivation developed. Existential philosophy melded with the spirituality of death and became predominant. We experimented with the concept of total possibility. Instead of the requisite Lady Macbeth, I got Messalina. Apart our futures would have taken radically divergent courses.

Carol Bundy and Douglas Clark—the Sunset Boulevard Killers

In 1980, in Los Angeles, Douglas Clark murdered at least six young women who were either hitchhiking or working as prostitutes in the Sunset Boulevard area. Clark apparently enjoyed shooting his victims in the head as they performed oral sex on him. He would then have sex with their corpses. His girlfriend, Carol

Bundy, accompanied Clark on at least one of the murders, sitting in the backseat of the car and watching as Clark murdered the victim in the front. When she felt that Clark was no longer interested in her, she committed a murder of her own.

Carol's Childhood

Carol Bundy was born in Louisiana in 1943, the second of three children. When she was a preschooler, her family lived briefly in Los Angeles because her older brother began getting small bit parts in movies as a child actor. He can be seen sitting on Santa Claus's lap in the classic *Miracle on 34th Street*.

Accounts of Carol's childhood are truly perplexing.[208] As a small child, Carol appears to have been loved and cared for by her parents. When she began to lose her baby teeth, her father dipped a doll's feet in mud and left a trail of little fairy footprints from the window to her bed. Carol remembers her mother telling the girls magical fairy tales as they lay in bed every night. Even though the family was short of money, one Christmas her younger sister received a bicycle while Carol got her own television set. All the children were intelligent and vacations were often combined with academic goals. When Carol began studying American history in school, the family went off in a car for a vacation in Washington with visits to the Smithsonian and to the New England states. Both her father and mother affectionately called Carol "Petunia."

Unlike her mother and younger sister, Carol was not a particularly graceful or beautiful girl. She was a little chubby with a dumplinglike body and thin, mousy-brown hair. At the age of nine, she was fitted with thick-lensed glasses and at school was taunted with, "Miss Encyclopedia" and "Four Eyes" by other kids.

Something then went terribly wrong at home. When Carol was 8, for reasons she cannot explain, she was suddenly cut off by her mother. Her mother locked her outside the house. As the little girl pounded on the door and windows to be let in, she says her mother said, "Go away little girl. You don't live here. You aren't my little girl."

Little Carol walked two miles to her father's place of work and he brought her home. Her parents fought into the night, and Carol claims that after that it was as if she no longer existed for her mother. Carol's younger sister, Vicky, recalls that their mother was not well mentally. She recalls that their mother was never allowed to administer physical punishment to the children, because once she began beating them, she would not stop until she was pulled off. Vicky said that Carol had already developed a defensive psychology toward her mother. She remembers watching Carol calmly smiling and reading a comic book while her mother beat her around the face and body with a belt.

Carol grew to be an intelligent but withdrawn child who read the dictionary for pleasure and buried herself in science fiction books. When she turned 14, her family life took another seriously nightmarish turn. Her mother suddenly died from a heart attack. That night, her father raped her and her younger sister. He abused her sister for several months and raped Carol one more time. Eight months later, he remarried, and the sexual assaults were replaced by beatings and verbal abuse. It was not long before her father's new wife left him. After a period in a foster home, Carol and Vicky were reclaimed by their father and they settled in Los Angeles. There, in her first year of high school, Carol engaged in promiscuous sex with boys. She learned that while she was largely unattractive, her sexual willingness would quickly attract attention—although that attention would quickly fade and turn to scorn as soon as the sexual encounter was over. When a rumor spread through her school that Carol was pregnant in ninth grade, she dropped out.

At the age of 17, Carol married a 56-year-old drunk. She left him, she says, because he wanted her to prostitute herself. She admitted, however, that she took small sums of money in exchange for sex during this period.

That same year, Carol met 32-year-old science fiction and erotica writer Richard Geis. He liked Carol's intelligence and wit and the two began a casual relationship. Geis edited Carol's first short story, which was published in a mainstream magazine; it was about a policewoman who rode to work on a bus. Carol also put out one issue of a science fiction magazine and published several cartoons.

When Carol was 19, her father committed suicide. Carol began to engage in lesbian relationships, but found that hurt and rejection came as easily from her female lovers as from her male ones.

One day, Carol asked Geis to pay her way through nursing

school. Geis agreed, provided she maintained good grades. In 1968, at the age of 25, after graduating as class valedictorian, Carol was certified as a nurse. In the ensuing years, Carol drifted apart from Geis, but they always remained in touch. (Geis would go on to win the Hugo Award as Best Fan Writer in 1975 and 1976.)

Carol married Grant Bundy, a male nurse at a hospital where she worked. They bought a house in Van Nuys, a working-class district east of Hollywood. During her marriage to Grant, Carol gave birth to two sons, David and Chris. When Carol left Grant in 1979, taking her sons with her, they were 9 and 5 years old.

Carol moved into a squalid apartment complex. The manager of the complex was Jack Murray, a part-time country music singer from Australia. Although Murray lived at the complex with his wife, he quickly began an affair with Carol, who became convinced that Murray was going to leave his wife. As her divorce proceeded, the house that Carol owned jointly with her ex-husband was sold, and Carol came into a large sum of money—about twenty-five thousand dollars. Shortly afterward, Jack told Carol he could not leave his wife to marry her because he had discovered she had cancer. Carol quickly gave Jack ten thousand dollars for his wife's cancer treatment, hoping that he would move in with her. The remainder of her money, she placed in a joint account with Jack, who then proceeded to empty it of an additional eight thousand dollars.

It was around this time that another scavenger moved in on Carol—Douglas Clark. Carol Bundy, who had a fairly promiscuous background and who often engaged in masochistic sex as a submissive partner, was perfect prey for Clark.

Douglas Clark

Douglas Clark was born in 1948, the third son of five children. His father was a senior naval officer and the Clark family lived in Pennsylvania, Seattle, Berkeley, and Japan. In 1959, the father left the navy and went to work as an executive in the private sector as a supply specialist. The family then lived in the Marshall Islands of the Pacific and in India. Neighbors from that period remember Doug as a handsome and normally mischievous child. At home, the only strange incident the family recalled was Doug being caught by his mother at the age of 9 wearing her and his sister's underwear.

As an adolescent, Doug was sent to a private school in Switzerland, while his parents moved on to other locations. His fellow students remember him telling exaggerated stories of his family's wealth. Nonetheless, his classmates were impressed by his ability to seduce older women at the age of 15. This was in 1963 and in Switzerland; the sexual revolution had not yet hit that part of the world, yet Doug was conducting adult sexual relations with local women who lived in Geneva. He was, however, expelled from the school after writing what has been described as a "darkly disturbing" sexual letter to one of the female teachers at the school.

At the age of 16, Doug was returned to the United States and enrolled in a military academy. There he became famous for sneaking women back into the school for sex. He also would tape record and photograph himself having sex with the women and share the photographs with his fellow students. He was 19 when he graduated the academy.

Doug Clark then enlisted in the U.S. Air Force and was trained as an Intercept Analyst Specialist. He was stationed in Alaska, where his job was to decode Russian radio transmissions. It is a mystery why Clark left the air force before his term of enlistment ended. He told various stories: One was that he had reported a senior officer as a security risk; another was that he had uncovered a plot by white officers to kill a black enlisted man. His military records remain sealed and the only information available is that Doug Clark was honorably discharged, was awarded a National Defense Service Medal, and all his post-service benefits were intact. He moved to Los Angeles after his release from the air force.

Nothing in his history so far points to Clark as a potential serial killer. His family background was stable and supportive, he was intelligent, reasonably good-looking, and successful with women, albeit with a few kinks. He was slightly maladjusted with a propensity for bragging, had a tendency to be rebellious, and was very self-centered and irresponsible. However, that hardly made him an incipient serial killer.

When Doug was 24, he married a woman who worked as a

bookkeeper. They started an upholstery business together, but it failed. In one of those strange coincidences, Doug Clark used to buy upholstery supplies from serial killer Angelo Buono, one of the Hillside Stranglers, who with his cousin, Kenneth Bianchi, raped and killed at least ten women in Los Angeles. After Buono was arrested, Clark would talk often of having been in Buono's shop where the tortures and murders had taken place. Later, when he began to kill, Clark dumped the body of one of his victims opposite the site where Bouno and Bianchi left one of their victims.

After his business failed, Doug trained as a stationary engineer and went to work for the City of Los Angeles tending big power plant boilers in San Fernando. For some time he had a drinking problem, but he joined Alcoholics Anonymous and stopped drinking for two years.

Nonetheless, after four years the marriage broke up. His ex-wife was not too specific as to why the marriage ended other than commenting that he was "lazy around the house." She remained friends with Doug after their divorce and when he was arrested she could not believe it. She remembered Doug as a perfectly normal man—aside from them wearing each other's underwear to work one day and his suggesting several times they try wife-swapping and three-way sex. Considering that they were living in California during the early 1970s, those things could hardly be alarming or even unusual.

By the late 1970s, however, disturbing reports began to filter in about Doug Clark from the San Fernando power station, where he worked. His fellow employees always considered him a braggart, but he was also reported to have threatened his coworkers with violence on at least four separate occasions. His rate of absence was also very high—he failed to go to work 15 percent of his working hours. He always had some extraordinarily elaborate excuse for not going to work. Clark was finally fired in 1979, with the supervisors so nervous about the threats that the police were called to his worksite to ensure he did not come back. Clark applied for work as a stationary engineer at the Jergens Soap factory and was hired.

By this time Doug began to focus on seducing especially fat and unattractive women. He would quickly move in with them and establish highly domineering relationships. He often lived rent-free and had the women buy food and cook for him. When they became too demanding he would move on. There seemed to be nothing intense about these relationships. He would not go as far as emptying their bank accounts and stealing their property—it would be little things like borrowing their car and returning it with an empty tank of gas or not paying for the groceries or the long-distance calls. Clark developed his petty exploitation of overweight, unattractive women into an art. Women with those characteristics probably satisfied some pathological need in him.

One night in 1980, in a North Hollywood country music bar, Clark laid his eyes on an overweight woman with mousy hair and Coke-bottle eyeglasses. He asked her to dance, and that is how Doug Clark met Carol Bundy.

"By the Way, I'm Spending the Night with Your Mom."

Although Carol Bundy would have had sex with Clark the night they met, Clark took his time romancing and seducing Bundy. He told her he was an engineer and gazed seductively into her eyes. He was educated in a private school in Switzerland, he said, and was a former military cryptologist. Unlike a lot of serial killers who weaved fantastic stories of their pasts, Clark was open with the truth—the lies would come later.

He told her that he had to go to a dinner but asked for her phone number, appearing to be smitten by her. Carol, who was an intelligent woman, was impressed with Clark's own intelligence. When Clark telephoned the next day, Carol must have felt it was "true love."

Clark went over, played with her two sons, and helped her put them to bed. He told them, to their delight, "By the way, I'm spending the night with your mom."

When he made love, Carol testified, he genuinely attempted to please her. Carol commented that most men attempted to please her in bed, but that it was an effort that required that she heap praise on them. Clark, Carol said, seemed to enjoy pleasing her in bed, spending hours performing oral sex on her, telling her how beautiful and intelligent she was. His soft, intelligent voice was hypnotic, she said. When Clark woke up in her bed that morning, looking like a little lost boy, and asked her if she would mind if he moved a few of his things in with her, she readily agreed.

Before long, Carol noticed that Clark was actually very self-centered. Although he called her "Motor Mouth," he showed no interest in hearing about her life. When she tried to show him a short story she had written, he produced a two-inch-thick manuscript of his own of torture stories in dungeons. Their conversation often focused on serial killers and Clark told her of his encounters with Angelo Buono when he was in the upholstery business.

In the dark, as they lay in bed, Clark began to quietly purr his fantasies into Carol's ear. He would like to subdue and capture a young girl, take her to a country house with a torture chamber, and keep her there as a sex slave, he told her. On another night, Doug told her that throughout history people had been flagrantly slaughtering each other, which she agreed was true. It was fun to kill, Clark said, and any woman who loved him should be willing to kill for him.

On one occasion, Doug told Carol that he was an assassin for the Mafia and asked her to help him kill somebody in Denver. Carol immediately showed her willingness to help by asking him the flight schedules and what she should wear.

In April of 1980, Doug went into a pawnshop and had Carol buy a pair of small .25-caliber handguns. Clark told her that the guns should be registered in her name because he had been convicted of an armed robbery in Indiana and could not possess firearms. This was not true: Unlike many serial killers, Clark had no previous criminal record.

Their fantasies began to spiral. Clark became mildly abusive and disdainful of Bundy, which only made her more desperate for his attention. Tension also had developed between Clark and one of her sons. Carol sent her sons away to live with their paternal grandparents. She sold the children's furniture and began to look for an apartment near Doug's place of work.

"How Am I Going to Turn You into a Murderer If You Are Clumsy and Not Observant."

Police believe that in the late spring of 1980, Clark began to murder young women with Carol's pistols. On May 31, he picked up a prostitute in the Sunset Strip area and shot her dead. He dumped her body in the Los Angeles hills. On June 11, he lured two young teenage girls into his car and shot them both dead. He took their bodies back to a garage he had rented, had sex with their corpses, and photographed them before dumping their bodies near a road in the Hollywood Hills. Clark told Carol nothing until she discovered a bag of bloodied clothing in her car, which she would often loan him. Carol carefully laundered the clothing.

After Doug told her he had killed the two girls, Carol immediately called the police—not to turn Clark in, but to confirm that indeed he had committed the homicides. She questioned homicide detectives over the phone, saying that she thought her boyfriend was the killer but did not want to turn him in unless she was sure. Could they give her a few details of the homicides? The conversation ended when the police switchboard inadvertently cut her call off.

Clark meanwhile took Carol on a guided tour to show her where he had dumped the bodies of the two teenagers and the body of the first victim, who still had not been discovered. He told Carol he had slit the corpse's stomach open to encourage the "wiggly-squirmies" to consume it. He took the prostitute's clothes, which he gave to an 11-year-old-girl in the apartment complex (with whom Carol and Clark were having sex), but kept her underwear for himself.

Carol, correctly, told Clark that he was a sociopath and he took offense at the idea.

Clark focused his trolling on the part of Sunset Boulevard area that straddled Hollywood and West Hollywood—a "ground zero" of the Los Angeles street-hooking scene in the 1980s. This was and is a drab but busy area choked in car exhaust and lined with small, shabby stores, low-income apartments, dingy motels, fast-food joints, and supermarkets, whose parking lots were favored by prostitutes. It was a barren and sun-baked plateau between the downward slope south toward central L.A. and the upward slope north toward the cool of the Hollywood Hills. The prostitutes counted on the rather heavy east-west traffic slowly passing through the area on its way between the various districts of Los Angeles.

On the night of June 20, Clark took Carol along with him on

his next kill. Near a supermarket on Highland Avenue, while Carol sat in the backseat of the car, Clark picked up a prostitute who did not mind servicing him in the car while the fat woman in the back watched. As the girl performed oral sex on Clark, he held up his hand, a signal to Carol to slap one of the small .25-caliber handguns into his open palm. Clark then shot the girl once in the head. She lost consciousness but did not die. Carol jumped over into the front seat as Clark drove away. The girl's head lay in Carol's lap, pumping blood, as Carol stripped off her jewelry and clothes. Using a paper towel, Carol wiped away the blood that was bubbling out of the girl's wound and nose. When they got to the northern fringes of L.A., they rolled her body out into the desert and left her there to die. The identity of the girl, somewhere between the ages of 17 and 20, has never been established to this day.

Carol remembers that she was not turned on nor repulsed by the murder—she said that she was riveted to the scene unfolding before her eyes by an intellectual curiosity. As she stripped off the girl's clothes, she thought how difficult it was to undress an unwilling subject, and that the girl had a good body with nice blonde pubic hairs. When she took the girl's boots off and found a knife tucked inside beneath her cigarettes and comb, she said that she thought to herself, "Dumb broad—the knife won't do you any good tucked away like that."

After the murder, Carol put her intellect behind Doug's killing. She suggested that he carry with him a "kill bag"—a paper sack containing a knife, paper towels, rubber kitchen gloves, and liquid cleanser. He should clean up the car immediately after each murder. She also suggested that he make each killing progressively more gruesome, so that it appeared to the police as if a psychopath was committing the crimes as opposed to somebody "sane" like Clark. Riding in the car with Doug as he trolled for victims, she tagged them as either "bitches, botches, or butches."

To confuse the police, Carol called a rape crisis line and said that her black boyfriend had killed the girls. She also tried to get a black nurse at the hospital where she worked to give her one of her pubic hairs. Doug was going to plant it at the scene of the next murder. The nurse was offended and refused.

Doug Clark was killing at a rapidly accelerating rate. On June 22, he went out again—alone this time. He spotted three prostitutes—two white girls and one black girl in the Sunset area. By then the girls were alert to the killings and only the black girl would agree to enter Clark's car alone. Clark turned her down. Like the typical serial killer, he was only interested in killing within his own race. Clark drove around some more, but could find no victims. He was on his way home, when he spotted one of the white prostitutes walking alone now, a young woman with frosted blonde hair. This time he convinced her to enter his car. As she performed fellatio on him, he shot her through the back of her head. He drove behind a closed restaurant—it was Sunday night. After dragging her body out of his car, he cut and sawed the girl's head off in the parking lot. He put the head into a plastic bag that Carol had so thoughtfully outfitted him with and tossed it into the back of the car—a station wagon. He drove off, leaving the headless corpse behind the restaurant.

Doug then began to worry that the other two prostitutes might identify him. He returned to the Sunset area and began to look for them. He found the black girl and lured her into the car. He quickly shot her dead, stripped her of her jewelry and money, and rolled her body out into the street. Her murder is an example up how a serial killer's every homicide has its own method and madness to it. Clark murdered the black woman only because he felt he needed to eliminate her as a witness. Otherwise, however, she was completely outside his killing profile. Clark then went looking for the third girl, but could not find her.

He went home with the blonde girl's head in the plastic sack, but despite Carol urging him to show it to her, he refused, saying it was "too gross." Carol argued that she was a nurse and was used to working with corpses, it would not freak her out, but Doug refused just the same.

The next morning, Carol found the head sitting on the counter by the kitchen sink, its frosted blonde hair all damp and soggy and the mouth gaping open. Doug told her that he had taken the head into the shower with him and had copulated with it. He stuck the head in the freezer.

After two days, Doug decided they needed to get rid of the

head. Carol went out and bought an elaborate but common wooden chest made in Mexico. At Doug's request, she combed and fashioned the hair with a blow dryer and applied makeup. Then Doug decided that Carol might have left her fingerprints on the head, so he ordered her to scrub it clean in the kitchen sink. Placing the head in the chest, they drove around until Carol tossed it out of the car into an alley. It was found later that night by somebody parking their car.

Doug was angry that she had not picked a better place to throw the chest. "How am I going to turn you into a murderer if you are clumsy and not observant," he snarled at her.

Doug Clark continued to humiliate and deride Carol. She must have believed that her participation in the murders would bring her closer to Doug. As carefully as she packed his lunch for work, she would also pack his "kill bag" when he went out at night to "take care of business." But her slavish attention to Clark's crimes only reinforced the sense of control he felt he had over her, and led him to be more distant and abusive.

The police had linked all the crimes by the .25-caliber bullet used to kill the victims. They accumulated lists of people who had recently purchased .25-caliber handguns, and of course, upon coming to Carol's gun registration, they gave it a low investigative priority—the suspect was not going to be a woman, the police surmised.

Clark was by then talking about killing a hundred women. Police suspect he killed, in addition to the five women described above, anywhere from another two to five more women that summer of 1980. He was eventually charged with six homicides, but several more bodies of young women with .25-caliber head wounds had been found. The bullets, however, had been fragmented and could not be conclusively proven to have come from the weapons he used. Carol, in the meantime, was feeling sexually rejected. She noticed that after every murder, Clark was unapproachable for sex. It was not that he seemed satisfied—he was edgy and in a state of euphoria, but he was withdrawn. He was even more critical and derisive of her. He never beat her, but in Carol's twisted psychology, a beating would have probably indicated to her he still cared. Carol was getting desperate.

"The Honest Truth Is, It's Fun to Kill People . . ."

On August 4, to prove her worth as Doug's mate, Carol decided to commit a murder all on her own. She looked up Jack Murray, the man who had been her lover before Clark and who had cleared out a major portion of her bank account. She convinced him that she wanted to have sex with him in his van. Once inside the van, she shot him in the head. Like a good nurse, Carol checked his pulse and found it to be still strong. She shot him again in the opposite side of his head. She then stabbed him six times in the back. She says she then slashed his anus and carved a piece of his buttocks away to make it look like a "psycho murder." As she slashed away at him, she remembers saying, "If you want a piece of ass, here's a piece of ass."

After carefully cleaning away her fingerprints, Carol realized that the two bullets in Jack's head would link his murder to the others—so she cut his head off and took it home in a plastic bag. Doug then took Carol out driving in the car. He asked her what she wanted to do with the head. Carol replied, "It's got three holes. We could go to a bowling alley and bowl down the lane."

Doug pulled up in front of an industrial garbage bin and told her to throw Jack's head in the trash. It was never found. Instead of being proud of her, Doug was—to Carol's disappointment—even more insulting. He told her she was an idiot for taking the head with the slugs in it but leaving behind the spent .25-caliber casing on the floor of the van.

On Saturday night, after neighbors reported a foul smell coming from a van parked nearby, the police discovered Jack's body. Since witnesses had seen Jack talking to Carol in the North Hollywood bar he frequented, and everybody there knew Carol was one of his ex-lovers, the police questioned her Sunday afternoon. Carol admitted that she had seen Jack earlier the day he disappeared, but denied knowing anything about his murder. When asked whether she owned a .25-caliber handgun, she said that she had owned two, and had sold both in May. No, she did not remember the name of the man she had sold them to.

Doug Clark distanced himself even further from Carol, saying to her, "Whatever you do, don't get me hung for Jack. I didn't do Jack and I don't want to take the rap." After the police left, Carol

Bundy was almost hysterical. She called her sons at her ex-mother-in-law's home in the north. She talked with them for about twenty minutes. She also called Dick Geis, and asked if she could go up to Oregon to stay with him. He told her he did not want to see her. Doug, in the meantime, had gone out with another woman without telling Carol where they went. She felt alone and abandoned that Sunday night.

It is often some minor thing that finally makes these cases break open. In the case of Doug Clark and Carol Bundy, it was Carol waking on Monday morning and discovering she had run out of Librium, a tranquillizer she took. After driving Doug to work that morning, with him complaining about her the entire drive and calling her "Motor Mouth" for telling the police too much, Carol arrived at the Valley Center Hospital where she worked as a nurse.

At Valley Center she was already considered by her fellow workers to be weird and annoying, but satisfactorily competent at her job. That day her fellow nurses noticed that Carol Bundy was in a state of agitation. Late in the morning, Carol cornered another nurse and babbled out to her the entire story of the murders in all their gory detail. As Carol recounted the minute nuances of cutting off Jack's head but forgetting to pick up the shell casings, the stunned nurse noticed that Carol's hand kept groping around inside the pocket of her uniform. The nurse became frightened and thought that Carol might have a handgun in her pocket. Finally, Carol finished her story and said she was going home to gather up the evidence of the murders and turn herself in to the police.

The nurse ran off to call security, and as police descended on the hospital, Carol Bundy calmly went down to the basement, changed her uniform, and oblivious to the panic upstairs, left the hospital unnoticed. Once home, she gathered together the clothes of the victims, some of the bullets, photographs, and other evidence (the handguns were hidden at Jergens where Doug worked) and tried to call the police.

Remarkably, as Bundy dialed number after number, she either got busy signals or answering machines or was told to call other numbers. She finally located a homicide officer from a district far away from where the crimes occurred, who was only vaguely familiar with the murders. He had not even read about them in the newspaper. Nonetheless, he held her on the line as she related to him everything she knew. When he asked her why she was turning in her lover, she replied, "Oh, for quite a hell of a long time he's been treating me like shit. It's been worse and worse and worse. And now I've done one on my own. Done one completely on my own and he's falling apart over it and I'm just plain sick of it."

The detective asked her if she felt bad about the murder she had committed. Carol asserted, "The honest truth is, it's fun to kill people and if I was allowed to run loose I'd probably do it again. I have to say—I know it's going to sound sick, it's going to sound psycho, and I really don't think I'm that psycho—but it's kind of fun. Like riding a roller coaster."

Later Carol wrote to Richard Geis from prison:

> Dick, here is one simple truth. It is very easy to kill. We all have the potential. Only social conditioning from childhood prevents each of us from being murderers . . . I have been told that murder is the easiest of crimes to get away with. I believe it. If I hadn't confessed . . . ah, well. Too late. Too late.

As soon as Carol Bundy finished talking on the phone, the police arrived. They had been alerted by her confession at the hospital. As Bundy was already a suspect in the Jack Murray killing, she was quickly picked up. Later that day, Doug Clark was arrested coming out of the Jergens factory. The two handguns were found hidden in the factory.

Doug Clark, after acting as his own defense counsel à la Ted Bundy, was sentenced to death in 1983. He still sits on death row insisting that Carol and Murray committed all the murders and that he was framed.

Carol pleaded guilty and received two consecutive terms of twenty-five years to life for the murders of the unknown prostitute and Jack Murray. She would have been first eligible for parole in 2012, when she turned 69 years old, but she died in prison at age 61 on December 9, 2003.

No sooner had the Los Angeles police arrested Doug Clark and Carol Bundy in August 1980, when the police in Sacramento, California, got a strange call early in the morning of November 2, 1980. College students were out at a formal dinner that night, following a Founder's Day dance. As 22-year-old Craig Miller and his date, 21-year-old Mary Beth Sowers, left the restaurant, they were followed by a friend, Andy Beal, who was intending to play a practical joke on them. In the parking lot, before he could pull the joke, he watched as the couple was approached by a young blonde woman. For some strange reason, they accompanied the woman to her car and got into the backseat. Andy Beal then ran to the car and laughing jumped into the driver's seat. He was surprised to see that sitting in the dark on the passenger side was a sullen man. Looking back at the faces of his friends, he saw that something was wrong. Suddenly the blonde woman leaned in through the driver's side, slapped his face, and shrieked at him to get out. Shaken, Andy climbed out of the car and watched the woman get in and screech away with his two friends. He had, however, the presence of mind to note down the license plate number of the car.

When the police ran a check of the license number, they found it registered to Sacramento resident Charlene Gallego, a 24-year-old college graduate, married, from a wealthy and respectable Sacramento family—seven months pregnant. When interviewed, she told the police that she was alone that night and nobody had touched her car—it was parked in the driveway. Not knowing whether any kind of foul play had actually occurred in the parking lot and seeing the pregnant Charlene as not particularly suspicious, the police left. The kid must have been mistaken when he wrote the license plate number, or perhaps he had just had one too many to drink and nothing had happened, the police thought. But within hours, the body of Craig Miller was discovered in a field, shot in the back of the head three times with a .25-caliber pistol.

Police then ran a check on Charlene's husband, Gerald Gallego, and discovered an individual with a lengthy record of sex offenses beginning at the tender age of 13, when he had raped a 7-year-old girl. Gallego, in fact, was wanted for sodomizing his 14-year-old daughter and raping her friend. Moreover, he had a criminal pedigree going back to his father—a man who had killed two law-enforcement officers and was the first person executed in Mississippi State's gas chamber when Gerald was 9 years old.

The police rushed back to the home of Gerald and Charlene Gallego, but found both them and the car gone. The two had been kidnapping and killing young women, often two victims at a time, since 1978.

The bisexual Charlene tested in prison at an IQ of 160. She was a talented violin player and college graduate from a wealthy California family. One evening, while buying drugs at a club, she met Gerald Gallego. Charlene was instantly attracted to Gallego's "outlaw" persona and married him.

Once again, she was probably a high-dominance woman who needed a high-dominance man—Gerald was perfect. He fantasized along with Charlene about keeping virginal young sex slaves at a remote country house. On his daughter's (from another marriage) fourteenth birthday, he sodomized her and raped her friend as Charlene watched.

Things went wrong when one night the both of them seduced a 16-year-old go-go dancer. The three-way sex was fine, but the next day, after coming back from work, Gallego found Charlene and the dancer having sex together. He became enraged, threw the girl out, and stopped having sex with Charlene. Charlene then suggested that they kidnap, rape, and murder young girls.

Killing between September 1978 and November 1980, they often kidnapped girls from Sacramento shopping malls. They also killed in Nevada and Oregon, often beating in the heads of their victims with a tire iron or shooting them with a .25-caliber pistol. They buried alive one victim, a pregnant woman. In three instances, they kidnapped two women at a time. Gerald shared the victims with Charlene, who liked to bite one girl as another performed oral sex on her. She bit the nipple off one of the victims.

At one point, Charlene got into a gun fight with Gerald when he started raping their two young teenage captives in the back "without waiting for her" while she was driving the van. The couple shot at each other until Charlene grazed Gerald's arm.

The were eventually apprehended, and Gerald Gallego was sentenced to death, while Charlene Gallego, in a familiar pattern, received a sixteen-year sentence in exchange for testifying against Gerald.

While in prison, she continued her education, studying a range of subjects from psychology to business to Icelandic literature. "She's a pretty intellectual woman," said Nevada District Judge Richard Wagner, who was the lead prosecutor in Gallego's Nevada trial. "She has a phenomenal mind, which made her a tremendous witness . . . She had almost a photographic memory about the victims, down to their shoes and clothes."

On July 17, 1997, Charlene was set free and reverted to her family name of Williams. In an interview, she claimed that she was as much a victim of Gallego as the other girls: "There were victims who died and there were victims who lived. It's taken me a hell of a long time to realize that I'm one of the ones who lived."

Charlene said of Gerald Gallego, "He portrayed to my parents that he was a super family guy. But soon it was like being in the middle of a mud puddle. You can't see your way out because he eliminated things in my life piece by piece, person by person, until all I had around me were members of his family, and they're all like him, every one of them. . . . Prison was freedom compared to being with him."

Gallego recently died of cancer in the midst of his attempts to get a new trial. On November 20, 1999, a Nevada farmer uncovered a shallow grave containing the bodies of 14-year-old Brenda Judd and 13-year-old Sandra Colley, missing since 1979, two of the ten suspected victims of Charlene and Gerald.

* * *

In the psychopathology of male-female serial killer couples, certain distinct patterns are clear. One is that in most of the cases described here, the male partner has a fantasy of holding virginal sex slaves at a remote location—the "Collector" fantasy. The female partner is harder to typify. There seems to be a distinct hatred or anger toward fellow women, mixed with homosexual or bisexual tendencies. The murders were all sexualized by the women, either through direct sexual contact with their victims or through sex with their killer mates.

In each of the cases, even though there was evidence that the female partner contributed equally to the crimes—or even exceeded her male partner—the female always received a lighter sentence. Society is not ready to recognize that a female can be as potentially sadistic and murderous as a male—especially within a male-female couple context.

Karla Homolka and Paul Bernardo—the Ken and Barbie Killers

In Ontario, Canada, the case of Paul Bernardo and his wife, Karla Homolka, was hauntingly similar to the Hindley-Brady, Gallegoses, and Bundy-Clark killings. The difference was that they had more advanced technology with which to document the rapes and tortures of their victims: They filmed everything on videotape, leaving behind a horrific record of exactly what an organized, sadistic serial killer does to his victims. In criminal history, never have homicidal videotapes as detailed and extensive as those recorded by Homolka and Bernardo been entered into evidence—not even the notorious videotapes of Leonard Lake and Charles Ng.

Paul Bernardo and Karla Homolka have been called the "Ken and Barbie Killers," after the perfect little dolls that so many girls play with. When arrested, he was 28 and she was 22 years old. Paul Bernardo was blond, blue-eyed, tall, athletic, intelligent, and handsome with what many described as an angelic face. She, too, had a head full of thick blonde tresses, was blue-eyed, smart, petite with a well-proportioned body, and good looks. He was a university-educated accountant and she was a recent high school graduate who worked as a veterinarian's assistant. Both were brought up in anonymous, middle-middle-class suburbs, attended typically middle-middle-class suburban schools. They frequented typical high school and college student events and parties. Everything about them was "middle-middle" typical—their tastes and styles were not too high class and not too low class. They were upscale, shopping-mall mediocre.

Paul and Karla were married in a lavish, but again typically mediocre-in-taste ceremony that could have, and probably did, come from the pages of a popular bridal magazine. They left the church in a horse-drawn carriage and honeymooned in Hawaii.

They settled in one of those typical, wealthy, middle-sized towns that dot the fertile belt of southern Ontario known as the "Golden Horseshoe" between Toronto and Niagara Falls near the border with the United States. They rented a perfect little lakeside Cape Cod–style house for twelve hundred dollars a month, about thirty minutes from Niagara Falls, and furnished it with typically Canadian pine furniture.

Atypically, by the time Paul and Karla left for their honeymoon, they had already raped, tortured, and murdered two adolescent girls, including Karla's younger 15-year-old sister. Both crimes they recorded on videotape. So perfectly respectable, attractive, and inoffensively middle-class was the couple, that nobody suspected them of anything as schoolgirls began disappearing in the region—only to be found dismembered and encased in blocks of cement by a pond or dumped in a ditch naked.

Karla Homolka—the Mean Girl

Karla Homolka was born in 1970 and brought up in St. Catharines, an affluent town of about 130,000 people, nestled between Toronto and Niagara Falls. The town is nicknamed the "Garden City" because of the lucrative local agricultural industries—wine grapes, apples, and vegetables. Karla was the oldest of three sisters. Her mother was Canadian—a hospital administrator. Her father immigrated from Czechoslovakia and was a dealer of lamp fixtures and black velvet paintings—the kind that feature Elvis Presley or the Beatles.

Very little is known about Karla's home life. Her friends remember her as a bossy little girl who was, with no irony intended, called "The Princess." She had long golden blonde hair and was a very intelligent child. She had a huge collection of Barbie dolls and read children's mystery novels like Nancy Drew and the Hardy Boys. She wanted to be a detective when she grew up, she said. Her childhood friends remember her as always being extremely dominant in their friendships.

Many said that in high school Karla was the cleverest, prettiest, and most popular. Her only weakness was her lack of athletic aptitude. Yet Karla often appeared to be unhappy. Her marks slipped and she seemed to be obsessed with boys—nothing else interested her. She seemed to urgently want to get married and leave school, and she went through several boyfriends.

When Karla was 15 and 16, she would dye her hair in garish punk shades of red and black. She was on the Pill and having sex, but so were hundreds of thousands of teenage high school girls. There were arguments at home, but nothing serious. When she was 17 she wanted to visit a boyfriend who had moved to Kansas, but her parents refused permission for her to go. She booked a flight and went anyway, but made sure to phone her parents when she arrived there to tell them she was coming back in two weeks and not to worry.

To one girl, Karla showed tiny little scratches on her wrists and said that she had attempted suicide, but the girl, who herself had seriously slashed her wrists, recalls that she did not think Karla was serious about taking her life—it was attention she wanted.

There were a few dark tones to her adolescence. In one student's yearbook she wrote, "Remember: suicide kicks and fasting is awesome. Bones rule! Death Rules. Death Kicks. I love death. Kill the fucking world."

Another girl recalls Karla once whispering in her ear as they sat in the school cafeteria, "I'd like to put dots all over somebody's body and take a knife and then play connect the dots and then pour vinegar all over them."

Karla read voraciously and her reading material during her high school years reflected a gothic taste: true-crime, occult, horror, and fantasy books were among her favorites.

Karla and her *Mean Girls* friends formed a little clique they called EDC—Exclusive Diamond Club. The objective, they said, was for each member to find a rich, slightly older, good-looking man, get a diamond, marry, and live happily ever after.

Other girls remember Karla simply as a bubbly, cheerful girl, who talked about going to university and becoming a veterinarian. She worked part-time in a pet store and liked animals.

Overall, nothing has been uncovered in Karla Homolka's adolescent history that is particularly different from the lives of millions of typical teenagers. No trace of abuse, family dysfunction, rape, abandonment, or trauma. Everything was middle-middle typical.

In 1987, when Karla was 17, she and several of her friends drove to Toronto to attend a pet-store convention during a weekend. They booked into a hotel in Scarborough. That Friday evening, after going drinking and dancing, Karla and her friend came back to their room after midnight. They were on the make because they brought back two men with them, but it didn't work out—they sent the men on their way. Karla had changed into her pajamas and was ready for bed when she suddenly had the urge for a sandwich. She called room service but was told they were already closed. However, the restaurant downstairs was still open. Karla, dressed in her pajamas, and her friend went down to the restaurant for a late-night snack. That is where she met Paul Bernardo.

"Bastard Child from Hell."

Hindsight can be cruel, but if there was nothing in Karla's past that signaled a potential for becoming a serial killer, everything about Paul Bernardo did. On the surface, Paul Bernardo seemed as middle-middle typical as Karla. Paul was born in 1964, the youngest of three children. His father, Kenneth Bernardo, was a successful accountant, while his mother, Marilyn, was a housewife, who in her spare time was an active Girl Guide leader.

Both came from middle-class backgrounds from the prosperous rural town of Kitchener-Waterloo, home of one of the world's leading computer science universities, located in the heart of Ontario's Mennonite farming country. Marilyn's family traced their origins to the United Empire Loyalists—British citizens who rejected the revolution in 1776 in the Thirteen Colonies and moved to Canada to become a ruling elite there. Her father was a lawyer and a colonel in the Canadian Army, who had distinguished himself during the war in Italy. Kenneth Bernardo's father came from more humble roots: He emigrated from Portugal, but once in Canada, he had built a highly successful tiling company that specialized in fine marble.

After they got married, Kenneth and Marilyn Bernardo settled in a wealthier part of Scarborough, a suburb east of Toronto built during the 1950's boom in Canada. Their house had a swimming pool out back—a luxury, considering that Canada's summers barely lasted two months.

Beneath this optimistic family portrait lurked dark shadows.

When Paul was a child, his father had repeatedly sexually abused Paul's 9-year-old sister. On one occasion, neighbors called police after catching him peeping into their windows dressed in his pajamas. This places Paul into a category that 50 to 53 percent of serial killers in the FBI study can be found in: parents with criminal and psychiatric records. (In a bizarre twist, on the same day that Paul was arraigned in court after his arrest, his father, Kenneth, by then aged 58, was appearing in an adjoining courtroom for his sentencing hearing after pleading guilty to repeatedly and indecently assaulting his daughter 20 years earlier, between January 1969 and June 1974. She pressed charges as an adult after she became convinced that he was molesting her own daughter.)[209] Witnesses recalled that the Bernardos' home life was "stormy" and that husband and wife had separate bedrooms. Paul's mother grew obese, passive, and depressed.

When Paul was about 5 or 6 years old, he apparently ran away from home and remained absent for several days. Paul's older brother, David, said that nobody in the family even asked him where he had been.

Like many serial killers, Paul Bernardo had an early illness—a form of aphasia as a result of a lack of oxygen to the brain during birth. As a result, he did not speak until the age of 5 and for several years following he stuttered and had speech impediments.

Like Ted Bundy, Bernardo learned in late adolescence that his origins were not those he had thought they were. He was 16 when apparently his mother, after another in a series of bitter arguments with his father, burst into Paul's room with a picture of a man and declared that he was Paul's real father. She would refer to her son as the "bastard child from hell." In a recent interview, his father confirmed that Paul was not his biological son, but said, "That's his hang-up. That's never been a hang-up with me."

As a child in school, Bernardo was isolated and tormented by other children, who chanted "smelly Barnyard, dirty Barnyard." Nonetheless, Paul grew up to be a popular and athletic youth in his teens. He was remembered as a popular summer camp counselor, who was very kind, gentle, and helpful to children. Again, everybody remembered his angelic face.

Bernardo was, however, developing a secret life. Since about the

SEX, DEATH, AND VIDEOTAPE

age of 10, he was collecting women's lingerie advertisements, although so were probably millions of other 10-year-old boys. But there were other things—the neighbors caught him window-peeping several times, and on one occasion the police were called. Friends recall that by the time Bernardo was in his late teens, he was an avid aficionado of pornographic videos and slasher horror movies.

When he was 19, he entered the University of Toronto to study accounting like his father. His girlfriend from that period testified that he would enjoy having rough sex with her. He would take her in his car to deserted factory parking lots, choke her with a cord, force anal sex on her, and order her to masturbate with a wine bottle. By the age of 19, he was, as the popular saying goes, "one sick little puppy."

During his college years, Bernardo began supplementing his income by smuggling tax-free cigarettes from Niagara Falls, New York, into Canada. He became intimately familiar with the area that lies between Toronto and the Falls. He also began to develop a sense of himself as an "outlaw."

"You Have Opened My Eyes to a New Way of Thinking and Being."

On night, Bernardo and a friend walked into a hotel restaurant for a late-night coffee. The instant he laid his eyes on the blonde in the pajamas he immediately went over to her. They chatted for about an hour, Bernardo spinning stories of his business ambitions. Homolka was enthralled by the handsome, aggressive, confident, blond, 23-year-old Paul; she called him the "big, bad businessman"—like in "the big, bad wolf." Homolka and her friend invited the two men upstairs to their room. An hour later, Bernardo and Homolka were in bed together. They had mated immediately in an animal lust for each other.

Psychiatrists are still trying to fathom the relationship of Bernardo and Homolka. Karla was a dominant, aggressive young woman, yet she became totally submissive to Paul. Karla was no doubt a high-dominance personality, and believed that she needed a strong and willful man in her life. The psychopath Bernardo matched the bill. The final link in the formula was Homolka's total lack of any sense of morality. Despite her intelligence, for whatever reasons, she lacked a moral compass. When she came together with the psychopathic, amoral Bernardo, and went along with him into his fantasies, the path to murder was laid.

By the time Paul Bernardo arrived in St. Catharines the next weekend to see Karla, she had told all her Exclusive Diamond Club friends that she had met her Prince Charming. He called at her home and met her parents and then the two went out to see a movie: *The Prince of Darkness,* a horror film about the unleashing of an evil spirit into the world. Afterward, Karla had invited some of her friends home for a small party. All who met Bernardo agreed with Karla—he was a dream boy.

During the party, Karla and Paul slipped away into her bedroom upstairs. When they closed the door, Bernardo noticed Karla's jean jacket hanging on the handle: It had a pair of handcuffs sewn to it as decoration. Karla told Paul that he could use those on her. He handcuffed her to the bed and they had sex.

Paul was bright and charming with her parents and appeared to be an attentive boyfriend. He called Karla his "Little Princess." He would visit every weekend and Wednesday, bringing flowers and gifts. Homolka would always be ready for him with a syrupy-sweet little note. Hundreds of these notes would be entered into evidence later at his murder trial. After some time, Homolka convinced her parents to allow Paul to spend the night at their house on the couch, so that they could spend more time together during his visits from Scarborough. During the night, Paul would sneak up to Karla's bedroom and make his way back down to the couch before her parents got up.

Karla noticed that Bernardo seemed to want to have less vaginal sex with her and preferred that she fellate him instead. Whenever they had vaginal sex, Bernardo seemed to be unable to climax. They would drive to a popular fishing location, Lake Gibson, and there Bernardo would have Karla perform fellatio on him in the car.

One night at her house, Bernardo rose at night and went around the back to watch Karla's 12-year-old sister Tammy undressing to go to bed.

In December 1987, two months after he met Karla, Bernardo committed what is believed to be the first of a series of rapes in

Scarborough. It was every woman's nightmare: The victim got off the bus near her home late at night. She was jumped by a stranger from the dark, dragged out of view, raped, and sodomized. This means that by the time Karla had met Paul, or shortly afterward, he was already committing brutal rapes. When arrested for murder, Paul was also charged with twenty-three rape-related counts that occurred in Scarborough.

In the meantime, Bernardo was letting his true colors show to his 17-year-old girlfriend, Karla. He now ordered her to call herself names when she gave him fellatio: "cocksucker, cunt, and slut." They had to be in that precise order. In the car at Lake Gibson, Karla would have to say as she began fellating him, "My name is Karla. I am 17. I'm your little cocksucker. I'm your little cunt. I'm your little slut."

Then in December, Bernardo announced that since Karla was not a virgin when they met, they should have anal sex. Karla refused and this became a source of stress in their relationship for two months. Bernardo demanded that Karla invent a name for his penis. She came up with "Snuffles."

A letter sent by Karla to Paul included a love coupon, which stated: "The bearer will receive one cute little blonde 17-year-old to put on her knees between his legs and satisfy his wishes." In an accompanying note, Karla wrote:

Dear Paul,

You're a dream come true. You are the best, my Big, Bad, Businessman. I've been fantasizing what playful things to do with your body all day. Your strong chest. Your muscular arms. Your beautifully shaped legs. Your hard, flat stomach. And Snuffles, oh wonderful Snuffles. The pleasure I get from touching, from licking, from sucking Snuffles, is indescribable.

You know what I love? Having you stick it inside me and making me gasp for air while my parents are in the next room. I love it when you shoot it into my mouth. I want to swallow every drop, and then some. The power you wield over me is indescribable. When we sit together on the couch I have to use all my strength to keep from ripping off your clothes. You make me so horny . . .

I love you an amount I never thought possible. Words can't

even come close to expressing my feelings. With you in my life, I feel complete. Whole. With you by my side nothing can go wrong. You have opened my eyes to a new way of thinking and being. I will love you forever, no matter what.

Karla XOXOXO

In the car at Lake Gibson, Karla was then expected to follow this script: "I love having Snuffles in my mouth."

"And what are you?"

"Your little cocksucker."

"What else?"

"Your little cunt. Your slut. I want to suck on Snuffles all the time."

In February 1988, after Paul Bernardo threatened to drop her, Karla finally agreed to anal sex. He brought Karla back to his parents' house while they were away on vacation. As usual, by the time Karla had agreed to anal intercourse, Bernardo was ahead of her. Now he wanted to take pictures as well. Setting up his Polaroid camera, he had Karla masturbate with a wine bottle. He then had her get on the bed and he penetrated her anally. At one point, he tied a black electrical cord around her neck and yanked on it. In his hand, he held an eight-inch-long hunting knife. He told Karla not to worry, that the two props excited him more. The dated photographs were later entered into evidence.

Instead of running as far away from Bernardo as she could, Karla actually became excited by these games and told Paul she hoped that he would marry her.

In the autumn of 1988, about a year after they had met, Homolka said that Bernardo struck her for the first time. He told her he wanted her to wear a dog collar, and when she laughed, he slapped her. The next time they had anal sex, Karla was tugging on a dog leash while Bernardo tenderly whispered, "You're my little mutt." That was shortly followed by Bernardo's demand for "anal-ingus" and that Karla now also add "ass-licker" to her vocabulary of scripted words.

In one of Homolka's cards to Bernardo (which she wrote and mailed almost every day), she wrote—around her first anniversary:

Thanks for the best year of my life. You enriched my life beyond belief . . . I want to suck Snuffles and get him so hard that he can't take it anymore. And then I want to ease your pulsating penis into my tight little cunt. Your little girl wants to be abused. She needs her Big Bad Businessman to dominate her the best he can.

Love, Kar

In 1989, Karla Homolka graduated from high school. She wanted to become a policewoman and was planning to enter the Faculty of Criminology at the University of Toronto. Bernardo told her that he did not want "his wife" working in a job as dangerous as a police-woman's. Thus instead of school, Homolka went to work as an assistant in a veterinarian's office in St. Catharines. She had thought first of going to Toronto, but by then, Bernardo was smuggling cigarettes almost full-time, and told her that he wanted to live in the St. Catharines area, conveniently in the middle between the U.S. border and Toronto.

During Karla's graduation party, Bernardo displayed another side of himself. He drunkenly accused some of her fellow male students of flirting with Karla and got into a fight with several of them. Although they were members of the school football team and were quite athletic, Bernardo showed no fear in fighting them. Despite being outnumbered by big football players and receiving a few blows that bloodied his nose, Bernardo continued to throw punches and seemed to enjoy the confrontation. Unlike many serial killers, Bernardo was not afraid or physically meek in the presence of other males.

Bernardo wanted to produce a rap record and recorded an album he titled *Deadly Innocence* in his home studio. During his trial, the judge refused to allow the lyrics of the songs to be entered into evidence. In the eyes of the law, the poetry or lyrics that one writes do not necessarily reflect the actual state of mind of the artist. Perhaps . . . but here is what Bernardo wrote anyway:

You think I'm innocent?
But behind this I'm packing a lot of deadliness
So come at, come at me
I got a fucking nice face

I look like a pretty boy
Why don't you come at me, man?
Take your best shot
See what happens to you, pal
You're outta here, man
You come at me with your beer belly
And you think you're really tough
I come back, looking like I'm 13 years old
I'll kick your ass
I'll kill your parents
I'll shoot your girlfriend
And fuck your wife
That's me, Deadly Innocence.

Bernardo was as completely aware of the angelic image he projected as he was of the violent rage that seethed inside.

Karla's parents and her younger sister, Tammy, were enthralled with the baby-faced Paul Bernardo. Her mother referred to him as her "weekend son," while 15-year-old Tammy was in love with her sister's boyfriend. In the winter of 1990, Paul Bernardo and Karla Homolka became engaged to be married. They began to slowly plan a wedding for June of 1991.

The Christmas Present

Bernardo, in the meantime, became obsessed with Tammy. He would enter her room at night while she was sleeping and masturbate on her pillow. He began to demand that Karla dress in Tammy's clothes and developed a new script for her. ("Scripting" is a typical trait of a sexually sadistic offender.) Now Karla had to say, "I'm your 15-year-old virgin. I love you. You're the king." While Karla would perform oral sex on Bernardo, he'd stare at a photograph of Tammy. He would insist that he and Karla have sex in Tammy's bedroom while she was out. None of this seemed to offend Karla and she went along with the game.

Sometime in 1990, Bernardo bought a video camcorder. He said they would need it for the wedding. Bernardo began to obsessively record everything on videotape.

One day, Bernardo and Tammy drove over to the U.S. to buy

some liquor without Karla. On the way back, they stopped and necked. Karla somehow became aware of this and lashed out angrily at Bernardo: "She's a virgin. She wouldn't know what to do with Snuffles."

Bernardo charged into the opening that Karla had inadvertently made: "Maybe I should have sex with Tam and teach her the proper way. Wouldn't it be great if Tam got to feel Snuffles inside of her? Wouldn't it be great if I took her virginity?"

Homolka refused to entertain the idea, and as with Bernardo's demands for anal sex, her refusal strained their relationship. Homolka became afraid that the June wedding might not take place despite the $4,500 engagement ring Bernardo had given her.

Finally, Homolka gave up in December of 1990—she agreed to give Tammy's virginity to Bernardo as a "Christmas present" as compensation for not being a virgin herself. From the veterinarian clinic where she worked, Karla stole some halothane, an etherlike substance used to sedate animals. Telling a pharmacist she was ordering sedatives for the animal clinic, she also ordered some Halcion, a powerful triazolam sedative.

On Christmas Eve of 1990, Bernardo and his video camera showed up at the Homolka's house to spend the holidays. Years later, television audiences would be horrified by the home videos of 15-year-old Tammy drinking down eggnog spiked with Halcion while Bernardo and Karla hovered over her. She had less than a few hours left to live.

At the end of the evening, the parents retired to bed and told Tammy she should turn in as well. Little Tammy protested: Karla and Paul had invited her to stay up with them and watch a movie on the VCR and spend some time together. The Homolkas went to bed while Bernardo slid a cassette into the VCR. The movie was *Lisa,* about a young woman who falls in love with a man she does not know is a serial killer. By the time the movie finished, Tammy had passed out from all the Halcion she had consumed.

Karla quickly ran to her room and got the halothane. She poured it onto a cloth and held it around Tammy's face to make sure she was more deeply sedated. Bernardo meanwhile unbuttoned Tammy's blouse and fondled her breasts. Karla stripped naked while Bernardo pulled off Tammy's track pants and underwear. He then switched on the video camera. This part of the videotape was never broadcast on television, but it was shown to the jury in the courtroom five years later at Bernardo's trial for murder. The tapes presented in court reveal what took place as recorded by Bernardo's video camera:

(*Video recording starts.*)

HOMOLKA: Put on a condom.

(Bernardo vaginally penetrates Tammy Homolka.)

HOMOLKA: Paul, hurry up.
BERNARDO: Shut up!
HOMOLKA: Please, hurry up, before someone comes down.
BERNARDO: Shut up. Keep her down.

(Homolka pours more halothane onto the cloth pressed against Tammy's face. Bernardo again enters Tammy. Homolka urges Bernardo to put on a condom.)

HOMOLKA: Put something on.
BERNARDO: Shut up, Karla.
HOMOLKA: Put something on. Do it.
BERNARDO: You're getting all worked up.
HOMOLKA: Fucking do it. Just do it.

(Bernardo penetrates Tammy anally. He continues for about a minute.)

BERNARDO: Do you love me?
HOMOLKA: Yes.
BERNARDO: Will you blow me?
HOMOLKA: Yes.
BERNARDO: Suck on her breasts.
HOMOLKA: I can't.
BERNARDO: Suck on her breasts. Suck. Suck. Suck.

(Homolka sucks Tammy's breasts.)

HOMOLKA: Hurry up, please.

BERNARDO: Lick her cunt.

(Bernardo pushes Homolka's head between Tammy's legs.)

BERNARDO: Lick. You're not doing it.

HOMOLKA: I am so.

BERNARDO: Do it. Lick her cunt. Lick it. Lick it up clean. Now put your finger inside.

HOMOLKA: I don't want to.

BERNARDO: Do it now. Quick, right now. Put three fingers right inside.

HOMOLKA: No.

BERNARDO: Put it inside. Inside! Inside!

(Homolka inserts her finger into Tammy's vagina. When she withdraws her finger it is smeared with menstrual blood.)

BERNARDO: Okay, taste it. Taste it. Inside . . . inside.

HOMOLKA: I did, I . . . did!

BERNARDO: Now do it again, deeper. Inside. Deeper. Right inside. Okay, taste good? Taste good?

HOMOLKA: Fucking disgusting!

(*The video recording stops.*)

Homolka later testified that at this point Bernardo struck her and told her to be more cooperative before the camera. Bernardo then switched the camera back on and had Karla hold it while he again had vaginal and anal sex with Tammy. He had not climaxed when the video recorded him suddenly stopping and withdrawing. Homolka put the camera down and switched it off.

She testified that Bernardo said that something seemed wrong—it appeared like Tammy wasn't breathing.

Tammy was dead. She had vomited and choked to death during the rape. The emergency crews had arrived at the house at about 2:00 A.M. that night, but there was nothing they could do. A police officer, who responded to the call, remembers seeing a strange, huge, burnlike red mark around Tammy's mouth and nose. In the autopsy photograph it is cherry-red bright. He noted that Tammy had been moved from the living room to a bedroom. Bernardo said they had moved Tammy because the light was better in the bedroom—they could see better there. The police officer checked the lights in both rooms and saw that they were equally bright, but then thought that people under stress can react in all manner of inexplicable ways. He asked about the red marks on Tammy's face, and Bernardo replied that they probably were caused by the rug when they dragged Tammy to the other room. They would have had to drag her facedown, the police officer thought—which was odd. But the officer's duties were to merely file the response report and not to investigate the accident. Moreover, he was a rookie who had just come on the job. He kept his suspicions to himself and left it to the senior detectives and coroner to investigate.

After interviewing the Homolkas and being told that Bernardo was a fine, upstanding young accountant, who was scheduled to marry Karla in June and who was loved by the family like a son, the police developed no strong suspicion of him.

Forensic pathology is as much an interpretive art as it is a science. The extent to which a pathologist will explore a death in an autopsy depends upon the external circumstances presented to him by the police. Had Tammy's body been found abandoned by a roadside, perhaps the autopsy would have been more extensive, but Tammy's body was found by her concerned, loving sister and future brother-in-law. Tests were made for illicit drugs, but the recreational kind—not for animal sedatives. The burns around her mouth, the pathologist concluded, were the result of acidity in her vomit. Her rectum and vagina were inspected, but showed no indications of rape. Bernardo had not had time to ejaculate. Again, even if no seminal fluids were found, Tammy's vagina and anus should have been dilated enough to signal the pathologists that something was wrong, *had they been looking for such signals*. But they were not. The official autopsy result was death by aspiration of vomit.

* * *

During Bernardo's trial five years later, Homolka was cross-examined about her role in the death of her little sister:

"The first time he mentioned having sex with your sister I would have thought you'd spring out of bed and say, 'There's no way I'm going to let you touch my baby sister.' Wouldn't that be the right reaction?"

"Yes."

"But you didn't do that?"

"No, I didn't."

"You thought, 'Knock her out and have some sex with her. What's the harm'?"

"I didn't know her safety would be in danger. I was afraid he would do it regardless. I was afraid he would just grab her off the street and rape her. This was the best way. I had no choice . . . I thought it would happen once and it would be over."

Homolka claimed that because of Tammy, Bernardo had something to hold over her head. She claimed that because she feared Bernardo would expose her role in Tammy's death to her parents, she became his unwilling slave.

Homolka said that after the death of her sister, she was numb. Obviously not numb enough to complain that her parents spent too much money on Tammy's funeral. Homolka wrote to a friend a few months after Tammy's death:

My wedding plans are great, except for my parents being such assholes. They pulled out half of the money from the wedding saying they couldn't afford it. Bullshit!!! Now Paul and I have to pay for seven or eight thousand dollars of the wedding. We've been compromising like crazy; a cash bar, no flowers on the table, etc. Finally Paul and I said fuck it! No paying for the bar. Cocktails. Everything!!!

Fucking parents. They are being so stupid. Only thinking of themselves. My father doesn't even want us to have a wedding. He thinks we should just go to the hall. Screw that! If he wants to sit at home and be miserable, he's welcome to it. He hasn't worked, except for one day, since Tammy died. He's wallowing in his own misery, and fucking me.

It sounds awful on paper, but I know you really see what I'm saying. Tammy always said she wanted a Porsche on her six-teenth birthday. Now my dad keeps saying, "I should have bought it" Bull! If he really felt like that he'd be paying for my wedding because I could die tomorrow, or next year. He's such a liar.

And for the real reason we moved out. My parents told Paul and I that they wanted him to stay at the house until the wedding. Then they said they wanted him to go after Tammy died because they needed their privacy. First they took away half the wedding money, and then they kicked us out. They knew how much we needed to be together, but they didn't care. What assholes!!!

About three weeks after the funeral, Karla's parents went away for a week to recuperate after Tammy's death while Karla's other sister went to stay with friends. Karla and Paul were alone in the house. Bernardo spent a lot of time masturbating to the videotape they had made of Tammy's rape. He and Karla went into Tammy's room, which had remained untouched since her death. Bernardo set the video camera up on a tripod facing Tammy's bed. While Homolka put on Tammy's clothes, Bernardo warned her, "Re-member, don't say anything stupid that will ruin the tape." He was still mad at Karla for saying she was not enjoying performing oral sex on her sister the night she died. Paul told her, "It's my only tape of Tammy and you fucked it up."

(*Video recording starts.*)

(Bernardo is lying naked on Tammy's bed. Homolka is with him, with her hair brushed forward over her face. Bernardo is holding a picture of Tammy. Homolka is performing fellatio on him.)

BERNARDO: Here's my little virgin Tammy. Fucked by me. I broke the hymen.
HOMOLKA: Tammy was a virgin.

(Bernardo turns over onto his hands and knees while Homolka performs analingus while rubbing his penis at the same time.)

HOMOLKA: I love licking your ass. I love sucking your cock. I love you. I love to be fucking you so much.

(Bernardo rolls over on his back and adjusts Homolka's hair so it covers her face. She is fellating him.)

HOMOLKA: I love you so much.

BERNARDO: I love you too, Tammy.

HOMOLKA: I want your cock in me. I'll give you the best orgasm of all. Together we're perfect. I want to lose my virginity to you.

BERNARDO: You didn't know I was filming you, Tammy, when you were in your room, undressing. But I was watching you through the window.

HOMOLKA: Can you ever stop thinking of me? Can you ever stop coming in my face? Take my virginity, Paul. Take it.

BERNARDOO: I will, Tammy. I love you, Tammy.

(Bernardo positions Homolka on her hands and knees and enters her anally. He is still holding Tammy's photograph in his hand.)

HOMOLKA: Oh, I'm losing my virginity. I love you, Paul. I love you so much.

(Bernardo repositions the video camera at the side of the bed. He motions to Homolka to enter the frame while he looks directly into the camera.)

BERNARDO: Hi, Tam.

HOMOLKA: Hi, Paul.

BERNARDO: Gonna make me happy?

HOMOLKA: I love sucking you.

BERNARDO: You're better than Karla, that's for sure.

HOMOLKA: I love you. Will you fuck me, Paul?

(While Homolka performs oral sex, Bernardo holds the picture of Tammy.)

HOMOLKA: I'm a virgin.

BERNARDO: Oh, Tammy. Oh, I love you. Yes. Yes. Yes, my little virgin. Yes.

HOMOLKA: I love you, Paul. I'm your virgin.

(Homolka performs fellatio on Bernardo for twenty minutes until he climaxes.)

(*Video recording stops.*)

* * *

The next night Bernardo went out driving. Before leaving, he told Homolka that if he came back with a girl, she was to hide or pretend to be his sister. He returned with a young woman about 16 years old and the two had sex while Homolka hid behind the drapes.

The next night, Bernardo made another tape. This one was made by a roaring fireplace in the same room where Tammy had died. Bernardo was stretched out on his back with a glass of wine in his hand as Homolka performed fellatio. In between, she would stop and talk:

(*Video recording starts.*)

HOMOLKA: I loved it when you fucked my little sister. I loved it when you fucked Tammy. I loved it when you took her virginity. You're the king. I love licking your ass, Paul. I'll bet Tammy would have loved to lick your ass. I loved it when you put Snuffles up her ass.

BERNARDO: How did you feel?

HOMOLKA: I felt proud. I felt happy.

BERNARDO: What else?

HOMOLKA: I felt horny. It's my mission in life to make you feel good.

BERNARDO: (Into the camera) That is why I'm going to marry her. Skoal to the king.

HOMOLKA: I'm glad you made me lick her cunt.

BERNARDO: Are you a fully fledged dyke?

HOMOLKA: No, I'm not.

BERNARDO: You were having sex with your little sister.

HOMOLKA: That was different. It was my little sister.

(Homolka strokes Bernardo's penis.)

BERNARDO: Love in the family. Do you believe in that concept?

HOMOLKA: You know I had fun doing it. You know I liked it.

BERNARDO: What did it teach you?

HOMOLKA: Well . . . we like little girls. I like you to fuck them. If you're going to fuck them, then I'm going to lick them. All the little girls.

BERNARDO: What age should they be?

HOMOLKA: Thirteen.

BERNARDO: Why?

HOMOLKA: Because it will make you happy.

BERNARDO: But why thirteen?

HOMOLKA: That's a good age.

BERNARDO: Because why?

HOMOLKA: Because they'll still be virgins.

BERNARDO: What are you saying?

(Homolka and Bernardo look at each other.)

HOMOLKA: I'm saying I think you should fuck them and take their virginity. Break their hymens with Snuffles. They're all our children, and I think you should make them ours even more.

BERNARDO: You're absolutely right. That's a good idea. When did you come up with it?

HOMOLKA: Just now.

(Homolka performs more oral sex on Bernardo and then gets up and walks out of camera range.)

HOMOLKA: I have a surprise for you.

(Homolka re-enters camera range, and holding a paper bag in her hand, sits down beside Bernardo. From the bag she takes out a bra and panties and hands them to Bernardo.)

HOMOLKA: It's Tammy's.

(Bernardo smells Tammy's bra while Homolka rubs his penis with the panties.)

HOMOLKA: I want to rub Tammy's underwear all over your body. It will make you feel so good. I'm so glad you took her virginity, Paul. I wish we had four kids, Paul.

BERNARDO: Yes?

HOMOLKA: So you could fuck each one of them. (Rapidly rubbing the underwear on Bernardo's penis.) How does the king like that?

BERNARDO: Yeah.

HOMOLKA: I think the king should turn over.

BERNARDO: Okay.

HOMOLKA: Because his little slave has some more things to say and do.

(Bernardo gets on his hands and knees while Homolka positions herself behind him. She probes his anus with one hand, licks it, while with the other hand she strokes his penis.)

BERNARDO: Oh, my little ass-licker.

(After several minutes, they change positions. Bernardo lies on his back while Homolka strokes his penis with a long-stemmed rose.)

HOMOLKA: You know what we're going to do with this? (Holding up the rose to the camera.) We're going to take this to Tammy's tomorrow, and put it on her grave.

BERNARDO: Why?

HOMOLKA: Because it will give you pleasure. You loved her. She loved you. You were her favorite, you know. The things that you did, you know I loved it. The way you fucked her in what, sixty seconds? She loved it. She loved it.

BERNARDO: Your titties are bigger than hers.

HOMOLKA: I know.

BERNARDO: They taste better. When Tammy was alive, what did you used to do?

HOMOLKA: You made me lick it and suck it. And now I'm doing it on my own because I loved it, Paul. I loved everything you did with her. She was our little play toy.

(Homolka resumes fellating Bernardo.)

BERNARDO: And we both loved her so much.

HOMOLKA: Yes, our little virgin. She loved us.

BERNARDO: What else?

HOMOLKA: I didn't give you my virginity, so I gave you Tammy's instead. I loved you enough to do that.

Homolka then began to talk about the girl Bernardo brought back to the house the night before.

HOMOLKA: (Clutching at Bernardo's penis.) You fucked her with this. You fucked her cunt. She sucked you. She sucked Snuffles. She put it in her mouth, like this . . . You put her on her knees. You fucked her. And I let you do that because I love you, because you're the king . . . I want to do it again.

BERNARDO: When?

HOMOLKA: This summer, because the weather is too bad in the winter. If we can do that then it's good.

BERNARDO: Good.

HOMOLKA: If you want to do it fifty more times, we can do it fifty more times. If you want to do it every weekend, we can do it every weekend. Whenever we can. Because I love you. Because you're the king. Because you deserve it.

BERNARDO: Virgin cunts for me.

HOMOLKA: Yeah.

BERNARDO: Virgins just for me. It'll make me happy . . . going from one cunt to another, from one ass to another. Will you help me get the virgins?

HOMOLKA: Yes, I'll go in the car with you if you want, if you think that's best. Or I'll stay here and clean up afterward. I'll do everything I can because I want you to be happy. Because you're the king.

(Homolka sucks on Bernado's toes.)

BERNARDO: Oh, footsies.

HOMOLKA: Got to treat the king like a king.

BERNARDO: Good and what else?

HOMOLKA: I'm your little cocksucker. My nipples are so hard. I'm your cunt. Your little slut. Your little ass-licker. Your little virgin.

BERNARDO: (Raising his glass to the camera.) It's good to be king.

HOMOLKA: I'm your cunt-licking slut, the keeper of your virgins. Your ass-licking bitch. And I love you. I want to marry you.

(*Video recording stops.*)

The tape ended without Bernardo climaxing. It was an extraordinary insight into the minds and dynamics of a serial killer couple. Not only did they record their crimes, but also their intimate moments in which the fantasies of these crimes were brought to the surface.

"Why Couldn't It Have Been the Same with Tammy?"

Karla's parents were indeed tired of having Bernardo around. They were also upset by how Bernardo constantly hovered over their daughter, never leaving her alone with them. When they would speak with her, Bernardo would speak in her place. They asked Bernardo to move out, explaining that they needed privacy to grieve over Tammy's death. To their dismay, Karla moved out with Bernardo in a huff.

The couple rented the house in the picturesque little lakeside town of Port Dalhousie, just outside of St. Catharines. Bernardo and Homolka were alone with their fantasies in their own private space.

Life with Bernardo was horrendous. Any time Karla made a mistake, Bernardo would unwind full punches to her upper arms—places where the bruising could be covered with a long-sleeved blouse. Another punishment he inflicted he called the "terrorist attack." He would wait until Karla had fallen asleep and then he'd suddenly jump on her, entering her anally and pummeling her with his fists. Her nights became long, restless stretches of semisleep, hovering between the nightmares of her dream-state and those of her waking life. One night, Bernardo was tossing and turning. Finding the bed too small, he pushed Homolka out on the floor. From that night on, he insisted that she always sleep on the floor while he occupied the entire bed. Not once did Homolka consider not marrying her Prince Charming. The wedding planning continued in earnest.

In the meantime, Paul prowled at night and in the early mornings, attacking women and brutally raping them. He would tell Karla about the attacks. She scolded him when he raped a young woman jogging one morning in Port Dalhousie. Too close to their home, she complained.

* * *

On June 6, 1991, while Bernardo was out, Karla invited a 15-year-old girl known only as "Jane Doe" for a sleepover at their house. Karla had met the girl when the girl was 12—she used to hang around the pet-food store Karla worked in. Jane looked up to Karla and thought of her as a beautiful princess. She was a little surprised at the invitation, but eagerly went over to the house in Port Dalhousie. As they watched the movie *Ghost,* Karla plied the girl with drinks spiked with sedatives. When the girl lost consciousness, Karla phoned Bernardo on his cell phone, telling him to come home because she had a "surprise" wedding gift for him.

When Paul got home, Karla offered up the unconscious girl to him. Bernardo was unsure at first, expressing concern over what had happened to Tammy. Karla reassured Bernardo that this time she had the drug dosage under control.

They videotaped themselves raping the unconscious girl. In the fifteen-minute videotape, Bernardo is seen forcing his way past the virgin girl's intact hymen, commenting, "Shit, I'll have to bust it." Karla rubbed her genitals against Jane's face, rotating her hips lasciviously, and then inserted the girl's limp fingers into her vagina while aping for the camera. Karla pretended to put a big, sloppy, fat kiss on the camera lens and performed cunnilingus on the girl.

The next day, Jane Doe awoke feeling sick but unaware of what had happened to her the night before. After driving the girl home that morning, Paul brutally punched Karla in the arm as he had a tendency to do when she did something he did not like.

"What was that for?" Karla whined.

"Everything went so smoothly with Jane," Paul complained. "Why couldn't it have been the same with Tammy?"

But Karla had shown Paul she was ready to play and could even take the lead.

The Murder of Leslie Mahaffy

A week later, on the night of June 14 or June 15, 1991—exactly two weeks before Bernardo and Homolka were to be married—Paul went out prowling as he often did. Bernardo had often told Homolka that if he saw an appropriate "virgin" victim, he would kidnap her and bring her back. It did not seem to particularly concern Karla. That night, however, Bernardo had another mission in mind as he prowled the quiet residential suburbs of Burlington, yet another anonymous and affluent town in the Golden Horseshoe between Toronto and Niagara Falls. He had left his accounting job and was now a full-time liquor and cigarette smuggler. He used stolen license plates on his car during his smuggling runs in the belief that Canadian customs agents were staking out the parking lots of duty-free stores on the U.S. side and radioing back the license numbers of Canadian cars parked there. Wearing a dark-hooded sweatshirt, Bernardo surreptitiously made his way between the dark yards and driveways of the sleeping housing tracts, looking for suitable license plates to steal. His prowling must have stirred all sorts of sexual associations for him of window peeping and pouncing on unsuspecting women to rape them. At about 2:30 A.M., Bernardo slipped into the backyard of Deborah and Dan Mahaffy's house. There he saw their 14-year-old daughter, Leslie, sitting alone in the dark of their backyard on a picnic bench.

Leslie Mahaffy was a cute girl with long, straight, honey blonde hair and braces gracing a warm smile. She was a highly spirited, independent, and rebellious girl—but reasonably responsible. After one argument too many with her parents, she had recently run away from home. Unlike most teenage runaways, she did not run to the streets, but instead to the home of her best friend. Her friend's mother allowed her to stay there and Leslie phoned home every day, assuring her parents she was fine. After about ten days, tired of her independence, Leslie returned home; there seemed to be less tension with her parents. The main issue had been that Leslie was expected to come home by 11:00 P.M. sharp.

On Tuesday night, four of Leslie's fellow high school friends were killed in a horrific car accident. That Friday, she and her friends had gathered together at the funeral home and later at a park to mourn their friends. Leslie's mother had dropped her off at the funeral home and told her that she could stay out a little later than 11:00 that night, but she was to phone home. Leslie stayed out until 1:30 A.M., and in a world still without pocket cell phones, she never telephoned.

A male friend of Leslie's walked her home. When they arrived at her house, everybody had gone to sleep. Her friend wanted to wait until she went inside, but Leslie assured him that she would go in through the side door, which was always left open. She told him to go home. Alone, she discovered that both the side and back doors were locked. Leslie used to have a key, but when she ran away her parents had changed the locks on the doors. When Leslie returned home, they had not given her a new key. It was an oversight that cost their daughter her life.

Afraid that her mother would not let her go to the funeral the next day because of how late she was getting home, Leslie decided not to wake her parents up. At 2:00 A.M., using a public phone near their house, Leslie phoned her friend at whose house she had previously stayed. She wanted to go over and stay the night there, but her friend's mother would have to get up and drive over to pick Leslie up. That was not a good idea, the two girls agreed. At about 2:20 A.M. Leslie hung up the phone and walked back to her house. She sat down on the family's picnic bench out back and must have been wondering what to do next when Bernardo emerged out of the shadows.

Standing before her was a handsome, blond, young man with an angelic face. Leslie asked, "What are you doing here?" Bernardo told her that he was burglarizing houses in the neighborhood.[210]

The rebellious 14-year-old's response was, "Cool."

They chatted for a while and Leslie explained to Bernardo that she was locked out of her house. She then asked Bernardo for a cigarette. Paul replied that he had some in his car, which was parked on the next street. They walked over to his vehicle. Bernardo invited her to sit down inside his car. She agreed, but cautiously told him that she would keep the door open. She sat in the passenger seat with her legs dangling out on the road, smoking the cigarette that Bernardo had given her. He sat in the driver's seat. At one point, Leslie turned toward the open door to blow some smoke out. At that instant Bernardo struck like a snake: He leaned over and placed a knife around her throat and ordered her to lift her legs into the car. Bernardo then pushed her into the rear seat, blindfolded her, and threw a blanket over her. He then calmly drove thirty-five miles back to his home at Port Dalhousie, assuring Leslie that if she did everything he told her, no harm would come to her.

As soon as Bernardo got Leslie into the house, he set up his videocamera and began taping his beating, raping, sodomizing, and tormenting the girl. As the video camera rolled, Leslie was punched, slapped, her nipples were twisted by Bernardo, she was forced to urinate before the camera, to perform fellatio (with warnings from Bernardo not to scratch him with her braces), and was repeatedly raped and sodomized. She was blindfolded all the time. Fearing that she would be killed if she got another look at her assailants, every time the blindfold came loose, Leslie would alert Bernardo. She is seen in the video begging Bernardo not to kill her and cries that she desperately wants to see her baby brother again.

During this time Karla sat downstairs reading the Bret Easton Ellis novel, *American Psycho*. Occasionally, when called, she would go upstairs and hold the videocamera while Bernardo repeatedly raped the girl. When asked in court during her cross-examination how she could possibly read while a girl was being tortured and raped upstairs, Karla missed the point of the question and incredulously replied that she was easily capable of doing two things at once.

It would be pointless, cruel, and perhaps even immoral to dwell on the detailed transcripts of the torture and rape inflicted on Leslie Mahaffy. From the video transcripts already quoted here, one can easily surmise what Karla and Bernardo put the girl through and what was said. If any reader should need the exact details of what was on the videotapes, they can refer to Toronto crime reporter Nick Pron's book, *Lethal Marriage*. Pron made the difficult decision to publish the transcripts in their entirety, and one such source should be enough.

* * *

Leslie Mahaffy suffered for nearly twenty-four hours. Sometime in the middle of the night, while Leslie lay handcuffed in the bedroom upstairs, Bernardo and Homolka went down to the kitchen and had a conference. There was a problem: It was Father's Day and Karla's parents were expected for dinner later in the day, their first visit to the house Karla and Paul had recently rented. According to Karla, Bernardo decided that he had to kill Leslie because she would identify him if he let her go. Homolka says that she insisted on going upstairs and feeding Leslie sleeping pills so she would not feel anything when she died. Karla gave Leslie a teddy bear named Bunky that Bernardo had given her, to comfort the girl as she curled up in a fetal position and went to sleep. Then, Homolka says, Bernardo entered the room with a black electric cord, wrapped it around Leslie's throat, and strangled her. A pool of urine formed under Leslie as she died on the carpeted floor of the Bernardo's bedroom.

Bernardo ordered Homolka to destroy the pillowcases and blanket stained with Leslie's blood. Homolka argued that they were her favorite set of bedding. She would carefully wash them instead.

Bernardo took Leslie's body down to the basement and hid it in a cool corner. Then the couple went to bed to sleep as Leslie's urine dried on their floor. Bernardo let Karla sleep in the bed that night. They got up toward noon and Karla bustled about preparing dinner for her parents. When the Homolkas arrived, Bernardo took them for a tour of the house, carefully avoiding the basement where Leslie's body still lay.

On Monday morning, while Homolka went back to work at the clinic, Bernardo set up a clear plastic sheet in the form of a tent in the basement. He lined the bottom of it with sheets of newspaper. He then dragged Leslie's body into the tent and carved it into ten pieces with a power saw. The entire interior of the tent was splattered from top to bottom with blood, tissue, and body fluid, which spilled out from the corpse. The electric saw was caked in flesh and bone. Bernardo attempted to wash it clean in the sink, but only succeeded in clogging up the drain with body matter.

Bernardo then went out and bought some quick-dry cement. Returning home, he encased the ten body parts into blocks of cement, and then stacked them in the basement. Leaving the bloodied tent still standing, he went to the animal clinic and picked up Karla. He took her down to the basement and had her put away the tent and clean out the body tissue and hair from the drain. Homolka testified that she used lemon-scented Lysol cleaner to clean up the basement.

The couple then went upstairs and had dinner. Bernardo asked Homolka not to serve any meat for a while, but laughed and joked how light Leslie's head was when he had cut it off.

The next evening, when Bernardo picked up Homolka from work, he told her that the concrete blocks were in the trunk of the car. The couple drove out to Lake Gibson, where they used to have sex when they were first dating, and threw the blocks into the water.

The remainder of the two weeks was busy for Homolka as she prepared the last details of her wedding. When she was being fitted for her wedding dress, several of her friends noticed the bruises on her arms, but Homolka explained that she got them from handling dogs at the clinic.

On Saturday, June 29, 1991, the lavish wedding took place at the exclusive tourist town of Niagara-on-the-Lake. While Niagara Falls is a trashy and carnivallike town, full of cheap motels, casinos, and souvenir stands on the site of the famous waterfalls, Niagara-on-the-Lake, twenty minutes away, is an elegant, Loyalist colonial settlement with an important theater center. At about the same time that Bernardo and Homolka were getting married, a fisherman was pulling out of Lake Gibson one of the concrete blocks Bernardo and Homolka had tossed in—the one they had not tossed far enough away from shore. That night, unaware that the police were piecing together Leslie Mahaffy's body, Bernardo and Homolka counted the money they had collected during the wedding. They had nine thousand dollars to spend on their honeymoon in Hawaii.

* * *

On November 30, 1991, it is suspected that Karla and Paul might have kidnapped, drugged, and murdered 14-year-old Terri Anderson as she was leaving her church parking lot. Her body was found floating in the waters of Port Dalhousie. After finding traces of

LSD in her system, however, the coroner officially ruled her death as accidental drowning.

The Murder of Kristen French

After the murder of Leslie Mahaffy, Bernardo spent the next ten months beating Homolka and stalking and raping other victims. On the Thursday afternoon before the Easter weekend of April 1992, Bernardo decided he needed another "virgin." He told Homolka to put her hair into a nonthreatening ponytail and the two drove over to the Holy Cross Catholic high school, about half a mile from where Terri Anderson disappeared. Bernardo had already staked out the school. He was aroused by the school uniforms the girls wore: short plaid skirt, white blouse, and knee socks—a fairly common theme in erotic and pornographic media.

As students poured out of the school, Bernardo scanned the girls looking for one that suited his desire. He picked out 15-year-old Kristen French, a serious and studious young woman in grade 12. Bernardo followed her in his car. When he saw that she was walking alone, he passed her and pulled into a church parking lot just ahead. As Kristen came up toward the car, Karla called her over asking for directions. Standing in the open door of the auto, Karla had spread a map on the car's roof and asked Kristen to show her where they were. Kristen felt no fear in approaching the handsome young couple. As she began to scan the map, Bernardo circled behind her and pushed her into the vehicle. While Homolka held Kristen down in the backseat, Bernardo drove to their home.

Bernardo and Homolka both sexually assaulted Kristen for a period of three days. As before, everything was videotaped. During the nights, they kept her drugged on sleeping pills, tied and locked in the closet.

In the video, Bernardo urinated on and attempted to defecate on Kristen and had her chant, "I'm your 15-year-old Holy Cross sex slave," and "You're the most powerful man in the world. You deserve anything you want . . . You're so nice, powerful, sexy. So much in control of everything. Nobody can overpower you. Nobody . . . you're the king. The master. The king of all kings. The best man in the whole world. It's good that I'm getting punished."

Bernardo had Karla put on Tammy's similar schoolgirl uniform–type outfit and climb into bed with Kristen. He then ordered them to perform oral sex and masturbate each other. Bernardo barked out commands from behind the camera like a psychopathic film director: "Start licking at the bottom and work your way up to the top . . . Come on, let's hear some love stuff."

Karla told police in her interview:

"So we dressed in almost identical uniforms and we put on makeup and we were giggling and laughing and it seemed like we're just friends getting ready to go out, kind of thing, we were doing what Paul had told us to do. I had all little perfume samples and she wanted to try some."

One is immediately incredulous—the raped and beaten, captive victim wanted to try perfume samples! Ridiculous. But there it was in the videotapes, which surfaced later. As Homolka and Kristen stood in front of the bathroom mirror with cosmetics lined up on the counter, Bernardo switched on his video camera.

(*Video recording starts.*)

HOMOLKA: So what kind of perfume do you like?

KRISTEN: Eternity or Giorgio.

HOMOLKA: Yeah, I like Giorgio as well. I have some of that new perfume, Halston. I haven't worn it yet, but maybe I will today.

BERNARDO: Okay, girls, you know what I want you to do. Each one of you pull up your skirts at the same time. Okay, now bend over. Give me a nice ass shot.

(Kristen does what she is told.)

BERNARDO: Good girls. Okay back to work.

HOMOLKA: Let's see what we have here.

KRISTEN: Eternity.

HOMOLKA: Oh, Eternity. I like it. That's Escape. I hate that one.

KRISTEN: Really? Can I smell it?

HOMOLKA: It's gross.

KRISTEN: I've never used it.

HOMOLKA: I was at work one day, and I bought one of those maga-

zines, like Mademoiselle, and then the whole place stunk because of
that perfume in a page. I've got others here to try, like Alfred Sung.

KRISTEN: Can I try this one?

HOMOLKA: Sure.

Explaining the scenes recorded on the videotape, Homolka recounted in court how Bernardo held a contest between her and
Kristen. They were instructed to select and put on makeup and
perfumes. Bernardo explained, "The one who smells the best is the
winner and won't get fucked by me up the ass."

BERNARDO: Tell the camera. Mmm, gorgeous, gorgeous.

(Bernardo leans forward and smells Kristen. He then smells
Homolka.)

BERNARDO: No way, lady. This is not a nice smell.

HOMOLKA: (Sniffing Kristen's neck.) That is a nice smell.

BERNARDO: (To Kristen.) Even though you smell the best, I'm still
going to fuck you up the ass anyways. She's my wife, after all.
And she's got brownie points on her side.*

The videotape revealed some surreal episodes in Kristen French's
three-day ordeal at the hands of Bernardo and Homolka. There
were moments when one would not guess that Kristen was a captive in the hands of homicidal psychopaths who were raping her
and were about to murder her.

Some of these horrific episodes are reproduced here because
they illuminate the subtle dynamics between a victim and her
killers—the razor's edge between life and death at the hands of a
serial killer. In the midst of her nightmarish ordeal, Kristen French
cleverly and desperately attempts to survive and manipulate her
captors. In one video segment, Kristen and Karla are videotaped
by Bernardo having sex with each other:

---

* "Brownies" are Girl Scouts. They wear brown and tan uniforms and earn
"points" for good performance.

HOMOLKA: I like you, Kristen.

KRISTEN: I like you, too.

HOMOLKA: Do you want to have some fun?

KRISTEN: Sure, okay. How come your teeth are so straight?

HOMOLKA: I don't know. How about yours?

KRISTEN: (giggling) You're silly.

HOMOLKA: (Undressing Kristen.) Don't be so nervous. It's okay.

KRISTEN: Am I shaking?

HOMOLKA: No. Just try to feel at home. You have nice legs.

KRISTEN: This one's kind of short.

HOMOLKA: That's okay.

KRISTEN: Can I ask you a favor? Before I leave, can I see your dog . . . without it attacking me?

(Homolka looks up toward Bernardo behind the camera.)

HOMOLKA: It's up to him.

BERNARDO: Yeah, sure. Before you leave.

KRISTEN: I like dogs.

BERNARDO: Me, too.

Some interpreted Kristen French's easygoing banter with Homolka and Bernardo as symptoms of her succumbing to Stockholm syndrome—where shocked and disorientated captives begin to relate to and associate themselves with their captors. In Kristen's case, it is unlikely. It is clear from Kristen's dialogue that she had her wits about her and was cleverly attempting to create a context in her relationship with her captors in which her release would be inevitable. Kristen positively said, *"Before I leave, can I see your dog?"* A courageous and brilliant attempt at survival and one that could have potentially worked had she been in the hands of serial killers with a slightly different profile.*

While Kristen was held captive, Bernardo would go out of the house on two occasions to get takeout food, leaving her alone with

---

* See Peter Vronsky, *Serial Killers: The Method and Madness of Monsters,* for material on how to enhance chances of surviving capture by a serial killer or rapist.

Homolka. The moment Bernardo was out the door, Kristen desperately pleaded with Karla to let her escape, but Karla refused.

"What Do You Know About Dying?"

On the third day, Kristen French began to openly resist Bernardo, refusing to obey his commands—not the behavioral path a Stockholm syndrome victim takes. Bernardo then showed her the videotape of Leslie Mahaffy being raped and tortured, saying to Kristen, "You know who that is, don't you? What happened to her will happen to you if you don't do what I tell you."

Kristen was horrified to recognize the face of the girl who had been reported missing and had been found dismembered at Lake Gibson.

Despite the horror of recognizing Mahaffy, the courageous 15-year-old Kristen French refused to comply further with Bernardo's perverted demands and defiantly countered, "There are some things worth dying for."

Bernardo responded with a sustained cycle of vicious punches and kicks to her body. Homolka and Bernardo raped her again several more times before Bernardo commenced beating her yet again. One of the last images on the video was of Kristen lying tied up and battered almost into unconsciousness. On the video, she spits out at Bernardo: "I don't know how your wife can stand being around you."

"Just shut up, okay. Just shut up," Bernardo is heard saying on the video, just before turning the camera off.

Shortly afterward, Bernardo took an electrical cord and wrapped it around Kristen's throat. He carefully timed himself for seven minutes as he held his grip. Karla says she heard Bernardo whisper in Kristen's ear as he killed her: "What do you know about dying?"

* * *

If in *Dante's Inferno* there was a "He-Said-She-Said Psycho Newlyweds Game Show," then Bernardo and Homolka would have been star contestants. While Homolka testified that Bernardo killed the girls, Bernardo stated that Homolka killed both of the girls when he left them alone with her. Bernardo said he wanted to keep Kristen French as a sex slave and not kill her. Homolka became jealous, he asserts, and killed Kristen. This is conceivable, for along with *American Psycho,* the other book that Bernardo had on hand at the time was *Perfect Victim,* by Christine McGuire and Carla Norton. The book was a true-crime account of a 20-year-old woman who was kidnapped in California and kept as a sex slave for seven years by a married couple. Furthermore, the autopsy report on Leslie Mahaffy showed bruising on her back consistent with a pair of knees pressed there the size and shape of Karla's.

Karla testified that Bernardo had killed Kristen because the couple was due at her parents' house for Easter dinner. She stated that Bernardo had forced her to clean up the evidence. Because there might be carpet fibers in Kristen's hair from Bernardo's rug, rather than destroying her precious rug, Karla stupidly hacked off Kristen's hair and collected it in a bag. She and Bernardo then carried her body into the bathroom and submerged it in the tub. She was scrubbed clean, because Bernardo told Karla that the police were able to lift fingerprints from flesh. He ordered Karla to douche Kristen's vagina and anus of Bernardo's seminal fluids. Bernardo burned her clothes, hair, and the sports bag she was carrying in the fireplace, and then collected the ashes. He meticulously wiped clean the glass face of Kristen's watch, and then shattered it.

To make it seem like the killers lived in Burlington, where Mahaffy had been kidnapped, Homolka and Bernardo planned to dump Kristen's body on Leslie Mahaffy's grave, but they couldn't find it. In the end, they tossed Kristen out by an illegal dumpsite. She was found naked and shorn of her hair fourteen days after she had gone missing.

* * *

Bernardo and Homolka went on for another eight months. There were beatings, Bernardo was out stalking and raping women, Homolka and he engaged prostitutes for three-way sex. Bernardo was drinking heavily and beating Karla almost daily, and was now striking her in the face and pulling out clumps of her hair. Once Bernardo threw her down into the cold cellar, turned off the light, and bolted the door, screaming down to his terrified wife, "Leslie's coming for you! She's down there in the basement. Right where I cut her up." Karla spent the night locked in the dark basement.

Bernardo drove around with Karla in the car, pointing out women he was stalking and telling her he was going to rape them next. Once, while watching a woman on the street, he masturbated, making Karla look the other way. At other times, he had Karla perform fellatio on him as he watched his potential victims. She stupidly stood by her man.

"I Hope They Let Me Do My Hair in Jail. I Would Just Die If My Hair Went to Hell."

Bernardo owned a Mag-Lite—a long-handled flashlight manufactured out of solid gun barrel–hard steel. They are carried by many police officers because of their durability and usefulness as a baton. There are several cases of individuals being killed from blows of a Maglite wielded by a police officer. When Bernardo began to beat Karla with the flashlight, she finally ran. Bruised and swollen, she showed up at her parents' house on January 5, 1993. They immediately took her to an emergency ward at a hospital and Bernardo was charged with assault that night.

So that Bernardo could not find her, the Homolkas sent her to Toronto to stay with her aunt and uncle. There the tenants of the building nicknamed the mysterious blonde with the bruises under her eyes "Raccoon Face." Within weeks, however, Homolka was out partying at a disco and quickly found herself a new lover. She told him nothing about her past other than that she was going through a "bad divorce."

In the meantime, Bernardo was rambling around the empty house, shouting for Karla. "Snuggle Bunny, are you home, Karly Curls?" He recorded a videotape directed to Karla in which he threatened suicide: "I need you, Kar. I love you, my princess, my queen, my everything. I think about you every day now . . . I realize now you're never coming back. Fucking kills me, pal. I wish I just could have been given a second chance to make things right . . . I know you had to leave, and I don't blame you. In fact, it was the best thing you could have done for me. It snapped me out of whatever state I was in. It made me realize how much I care for you . . . You are the most special person who ever touched my life. Yes, even more than Tammy. When you know you've lost it all, and there's no one to turn to, death's welcome mat is the only place you can go . . . Okay, I fucked up this life, right? When I go to the other side, okay, I'm going to make it better for you there. I'm going to set something up real nice. So when you come, it'll be all right. You know what I'm saying?"

When it ended, it ended fast, but dirty. Bernardo had been one of the many suspects in the Scarborough rapes and had resigned himself to giving police his DNA sample when his description matched that of the rapist. Three weeks after Karla left Bernardo, a DNA sample finally came back to the police. In the wake of government-funding cutbacks, it had taken twenty-six months to run the tests. Paul Bernardo, the polite young accountant, was their man. The police immediately erected a twenty-four-hour surveillance around Bernardo. They followed him as he stalked women in his car.

When the police discovered that Bernardo was living in the Niagara region, it was not long before they began to suspect him of the Leslie Mahaffy and Kristen French murders. Detectives visited Karla Homolka and asked her if she had ever cut anyone's hair and whether she was ever in the church parking lot from which French was kidnapped (without telling Homolka why they were asking). Homolka was in a state of panic. On February 17, 1993, Bernardo was arrested and charged with the Scarborough rapes.

Homolka broke down and made a full confession to her aunt and uncle. She was immediately taken to a lawyer. The police, meanwhile, began a forensic search of Bernardo's house for evidence. Wearing spacemanlike suits so that they did not contaminate the site, the police forensic technicians tore out the walls, they drilled holes in the floor, they wrenched out the plumbing, they ripped out the carpeting, pried loose the baseboards, vacuumed up every loose hair and piece of lint, and dusted every square inch for fingerprints. The police technicians spent seventy-two days inside the Port Dalhousie death house—and found little to nothing with which to link Bernardo to the murders of the two girls.

Karla Homolka, in the meantime, had been told by everybody—doctors, police, nurses, social workers, family, and friends, all unaware of her role in the crimes—that obviously she was a battered wife. She was a victim here. Soon Homolka began to believe it herself and cleverly read up on battered woman syndrome and post-traumatic stress disorder, mastering the jargon and its symptoms. In describing her relationship with Bernardo, Karla frequently used the terms "cycle of abuse" and "learned helplessness," terms set out in Lenore Walker's definitive 1979 book, *The Battered Woman*. Whenever police would come up with something Homolka had neglected to mention, like, for example, her luring and drugging—on her own initiative—of Jane Doe for Bernardo to rape, Homolka would claim post-traumatic stress–related memory loss as a result of her victimization by Bernardo. Despite the fact that Karla was living at home with her family and Bernardo was visiting her only on weekends, Karla claimed she was helpless to resist Paul's demands to assist him in the Christmas drugging and rape of her little sister.

When Karla Homolka's lawyer came forward with her offer to testify against Bernardo in exchange for a lenient sentence, the prosecutors readily accepted for they had come up with no evidence in the house linking Bernardo with Mahaffy and French. For a guilty plea to manslaughter and her testimony against Bernardo, Homolka negotiated a sentence of twelve years. She would be eligible for parole in four years, and if denied, eligible for automatic statutory release in eight under Canadian penal law. The prosecution agreed not to contest her parole application.

While these negotiations with Homolka were taking place, Bernardo sent his lawyer to the Port Dalhousie home with a hand-drawn map he had prepared, once the police search was over. Left alone in the house, the lawyer went up to the bathroom, got up on the vanity, unscrewed a ceiling lamp, reached in with his hand under the roof insulation, and withdrew a bundle of six small Hi-8 video cassettes—the rape and torture videos that the police failed to find in their seventy-two-day search of the small house! The lawyer then promptly concealed the existence of the tapes for fifteen months. He had recovered the tapes a week before the deal with Homolka had been made by the prosecutors. Had the tapes been turned over to them then, a deal with Karla might not have been necessary.

Karla testified against Bernardo, portraying herself as just one more of his victims. Her testimony, however, was hardly necessary—the tapes that Paul and Karla made were entered into evidence in court, shown only to the jury, while the spectators and press heard the audio. The jury saw Karla willingly participating and enjoying the rapes and tortures of the victims. But there was nothing they could do. The deal was done.

Paul Bernardo admitted to raping the girls. In view of the video-tapes, he could take no other position. He denied, however, killing Mahaffy and French. He insisted that both girls died while in Karla's custody. Near the end of his testimony, Bernardo admitted that he had some "problems" with his sexuality. "Down the road, I'm going to have to seek professional help for it," Bernardo flatly stated, not understanding why a wave of scornful laughter rippled through the courtroom.

Bernardo was sentenced to life imprisonment in 1995 (Canada has no death penalty) and he will not be eligible for parole for twenty-five years. It is unlikely that he will ever get it.

In chatty letters from prison to her friends, Homolka wrote on her arrival there: "There are some people, like you, who know that this horror is not of my own making." She wrote that prison was an opportunity for her to take some university courses: "I want you to know that life in here isn't as bad as most people think . . . Hopefully, I'll be able to finish my degree while I'm here. I'm eligible for parole in four years and intend to be out—for sure!" Her only worry about prison: "I hope they let me do my hair in jail. I would just die if my hair went to hell."

* * *

Karla did not get out in four years, nor in eight. Public indignation over the deal and a constant barrage of media coverage of Karla's every prison party, her lesbian relationships, her love affair with a male prisoner convicted of murdering his girlfriend, her prison psychiatric file, her personal letters and photographs, forced the correctional system to keep Karla in prison until she had served her full term of twelve years. Her mandatory release on Independence Day in July 2005 received frenzied helicopter-convoy coverage in Canada. The media dogged her for another six months or so and then tired of it. She lives somewhere in Montreal under the name of

Teale, a name she and Paul Bernardo had adopted shortly before their arrests, based on the serial killer portrayed by Kevin Bacon in the movie *Criminal Law*—Martin Thiel, one of their favorites.

Despite the public fear that Karla will reoffend or become a homicidal muse for another serial killer, the prognosis for never hearing about her again is good, unless the press ferrets her out at a bus stop, doing nothing other than waiting for a bus, which is what they precisely did recently.* Statistically speaking, high-profile female offenders like Karla, who either escaped prison or were released, have not been discovered committing a new series of crimes. Charlene Gallego continues to live in anonymity—hopefully in innocent anonymity.

Everest

Explaining Karla is a more difficult task. There is nothing in her history prior to meeting Bernardo that is common to that of other serial killers (or psychopaths for that matter). In prison, Karla had been administered practically every psychological test known to man and scored normal profiles. Her score on the Hare Psychopathy Checklist-Revised (PCL-R) was five; a score of at least twenty is required to designate the subject as a psychopath.[211] On the other hand, while in prison Karla completed a degree from Queen's University in psychology, including courses in deviant psychology. She could have manipulated her responses to the tests.

Homolka remains a mystery. It was not so much that Homolka was evil, as she was vacant. She was as colorless and as soul-dead as the anonymous housing tracts and shopping malls she and her Exclusive Diamond Club friends inhabited. Karla was conscious of only her Beastie Boy "right to party." Her family was a numb and shriveled middle-middle-class hive of greed. All her poor sister Tammy wanted for her sixteenth birthday was a Porsche—something usually just beyond the means of the middle-middle. Karla Homolka could

---

* As this book was being prepared for print, Canadian media breathlessly reported rumors that since her release Karla had acquired a dog, secretly married, and had recently given birth to a baby boy. A *Toronto Sun* headline on February 8, 2007 screamed: "Say It Ain't So: Karla's a Mom! A New Puppy, Hubby and Baby Within 2 Years."

rattle off cosmetic-counter brand names in the midst of an unfolding rape-homicide, but was incapable of the simplest moral judgment—of not submitting her sister to a rape; of releasing a frightened and battered girl when she had the power to. Her capacity to do the right thing was totally extinct.

For Homolka, Bernardo was as perfect as the cover of a cheap romance novel—a blond, large, nicely styled Big Bad Businessman. His values were as vacant as hers and as such, they made a perfect couple. The walls of Bernardo's study were covered with pictures of expensive sports cars and slips of paper with slogans like "Poverty is self-imposed." "Time is Money." "Money never sleeps." "Think big. Be big." "I don't meet the competition—I crush it." "Poverty sucks." *Wall Street* was his favorite movie.

The horror is that there probably was not an ounce of murder in Karla Homolka's heart before she met Bernardo, and probably none remains today. Yet on contact with a Bernardo, a vapid and vacant little Barbie princess like Karla becomes an effective homicidal bitch. We know that there are lots of Paul Bernardos out there, but one wonders: How many young men and women are out there—with moral discretion as malnourished as Homolka's—waiting to meet their mate?

* * *

Some might argue that until Bernardo met Karla he had not committed any rapes or murders; until Ian Brady met Myra Hindley; until Doug Clark met Carol Bundy. Were these women—as women sometimes tend to do when killing—using these men as their proxies for their own homicidal desires? Possibly. Would these men have gone on to rape and kill if they had not met these women? Very likely. One thing we know for sure, however, in modern history there has not been a single known case of a Karla Homolka or a Myra Hindley or a Charlene Gallego without a male. (The notable exception, perhaps, is the lesbian female team of Gwendolyn Graham and Catherine May Wood, who murdered elderly patients in a retirement home for sexual thrills.)

Although he applied it to the victims as well as accomplices of females, as Patrick Wilson concluded in his study of Home Office statistics of nearly every woman executed in Britain since 1843, "The husband or lover of a murderess invariably plays a part in causing the murder, if only, because, like Everest, he is there. The same cannot be said of male crimes of violence."[212]

7

NAZI BITCHES AND THE MANSON KILLER GIRLS

Making Female Missionary Cult Serial Killers

When the movie *Ilsa, She Wolf of the SS** was released in 1975, it reminded us of our belief that women did not kill or torture—unless they were Nazis. This infamous exploitation movie was set in a Nazi slave labor camp (actually shot on the set of *Hogan's Heroes*). Ilsa (played by Dyanne Thorne) is the female camp commandant, a deranged sex maniac and SS mad scientist. She enjoys forcing male prisoners to have sex with her, castrating those who fail to satisfy her. She also conducts medical experiments designed to test whether women can withstand more pain than men, which, of course, involves lots of graphic footage of the torture of buxom, naked women. This genre was not new. It was firmly rooted in a torrent of men's pulp adventure magazines from the 1950s and 1960s with titles like *Argosy, Stag, Man's Action, True Adventure,* which sometimes ran stories with sexy evil torturous Nazi females who demanded sexual satisfaction from their male sex slaves, whose lives depended upon their performance.

A year after *Ilsa*, Italian film director Lina Wertmüller followed on the same theme in *Seven Beauties (Pasqualino Settebellezze)*,

---

* SS—*Schutzstaffel*—"protective units"—the fanatical black-uniformed German Nazi paramilitary who wore skull-and-bones death heads on their caps and served as concentration camp guards, among other functions in the Third Reich.

with Shirley Stoler (who played Martha Beck in *The Honeymoon Killers*) portraying a female SS camp commandant who demands sexual service from inmate Giancarlo Giannini, in a sequence that the website IMDb claims, "Remains one of the most harrowing and fascinating scenes ever filmed."[213]

One can debate endlessly the meaning of the mostly male sexual fascination with beautiful blonde Nazi killer bitches, but its roots are indisputably founded in historical events—recent ones at that—unfolding in Nazi Germany between 1933 and 1945.

STATE SERIAL MURDER IN THE THIRD REICH

By now we realize that serial killers are neither exclusively male nor are they exclusively driven by sexual impulses. They include profit and power killers and Mafia contract killers and although it would have been argued a decade ago that the definition of a serial killer did not include military and genocidal killers, it especially includes them—and particularly those of the Third Reich. In fact, the Third Reich practiced state serial killing—serial mass murder. Probably the first state in history to do so in the way it did.

In the twelve years that it existed, Nazi Germany murdered approximately twelve million people—that includes the Jews, who made up nearly half of those victims. We are not talking here about people killed by aerial bombing, in sieges, by starvation or deprivation by occupied populations at home, or in urban battle crossfire. What we are talking about is one-on-one collective acts of murder—teams of killers firing single gunshots from small arms into the backs of victims' heads; hangings; beatings; injections of phenol into the heart; stompings; burning people alive; killing by medical experimentation and through so-called "sport" killing, and other individual acts of brutality. Toward the end the Nazis picked up the pace with mass killing in gas chambers, but those never really worked very well and broke down often. But still, they worked well enough to kill three million victims. But most of the remaining nine million were murdered person-to-person by thousands of serial killers who killed day after day, victim by victim, shot by shot, until they could kill no more.

For the longest time, we believed in the Nazis' defense that they were "only following orders." We did not forgive it, but we believed in it as an explanation, and that is one of the reasons that we have until recently excluded Nazi war criminals from the category of serial killer. We presumed they were not doing what they did by choice and that their victims were selected for them, the act of killing ordered at the pain of dire punishment if refused. Recent scholarship has completely put that notion to rest. We now know that direct participation in killing was mostly an optional and voluntary choice and no German trooper was punished for refusing to shoot unarmed men, women, and children. If they refused, and some did, they were not shot themselves, they were not sent to a concentration camp, nor were they even sent to the Eastern Front. At worse, they were teased by their fellow troopers for being "weak" and perhaps passed over for promotion.

Some would categorize Nazi perpetrators as missionary type serial killers who are politically, morally, religiously, or ideologically motivated to murder particular types of victims, who they feel deserve to be eliminated from society. But in many cases they did not commit these crimes because they were fanatical Nazis. Historian Christopher Browning studied a mobile killing unit that hunted down and killed thousands of men, women, and children in eastern Polish country villages, shooting them into mass graves one by one. Browning discovered that the killers were mostly reserve police officers approaching middle-age, from the rank and file, of which only 25 percent belonged to the Nazi Party.[214] This unit did not consist of indoctrinated, elite, black-uniformed SS troops, security police units, specialized *Einsatzgruppen* killing commandos, or even vigilante Nazi fanatics; they were ordinary Hamburg traffic cops on temporary assignment in the Polish countryside behind German lines. Thus Browning called his book on the subject *Ordinary Men*.

What we are beginning to understand is that the Nazis were able to induce a kind of temporary state of psychopathy in its citizenry, where ordinary, sane, "normal" people were made capable for brief periods of committing serial murder. Brief periods, because with time many began to have mental breakdowns, resorted to alcohol abuse, had nightmares, and even committed suicide, and developed what has been recently termed "perpetration-induced traumatic stress"—a type of post-traumatic stress disorder suffered by perpetrators of atrocities.[215] Thus the Nazis introduced the gas chambers in the winter of 1941–1942, not for more efficient killing necessarily, but for a less traumatic experience for the perpetrators. Gas was seen as a "humane" way to kill victims, reducing the psychological toll on the killers, who were murdering by the hundreds of thousands in the East.

While we have come close to understanding how the Third Reich made ordinary men into serial killers, we have yet little information on the "ordinary" women involved in the killing. And they did indeed exist in Nazi Germany, to some degree authentically reflected by the pulp fictional *Ilsa, She Wolf of the SS*.

The fictional Ilsa is inspired by a combination of two actual notorious blonde/redhead Nazi serial-killing women, both initially products of the state: Ilse Koch, the "Bitch of Buchenwald," and Irma Grese, the "Beast of Belsen." Both these women were accused of taking personal pleasure in the sadistic torture and mutilation of concentration camp inmates beyond their call of duty. They were more than just state-nurtured serial killers: They were freelancing, opportunistic murderers who excelled in killing because they personally found pleasure in it. As such, they would have been, and to some degree were, condemned by the Nazis, too. Yet, very much like female serial killer accomplices described in the previous chapter, it is doubtful whether Ilse Koch or Irma Grese would have committed the atrocities they did if they were not introduced and prepared for it by the state.

Ilse Koch—the Bitch of Buchenwald

Ilse Koch was a 41-year-old, red-haired, green-eyed, buxomly woman when she was put on trial in 1947 for crimes committed in the Buchenwald concentration camp, where some 50,000 inmates had died. Interestingly enough, Ilse was tried three times for different crimes in Buchenwald—by the Nazis in 1943, by the Americans in 1947, and again by the new West German government in 1950.

The charges laid against her in her trial by the Americans, the most famous of the three trials, were monstrously spectacular. It was alleged that Ilsa, who was the camp commandant's wife, would assemble newly arriving inmates and order that they remove their shirts. Ilse would then walk the ranks of the prisoners selecting those with tattoos she liked. She would then have them killed, skinned, and have household artifacts made from the tattooed skin like lamp shades, photo album covers, handbags, and gloves. Her house at the concentration camp was alleged to have light switches made from human thumb bones and furniture and decoration made from body parts and shrunken heads. It was alleged that she had murdered approximately forty inmates for this purpose.[216]

It was all incredibly creepy stuff and would ten years later inspire a real serial killer back in the U.S. In 1957, Ed Gein, after reading too many men's pulp true adventure magazines, adopted Koch's reported decorating style and furnished his own lonely Wisconsin farmhouse in the same way, using the body parts of women he killed or dug up from graves.[217]

That would make Ilse Koch a very unique serial killer. She was a hedonist lust type—a rare species among women, the only one known in modern times—a female killing to harvest body parts through some kind of compulsive sexual deviance. The closest thing to Ilse on the historical record is Elizabeth Báthory, some four centuries earlier.

There were other charges leveled against Ilse. Any male prisoner who dared to cast his eyes in her direction was beaten to death for impudence and "sexual harassment." She had crews of inmates worked to death building her personal riding stables on the grounds of the camp. She wandered around the camp reporting prisoners for real or imagined infractions, resulting in their deaths by beating, which she enjoyed watching. There was a distinctly sexual edge to the charges. Ilse was described as a "nymphomaniac," although her sexual indiscretions were confined to other SS staff at the camp and not inmates. But the accusations that she collected human skin and had had a tattooed skin lamp shade made, distinguished her from the other thirty defendants from Buchenwald standing trial with her. The crimes were so depraved that they became a symbol of Nazis genocidal madness at its most evil and extreme. Newspapers and magazines reproduced photographs of leatherlike patches of tattooed skin, one with a pair of clearly discernible nipples, shrunken heads, and other artifacts, including

lampshades, allegedly made of human skin and found in Buchenwald when U.S. troops liberated the camp in 1945. There was
newsreel footage of it in movie theaters.

Ilse Koch, the Bitch of Buchenwald, was sentenced to life imprisonment in 1947, but a year later American occupational authorities
suddenly commuted her sentence to four years' imprisonment, to
the shock of the public worldwide. Having served a year, she had
three years remaining on her sentence when public pressure resulted in her being tried again by West German authorities, who
then sentenced her to life. Today, Ilse Koch has a legion of
defenders—not all of whom are neo-Nazis or Holocaust deniers.
Yes, you guessed it—some are feminists who portray Ilse as a victim of male inmates, who slandered Ilse Koch for her "trangression
of gender stereotypes."[218]

I'm not joking!

Background

Ilse Koch was born Ilse Kohler Schnitzel, September 22, 1906, in
Dresden. After graduating high school, she was employed in a
bookstore and later worked as a secretary. She joined the Nazi
Party relatively early—in May 1932. This placed her in a doubly
exclusive category—joining before the seizure of power by Hitler
in January 1933 and being one of a small minority of females who
were members of the party. Only 7.8 percent of the Nazi Party at
that time consisted of females.[219] The Nazis did not anticipate any
role for women in the Third Reich other than that of wife and
mother of Aryan soldiers. Women in the German workplace outside of traditional female jobs like schoolteacher, nurse, shop clerk,
or secretary were encouraged to return home and start a racially
pure family.

Ilse was employed as a secretary in the Nazi Party. As a trusted
party member, she was eventually assigned to the Sachsenhausen
concentration camp near Berlin in 1936. It is important to note
that first-generation concentration camps in Germany like Sachsenhausen and Buchenwald were not "death camps" per se. Unlike
the second generation of "annihilation camps"—places like Treblinka, Sobibor, and Belzec, built in Poland, the only purpose of
which was to kill the many arriving deportees as fast as possible,

mostly Jews and Gypsies—first-generation concentration camps in Germany generally kept inmates alive in confinement for long periods of time. They were, indeed, brutal, and inmates were routinely shot, worked, and beaten to death, experimented upon, or killed just to make space. Nonetheless, the primary purpose of these camps was to confine political opponents. Fifty-six thousand victims died in Buchenwald in the ninety-three months it was in operation between its founding in 1937 and its liberation by the Allies in April 1945.[220] Some 240,000 prisoners passed through the camp, and although some were killed later in other camps, many, probably most, survived: That's a concentration camp. At the three annihilation camps of Treblinka, Sobibor, and Belzec, a total of 1.5 million were murdered in twenty-one months and only a few dozen are known to have survived, a big difference in the homicidal environment between the categories of camp. Ilse's assignment to the Sachsenhausen camp in 1936 was akin to being assigned to an extremely brutal prison but not necessarily part of a killing function of the "Final Solution," which did not get officially underway until the late autumn of 1941.[221]

While working as a secretary in the office at Sachsenhausen, Ilse met Karl Otto Koch, the camp commandant. They were married in an SS pagan marriage ceremony and had two children. In 1937, Koch was transferred to the newly opened Buchenwald camp and he and Ilse moved into a new house inside the camp. It was in this house that American troops were said to have found the gruesome human-skin souvenirs.

The Feminist Defense of Ilse Koch

Ilse Koch was never an official functionary of the camp. She was the commandant's wife. While that gave her a tremendous degree of authority, it was entirely unofficial. Here, according to one German historian, Alexandra Przyrembel, was the first key to the vehemence with which Ilse was prosecuted after the war and the sexually depraved nature of the crimes she was accused of. According to this historian's feminist perspective, Ilse was prosecuted because she defied traditional gender roles and offended the male inmates' patriarchal sensibilities by doing so. Przyrembel argues that Ilse as a woman impacted on the "male society of inmates." She states:

> . . . Ilse Koch appeared—in the perception of inmates—to have penetrated the domain of power reserved for the male members of the SS or at most certain *Kapos* (inmates who supervised inmate labor). This interaction between the (apparent) confirmation and transgression of gender stereotypes is, in my opinion, the root of the 'Ilse Koch phenomenon' after 1945.[222]

It appears that when it comes to women murderers, radical feminism has no bounds in its assertion that female serial killers are essentially a social construct of the oppressive and conspiring male patriarchy—even a patriarchy confined to a concentration camp. For radical feminism, Ilse Koch is as much a victim of the patriarchy as Aileen Wuornos.

". . . Kill Them in a More Decent Way."

But it is not as simple as all that. The Nazi hierarchy had actually already criminalized Ilse and her commandant husband during the war. SS commandant Karl Koch was arrested by the Gestapo in 1942 on charges of financial corruption and the murder of two inmates to cover up his crimes. He was tried by an SS tribunal and sentenced to death. He was executed, ironically, in the Buchenwald concentration camp, by the SS in April 1945, just days before the camp's liberation.

Ilse was arrested two years before the war ended by the SS in August 1943, and also charged with corruption, but acquitted in her trial. (Although, as she complained to her American captors later, not before her sizable cash deposits were confiscated by the Third Reich in a type of forfeiture of criminal enterprise gains. The amount seized from her was 12,000 Reichsmarks—about $30,000 in today's buying power.)

It was during this internal 1943 SS investigation that allegations were first made that Ilse Koch made human lamp shades. This was an offense under the Nazi code of conduct, which insisted that killing be conducted with decorum or "decency." Even the taking of photographs was a serious offense, despite the fact that thousands of perpetrators snapped pictures of themselves committing atrocities. SS men were tried and imprisoned if they were caught taking photographs of atrocities or if they killed Jews without orders or killed them for depraved personal motives.[223] During one SS court-martial, an SS private testified that the SS defendant had killed children by holding them off the ground by the hair and shooting them. He testified, "After a while, I just could not watch this anymore and I told him to stop. What I meant was he should not lift the children up by the hair, he should kill them in a more decent way."[224]

The SS defendants ended up on trial because they were passing around photographs of the atrocities like trading cards while on leave in Germany. (Some sent photographs to their wives, girlfriends, and mothers.) SS Chief Himmler was very vocal on the issue of killing with decorum. When he addressed a gathering of his senior SS killers, he said, "Most of you know what it is like to see a hundred corpses laid out in a line, or five hundred or a thousand. To have stood fast through this and—except for cases of human weakness—to have stayed decent, has made us hard."[225]

In other words, when the tattoo skin artifacts were supposedly found in her former house at Buchenwald in 1945, Ilse had not been living in it for two years and had been thoroughly investigated for it back in 1943. If, indeed, she had such fetishized trophies in her home, the SS investigators would have confiscated and destroyed them, and Ilse would have been severely punished for the offense—especially since she was not even a member of the SS but a civilian wife of an SS offender.

The Tattooed Skin Collection

Despite holding the center-stage in allegations that she had murdered and "skinned" inmates for their tattoos for decorative purposes in her 1947 trial by a U.S. Military Tribunal, Ilse Koch was not specifically charged with those offenses. Ilse, like the other defendants, was indicted with participating in a "common design" to subject the inmates of Buchenwald to "killings, tortures, starvation, beatings, and other indignities." Any association as perpetrator with the camp was sufficient for her conviction without a specific case necessarily proven.

But the specimens of tattooed skin were not a propaganda invention. They existed—and were indeed found in 1945, along with shrunken heads, perhaps at the house where Ilse once lived or perhaps in the camp pathology department. In fact, such samples were indeed being collected, but with official SS sanction! The culprit was an SS doctor, Erich Wagner, who had been writing a thesis on the link between criminality and the desire to be tattooed. Wagner photographed numerous inmates with tattoos and apparently—either upon their deaths or after ordering their deaths—detached pieces of their skin bearing the tattoos, and cured and saved them, not as decoration, but as academic specimens. According to historian Przyrembel, Ilse Koch did not attend the photographing and might not have even been aware of the existence of the tattoo project.[226]

A photograph of a lamp shade—allegedly made of human skin and placed next to shrunken heads and samples of preserved tattooed skin—was entered into evidence at her trial, but the actual lamp shade itself apparently was misplaced. While forensic analysis definitively identified the skin samples as human, no test reports on the lamp shade were entered into evidence.

Dr. Sitte, a Ph.D. in physics and a former inmate, was one of the star witnesses against Ilse Koch. He had been confined in Buchenwald from September 1939 until the liberation in April 1945. He stated that he had worked in the camp's pathology department and that tattooed skin was stripped from the bodies of dead prisoners and "was often used to create lamp shades, knife cases, and similar items for the SS." Sitte told the court that it was "common knowledge" that tattooed prisoners were taken away after Ilse Koch had selected their tattoos and they would be murdered and skinned for her.

But under cross-examination, Sitte admitted that he had never himself personally seen any of the lamp shades allegedly made of human skin and that he had no personal knowledge of any prisoner who had been reported by Ilse Koch and was then killed so that his tattooed skin could be made into a lamp shade. He also admitted that the lamp shade that was on the display table in the photograph was not the lamp shade made from human skin that he was referring to, allegedly delivered to Koch. Later, in a 1948 letter to the *New York Times* after Ilse Koch's sentence had been commuted, Sitte further admitted that:

> I began to work in that pathology department only after the Koch era (Koch had been arrested for embezzlement and corruption) and by this time the SS leaders had abandoned their custom of displaying objects adorned with the tanned skin of tattooed prisoners.[227]

In his letter Sitte concluded, "This was not evidence against Ilse Koch, but against the SS officers in the camp, who killed prisoners for their tattooings."

But Sitte pleaded nevertheless against the reduction of Ilse Koch's sentence: "Is justice to the victims of Ilse Koch and her kind so much less important than technical justice to this pack of murderers?"

What was the "technical justice" at issue here? The U.S. Military Governor of Germany, General Lucius D. Clay, explained his decision to commute Koch's sentence. He stated that Koch "could not be proved guilty of the serious war crimes that had been initially cited against her by the evidence presented at her trial. Among the specific charges was that she had used tattooed human skin for lamp shades and other household articles."[228] The problem, according to Clay, was that U.S. Military Tribunal procedures allowed not only for hearsay evidence to be entered, but also for written affidavits without the defense being given opportunity to cross-examine the witnesses.

In 1976 Lucius Clay recalled:

> We tried Ilse Koch . . . She was sentenced to life imprisonment, and I commuted it to three years. [She had already served one year.] And our press really didn't like that. She had been destroyed by the fact that an enterprising reporter who first went into her house had given her the beautiful name, the "Bitch of Buchenwald," and he had found some white lampshades in there, which he wrote up as being made out of human flesh.

Well, it turned out actually that it was goat flesh. But at the trial it was still human flesh. It was almost impossible for her to have gotten a fair trial.[229]

None of this in any way mitigates Nazi atrocities nor the specific charge that inmates were murdered for the collection of their tattooed skins. Holocaust deniers make a big deal out of Clay's assertion that the lamp shade turned out to be made of goat skin. (And that it was never determined in a test for the U.S. National Archives—where Ilse's photo albums are today stored—from what "animal" the suede covering the albums was made.) But there was never any doubt that some mad scientist at Buchenwald had collected those human tattoo skin specimens and shrunken heads. The inmates were unaware of the purpose. They assumed they were acts of personal depravity and laid them squarely on the doorstep of Ilse Koch, whom they despised.

While this may clear Ilse from those specific charges, it does not exonerate her as a member of the Nazi party, a corrupt commandant's wife living on the grounds of a concentration camp, and committing other offenses. The other charges against her—that she exploited inmate labor for her own purposes, that she vindictively reported prisoners, resulting in their punishment and sometimes executions; and that she had inmates, who dared to glance at her punished or murdered for their "impudence" toward a German woman—are entirely plausible and very likely. They are, in fact, the very source of the inmates' hatred for her—not her gender role transgressions. The senior SS staff had inmates working as servants, cooks, housekeepers, and gardeners at their homes. The SS wives set the degree of discipline for these slave domestics.

To the end, Ilse raged against an imagined "Jewish conspiracy" that she claimed was behind her charges. Ilse was an old-time Nazi Party member and one can easily imagine her attitude toward Jews and communists and other "enemies of the state" confined in her husband's camp. She deserved the life sentence she got, but her actual crimes made her more typical of other offenders, many of whom found their sentences commuted in the 1950s.

The public outcry over the commutation of the Bitch of Buchenwald's sentence to a mere four years, with one already served, led to

Ilse Koch being tried a second time, this time by the newly reconstituted West German judiciary. The trial was *very* political. The cream of German establishment opposition to Hitler had been confined in Buchenwald and camps like it. The entire echelon of the huge Social Democratic Party and the German Communist Party had been thrown into concentration camps from 1933 to 1937. Many survived by forming powerful and rival underground resistance groups inside the camps. These groups remained unified and politically active after the war. They emerged in post-war Germany, determined to make up for the lost twelve years during which they had been outlawed and brutalized by the Nazi state. There was no way that a high-profile example of Nazi depravity like Ilse Koch was going to escape punishment. These powerful German camp survivor associations relentlessly lobbied and protested for a second trial of Ilse Koch. And in the end they got their wish.

"Lamp Shade Ilse," as she was dubbed in the press, was retried in Bavaria in December 1950. In 1952, she was sentenced to life imprisonment after it was proven that she had "contributed" to the specific death of one inmate. The issue of collecting tattooed skin samples was not as central in her last trial. She vehemently appealed her sentence, claiming to be innocent of all the charges, but in 1967 she gave up and committed suicide at the age of 61 by hanging herself in her cell.

Ilse was an evil and awful human being and got the end she deserved. But as far as the extraordinary charges of using human skin as household decoration for which she became so notorious, Ilse Koch might have actually been innocent. The accusations are reminiscent of the myths around Elizabeth Báthory—of her bathing in victims' blood. But as the classic John Ford western *The Man Who Shot Liberty Valance* declares, when there is a choice between printing the truth or the legend, the legend always wins out. As repulsive as historian Przyrembel's feminist argument might be—that Ilse Koch was railroaded on those specific charges because she offended patriarchal sensibilities of the camp inmates—it is a charge one cannot completely dismiss as easily as one wishes. In one way or another, how we perceive and define female serial killers is often defined by social constructs and politics, including those of gender stereotyping.

Irma Grese—the Beast of Belsen

In real life, Irma Grese, nicknamed the "Beast of Belsen," is the more authentic inspiration for *Ilsa, She Wolf of the SS* than the camp housewife Ilse Koch. Grese was young, blonde, and beautiful, and she was part of the concentration camp system, employed as a female *SS-Aufseherin*—"supervisor" or matron. These were not members of the SS—females were not allowed to join—but paid female employees of the SS, auxiliary workers. She was only 22 years old when she was executed by the British occupational authorities for a series of brutal murders she committed while working in the concentration camp system.

In many ways, Irma Grese is easier to explain. She was born into a family of four siblings on October 27, 1923, to Alfred and Berte Grese, farm workers in Mecklenburg in northern Germany. Very little if nothing is known of her childhood. Her mother committed suicide in 1936 when Irma was 13 years old. Her father, Alfred, vehemently hated the Nazis but wisely kept his opinion to himself. (Some sources claim he joined the Nazi Party in 1937.)

Irma was 10 years old when the Nazis took power in Germany. She was educated in the Nazi school system, which ensured that she was indoctrinated at an early age in racial theory, which espoused the superiority of the German Aryans and the immanent threat from the "subhuman" Jews and "the Judeo-Bolshevik-Masonic conspiracy." Irma was raised on colorful Dr. Seusslike children's books with titles like "The Jew Is a Poisonous Mushroom" or "The Jew Is a Fox," heavily illustrated with lurid color drawings of beautiful, blonde, blue-eyed German children chasing stereotypically ugly, dark-skinned, hook-nosed Jewish children out of the school and out of town.

Irma was not a popular girl in school and was apparently bullied. She led a lonely existence typical of a serial killer's childhood. Her sister, attempting to defend Irma against the accusations leveled at her, testified that Irma was cowardly and would run away when threatened, and therefore was incapable of committing violent acts. Of course, we know better. If she ran away she might have stored enormous reserves of rage until she had an opportunity for "payback" as a camp guard over helpless inmates.

Irma was obsessed with her activities in the *Bund Deutscher*

Mädel (League of German Girls [Maidens])—the Nazi version of the Girl Scouts. Perhaps this is where she found acceptance, having been rejected by her schoolmates. Consequently, her already low marks at school suffered even more. She quit school in 1938 at the age of 15. She worked as a nurse's aide in the SS sanatorium Hohenlychen for two years and unsuccessfully tried to find an apprenticeship as a nurse.

After she failed to secure the apprenticeship, probably because of her low school grades, Irma was recommended by her boss at Hohenlychen in 1941 for a position in the SS female concentration camp service. She was interviewed, but told that at 17, she was still too young. For a year she ended up employed as a machine operator on a dairy farm.[230]

When Irma turned 18 in 1942, and became eligible, she successfully entered the *SS-Helferinnenkorps*, the female volunteer auxiliary service in the SS, which provided a range of services from secretarial to prison and camp custodial in the SS and security police. Irma claims that the German Labor Service, which enforced mandatory employment for all young Germans, arbitrarily assigned her to the job. This is unlikely, as women who were drafted into the service were classified as *SS-Kriegshelferinnen* ("war auxiliaries") to differentiate them from the more worthy *SS-Helferinnen* volunteers.[231]

Irma began her training as a guard in July 1942 at the Ravensbrück concentration camp for women. The ethos of Nazi concentration camp guards was brutal: Pity or mercy were seen as signs of weakness. It was drummed into the trainees' heads that inmates were enemies of the state and must be treated brutally at all times. In a kind of distillation of psychopathy, guards were not permitted to speak to inmates other than in an official capacity to ensure that inmates remained anonymous subjects for their brutality.

To ensure the unemotional performance of torture and punishment of inmates, usually by whipping with a stick or rod, with twenty-five strokes as the minimum for minor infraction and a thousand as the maximum, punishment was carried out by guards other than those who assigned it or reported the prisoner. This ensured that the guard had no personal or emotional sadistic investment in assigning punishment and that at the same time no guards could escape meting out beatings, even if they did not themselves report prisoners for infractions. Everyone had to participate.

SS guards were required to be uncompromisingly tough and to hate the inmates under their charge. When it rained, guards were prohibited to seek shelter when supervising outdoor work details. They had to show themselves to be as tough and/or tougher than the inmates they supervised.

A female inmate at Ravensbrück recalls the teenage girls arriving for training as guards:

> The beginners usually appeared frightened upon first contact with the camp, and it took some time to attain the level of cruelty and debauchery of their seniors. Some of us made a rather grim little game of measuring the time it took for a new *Aufseherin* to win her stripes. One little *Aufseherin,* twenty years old, who was at first so ignorant of proper camp "manners" that she said "excuse me" when walking in front of a prisoner, needed exactly four days to adopt the requisite manner, although it was totally new for her.
>
> It would be a reasonable estimate that about half of the guards took visible pleasure in striking and terrorizing their prisoners, especially the weak, ill, and frightened. Others dealt their blows with the coarseness and simplicity of a peasant whipping her donkey, some simply acted for the sake of conformity particularly in front of their colleagues or the SS men. In any case, even the best of them showed no adverse reaction when a prisoner was beaten in their presence.[232]

No "adverse reaction:" no subjectivization of the victim, no emotion, no empathy, no mercy or feeling—a psychopathic state artificially induced through indoctrination from childhood, hard conditioning, and discipline. But blatant sadistic behavior in concentration camps was paradoxically condemned by the Nazis as "indecent." Murder was to be committed coldly for noble state reasons, not for personal, depraved satisfaction, and SS men who killed for their own pathological gratification or material gain (as Ilse's husband, Karl Koch, had) were tried and sentenced to prison terms or executed by SS tribunals.[233]

On her first visit home, Irma arrived wearing her camp guard uniform and was promptly beaten by her father and told to never return, her sister testified at Irma's trial.

* * *

After a year's service at Ravensbrück, Irma was sent in March 1943 to what some SS doctors bitterly called "anus mundi"—the "asshole of the world"—a swampy hellhole the size of about forty American city blocks: the Auschwitz-Birkenau megadeath camp. This was a third-generation camp combining a forced labor concentration camp with a huge annihilation facility. Double railway spurs snaked directly into the camp with packed cargo trains backed up along the line attempting to unload thousands of Jewish deportees daily from the most distant towns and cities of occupied Europe—places like Greece, Romania, Hungary, Italy, Yugoslavia. (The Jews of Germany, Poland, Russia, and northern and central Europe had already been mostly murdered—either shot on location or in the second-generation annihilation camps.)

They would be forced off the train on "the ramp" and they would undergo "selection"—those to live sent in one direction and those to die sent in another, toward four huge combination crematoria / gas chambers the size of railway stations. One can see them today in aerial photographs filmed by passing USAF B-17 bombers on the way to targets in the vicinity. One can easily compare the immense size of these killing facilities next to train cars parked nearby on the spur in the photos. Two of the huge underground gas chambers could easily accommodate 1,200–1,500 victims each.

SS doctors on the ramp "selected" the very old, the very young, the weak, sick, or infirm to walk about a five-minute distance from the ramp to the nearest gas chamber. Of course, one did not need a medical degree to tell who was fit for slave labor—anybody could do that. But by their "selection" of who lived or died, the physicians were now actually taking the responsibility unto themselves for the killing, rendering murder into the realm of a medical procedure ordered by a doctor. As Victor Brack, chief of Germany's "euthanasia" program said, "The syringe belongs in the hand of the physician."

Those "ordinary" men—the cops who blew out the brains of kids and their screaming mothers one by one—ended up as mental cases. The Nazis discovered they could synthesize psychopathy temporarily, but they couldn't make it persist: The killers were bothered by what they were doing. So at Auschwitz they medicalized and assembly-lined the procedure. It was no longer murder— no more than a surgeon plunging a razor-sharp instrument inside a patient's body is murder. It was "racial hygiene," practiced by professional physicians. They were healing the German race by destroying the Jewish bacillus infecting it. There were always physicians on the ramp, with a second shift of physicians on standby in case the first needed to be relieved.[234]

Again we see a type of state-induced "artificial psychopathy"— a pseudoscientific medical rationalization for serial killing. One survivor, a scientist himself, stated that the ramp physicians began using a medical term, *therapia magna*,* as a joke at first but then seriously:

> They considered themselves performing *Therapia Magna Auschwitzciense*. They would even use the initials TM. At first it was mockingly and ironically, but gradually they began to use them simply to mean the gas chambers. So that whenever you see the initials T M, that's what it means. The phrase was invented by Schumann who fancied himself an academic intellectual among the intelligentsia of Auschwitz doctors.[235]

The physicians "selected" mostly old and middle-aged men, women, and children under 14 to die. Healthy young men and women and those with needed skills were sent to work, unless the young woman was carrying an infant in her arms, in which case she was selected to die with her child. (Somebody had to carry the infant into the gas chamber.) Occasionally, trusted inmates working on the ramps would discreetly whisper to a young mother to give her child to an elderly relative to carry when approaching the selection. This would save her life, but not that of her infant. Other mothers understated their child's age, hoping to save them from

---

* *Therapia sterilisans magna*—treatment of infectious disease by the administration of large doses of a specific remedy for the destruction of the infectious agent in the body without doing serious harm to the patient.

hard labor, unwittingly condemning their own child to death in the gas chamber.

Those "selected" by the physicians would become walking dead, sent directly from the ramp to the gas chambers. They would be ushered into huge subsurface undressing rooms to prepare for a "shower." There they would be told to hang their clothing carefully on numbered pegs and reminded to tie their shoes together by the laces so they would not get lost. (It made it easier to sort the victims' clothing afterward if it was already sized and the shoes paired.) They would be told to hurry along into the shower in the next room before the hot water ran out or before the coffee and breakfast that awaited them grew cold. And off they went.

Once packed into the huge concrete chamber with dummy shower heads, the airtight door would be suddenly slammed shut behind them, the lights turned off, and cyanide gas pellets would be poured by medical orderlies (again medics) from the roof into four vented, metal mesh columns dispersed along the length of the chamber. The cyanide gas was a commercial product that was released from the pellets once exposed to warm air. Called *Zyklon-Bl* (Cyclone B), it was designed to kill rats in granaries by gas so as not to contaminate the grain or storage facility with pesticides. The SS demanded that the manufacturer produce special batches of the gas without the "irritant" warning odor intended to alert people of its presence. The manufacturer balked, claiming it would endanger the patent they held on *Zyklon-Bl* if they did that. The SS insisted. Special custom-made batches were delivered without the irritant. The gas was odorless and painless to the victims, killing them through rapid respiratory and cardiac arrest and oxygen depletion in the blood. Victims did not "choke" on the gas, they just dropped dead with seizures. But it was a horrible death, nonetheless, with victims packed tightly among naked, dying strangers in pitch-black dark, clawing on each other in respiratory and cardiac paralysis in ever gradually expanding circles from the mesh columns.

The four crematoria gas chambers were capable of easily killing approximately 10,000 people a day—*each*. The problem was not killing, but disposing of the bodies. At maximum capacity, the crematoriums combined together could only burn 5,000 bodies every twenty-four hours. But furnaces frequently broke down, forcing corpses to be burned in huge, hellish, smoking, open-air pits at the camp's perimeter. Bones and ash would be ground to dust and hauled away in dump trucks for disposal in the nearby river. Somewhere between 1.1 and 1.5 million people were killed this way at Auschwitz, mostly Jews, but Gypsies, Poles, Russians, and other "subhumans" as well.

The Auschwitz camp and its satellites were like a small slave kingdom, with the registered inmate population totaling 155,000 at its maximum. These inmates were put to work "processing" the corpses, emptying the gas chambers, extracting gold teeth, and sorting the belongings of the dead to be shipped back to Germany for profit. They also worked in the kitchens, gardens, warehouses, clinics, and artisan shops that supported the enterprise of death or on construction gangs expanding the already huge camp perimeter to accommodate more and more victims to gas and burn, day in and day out, trainload by trainload.

"Sport"

So it was here at Auschwitz that little blonde Irma Grese—the former Nazi Girl Scout and wannabe nurse—at the tender age of 19 was assigned to supervise a camp section with thirty thousand female inmates, those chosen from the ramp to temporarily live a little longer. That is, as long as they did not get sick or collapse, could do the work assigned to them, committed no infraction real or imagined, and were lucky not to have encountered some idle SS man or female *SS-Aufseherin* like Irma in a bad mood swing looking to "sport" with inmates.

To "sport." It was a guard's term, meaning to idly brutalize prisoners for no reason other than to relieve the boredom; technically an offense, but as long as it did not "get out of hand" the authorities looked the other way. Irma's "sport" was to order women to retrieve something thrown beyond the safety line, which delineated, at the camp perimeters, an area beyond which prisoners were not allowed to venture. Guards were under strict orders to shoot to kill, with no warning shot, any prisoner who stepped beyond this perimeter. On average, Irma was reported sending thirty women a day to die in this manner, until one SS guard refused to shoot a woman ordered out by Irma into the kill zone. He was charged with a violation of camp regulations, but when the SS inquiry discovered the circumstances, he was returned to duty and Irma was transferred from the detail.[236] Irma was too much even for the SS.

One surviving inmate recalls that when Irma arrived at Auschwitz she appeared to be "a young girl in my eyes about 18–19, with a round, full face and two long braids." The inmate was transferred to another section and did not see Ilse for several months. When she saw her again she was stunned by the dramatic transformation. She had "slimmed down, her hair was up in a bun, the uniform immaculate and she had a cap over her head and on her waist was a belt and a pistol."

With her stunning blonde good looks, the teenage Irma had become the center of attention. Some sources allege she became the lover of the notorious Dr. Josef Mengele, a handsome, wounded war hero physician who worked on the ramp in an immaculately tailored uniform and conducted horrific medical experiments on dwarfs and child twins in his spare time. One of his experiments consisted of attempting to change eye color by injecting dyes directly into the iris. Mengele, nicknamed the "Angel of Death," would whistle Schumann tunes as he "selected" on the ramp or scrapped bone marrow samples from screaming children without an anesthetic. Witnesses placed Irma on the ramp when Mengele was there. She brutally beat and kicked people who were attempting to bypass the selection or to switch lines afterward.

An inmate physician stated that Irma had a fixation on women with large breasts and would inevitably whip their breasts to the point that they would become infected. She would always make a point of being present when the physician treated the painful infection, "swaying back and forth with a glassy-eyed look" as the inmate cried in pain.

Irma carried a special lightweight cellophane whip that was particularly painful and cutting that she had custom-made in one of the camp workshops. She kept prisoners standing for hours during roll call, mercilessly beating and stomping any inmate who collapsed. She forced prisoners to kneel for hours, killing anyone who keeled over. She rode around the camp on a bicycle, shooting prisoners with her handgun.

It is hard to sort fact from fiction in some of the testimony. One witness testified that Irma was accompanied by a German shepherd—trained by her to bite the breasts of female inmates—which she would unleash on prisoners who fell behind in convoys. But this is unlikely as specially trained dog handlers were in charge of the animals, each paired with its handler. One could not just "borrow" a guard dog.

It was said that Mengele broke up with Irma when he learned that she was having lesbian affairs with other inmates, something strictly prohibited by not only camp regulations but German law as well. Again, the portrayal of the female defendant as somehow sexually depraved is reminiscent of the charges leveled against Ilse Koch. The witnesses against her were mostly female and accusations of Irma's lesbianism might be reflective of female taboos of the period if we follow historian Przyrembel's logic.

When Auschwitz was closed down as the Red Army approached in December 1945, Irma accompanied prisoner transfers to Ravensbrück and then to the temporary transit camp of Belsen. By then the Third Reich was collapsing and the camp administration basically ignored the needs of the overcrowded, sick, and starving camp population. When British troops liberated Belsen, they found Irma and other female and male guards surrounded by mountains of emaciated corpses, most dying from deadly typhus. Bulldozers were used to push the tangled piles of corpses into mass graves. Irma was arrested on the spot and put on trial in September 1945 along with forty-four other defendants in one of the earliest war crimes trials after World War Two.

During her trial, the press was mesmerized by the beauty queen looks of the now 21-year-old defendant. She had chosen to remain at Belsen because she had fallen in love with one of the SS men there and now he was in the dock with her. Every day Irma brought a comb with her to carefully set her hair in blonde ringlets during the trial breaks.

In the trial Irma denied some of the specific or more lurid charges, but freely admitted to beating and torturing prisoners because it was the only way she "could keep order." She denied using a whip at Auschwitz, claiming she "only" beat prisoners with her hands, but admitted that she used a whip at Belsen because the prisoners were in such derelict condition that she would not want to touch them.

Throughout the trial Grese appeared contemptuous of the proceedings. She showed no emotion as the prosecution rolled films of the piles of corpses discovered at Belsen.

Irma Grese was sentenced to death and executed by hanging on December 13, 1945—the youngest woman hanged by the British in the twentieth century.

The Making of State Serial Killers

Irma Grese was not "following orders" when she beat and murdered her victims. She was clearly freelancing—to the point that the SS themselves thought she was excessive and had her transferred from perimeter duty after one too many "sporting" killings of inmates.

Both male and female guards in Nazi concentration camps were conditioned to suppress any empathy they may have had with the inmates, a primary characteristic of psychopathy. They were stripped of the ability to perceive the inmates in any way other than the generic "enemy of the state." No private communication was allowed between the prisoners and guards. Auschwitz was a murderous kingdom where killing was the norm. How could Irma Grese be anything but what she was in an environment like that with the conditioning she had?*

Nazism was to a great extent a cult, but its ideology seemed to play almost no role in the crimes of Ilse Koch and Irma Grese, nor did "following orders" appear to have much to do with it in the two women's cases, since they were acting mostly on their own initiative. Historians, sociologists, and psychologists have been strug-

---

* The more extensive story of female serial killers in Nazi Germany, beyond the scope of this book, is about the hundreds of doctors and nurses who participated in the murder of at least 150,000 mentally and physically handicapped German children and adults in a medical killing campaign disguised as euthanasia.

gling to explain how so many "ordinary" people in Germany ended up serially murdering so many victims. We are not talking about the "banality of evil" bureaucrats who killed from behind their desks, never actually seeing their victims, but of the thousands of people who were killing one on one, with blood splashing into their faces—all serial killers.

One of the earliest theories, suggested by Theodor Adorno, was that there was a type of testable "Authoritarian Personality Type" that could be scored on a so-called F-scale. Some of the personality features consisted of:

- rigid adherence to conventional values

- submissiveness to authority figures

- aggressiveness toward out groups

- opposition to introspection, reflection, and creativity

- preoccupation with power and "toughness"

- destructiveness and cynicism

- projectivity—a disposition to believe that dangerous conspiratorial things go on in the world

- an exaggerated concern with sexuality

Some of these characteristics are reminiscent of some of the psychopathology found among serial killers. According to Adorno, fascist cult movements encourage such personalities to express themselves in cruel and violent ways against ideologically targeted out groups.[237]

This approach has come under severe criticism. Historian Zygmunt Bauman dismissed it, arguing that it was as if saying: "Nazism was cruel because Nazis were cruel; and Nazis were cruel because cruel people tended to become Nazis." Bauman rejected Adorno's authoritarian personality type because it implied that ordinary people did not commit atrocities.[238]

John Steiner suggested a version of the authoritarian personality type, the so-called "sleeper," a latently violent personality that is unleashed by circumstance, such as an encounter with the violent subculture of the Nazi movement.[239]

Ervin Staub accepts Steiner's idea that people can be latently violent, but believes that the so-called "sleeper" is a very common trait to most people—that all human beings have a primary capacity for violence. There is a little bit of a serial killer in all of us. Staub says, "Evil that arises out of ordinary thinking and is committed by ordinary people is the norm, not the exception."[240]

Bauman disagrees. He argues that most people slip into the roles society provides them, and he is very critical of the "faulty personality" as a cause behind cruelty. Evil is situational, according to Bauman. Serial killers are made.

There is some evidence for this. Philip Zimbardo at Stanford University conducted an experiment where he set up a mock prison. Using personality tests, he filtered out sadistic personality types among those volunteering as guards. Yet within six days, volunteers who did *not* test for sadistic traits began to devise rapidly escalating brutal and cruel methods to control and deal with the volunteer prisoners. Zimbardo concluded that the prison situation alone was a sufficient condition to produce aberrant, antisocial behavior.

Zimbardo discovered that a third of the eleven guards emerged as cruel and tough, constantly inventing new ways to torment their prisoners; a middle group tended to be tough but fair and played by the rules, even if they were cruel, but did not exceed that cruelty on their own initiative; and only two guards actually went out of their way not to be cruel or showed acts of kindness to the prisoners.

If brutality and serial killing can be situational, then before we dismiss Ilse Koch and Irma Grese as Nazi bitches, we need to take a closer look into the face of the former Kentucky-born and -bred chicken factory worker and IGA cashier Lynndie Rana England, who, at the age of 21, found herself caught on camera while tormenting and abusing naked prisoners as a reservist in a military police company in Iraq assigned to the notorious Abu Ghraib prison. Lynndie never killed anybody, but is that the difference between her and Grese? How far did Lynndie have left to go? How many of us have a serial killer inside ready to be unleashed in the right situation? Is the process of becoming a serial killer much simpler and easier than we suspect?

The Manson Cult Women—Charlie's Hippie-Killer Girls

Let's fast-forward from the gloomy, musty, barbed-wired Europe of our grandmothers to where *surf Nazis must die*—to the sunshine of California twenty-five years later, to Charlie Manson's apocalypse and the killer girls who followed him into it. It's a very witchy story in a witchy place at a witchy time—the West Coast in the sixties. It was the Age of Aquarius: sex, drugs, music, freedom, sunshine and ocean and mass graves.

The girls met Manson when they were mostly in their late teens. They were in their early twenties when they descended down from the dark of the night onto upscale homes in Los Angeles, beating, garroting, shooting, and stabbing to death the wealthy occupants, finger-painting slogans in their blood on their white walls and brand-new appliances. One of the victims was an eight-month pregnant starlet, Sharon Tate, the wife of movie director Roman Polanski. Charles Manson, himself, did not kill any of the victims and was not even present at the actual killings. But Manson is the ultimate "Everest" in the tale of these female killers—simply always there.

Today Manson won't let anybody forget that he has been in prison since 1969 for seven murders—none of which he physically committed. He is right about that. It's a *fact*. But as somebody once said about him, "Charlie had a way of taking the truth and making it into a lie." What Charlie did was he got a whole bunch of young women and a few men to go out and do the killing for him.

Nearly forty years later, we cannot get Charles Manson and the Manson women out of our minds: They are the shadow in every baby boomer's sweet memory of another time long past. Manson represents in our collective consciousness how the sixties came to die: Manson with a swastika hand-tattooed into his forehead, and his killer girls, chanting and screaming at their trial, "Why don't you just kill us all now," each one with an X branded into her forehead with hot hairpins, right between the eyes. And all the raggedy, hippie Manson girls outside, barefoot on the court building lawn, some with their heads shaved, with their own X carved into their foreheads as well. And several years later, the Manson girl, Squeaky, pulling a gun on President Gerald Ford. All the other murders attributed to shadowy Manson followers still unsolved. The nightmare did not stop with Manson's imprisonment. There was the Geraldo Rivera TV specials with Manson, including one live from prison in 1989, twenty years after the event.

GERALDO: "Mostly the devil in your world, eh, Charlie?"

MANSON: "Okay. I'll play. I'll be the devil."

GERALDO: "You look more guilty than anyone I've ever looked in the eye in my whole entire life."

MANSON: "Really? Oh boy, that mirror is gonna be heavy for you to carry, ain't it?"

Charlie Manson was, and is, as I write this in the winter of 2007, a clever, mean old snake. But Manson does not, and did not, know what he said from day to day—and that's the problem. But he said it all beautifully with a mad poet's flurry. Unfortunately, Manson had a dark, nasty core that burned deep within him. He was an old-time hillbilly who did some real hard time from the age of eight in the American reformatory and prison system of the 1940s . . . and throughout the 1950s . . . and for the first six and a half years of the 1960s. Prison was his home. Other than that, Charlie was like most of us. He had his good, sweet days when he saved lives and he had days that were not so sweet—those low, dark times when Charlie raged a deep, black rage and destroyed and killed those he had earlier saved.

Charlie was a spoken hurricane—his poet's rap powered by a charismatic sincerity rooted in a backwoods tradition of old-time religion, the kind that comes with the zeal of speaking in tongues or snake handling, honed once in the California prison system by cellblock lessons in the techniques of Scientology and fine guitar playing. Charlie had it all and too much.

Manson still inspires a cadre of followers today: "ATWA—air trees water animals" is still the mantra for a third generation of Manson defenders, many born long after the sixties died. Just google "ATWA" for the key into that dark kingdom on the Internet. ATWA is a sort of environmentalist fundamentalism—the Charlie*ban,* the *black* green vowing holy war on the "piggies" chopping down our forests, pissing into our water, and unjustly imprisoning Manson.

Charlie Manson really was a good poet and lyricist, and a kind of savant philosopher who could have today, in the age of Amazon.com, made a million had he not gone over the edge back then. He would say things like, "Time is a game that's played with money." Or "Do the unexpected. No sense makes sense." But he mixed it with LSD and weed—his psyche already whacked by pools of his own natural body meth—perhaps kryptopyrrole from his piss, when in his head, rotting away all semblance of reason and compassion. The broken Boys Town childhood buried what was left in layers of rage, which would jack-in-the-box out of him in bad times, along with the brilliantly clever turns of phrase and poetry.

With his dark man-boyish looks—all denim and leather and suede and whisky, incense and bullshit, mental crank and Bowie knives—Charlie got laid a lot in the sixties. He called himself the "Gardener," planting his seed among the flower children, a sex-preacher man in the Age of Aquarius darkened by Altamont. Charlie took Woodstock and dune-buggied it out into Death Valley for us. Both men and women followed Charlie Manson into the abyss, but mostly it was the women who were loyal to the end. They closed up the sixties for us, in that last summer of 1969, finger-painting obscenities in blood on the naïveté of the age. We will never get the sixties back again—it's an impossibility that the Mansonites had as much to do with as anything.

The Tate Murders: "Have You Ever Tasted Blood? It's Warm and Sticky and Nice."

On the night of August 8, 1969, 26-year-old Sharon Tate had everything going for her. A harmless and pretty actress, she had married a tortured and brilliant successful film director—Roman Polanski. Her husband had just bought her a white Rolls Royce in England, and her only problem was that her red Ferrari in L.A. was out for repairs. Sharon was in the final stages of her pregnancy and she and Roman settled in a rented house in Los Angeles—not just any house, but one of those palatial, gated and walled estates with a swimming pool and guesthouse on the hill-side of Bel Air. The house had been previously occupied by actress Candice Bergen and record and television producer Terry Melcher, Doris Day's son.

Feeling lonely while Polanski was finishing a script in England, Sharon Tate invited three of her friends to stay over at the house. They, too, were "beautiful people" in what today would be that Paris Hilton way: Abigail Folger, 25, the heiress to a multimillion-dollar coffee empire; Voytek Frykowski, 32, Folger's lover and a friend of Polanski's from Poland, and Jay Sebring, 35, a highly successful entertainment industry hairstylist and Tate's former boyfriend.

They were vapid and wealthy but reasonably decent people. They were settling into their beds for an early night when what would later be described as a crazed, howling, drugged horde of murderous hippies vaulted the walls of the estate and butchered them all.

It was around 12:30 A.M. The doors of the house were locked, but the baby's nursery had just been painted that day, and the window was left open to air the drying paint. The killers slit the screen in the window and wiggled into the house—"creepy crawling" was the term they used.

According to the summary given by authorities at Manson's 1992 parole hearing:

Shortly before midnight on August 8, 1969, the prisoner [Manson] informed his crime partners that now is the time for helter skelter. The crime partners were directed to accompany Charles ["Tex"] Watson to carry out the orders given by the prisoner. The crime partners at the time were Linda Kasabian, Susan Atkins, and Patricia Krenwinkel. As the crime partners were in the car getting ready to leave the area, the prisoner informed them, "You girls know what I mean," something to which he instructed them to leave a sign. Crime partner Watson drove directly to 10050 Cielo Drive, where he stopped the car. Linda Kasabian held three knives and one gun during the trip. Watson then cut the overhead telephone wires at the scene and parked the vehicle.

Crime partners Atkins and Krenwinkel had been in the backseat with Linda Kasabian, the passenger in the right front seat. Watson then carried some rope over the hill and to the outer premises of 10050 Cielo Drive.

The vehicle containing victim Steven Parent approached the gate opening into the street. Watson stopped him at gunpoint and Parent stated, "Please don't hurt me, I won't say anything." Watson shot Parent five times and turned off the ignition of his car.

All of the crime partners then proceeded to the house where Watson cut a window screen. Linda Kasabian acted as a lookout while another female crime partner entered the residence through an open window and admitted the other crime partners.

Within the residence the prisoner's crime partners, without provocation, logic, or reason, murdered Abigail Anne Folger by inflicting a total of twenty-eight multiple stab wounds on her body. Victim Voytek, count two, was killed by multiple stab wounds. A gunshot wound to his left back and multiple, forced trauma of a blunt nature to the head. Victim Sharon Tate Polanski was killed with multiple stab wounds. Victim Jay Sebring was killed by multiple stab wounds.

Jay Sebring was actually stabbed seven times and shot once; Voytek Frykowski was shot twice, received thirteen blows to the head, and was stabbed fifty-one times; Sharon Tate was stabbed sixteen times—her unborn child, was of course, dead. Sharon and Sebring were also hung by the neck from a rafter in the house before they were killed. Written in Tate's blood on the front door of the house was a single word: "Pigs."

Sharon Tate had been killed by 21-year-old Susan Atkins, nicknamed Sadie Mae Glutz. According to her own testimony, she held Tate in a headlock while the other victims were being stomped and stabbed. Then Sharon's turn came. She begged Atkins not to kill her. Atkins testified: "She said, 'Please let me go. All I want to do is have my baby.' I looked at her and said, 'Woman, I have no mercy for you.' And I knew that I was talking to myself, not to her."

In jail, bragging to a cellmate, Atkins was more effusive, saying that she looked Tate in the eyes and said, "Look, bitch, I don't care if you're going to have a baby. You better be ready. You're going to die, and I don't feel anything about it."

Atkins also revealed to her cellmate that she licked Sharon Tate's blood off her fingers, "Wow, what a trip! I thought, 'To taste death, and yet give life.' Have you ever tasted blood? It's warm and sticky and nice."

Atkins dipped a towel into Tate's blood, and wrote "Pigs" on the front door of the house with it. Atkins said she wanted to cut Sharon's baby out of her womb and bring it back for Charlie, but that there just was not enough time. Atkins explained to her cellmate, "You have to have a real love in your heart to do this for people . . . I loved her, and in order for me to kill her I was killing part of myself when I killed her."

It would be a long time before the killers were identified. The massacre was a shocking news story, and in the subsequent days, all sorts of rumors of ritual or satanic rites were circulating in Bel Air and the Hollywood Hills. The fact that Polanski had just finished directing *Rosemary's Baby,* a movie with a satanic theme, only heightened the speculation.

The LaBianca Murders

The next day, on August 10, at around 10:30 P.M. in Los Feliz, another upscale neighborhood in Los Angeles just east of Hollywood next to Griffith Park, police were called to the house of Leno and Rosemary LaBianca, the wealthy owners of a supermarket chain. Rosemary, age 38, was found in her bedroom, stabbed forty-one times in her back and buttocks. A lamp cord was wrapped around her neck and one of the knife blows had severed her spine. Her husband, Leno, age 44, was found downstairs in the living room, stabbed twelve times with a knife and fourteen times with a large serving fork. It was left protruding from his ample stomach. Across his abdomen, the word "War" had been crudely carved into his flesh. In his blood, the words "Death to Pigs" and "Rise" were written on the walls, and on the refrigerator door, "Helter Skelter."

Again, according to Manson's parole hearing record:

On August the 10th, 1969, the prisoner drove his crime partners to a location near the residence of victims Leno and Rosemary LaBianca. The prisoner entered the LaBianca home alone at gunpoint and tied up the victims.

He impressed them with the statement that they would not be harmed and that a robbery was taking place. He then returned to the vehicle containing his crime partners and then directed them to enter that residence and kill the occupants. He informed them not to notify the victims that they would be killed.

Crime partners Charles Watson, Patricia Krenwinkel, Leslie Van Houten, then entered the residence and the prisoner drove away from the scene. The crime partners entered the residence and in a callous manner killed Leno LaBianca by inflicting multiple stab wounds to his neck and abdomen. Rosemary LaBianca was killed by multiple stab wounds, which were inflicted to the neck and trunk [sic].

The crime partners carved the word "war" on Leno LaBianca's stomach with the use of a carving fork. At both of the above murder scenes, the prisoner's crime partners used blood of their victims to write the words.

Under case number A-267861, the prisoner was received into the institution on December 13th, 1971, for violation of first-degree murder concurrent with prior term.

The Murder of Gary Hinman

The Tate and LaBianca murders were not the only killings, nor were they the first ones.

[A] pistol, knives, and swords were used in the following crimes, which the prisoner committed with crime partners Beausoleil and Atkins and [Brunner] and Davis. The prisoner directed the crime partners to go to the home of victim Gary Allen Hinman and have him sign over his property. The crime partners followed the prisoner's directions and on July 26th, 1969, they contacted the prisoner from the Hinman residence. Prisoner and Davis then went to the Hinman home and the prisoner struck Hinman with a sword, severing a part of the right ear and causing a laceration to the left side of his face from his ear to his mouth. The prisoner and Davis then drove away from the crime scene in Hinman's automobile.

On July 27th, 1969, after suffering three days of torturous treatment, Hinman was killed by a stab wound through the heart, which was inflicted by Beausoleil.

402   FEMALE SERIAL KILLERS

When Hinman was found in the Topanga Canyon home on July 31st, 1969, he had been stabbed through the heart in addition to suffering a stab wound in the chest, a gash on the top of his head, a gash behind the right ear, and a laceration on the left side of his face, which cut his ear and cheek.

The complicity of so many young women in these brutally violent crimes mesmerized the media as did the image of the female Manson followers who were not charged and who loitered, chanting and singing and demonstrating outside the court building.

The Manson killings are an anomaly in the history of serial murder. Except for the murder of a drug dealer in a dispute, for which Manson was never charged, Manson did not physically kill any of the victims nor was he present at the moment of death of any of the murders. Two of the incidents were a type of serial mass murder—the people killed together in the Tate house and the La-Bianca house. Some of the killers, while actually committing Manson's serial murders, themselves personally killed only once, while others did not kill at all but participated as accomplices. The leading presence of a male in charge, Tex Watson, at the killings further clouds the issue. But in the end, three women were convicted of murder along with Manson, and today still sit in prison.

Who Was Charles Manson?

One cannot really begin to tell the women's stories without telling Charlie's first. The man the women followed had come from far away and had been kept locked up for decades before he burst on the scene. When Manson said at his trial that he went to jail when he was 8 years old, and got out when he was 32, that was not an exaggerated claim. The last time Manson had been released from prison, in March 1967, he was, in fact, 32 years old, and he had spent by then an accumulated total of seventeen years in various reformatories, jails, and prisons—more than half his life. He was 8 years old the first time he was arrested for theft, and he was 9 when he was confined to a reformatory.

It was not just how much time Manson did, but how and *when* he did it. Charlie likes to say he had gone to prison the last time on a ten-year sentence for attempting to steal $37.50. And it's true.

He tried to steal a check from a mailbox, and mail theft is a heavy federal offense. But his sentence was suspended. Then he went out and committed more offenses, so the sentence was automatically *reinstated* and he ended up serving seven years of it. Again— remember the warning: "Charlie has a way of taking the truth and making it into a lie."

When they locked him up in 1959, Charlie was 24 years old and Eisenhower was President. When he got out in 1967, he was 32 and Kennedy was long dead. What more can one say? Manson had sat out in prison more than half of the sixties and more than half of his own twenties.

But Manson did not waste his time in prison. He learned Scien tology techniques. The Church of Scientology looked into it after Charlie made the news. An internal document from the church's security unit, seized by the FBI during an unrelated investigation and released through the Freedom of Information Act, reads as follows:

(22 June 1970)
Report of interview with Raul Morales, Re: Charles Manson.
  According to Raul: Raul arrived in prison on McNeil Island, Washington, in 1962 and became a cellmate of Lafayette Raimer, allegedly a trained Scientology auditor (about Level I in Raul's estimation) and was introduced to Scientology at that time. Raimer was auditing in prison at that time and in one ten-man cell had managed to gather a group of about seven, all in Scientology. Charles Manson entered later and studied, did TRO, etc., along with his cellmates and received approximately 150 hours of auditing from Raimer. Processes used were CCH's, Help processes (Who have you helped—Who have you not helped), and other Dichotomy processes (Raul's terms, such as What can you confront, what would you rather not confront), Havingness (such as What can you have? Look around and find something you can have. Look around and find something you're not in.) Raimer kept records of his auditing. Manson got super-energetic & flipped out when he'd been audited and would, for a time, talk about nothing but Scientology to the extent that people avoided his company. After a while, however, Manson was screaming to get away from his auditor (in

Raul's opinion, he'd been severely overrun or something). He eventually managed to get put in solitary confinement to get away from his auditor. Eventually prison officials got suspicious of the group's strange activities and broke up the group. Subsequently, Raul was released from the prison in 1965.

Raimer's wife was in training here at the L.A. Org in 1965–66; she had disconnected from Raimer. Raul just found out yesterday that another friend, Marvin White, later sent Manson books (after the Scientology group was broken up) on hypnotism and black magic.[241]

Manson's story gets wilder: at McNeil Island Penitentiary he also learned how to play the guitar. His teacher was Alvin "Creepy" Karpis, one of the few surviving gangsters of the classic era of Public Enemy, Bonnie and Clyde, John Dillinger, and Machine Gun Kelly. Karpis had been a member of the murderous Ma Barker Gang and held the record for the longest imprisonment on Alcatraz Island. He had been in prison since 1936, serving a life sentence for bank robbery and kidnapping and had recently been transferred to McNeil Island where he met Manson. Karpis was a bad-boy talented guitar player and taught the eager Manson all he knew.

* * *

At 8:15 A.M. on March 21, 1967, Manson was released from Terminal Island Reformatory in Long Beach. One can wax all manner of lyric about what the world was like in 1959 when Charlie went in and what it had become by 1967 when he came out, but enough said.

He claims that he never wanted to be released. That he was content in prison. On his release, Charlie was given thirty-five dollars, exactly two dollars and fifty cents less than the amount for which he had been locked up seven years before. Manson was transported to nearby Los Angeles. He carried a little suitcase with the clothes in which he had been arrested, and rode the bus for three days. He slept on the buses until the drivers kicked him off. Manson said it kept reminding him of being kicked out of prison. Then, because he had some acquaintances in San Francisco, Manson headed north.

Charlie crash-landed in the epicenter of America's countercul-
ture movement—the Haight-Ashbury neighborhood of San Francisco in March 1967 on the eve of the "Summer of Love," when
the hippie movement came into being. This was the time of Flower
Power, Make Love Not War, Turn On / Tune In / Drop Out, peace
rallies, sit-ins, love-ins, share-ins, guerrilla theater, communes, underground newspapers, Day-Glo posters, Owsley's acid, and music
and music and music. And Charlie hadn't even smoked a joint
yet—he had been strictly a Jack Daniel's man. The rest of Manson's history is pure legend, myth, and speculative bullshit.

Flowers and Acid—Manson in the Valley of Thousands of Plump White Rabbits

There are two versions of how Charlie Manson *became*. One is
that he dropped LSD for the first time at a Grateful Dead concert
at the Avalon Ballroom, curled up in the middle of the crowded
dance floor into a fetal position, and was reborn, "innovating" to
the music and drawing applause as he neuro-spun like a dervish
acidhead.[242]

The other version is that a young girl named Nancy Hart, a
petty check forger and would-be folk singer, introduced Manson
to LSD. She says that she was sleeping in the park under a pile of
blankets one spring night, when Manson approached her and asked
if he could get in under with her, because "she was giving off this
tremendous heat."[243]

"Charlie wasn't a great lover, but he acted out the role of it,"
Hart recalled. "And he was a great con artist, perhaps the best I
have ever seen or come across in the business. He went around
with me and hung paper [passed bad checks] around San Francisco
and he'd rap on all the con tricks he'd gathered. What he knew
could blow minds . . ."

"We'd ball and he'd get bored with what we were doing, so he
screwed me with a broom handle after he got tired and had me do
it with a Coke bottle, both sides, and to myself *so,* while he jerked
off. And he had me rap it all, like relating to him how I was experiencing and what it was that I felt from him—from his *nearness,* if
you can dig it. On acid it was that especially, that no contact thing
and his relating what was happening."

When she gave Charlie his first tab of acid, Hart told him, "You're already there, you don't need it, but it'll help straighten the currents." After spending several days with Manson, Nancy Hart was arrested and Manson went on his own way.

Manson said, "My awareness after acid of what was going on became that much more enlightened. I was with them, part of them. We were all really a part of one another."

LSD—lysergic acid diethylamide—acid. It was discovered in Switzerland in 1938, four years after Manson was born. It was of no interest to anybody and was filed away without any further testing. Then, on April 16, 1943, one of its discoverers, Dr. Albert Hofmann, a chemist working at the Sandoz Pharmaceutical Laboratories in Basel, accidentally ingested a small amount of the substance. Hofmann later wrote in his notebook:

Last Friday . . . I had to interrupt my laboratory work in the middle of the afternoon and go home, because I was seized with a feeling of great restlessness and mild dizziness. At home, I lay down and sank into a not unpleasant delirium, which was characterized by extremely excited fantasies. In a semiconscious state, with my eyes closed (I felt the daylight to be unpleasantly dazzling), fantastic visions of extraordinary realness and with an intense kaleidoscopic play of colors assaulted me. After two hours this condition disappeared.[244]

LSD is classified as an hallucinogen—from the Latin *halucinari* (to wander mentally) and the Greek *genes* (to be born). It is also classified as a psychedelic—from the Greek *psyche* (soul) and *delos* (visible or evident).

Psychedelic drugs, those that make the "soul visible" can be found in natural substances, and have a long history of religious and mystical use among Mexican and Central American Indians prior to the arrival of Europeans. Peyote cactus buds, when chewed, produced a psychedelic effect. Mescaline is derived from peyote, and is named for the Mescalero Apaches, who first brought it north from Texas and New Mexico. Mescaline has fewer unpleasant side effects than peyote. Psilocybin produces similar psychedelic effects and is found in certain types of mushrooms—so-called "magic mushrooms," which were also consumed in religious rituals by native Indians (and gobbled down today by new-agers in the northwest).

The effect of these substances is difficult to describe. First, time slows down. A minute feels like ten minutes, but one does not perceive things in slow motion. One's way of thinking and brain functions are altered. One might see sounds and smell colors and hear smells and touch tastes. One might be able to look at oneself from the outside—make new connections between ideas and gain remarkable insights into oneself, if one is predisposed in that direction.

Among the Indians in the nineteenth and early twentieth century, peyote was used to treat alcoholism and to alleviate postmenopausal depression in women. Guided by Indian shamans, their awareness sensitized by the effects of peyote, many women who felt depressed about the passage of their childbearing capacities, found new meaning and hope in their existence.[245] Unlike antidepressants, which chemically simulate a "happiness" that wears off with the drug, psychedelics focus natural thinking processes in a search for a cerebral discovery, which can remain fused in the psyche long after the drug is gone. It is said the drug can reveal a new path in one's thinking process, which once learned, is not forgotten and is not dependent on further ingestion of the hallucinogenic substance. This is precisely why, during the 1950s and 1960s, LSD was adopted as a possible miracle drug by some psychiatrists.

LSD is about a hundred times more potent than peyote or mescaline. It is a very powerful drug that induces a psychedelic trip some ten hours in duration. Pharmaceutical LSD, only produced by Sandoz, was privately consumed in small, closed circles of psychiatric employees and their friends and relatives throughout most of the 1950s and early 1960s. It was unknown outside these circles.

In the meantime, Harvard instructor Timothy Leary was discovering psilocybin mushrooms in Mexico in 1960. He said, "It was the classic visionary voyage and I came back a changed man. You are never the same after you've had that one flash/glimpse down the cellular time tunnel. You are never the same after you've had the veil drawn."

Leary then turned to LSD, and in 1963 he began talking about it to the press. By 1965, thanks to Leary, it had become the demon drug and was banned and outlawed. Sandoz stopped making it and a whole army of small underground laboratories began manufacturing it. LSD became instantly popular.

In 1965, at a psychiatric conference on the therapeutic use of psychedelics, the following was reported about LSD and mescaline:

1. They reduce the patient's defensiveness and allow repressed memories and conflictual material to come forth. The recall of these events is improved and the abreaction is intense.

2. The emerging material is better understood because the patient sees the conflict as a visual image or in vivid visual symbols. It is accepted without being overwhelming because the detached state of awareness makes the emerging guilt feelings less devastating.

3. The patient feels closer to the therapist and it is easier for him to express his irrational feelings.

4. Alertness is not impaired and insights are retained after the drug has worn off.

Under skilled treatment procedures, the hallucinogens do seem to produce these effects and one more, which is not often mentioned. That is *a marked heightening of the patient's suggestibility.* Put in another way, the *judgmental attitude of the patient toward the experience itself is diminished.* This can be helpful, for insights are accepted without reservations and seem much more valid than under nondrug condition.[246] [My emphasis.]

Charles Manson, a 32-year-old outlaw, who spent seventeen years in jail, was now into LSD, jacked up on Scientology, and musically fathered by Alvin "Creepy" Karpis. It was like North Korea with a nuke. The "Gardener" was loose among the flower children who were desperately looking for themselves during the great Summer of Love—especially the lost young women. And there was Charlie, all bullshit and rage, and now a pocketful of acid.

It is hard to say when Manson transformed himself into his long-haired, shaggy, hippie persona. On July 29, 1967, Manson was arrested on a minor charge of "interfering with a police officer." It was nearly August of the great, hippie, flower-powered Summer of Love, but Manson's mugshot that day shows him with his hair styled quite conservatively. It is slightly long and curly on the top and front in that late fifties greaser kind of way, but neatly barbershop-trimmed short around his ears and neck.

Manson was keeping his wits about him. He didn't buy into any of it. Thirty years later, in 1997, he recalled:

> When I got out last time, I knew it was all a bunch of rotten apples. But I didn't figure I was any better than the worst of them, or any worse than the best. It's the same fucking thing, it's just a pile of shit anyway, so why not try to grow some flowers in it? That's when I got out, and I went through these other things, and then I got trapped up in these kids of the sixties. But I'm not a kid of the sixties; I'm a kid of the forties. Bing Crosby was my hero, not Elvis Presley.[247]

Charlie Manson began homing in on young, impressionable flower kids emerging alone into a truly brave new world, a world that had never existed before for the young—especially the girls who were double-locked and chained by society's old values, which discounted both youth and women exponentially. Charlie offered to throw off their chains, and nobody knew better, because there was nothing like the sixties before—not even the twenties. There were no rules—nothing from the past to compare the present to—anything seemed possible.

Charlie once said of those times:

> I could *see* these people on the street—see them with clean eyes, you know. These people on the street were like me—thrown out of life like your paper coffee cups and hamburger sacks and rags and stinking Kotex pads and dirty rubbers. They were the garbage floating around and shit sticking to the sides of your toilet and your drain holes . . . I took these people that were your garbage that'd been thrown away by society, and I put them to use.

I made them put water in cans and make things work in order to keep living on the outside.

Ed Sanders, from the band The Fugs, said that the Summer of Love in the Haight was free and beautiful, "but there was a weakness: from the standpoint of vulnerability the flower movement was like a valley of thousands of plump white rabbits surrounded by wounded coyotes."

When the whole hippie movement in Haight-Ashbury was overrun by speed freaks and bikers and got all nasty and syphilitic by the foggy cold autumn of 1967, Manson moved himself and his followers to warmer climes—down to Los Angeles.

Mary Theresa Brunner—the Manson Family Matriarch

In the spring of 1967, six months before the move, Manson was hanging out in front of the gates of the University of California at Berkeley, panhandling and playing his guitar. There he attached himself to a small poodle and then to the somewhat unattractive, bespectacled redhead walking it—23-year-old Mary Theresa Brunner. Born in Eau Claire, Wisconsin, on December 17, 1943, to parents John and Evelyn Brunner, Mary was a good Catholic girl, who graduated in history from the University of Wisconsin and had recently moved to California to accept a librarian's position at the UC Berkeley Library.

Charlie charmed Mary on the spot, and with the hippie campus abandon of that spring of '67 in her nostrils, Mary thought she'd take a taste. She invited the charismatic street musician to crash on the couch of her apartment. No sex—this was strictly platonic. Then Charlie starting bringing girls to her apartment for sex. And Mary, who by now was smitten, wanted some, too, and brought him into her bed. But Charlie kept on bringing girls home, first one, then two, and eventually there would be eighteen. That's how the Family got started—with Mary Brunner. It was never called the "Manson Family"—that's a media thing. They referred to themselves only as "the Family."

Brunner would become the Family matriarch, nicknamed Maryoch or Mother Mary Manson. She would have a child by Manson, which he delivered himself and named Michael Pooh

Hoo. She was one of the women that went to Hinman's house and at least witnessed, if not participated, in his three-day torture before he was stabbed through the heart.

After Manson was convicted in the Tate-LaBianca murders, the ex-librarian was involved in a dramatic shootout in 1971 at a gun store in Los Angeles on South Hawthorne Boulevard. She and several accomplices had forced the clerks and customers to the floor and had loaded hundreds of powerful weapons into a van. The weapons were to supply a plan to rescue Manson from prison by hijacking a 747 jet, whose passengers would be killed one at a time, every hour, until Manson was released. But instead of fleeing, they began to argue amongst themselves as to whether they should kill all the people inside the store. By then, police responding to a silent alarm surrounded the store and there was a ten-minute gunfight before the robbers surrendered.

Brunner became involved with the Aryan Brotherhood (AB), an ultra-violent white-power convicts' group. Several other Manson followers also moved on to the Aryan Brotherhood after Manson was sent away, and were close to the core founders of the AB. There developed a sort of Aryan Brotherhood breakaway faction of the Manson Family after 1970.

Brunner testified against the others on the Gary Hinman murder, and after serving some time for the Hawthorne gun store robbery while her parents took care of Pooh Hoo, she was released and subsequently vanished into obscurity in the Midwest to raise Charlie Manson's son, who must be turning forty soon.

Lynette Alice Fromme—Squeaky

Mary Brunner was joined by a second female recruit, a studious teenage girl from Redondo Beach, the slender, freckle-faced Lynette Alice Fromme, who became known as "Squeaky." Resembling Sissy Spacek in *Carrie,* Fromme was 17 when her unusually domineering father kicked her out of the house.

Lyn was born on October 22, 1948, to Helen Fromme and her husband, William, an aeronautic engineer employed in the Los Angeles aircraft industry. She had a younger brother and sister. She was a talented and smart girl, averaging B plus and A minus during most of her academic career. She was an editor of the high school yearbook and an "expert" on the poet Dylan Thomas. But at home her father was rigidly controlling, specifically of her. She would inexplicably be subjected to stringent codes of conduct and made to eat separately from the rest of the family members.

Lyn ran away from home several times, but would return, reconciling with her mother and controlling father. By 1966, she was hitchhiking up and down the California coast, drinking, dropping acid, and having sex, which she found unsatisfactory. In 1967, she returned home and enrolled in El Camino College, signing up for French, theater arts, psychology, and modern dance. Her plan was to keep her grades up and transfer the next year to the University of California. But she had a final break with her crazy father instead. "We argued over some kind of definition from the dictionary, that's how dumb it was," she later said. "His way or no way. I said, 'yes, but,' and he said, 'yes but nothing.'"[248]

Taking nothing but her schoolbooks, Lyn walked out of her home with no place to go. She hitchhiked down to Venice Beach. At Manson's sentencing hearing, she would testify, "I was in Venice, sitting down on a curb crying, when a man walked up and said, 'Your father kicked you out of the house, did he?' And that was Charlie."

They spoke only for a few minutes. Charlie played the wise, fatherly figure for her, telling her, "The way out of a room is *not* through the door. Just *don't want out,* and you're free." Cool, thought Lyn.

Charlie told her he was heading up north back to San Francisco. She could join him if she wanted to. When? Right now, he told her. Lyn was a little incredulous and Manson said, "I can't make up your mind for you," and walked off. Lyn had only three more weeks to go on her freshman semester. She said that she grabbed her books and ran to catch up with him.

Lyn joined Manson and Mary Brunner, who had by now quit her job as a librarian, and with her last paycheck financed a trip for the three of them to Mendocino County, north of San Francisco. There they rented a small cabin near the ocean and Charlie began to work his sex magic, breaking down both Mary's and Lyn's taboos, eventually taking them both to bed. After the stupid sex Lyn had been having with her clumsy high school lovers, sex with Manson was mind-blowing, she recalled. He led her to discover her clitoris—"a tiny, hard, supersensitive thing," she said. He was the first lover who had performed oral sex on her.

Manson told the bright 17-year-old, "The fact is that if a man loves, he makes a woman feel like the most beautiful creature in the whole world. And if a woman loves, she can accept and feel all of his love, making one love, in one motion, of all feeling at once."

Lyn testified on his behalf, "Charlie is our father in that he would—he would point out things to us. I would crawl off in a corner and be reading a book, and he would pass me and tell me what it said in the book . . . And also he knew our thoughts . . . He was always happy, always. He would go into the bathroom sometimes to comb his hair, and there would be a whole crowd of people in there watching him because he had so much fun."

Squeaky did not go out on the 1969 killings, but six years later she tried to make up for it. In September 1975, in Sacramento, armed with a loaded .45 semiautomatic handgun, Squeaky rushed at President Gerald Ford and got within two feet of him, before being subdued by the Secret Service. She was quickly put on trial, and in November, sentenced to life imprisonment for attempting to assassinate the President.

Squeaky's life sentence is sort of like Manson's seven years for the theft of $37.50. Few people believe that Squeaky wanted to actually shoot Ford. In fact, while there were four bullets in the handgun's magazine, there was no round chambered in the breech—which means that Squeaky could have pulled the trigger as many times as she wanted, but the gun would not fire. She would have to jack back the slide and chamber a round before the weapon would work. Lyn was familiar with weapons, so it is unlikely that she was ignorant of the necessary procedure to properly load the .45. On the other hand, she could have been stressed or drugged out, and just forgot to chamber a round—it can happen. And if she meant no harm, why was the weapon loaded? Many feel, however, that Lynette Fromme should have been convicted of assault at worst. She is still in prison today, almost 60 years old at this writing.

Susan Atkins—Sexy Sadie Mae Glutz

Susan Atkins, who became known as Sexy Sadie Mae Glutz, was 21 at the time of the murders and perhaps the most vicious of all the Family members. After chasing one of the escaping victims across the lawn at Cielo Drive and cutting him down, she then returned to the house to stab to death the eight-and-a-half-months pregnant Sharon Tate.

Susan Atkins was born in San Gabriel, California, on May 7, 1948. She was the middle child and only girl among the three siblings. The family, apparently, had problems with alcohol, and authorities once tried to take the children away. She was a religious girl, sang in the church choir, was a member of the Girl Scouts, and was a good student in primary school.

Susan, however, felt that she was left out of the family, with her parents preferring her brothers: her mother the youngest, her father the eldest. Atkins herself said, "I didn't like my mother. She tried to get along with me, but I just refused to get along with her. I didn't like my father either. Didn't like either one of them. I didn't like my mother because she was an alcoholic . . . my father also was an alcoholic, used to beat my mother up."[249]

In 1963, when Susan was 15, her mother was diagnosed with terminal cancer. Susan and the church choir sang beneath her dying mother's bedroom window. About her mother's death, however, relatives recall, "Susan had an almost indifferent air about it."

After her mother's death, Susan began to run wild. A friend of Susan's stated, "She just didn't seem to care. Like when her mother died, she didn't show any real sadness about it. I don't think Susan cared about anything very much. There was something wrong with her."

Atkins left home when she was 18—"On the day," she says. She held a few menial jobs, but mostly she turned to crime. Susan was arrested for car theft and put on probation. She committed a number of petty crimes and frequented the company of armed robbers. In San Francisco, she worked as a topless dancer and lived in a communal house. She also got into Satanism. According to her psychiatric report, read into the record at her sentencing hearing, Atkins, in 1966:

. . . entered into what she now calls her Satanic period. She became involved with Anton LaVey, the Satanist.* She took a part in a commercial production of a witch's sabbath,† and recalls the opening night when she took LSD. She was supposed to lie down in a coffin during the act, and lay down in it while hallucinating. She stated that she didn't want to come out, and consequently the curtain was fifteen minutes late. She stated that she felt alive and everything else in the ugly world was dead. Subsequently, she stayed on her "Satanic trip" for approximately eight months.

One day in the summer of 1967, when Atkins was 19, she met Charlie at a party. Atkins recalled that Manson was singing and playing his guitar and that she was mesmerized by his voice and lyrics:

And when he finished his song, I asked him if I could play his guitar. He just handed it to me without saying anything.

I looked at it and put my hand on it, and I plucked it. I knew only one chord. I thought to myself, "I can't play this."

I just thought that to myself, didn't say it out loud. But he turned around and looked at me, straight in the eye, and he said: "You can play that guitar if you want to."

I just looked at him, and I immediately knew who he was and what he was there for. In other words, what he was there for was to show me he was inside my head. There was no way I could get away from it.

And, wow, nothing like this ever happened before—and it blew my mind. I was just with him from then on.[250]

Several days later, Manson returned for Atkins:

---

* LaVey was the founder of the San Francisco–based First Church of Satan—a pseudosatanic cult for wankers with fat wallets and small brains.

† In point of fact, there is no connection between satanism and witchcraft. Either the psychiatrist was in error by linking the two, or the organizers of the event were themselves characterizing what they were staging as the "Witches Sabbath."

He told me he wanted to make love with me. Well, I acknowl-edged the fact that I wanted to make love with him and he told me to take off my clothes. So I uninhibitedly took off my clothes, and there happened to be a full-length mirror and I turned away and he says, "Go ahead and look at yourself, there is nothing wrong with you. You are perfect. You always have been perfect." He says . . . "You were born perfect and everything that has hap-pened to you from the time you were a child all the way up to this moment has happened perfectly. You have made no mistakes. The only mistakes you have made are the mistakes that you thought you made. They were not mistakes . . ."

He asked me if I ever made love with my father. I looked at him and kind of giggled and I said, "No." And he said, "Have you ever thought about making love to your father?" I said, "Yes, I thought I would like to make love with my father." And he told me, he said, "All right, when we are making love imagine in your imagination that I am your father and, in other words, picture in your mind that I am your father." And I did, I did so, and it was a very beauti-ful experience.[251]

Manson was giving little Suzy Atkins a pseudo-Scientologist total mind-and-body fuck.

Susan Atkins became Sexy Sadie Mae Glutz. She had a child by somebody from the Family, which Manson also delivered. The lit-tle boy was named Zo Zo Ze Ze Zadfrack (or according to other sources, as if it makes a difference, Zezo Zece Zadfrack).

Before Susan Atkins joined in on the murders at Cielo Drive, she had already participated in the torture and murder of Gary Hin-man on July 26, 1969. Thirty-two-year-old Hinman taught music in L.A. and was working on his Ph.D. in sociology at UCLA. He was a member of the Nichiren Shoshu Buddhist sect and owned several cars and a Volkswagen camper. Hinman was fairly well known in Topanga Canyon, and hitchhikers and hippies often stayed at his house, as did Manson in 1968. Hinman may or may not have been manufacturing synthetic mescaline.

According to witnesses, on Friday, July 25, Bobby Beausoleil, a new male member of the Family, Mary Brunner, and Susan Atkins went to Hinman's house armed with a handgun and knives. They demanded money from him and ownership papers to his cars. Hinman refused, whereupon the trio began to beat him. When they had no success getting what they wanted, they telephoned Manson.

Manson arrived brandishing a sword and demanding that Hinman turn over the cars and money to him. When Hinman refused, Manson struck him with the sword, cleaving his ear in two and cutting a deep wound into his jaw. Hinman quickly handed over the keys to his cars and Manson drove off in one of them, telling the girls to sew Hinman's wound up, and to continue attempting to extract cash from him.

Atkins and Brunner stitched Hinman's wound with dental floss and then proceeded to torture him all day Saturday and into Sunday. They would take turns sleeping. On Sunday, Hinman had still failed to relinquish any money. At that point, Beausoleil telephoned Manson again, who allegedly said, "You know what to do," or "You know what to do. Kill him—he's no good to us," or "He knows too much."

Manson steadfastly denies he gave any instructions to kill Hinman:

It would come from the witness stand that when on the telephone the only thing that ever connected me with Hinman's murder was Beausoleil called me and asked me what to do and I told him, "You know what to do." I didn't tell him like [raising voice], "You know *what* to do." I told him, "Man, you're a man, grow up, juvenile. Don't ask me what to do. Stand on your own two feet. Be responsible for your own actions. Don't ask me what to do."[252]

Shouting, "Society doesn't need you—you're a pig! It's better this way. I'm your brother," Beausoleil stabbed Hinman four times. As Hinman bled to death, one of the girls gave him his prayer beads and Hinman chanted, "Nam Myoho Renge Kyo—Nam Myoho Renge Kyo," the chant of his Buddhist sect.

Hinman lost consciousness, but continued to breathe. Susan Atkins and Mary Brunner then took turns holding a pillow over his face until he suffocated. Using his blood, they wrote, "Death to Piggies," on the wall and attempted to stage the scene to look like some kind of Black Panther hit. They even made a crude cat's paw print on the wall.* They left with the remainder of Hinman's vehicles.

Charlie's Apocalypse

In the days between the Hinman murder and the Tate murders, Manson was north of Los Angeles, driving up the coast in a 1952 Hostess Twinkies bakery truck. A series of witnesses and a traffic citation pinpoint his travels.

Manson was up in Big Sur at the Esalen Institute. Esalen was (and is today) a personal "growth center" and luxury resort for wealthy clients from San Francisco and Los Angeles, offering seminars in all sorts of alternative Eastern and Western philosophies presented by various guest speakers. The subject matter ranged from yoga to satanism. Abigail Folger often stayed at the Esalen Institute.

Manson traveled in high Hollywood movie and music circles. He was a guest for the longest time in Beach Boy drummer Dennis Wilson's home, had met producer Phil Kaufman when Kaufman was in prison for a marijuana possession charge, and Kaufman promised to produce Manson's record, *LIES* (and did so in 1970 after Manson went on trial). Manson has a whole history of broken deals and screwed-up opportunities with heavy players in the film and music industries. The industry was liberating itself of the old studio mogul dinosaurs, getting closer to the youth in the street. A lot of doors were open for a guy like Manson. (The Beach Boys had actually recorded one of Manson's songs, "Cease to Exist," which appears on their *20/20* album as "Never Learn Not to Love.")

Manson visited Esalen on numerous occasions, taking seminars himself, using their hot tubs and springs and looking for recruits. This last visit to Esalen, however, did not go well for Manson, according to witness Paul Watson, who testified that Manson had said he went "to Esalen and played his guitar for a bunch of people who were supposed to be the top people there, and they rejected

---

* The notion was entirely stupid, as the Black Panthers, if they committed any political murders, were not known to write slogans in victims' blood and leave bloody cat pawprints at the scene.

his music. Some people pretended that they were asleep and other people were saying, 'This is too heavy for me,' and 'I'm not ready for that,' and others were saying, 'Well, I don't understand it,' and some just got up and walked out."²⁵³

Manson rolled back into Los Angeles on Friday morning, August 8, 1969, feeling exposed and rejected after the experience in Esalen and in one dark and heavy mood. Sharon Tate and her friends had just a little over twelve hours left to live.

In the preceding six months, Manson had gone apocalyptic with the Family, purchasing dune buggies and planning to hide out in Death Valley when the race war he predicted between blacks and whites broke out. He was feeding his followers pure hatred and fear. The prosecution would claim Manson called it Helter Skelter, inspired by the Beatles song on the *White Album*. Maybe.

Or maybe Charlie's brain just melted with drugs and paranoia and Hollywood bullshit—calls not returned, promised deals vanished into smoke. Manson would say anything that came to him with his moods and drugs and forget the next day, but according to Tex Watson, another trusted male member of the Family, Manson specifically told him that afternoon to go to producer Terry Melcher's former house at Cielo Drive, and murder anybody he found there as a warning to Melcher. Manson had had some kind of music deal going with Melcher that had gone bad. Manson knew that Melcher no longer lived there and that Sharon Tate occupied the house. He ordered Susan Atkins and Patricia Krenwinkel to accompany Tex and do what he told them.

Patricia Krenwinkel—Big Patty

Patricia Krenwinkel was 18 years old when she met Manson. She was a former Presbyterian Sunday school teacher and an avid Bible reader. She was extremely homely—a manly face, excess body hair, and as revealed when she later shaved her head, jug-handle ears. She became known as Big Patty, Katie, or Yellow.

Krenwinkel grew up in Manhattan Beach in Los Angeles. Her father, Joe, was an insurance agent and her mother a housewife who was active in church and community programs. She did well in high school and attended one semester of the Jesuit Springfield

College in Mobile, Alabama. After her arrest her parents described her as a perfect, normal, happy, clever, studious, pious, well-behaved child who enjoyed her family life, school and church activities, and was never in trouble. "Pat was very enthusiastic about reading the Bible . . . Never saw her hostile or angry . . . never saw her fight . . . never saw her cruel to animals . . . never saw her physically violent . . . not a person with a quick temper . . . If she awakened first in the morning, when she was still in her crib, she was doing little drawings or playing with little things . . . she would play with them and not create a disturbance. She would not cry for anyone to get her up or to do anything for her . . . I never had any trouble with her . . . never disrespectful . . . was a model child . . . never in trouble with the police . . . never received a traffic ticket."[254]

Creepy!

At Cielo Drive, the former Sunday school teacher chased Abigail Folger out onto the lawn in front of the house and stabbed her twenty-eight times, as Folger whimpered, "Stop, I am already dead." The next night at the LaBianca house, she stabbed Rosemary so hard that she severed her spine. She then stuck a serving fork into Leno LaBianca's stomach and "pinged" it to watch the fork wobble.

She would describe to her prison psychiatrists a much less rosy picture of herself as a child than the one painted by her parents. She said she always felt unwanted and unloved and perceived herself as ugly and hairy (which one might argue she was). Feeling overweight, she crash-dieted when she was 14. She said that she was completely mind-controlled by her parents, internalizing her "bad" repulsive self while maintaining an artificially pious and obedient exterior. The need to suppress her real self made her angry, which she also needed to repress and conceal.

Her parents divorced when Patricia was 13 but they claim, "It did not involve the children. It was a very quiet something—very personal, and it was nothing that the children would have any part in or be hurt by it." More wishful fantasy.

Krenwinkel met Manson and Mary Brunner through her half-sister, with whom she was sharing an apartment and who was a heroin addict. (Another product of a perfect childhood under their roof that the parents fantasized about. Her sister would later die of an overdose.)

Patricia recalled that when she met Manson he told her that everything would be all right. He liberated her secret self. Manson was the first man to make love to her with the lights on—to her hairy, "bad" self. She said, "I cried that first night with my head in his lap. He was like my dad. It got pure, it was so good . . . I told him, I've got to go wherever you go." And she did.

Linda Kasabian—Yana the Witch

A new recruit to the Family, Linda Kasabian, was sent to accompany Watson, Atkins, and Krenwinkel to the Tate murders. Linda had the only valid driver's license among them. Linda was born on June 21, 1949, in Biddeford, Maine. Her parents divorced and remarried when Linda was still young. She grew up in Milford, New Hampshire.

Kasabian recalled, "My mother and father fought a lot. My first recollection of childhood was sitting on a couch crying . . . My father finally left the house for good after we had moved to New Hampshire. My mother insisted that he buy me some shoes before he left and he refused. But as he went out he slipped some pennies into my hand."

She remembers her father driving around to the house to see her later. He always had another woman in the car and Linda instinctively hated her.

"My mother and I grew close . . . She'd fix up my banana curls and dress me in a pinafore and take me around, showing me off to everybody. My father used to beat her on the behind as she stooped over the washing machine . . . But my stepfather was worse. His name was Byrd and he had children of his own and he was always telling my mother how much better his kids were. I screamed at my stepfather one day. I said, 'You hate me, don't you?' He said, 'Yeah, I hate you all right.' And I flipped. I just flipped."

In grade school, Linda was a cheerleader and a star athlete. Then her recollections take a slight twist, almost sounding like Aileen Wuornos's childhood:

We used to go down to the river and strip. There were boys and girls and we'd all roll in the sand and feed the ducks and have a ball. But there was this kid, Larry, with the big bug eyes. He liked me and I guessed I liked him, too. But we wouldn't let him come down to the river with us and this made him mad and one day he went to our teacher and then there was trouble. Then one day a girl I knew called me a dirty little river girl. But the boys liked me. Maybe because they thought of me as a river girl.[255]

When Linda turned 16 she dropped out from high school and got married but soon divorced. After meeting a hippie named Robert Kasabian she married a second time and the couple traveled the country staying at various communes. In March 1968, Linda gave birth to her first child, Tanya. The following year the couple were living in Topanga Canyon with Charles Melton, who was acquainted with some Manson Family members. When her marriage with Robert was disintegrating in 1969, Linda paid a visit to her friends at the Spahn's Ranch, where the Family was based. After spending a day with Manson, Linda returned to Topanga Canyon, packed her belongings, and after stealing five thousand dollars from Melton, left Robert to join the Family.

When the murders took place, she stood watch outside the house and later testified against the accused in exchange for immunity. After Linda was released, she reconciled with Kasabian and moved to New Hampshire where she had another child.

In a 1971 interview, she claimed to be a Jesus freak, telling the report, "Freedom is a union with that man," pointing to a picture of Jesus above a mattress that served as her bed.

In 1996, police arrested Linda and one of her daughters during a raid in which a gun and drugs were seized. Linda's daughter, aka "Lady Dangerous," was charged with possession of cocaine and sentenced to a year in prison. Linda Kasabian was found in possession of methamphetamine but stayed out of jail after agreeing to attend drug-counseling.[256]

* * *

Before sending them out to Cielo Drive, Manson told the girls to leave a sign at the house: "Something witchy." With Tex and Atkins snorted-up on speed (without Manson's knowledge—he despised amphetamines) and Kasabian and Krenwinkel stoned on who-knows-what, they drove in a 1959 Ford through the San Fernando Valley Friday night traffic up the back of the Hollywood Hills. The high hills at night are a magical place. Viewed from the dark and relatively rural heights, the lights of Los Angeles below stretch out forever on both sides to the horizons like a vast, twinkling, electric ocean. After crossing Mulholland Drive on the ridge of the hills, they rolled down the other side along North Beverly Glen Boulevard into Bel Air, turning east into a tangle of hillside streets just before Sunset Boulevard. They parked the car down the hill from the Cielo Drive gate and proceeded on foot, carrying with them a change of clothes, rope, knives, and a gun. They were all wearing black clothes that Charlie had them purchase for "creepy crawling," where they would practice trespassing across people's property in the middle of the night without being detected.

Kasabian understood little of what was going on inside the house while she stood guard outside in the bushes. She heard shouts and the sounds of a scuffle. At one point, she saw Voytek Frykowski burst out of the house, screaming, blood streaming from his body. He was chased down by Susan Atkins and Tex, who both stabbed at him with their knives. Frykowski tried to stay on his feet, clutching a garden lamppost, like a wounded animal surrounded by a killing pack. Finally, he crumpled to the lawn with thirteen separate blunt-trauma injuries to his head, two gunshot wounds, and fifty-one stab wounds.

When Kasabian saw Abigail Folger run out of the house, her white see-through nightgown a sticking-wet red, and chased by Krenwinkel wielding a knife and butchering her on the lawn, she had had enough. She left the Cielo Drive property and walked outside to sit in the car. Ten minutes later, she saw Tex, Atkins, and Krenwinkel descending the hill, like zombies, their dark clothes soaking wet and their hands and faces stained with red.

Leslie Van Houten—LuLu with No Nickname

The next night, Charlie, Tex, and Krenwinkel drove out to the house of Leno and Rosemary LaBianca. Accompanying them was yet another female member of the Family—19-year-old Leslie Van

Houten. Another "perfect" child from a Presbyterian family, Leslie was a Bluebird, Campfire Girl, and a member of a girls' religious group called Job Daughters. She was the youngest of two children. When she was seven, her parents adopted two Korean orphans.

Again, the family is portrayed as religious, an ideal family, but Leslie's father actually had problems with alcoholism. The marriage was on the rocks. When Leslie was 14, her parents divorced.

Leslie did well in school and was popular. She had been elected Homecoming Queen at her high school. But she led a double life. She began smoking marijuana, still something rare for middle-class kids back then. She became pregnant and had an abortion.

She graduated from business school, but never sought any work afterward. She ended up in San Francisco and hooked up with Bobby Beausoleil, the handsome star of underground filmmaker Kenneth Anger's *Lucifer Rising*. Beausoleil was socializing with Manson and was slowly being drawn into the Family. When he finally submitted to Charlie, he brought Leslie Van Houten with him.

Van Houten felt overlooked by Manson, who did not give her a nickname like the other girls. Moreover, he handed her off to be Watson's woman, which upset her even more. When she heard the girls who had gone to Cielo drive describe the murders they had committed, she decided she wanted to go the next time to prove her devotion to Manson. She got her opportunity the next night.

After Manson went into the house by himself and subdued Rosemary and Leno LeBianca at gunpoint, he departed, leaving them tied-up and at the mercy of Charles Watson, Patricia Krenwinkel, and Leslie Van Houten. After murdering Leno, they tied an electrical cord around Rosemary's throat. As Watson and Krenwinkel stabbed her, Van Houten held her down with a pillow over her head. She then assisted them in cleaning the house of evidence and writing "witchy" slogans on the walls and refrigerator. She finally earned a nickname—LuLu.

* * *

Manson, Krenwinkel, Van Houten, and Atkins were tried together and sentenced to death, but the sentences were commuted when the death penalty was temporarily suspended in 1970. One can surf the Internet and find complete transcripts of their parole hearings. Atkins claims to have found Jesus in a big way, while the other women found him in a small way. They are all sorry, boohoo. They are all up for their umpteenth parole hearing in 2006 and 2007. It's unlikely they will be released.

Manson rages on. For a while, he had his own website, ATWA.com, but it got pulled and a WHOIS search shows it as "locked" but available for sale. What isn't these days? Now others run it for him under different URLs, linking into archival caches of the former site.

The Method to Charlie's Madness

Charlie Manson demanded absolute obedience from the people around him. His word was never questioned. At first one might suspect that it was the drugs, especially the LSD that broke down the will of his disciples—but it wasn't. It was the sex. Dr. David Smith, who worked at the Haight-Ashbury Medical Clinic and saw the Manson group, said, "A new girl in Charlie's Family would bring with her a certain middle-class morality. The first thing Charlie did was to see that all this was worn down. That way he was able to eliminate the controls that normally govern our lives."[257] Manson's girls had become his followers, not *despite* their middle-class background and education, but *because* of it.

Manson controlled the men in the Family through the girls. The girls often lured the men to his circle, and afterward it was on Manson's command whether the girls would have sex with the men or not. Manson also liked young men in his group, to lure other girls, because he knew that as an older man he often scared young girls away.

Nor was Manson above using physical violence with any female that disobeyed him. He was particularly abusive of a 13-year-old girl by the name of Dianne Lake, nicknamed "Snake" for the way she moved when she made love. Her parents had already gone hippie, living on various communes, and had no objections to her joining the Family. Manson was seen beating her with a chair leg once, and with an electric cord another time. (After Manson was sent away to prison, Snake was adopted by a district attorney, returned to school, and today is a vice-president of a bank. I'm not sure how happy an ending that is.)

Manson orchestrated group sex sessions. One witness said, "Everything was done at Charlie's direction." He would dance with his followers trailing behind him like a train, stripping off their clothes. Manson would liberally distribute LSD and peyote and the Family would huddle into a group grope, with Charlie giving directions. "He'd set it all up in a beautiful way like he was creating a masterpiece in sculpture, but instead of clay he was using warm bodies."

Manson would use sex to break down people's "hang-ups." He sodomized the 13-year-old Lake in front of the group and performed fellatio on a young man to show he had no hang-ups himself.

But there was more to it than that. Sometimes it's the times. Today, a Charlie Manson running his kind of game might at best get a shrug and a laugh. But the sixties were a very special time— a type of loss of virginity for an entire generation of *Leave It to Beaver* kids, who found themselves not only dropping acid, smoking pot, and having sex, but also dying in Vietnam, in civil rights actions, and in campus protests, clubbed and killed by their *Father Knows Best* elders. Unlike the "lost generation" of young men who returned from the First World War and fueled the rebellion of the twenties, the sixties' kids mostly stayed close to home—their traumas unfolded not on the battlefield, but in their hushed, closed suburban homes, and it encompassed young men and women alike. The hypocrisy of the times was crushing. A figure like Charlie Manson was truly a Christlike savior in their eyes. He was something new. It was no coincidence how many of the women who joined Manson grew up in religious households. The entire ethos of modern California is built on the search for a new spirituality, and Manson was one of its epicenters.

Manson said at his sentencing:

You eat meat with your teeth and you kill things that are better than you are, and in the same respect you say how bad and even killers that your children are. You make your children what they are. I am just a reflection of every one of you . . . These children that come at you with knives, they are your children. You taught them. I didn't teach them. I just tried to help them stand up.[258]

That might be the one truth Charlie never turned into a lie.

CONCLUSION

RECOGNIZING THE PREDATORY WOMAN

Profiling Female Serial Killers

Is your mom, sister, daughter, grandmother, wife, girlfriend, babysitter, the nurse taking your kids' temperature, or the home-care worker who looks after your granny a serial killer just waiting for an opportunity to strike? Probably not, but she could be. What might be the warning signs, other than the burning sensation you might have in your throat after drinking a cup of coffee she sweetly offered you?

There are some warning signs—common behavioral traits that we have seen in the women featured in the case studies:

- The telling of exaggerated stories intended to inflate the teller's worth or importance in the listener's perception

- Compulsive lying

- Petty thieving, bouncing of checks, bad credit behavior

- Sudden shifts in mood or a permanent shift to a hostile and demeaning attitude from an affectionate and respectful one

- Promiscuous sexual behavior

- Morbid interest in death and true-crime literature

- Drug or alcohol abuse

- Eating disorders or obesity

- A history of abuse as a child
- A history of broken marriages

That's right—many are characteristics that millions of average men and women all might exhibit. In other words, there are very few warning signs without context. A bounced check might be nothing but an error in balancing a checkbook—but in a Black Widow it may be a warning of trouble to come. The problem is having enough information to have a context.

There are characteristic indicators of a psychopath:

- superficial charm
- self-centered and self-important
- need for stimulation, prone to boredom
- deceptive behavior and lying
- conning and manipulative
- little remorse or guilt
- shallow emotional response
- callous with a lack of empathy
- living off others or predatory attitude
- poor self-control
- impulsive lifestyle
- lack of realistic long-term goals
- promiscuous sexual behavior

But not all psychopaths are killers—many, especially the intelligent ones, cause all sorts of perfectly legal havoc, some from congressional seats and corner offices.

There are some warning signs for Munchausen syndrome by proxy, but again these can only be seen in context. They are helpful for the physician or health-care worker who can gather and evaluate this kind of information, but for the family it is of less help:

- persistent or recurrent illnesses for which a cause cannot be found; the child continues to be presented in a victim's role by the mother through "add-on" and newly "remembered" symptoms or details

- discrepancies between history and clinical findings; history given of abuse that should produce physical findings—for example, repeated rape—but a medical exams shows no evidence; factual contradictions in history given—for example, locations that police cannot confirm

- symptoms and signs that do not occur when a child is away from the mother or the child answers negatively about symptoms when away from mother

- a persistent failure of a child to tolerate or respond to medical therapy without clear cause or the child does not respond to psychological therapy

- a parent appears to be less concerned than the physician, sometimes comforting the medical staff, or a child recites allegations or symptoms in a rote manner or is eager to tell his or her story

- repeated hospitalizations and vigorous medical evaluations of mother or child without definitive diagnoses; mother has child repeatedly evaluated for diseases or abuse and is dissatisfied with negative results

- a mother who is constantly at the child's bedside, insists on staying in the room for child's therapy interview, excessively praises the staff, becomes overly attached to the staff, or becomes highly involved in the care of other patients

- a mother who welcomes medical tests of her child, even when painful; seems to welcome repeated sexual assault exams and interrogations of child

- frequent comparisons of the child's medical problems to those of the mother

- the complaining mother seems to know more about what allegedly the child feels than the child

While this is of help to the physician, it does not help the child's father at home. How much did Mary Beth Tinning's husband know about what his children were suffering or allegedly suffering while he was away at work in the factory; and even if he did, how many times did he accompany his wife into the physician's interview and examination? Would he have even been in a position to recognize any lies that she might have been telling the doctor had he been there?

* * *

Kim Iannetta, a Hawaii-based forensic handwriting examiner, looks for indicators of predatory characteristics revealed in people's handwriting. She has nearly three decades of experience in forensic behavioral profiling through written communication and forensic document examination and has reviewed the handwriting of many female singular and serial killers.[259]

When asked what differences she finds in profiling men and women, Iannetta says, "In the broadest sense the range of profiling differences between men and women or women and other women seems to be an element of style as a function of the killer's personality. That is, their methods of killing could be interpreted as an extension of their very personalities, which could reflect not only who they are but who they wish to be.

"More specifically, as men and women settle into society's cultural expectations, their handwritings give us an opportunity to assess their level of comfort or discomfort in their roles. Typically, women still function as the more passive sex, taking on nurturing, caregiving, caretaking, organizing, and administrative responsibilities. As society demands more assertive behavior from men: arrogance, pride, and aggression become more associated with male style. Common to both male and female killers, however, is that level of socio- or psychopathic detachment, which allows them to pursue the ultimate release of their anger, rage, and unfulfilled needs—the killing act itself.

"The most significant difference between men and women who kill is women's expert ability to act in a passive-aggressive manner with a carefully crafted persona. Comfortably playing a conventional role and accepted as 'normal,' they 'blend right into' society. Their goal then becomes easier to attain. This insidious behavior makes them particularly dangerous.

"Acting out in their conventional roles, some female killers often have a deep hunger for excessive attention. They may habitually invade other people's space, showing little or no respect for social or personal boundaries. They also tend to be emotionally immature, and like Karla Homolka, may play the role of 'cute little girl,' still trying to capture Mommy's or Daddy's attention. Like some male killers, they may have repetitive, obsessive sexual thoughts (Karla Homolka and Carol Bundy), which distort their value systems. Readily seen in Christine Falling's handwriting is a compulsively convoluted thinking style, which twisted her notions of values . . .

"The most outstanding difference I see in women who kill, as opposed to men, rests in their ability to fabricate a methodically crafted persona or mask of cultivated charm and seductive, ingratiating behavior. Men seem to be much less interested in role-playing, more drawn to sex in order to dominate, and often to avenge their 'honor' and pride."[260]

* * *

If women, indeed, have "expert ability to act in a passive-aggressive manner" as Iannetta suggests, then their predatory aggression might be truly invisible until it is too late. Aggressive behavior in men is more overt and easier to track—aggression is often *expected* and encouraged in men at work, sports, and duty. One judges the male by the nature of his aggression—and against whom he directs it. But when women from whom we expect *no* aggression at all—never—cloak their aggression entirely, it becomes more difficult to discern what is happening. There is no visible aggression to judge as appropriate or inappropriate as we do with men. We do not see it until it is truly too late.

We know a number of things about predatory aggression (as opposed to "affective" aggression—a response to being attacked).[261] Predatory aggression is a cerebral process. There is little autonomic "fight or flight" arousal in the predatory aggressor. It is a controlled and calm attack, although it could bounce back and forth between affective and predatory once underway in some cases—mostly with sexual offenders.

There is an absence of emotion. Male serial killers report that they are most emotional—feeling a sense of exhilaration—*prior* to killing, often during the stalking stage. The killing itself is often committed in an emotionally deadened state.

Females appear to invest their exhilaration into the murder itself. Genene Jones, Jane Toppan, Aileen Wuornos, for example, were all thrilled by the actual murders. That was their point of exhilaration, not the buildup to it. That is why murder could actually be the female serial killer's primary signature. The predatory violence is planned and purposeful. Rarely are there "disorganized" female serial killers. Most have a plan and it frequently involves some kind of deception or intimate seduction of the intended victim.

Predatory aggressors manifest an inflated self-worth—a grandiose perception of their self-importance balanced by a diminished perception of the victim's worth. Again, this was very evident in the case of Aileen Wuornos and her denigration of her victims as "rapists;" in Dorothea Puente, who perceived her derelict victims as worthless to society; in Jane Toppan, who thought many of her victims were too old to live on; and in the Manson women who saw their victims as wealthy "piggies."

* * *

There have been attempts to categorize female serial killers as Black Widows, angels of death, cult followers, missionaries, accomplices, vengeance killers, or Munchausen syndrome by proxy killers, etc. But we see that in many cases it is impossible to attribute such a singular motive to any female serial killer:

- Was Aileen Wuornos driven by profit or rage and vengeance for her past abuse?

- Was Jane Toppan a missionary killer, murdering people she felt were too old to live, a vengeance killer, or was she a sadistic sexual killer, deriving pleasure from watching her victims die?

- Was Velma Barfield killing for the meager profit or covering up crimes to save her self-esteem? Was she raging with hormonal imbalance after her hysterectomy or was she a Munchausen syndrome by proxy killer, seeking attention from her son to whom she was over-attached?

- Was Karla Homolka a compliant victim of her husband's depraved sadistic fantasies or was she his muse, using him to express her own predatory sexual desires?

Rarely do we have these kinds of ambiguities in our analysis of male serial killers.

The only thing we know for sure is that almost all serial killers, male or female, spawn in the cruel pool of their childhood, starting as victims. Every serial killer is the first victim in their own history—little girls and boys who should have been loved, cared for, and nurtured, but were not. It's not about excusing their horrific acts, but about the place where we could make it stop before it ever becomes—in the child's heart. If only we could.

The feminists are right about one thing: We live under a wealthy autocracy of some sort that strives to classify, divide, and rule us. The media and the mall are its henchmen droogs. This nebulous autocracy encourages mass consumption, social and intellectual degradation, and dumb, mindless acquiescence to force and violence. Women are victimized by it, as are equally men and children. There is no special *gynocide*. There is only democide—the murder of everyone equally. Not only the killing of people, but of ATWA as well—Air Trees Water Animals. Charlie Manson said, "You are either working for ATWA—life—or you're working for death. Fix it and live or run from it and die."[262]

Manson can seem to make sense because his hillbilly-boy pain was real. It was his acts that were evil. But if Charlie can take truth and make it into a lie, then perhaps we can at least take some of his pain-borne lies and redeem them for the truth. It's up to us.

Love each other and never kill for any reason no matter what. Just don't do it.

APPENDIX

SOME KNOWN FEMALE SERIAL KILLERS AND NUMBERS OF POSSIBLE VICTIMS

Name	Victims Confirmed (Suspected)
Agrippina the Younger	(100>)
Sara Aldrete	13 (15–30)
Beverly Allitt	4
Susan Atkins	9 (20>)
Kathleen Atkinson	4
Amy Archer-Gilligan	20 (40>)
Margie Velma Barfield	5 (6–7)
Elizabeth Countess Báthory	300 (<650)
Martha Beck	4 (20)
Marie Alexandrine Becker	12
Betty Lou Beets	2
Mary Flora Bell	2
Kate Bender	10 (12)
Marie Besnard	13
Catherine Birnie	4(8)
Elfriede Blauensteiner	5>
Cecile Bombeck	3>
Marie de Brinvilliers	50>
Debra Denise Brown	8
Mary Brunner	9 (20>)
Judias Anna Lou Buenoano	3
Carol M. Bundy	2 (6)
Mary Emily Cage	1 (6)
Patty Cannon	25(>)
Susan Carson	3

Name	Victims Confirmed (Suspected)
Sarah Chesham	1 (10>)
Cynthia Coffman	4 (>)
Faye Copeland	5
Mary Ann Cotton	15–22(+)
Theresa Cross	2 (3)
Anna Cunningham	5
Sarah Dazely	2 (4)
Minnie Dean	2 (3>)
Catherine Deshayes	? (2,500)
Nancy "Nannie" Hazel Doss	4(11)
Amelia Dyer	11>
Elizabeth Eccles	3
Marti Enriqueta	6>
Ellen Etheridge	4
Christine Falling	6
Susanna Fazekas	100>
Constance Fisher	6
Catherine Flannagan	(9)
Debbie Fornuto	6
Sarah Freeman	4
Caril Fugate	11
Mrs. Julius Fuzekos/Fazekas	7 (100)
Charlene Gallego	10
Tillie Gbrurek	5
Janie Lou Gibbs	5
Kristen Gilbert	5>
Amy Gilligan	9
Delfina Gonzales	91>
Maria de Jesus Gonzales	91>
Gesina Gottfried	16
Gwendolyn Graham	5
Ann Green	2 (?)
Caroline Grills	4
Maria Gruber	49 (300)

Name	Victims Confirmed (Suspected)
Belle Gunness	16–28 (48)
Anna Marie Hahn	5 (15>)
Margaret Higgins	(9)
Audrey Marie Hilley	3 (4)
Myra Hindley	5 (10)
Karla Homolka	3 (?)
Waneta E. Hoyt	5
Mary Jane Jackson	4
Marie Jeanneret	7 (8)
Helene Jegado	27>
Martha Ann Johnson	4
Genene Jones	1 (47)
Eliza Joyce	3
Linda Kasabian	9 (20>)
Claudette Kibble	3
Sharon Kinne	3
Tillie Klimek	9(>)
Patricia Krenwinkel	9 (20>)
Christa Lehman	3
Irene Leidolf	49 (300)
Juliane Lipka	7 (100)
Diana Lumbrera	6
Anjette Lyles	4
Sarah Makin	7>
Christine Malevre	7 (30)
Martha Marek	4
Rhonda Belle Martin	6 (8)
Mary May	2 (14)
Stephanija Mayer	49 (300)
Carolyn McCrary	11 (22)
Virginia McGinnis	4
Daisy Louisa C. De Melker	3
Valeria Messalina	(50>)
Mary Ann Milner	3

Name	Victims Confirmed (Suspected)
Alice Mitchell	<37
Blanche Taylor Moore	5
Patricia Moore	3
Judith Ann Neelley	12 (15)
Marie Noe	8
Susi Olah	7 (100)
Sandra Pankow	3
Bonnie Parker	12 (13)
Madame Alexe Popova	<300
Dorothea Puente Montalvo	9
Terri Rachals	6 (9)
Vera Renczi	35
Martha Rendell	3
Sarah Jane Robinson	8
Antoinette Scieri	6 (?)
Jane Scott	1 (3)
Lydia Sherman	10 (11>)
Della Sorenson	7
Mariam Soulakiotis	177
Hieronyima Spara	100>
Mrs. Szabo	7 (100)
Ginger Taylor (nee McCrary)	11 (22)
Bobbie Sue Terrell	12>
Marybeth Tinning	9
La Tofania	<600
Jane Toppan	31 (<100)
Lydia Trueblood	6
Debra Sue Tuggle	4
Lise Jane Turner	3
Sophie Ursinus	3
Leslie Van Houten	9 (20>)
Maria Velten	5
Louise Vermilyea	10
Waltraud Wagner	49 (300)

Name	Victims Confirmed (Suspected)
Rachel Wall (pirate)	1>
Margaret Waters	16 (35)
Jeanne Weber	8 (<20)
Rosemary West	10 (18)
Dorothy Williams	3
Stella Williamson	5
Catherine Wilson	5 (7)
Martha Hasel Wise	3
Catherine May Wood	5
Martha Woods	7
Aileen Carol Wuornos	7(>)
Lila Gladys Young	(100>)
Anna Zwanziger	3>

BIBLIOGRAPHY

BOOKS

Theodor Adorno, et al., *The Authoritarian Personality,* New York: Harper & Brothers, 1950.

M.D.S. Ainsworth, et al., *Patterns of Attachment: A Psychological Study of the Strange Situation,* Hillsdale, NJ: Erlbaum, 1978.

Susan Atkins (cowritten by Bob Slosser), *Child of Satan, Child of God,* Logos International: 1977.

Velma Barfield, *Woman on Death Row,* Nashville, TN: Thomas-Nelson Books, 1985.

Zygmunt Bauman, *Modernity and the Holocaust,* Ithaca, NY: Cornell University Press, 1989.

Geoffrey Best, *Mid-Victorian Britain 1851–1875,* New York: Schocken, 1972.

Daniel J. Blackburn, *Human Harvest,* New York: Knightsbridge, 1990.

Jerry Bledsoe, *Death Sentence,* New York: Onyx Books, 1998.

John Bowlby, *Attachment and Loss: Volume 1. Attachment,* New York: Basic Books, 1969.

Ian Brady, *The Gates of Janus,* Los Angeles: Feral House, 2001.

Jess Bravin, *Squeaky: The Life and Times of Lynette Alice Fromme,* New York: St. Martin's Griffith, 1998.

Edward M. Brecher, *Licit and Illicit Drugs,* Boston: Little Brown and Company, 1972.

Daniel Patrick Brown, *The Beautiful Beast,* Ventura, CA: Golden West Historical Publications, 1996.

Daniel Patrick Brown, *The Camp Women: The Female Auxiliaries Who Assisted the SS in Running the Nazi Concentration Camp System,* Atglen, PA: Schiffer Publishing, 2002.

Christopher Browning, *Ordinary Men: Reserve Police Battalion 101 and the Final Solution in Poland,* (2nd Edition), New York: HarperPerennial, 1998.

Christopher Browning, *The Origins of the Final Solution: The Evolution of Nazi Jewish Policy, September 1939–March 1942,* Lincoln, Nebraska/Jerusalem: University of Nebraska Press/Yad Vashem, 2004.

Vincent Bugliosi, *Helter Skelter,* Bantam Books, New York: 1975.

D. Cameron and E. Frazer, *The Lust to Kill: A Feminist Investigation of Sexual Murder,* New York: New York University Press, 1987.

Jane Caputi, *The Age of Sex Crime,* London: Women's Press, 1987.

John Cashman, *The LSD Story*, Greenwich, CT: Fawcett Publications, 1966.

Phyllis Chesler, *Patriarchy: Notes of an Expert Witness*, Monroe, ME: Common Courage Press, 1994.

Hervey Cleckley, *The Mask of Sanity* (5th Edition), privately printed, 1988. http://www.cassiopaea.com/cassiopaea/psychopath.htm

Joyce Egginton, *From Cradle to Grave*, New York: Jove Books, 1990.

Peter Elkind, *The Death Shift*, New York: Onyx Books, 1989.

Louise Farr, *The Sunset Murders*, New York: Pocket Books, 1992.

Jennifer Furio, *Team Killers: A Comparative Study of Collaborative Criminals*, New York: Algora, 2001.

V. Gerbeth, *Practical Homicide Investigations*, Boca Raton, FL: CRC Press, 1996.

John Gilmore and Ron Kenner, *The Garbage People*, Los Angeles: AMOK Books, 1995.

Peter Haining, *Sweeney Todd: The Real Story of the Demon Barber of Fleet Street*, London: Robson Books, 2002.

Lynda Hart, *Fatal Women: Lesbian Sexuality and the Mark of Aggression*, New York–London: Routledge, 1994.

Eric W. Hickey, *Serial Murders and Their Victims* (3rd Edition), Belmont, CA: Wadsworth/Thomson Learning, 2002.

Ronald M. Holmes and Stephen T. Holmes, *Murder in America*, Thousand Oaks, CA, Sage Publications: 1994.

Ronald M. Holmes and Stephen T. Holmes, *Serial Murder* (2nd Edition), Thousand Oaks, CA: Sage Publications, 1998.

Ann Jones, *Women Who Kill*, New York: Fawcett Columbine, 1981.

Ann Jones, *Next Time She Will Be Dead*, New York: Beacon Press, 1994.

Michael Kater, *The Nazi Party*, Cambridge, MA: Harvard University Press, 1983.

Michael D. Kelleher and C. L. Kelleher, *Murder Most Rare*, New York: Dell Books, 1998.

Dolores Kennedy with Robert Nolin, *On a Killing Day*, New York: S.P.I. Books, 1994.

Ernst Klee, Willi Dressen, Volker Riess, *"Those Were the Days": The Holocaust As Seen by the Perpetrators and Bystanders*, London: Hamish Hamilton, 1991.

Shelley Klein, *The Most Evil Women in History*, London: Michael O'Mara Books, 2003.

Judith Knelman, *Twisting in the Wind: The Murderess and the English Press*, Toronto: University of Toronto Press, 1998.

Robert Jay Lifton, *The Nazi Doctors: Medical Killing and the Psychology of Genocide*, New York: HarperCollins, 1986.

Clara Livsey, *The Manson Women*, New York: Richard Marek Publishers, 1980.

J. Reid Maloy, *The Psychopathic Mind: Origins, Dynamics, and Treatment* (2nd Edition), Northvale, NJ: Aronson, 1992.

Raymond T. McNally, *Dracula Was a Woman: In Search of the Blood Countess of Transylvania,* New York: McGraw-Hill, 1983.

Kelly Moore and Dan Reed, *Deadly Medicine,* New York: St. Martin's Press, 1988.

Belinda Morrissey, *When Women Kill: Questions of Agency and Subjectivity,* New York–London: Routledge, 2003.

Joel Norris, *Serial Killers,* New York: Doubleday (Anchor Books) 1989.

Jack Olson, *The Misbegotten Son: A Serial Killer and His Victims,* New York: Island Books, 1993.

Patricia Pearson, *When She Was Bad: How and Why Women Get Away with Murder,* Toronto: Random House Canada, 1998.

Raymond Phillips, *Trial of Joseph Kramer and Forty-four Others (The Belsen Trial),* London: William Hodge and Company, 1949.

Otto Pollack, *The Criminality of Women,* New York: A. S. Barnes, 1961.

J. Radford and D.E.H. Russell (Eds), *Femicide: The Politics of Women Killing,* New York: Maxwell MacMillan International, 1992.

Robert K. Ressler, Ann W. Burgess, John E. Douglas, *Sexual Homicide: Patterns and Motives,* Lexington, MA: Lexington Books,1988.

Sue Russell, *Lethal Intent,* New York: Pinnacle Books, 2002.

Ed Sanders, *The Family* (Revised and Updated Edition), New York: Signet Books, 1989.

Harold Schechter, *Fatal: The Poisonous Life of a Female Serial Killer,* New York: Pocket Books, 2003.

Lawrence Schiller, *The Killing of Sharon Tate,* New York: New American Library, 1970.

Gitta Sereny, *Cries Unheard,* New York: Henry Holt, 1998.

Patricia Springer, *Blood Rush,* New York: Pinnacle Books, 1994.

Deborah Schurman-Kauflin, *The New Predator: Women Who Kill,* Algora, NY: 2000.

Kerry Segrave, *Women Serial and Mass Murderers,* London: McFarland & Co, 1992.

Mark Seltzer, *Serial Killers: Death and Life in America's Wound Culture,* New York–London: Routledge, 1998.

Stacey L. Shipley and Bruce A. Arrigo, *The Female Homicide Offender,* Upper Saddle River, NJ: Pearson-Prentice Hall, 2004.

Ervin Staub, *The Roots of Evil: The Origins of Genocide and Other Group Violence,* Cambridge, MA: University of Harvard Press, 1989.

Germain Tillion, *Ravensbrück,* Garden City, NY: Doubleday, 1975.

Laszlo Turoczy, *Ungaria suis cum regibus compendio data,* Nagyszombat: 1729.

Peter Vronsky, *Serial Killers: The Method and Madness of Monsters,* New York: Berkley, 2004.

Michael Wagener, *Beiträge zur Philosophischen Anthropologie (Articles on Philosophical Anthropology)*, Vienna: 1796.

Katherine Watson, *Poisoned Lives: English Poisoners and Their Victims*, London: Hambledon and London, 2004.

Emlyn Williams, *Beyond Belief*, London: Pan Books, 1967.

Stephen Williams, *Karla: A Pact with the Devil*, Toronto: Seal Books, 2003.

Colin Wilson and Donald Seamen, *The Serial Killers*, London: Virgin Publishing, 1992.

Patrick Wilson, *Murderess: A Study of Women Executed in Britain Since 1843*, London: Michael Joseph, 1971.

Wayne Wilson, *Good Murders and Bad Murders: A Consumer's Guide in the Age of Information*, Lanham, NC: University Press of America, 1991.

William P. Wood, *The Bone Garden*, New York: Ibooks, 1994.

ACADEMIC, HISTORICAL, SCIENTIFIC, AND FORENSIC JOURNALS

Dr. Robert L. Bergman, Head of U.S. Public Health Service for Navajos, *Presentation Paper*, Annual Conference of the American Psychiatric Association: 1971.

Béla Bodó, "The Poisoning Women of Tiszazug," *Journal of Family History*, Vol. 27, No. 1, January 2002.

Steven J. Boros, M.D., and Larry C. Brubaker, "Munchausen Syndrome by Proxy: Case Accounts," *FBI Law Enforcement Bulletin*, Washington D.C.: June, 1992.

Yehoshua R. Buchler, "'Unworthy Behavior': The Case of SS Officer Max Taubner," *Holocaust and Genocide Studies*, Vol. 17, No. 3, Winter 2003.

Jane Caputi. "The New Founding Fathers: The Lore and Lure of the Serial Killer in Contemporary Culture," *Journal of American Culture*, 13, 1–12, 1990.

T. Edwards Clark, M.D., *The Galaxy*, Volume 6, Issue 3, Sept. 1868.

K. E. Cole, G. Fisher, and S. S. Cole, "Women Who Kill: A Sociopsychological Study," *Archives of General Psychiatry*, 19, 1968.

G. Cote and S. Hodgins, "The Prevalence of Major Mental Disorders Among Homicide Offenders," *International Journal of Law and Psychiatry*, No. 15, (1992).

S. A. Egger, "A Working Definition of Serial Murder and the Reductions of Linkage Blindness," *Journal of Police Science and Administration*, 12: 348–357, 1984.

K. Feldman, D. Christopher, and K. Opheim, "Munchausen Syndrome/Bulimia by Proxy: Ipecac as a Toxin in Child Abuse," *Child Abuse & Neglect*, 13, (1989).

A. Frodi, J. Macaulay, and P. R. Thome, "Are Women Always Less Aggressive Than Men?" *Psychological Bulletin* 84 (1977).

Ilsa M. Glazer and Wahipa Abu Ras, "On Aggression, Human Rights, and Hegemonic Discourse: The Case of a Murder for Family Honor in Israel," *Sex Roles* 30:3/4 (February 1994).

Kathryn A. Hanon, "Munchausen's Syndrome by Proxy," *FBI Law Enforcement Bulletin*, Washington, D.C.: December 1991.

Richard L. Jenkins, "The Psychopath or Antisocial Personality," *Journal of Nervous and Mental Diseases*, No. 131, (1960).

Nancy C. Jurik and Russ Winn, "Gender and Homicide: A Comparison of Men and Women Who Kill," *Violence and Victims*, 5:4 (1990).

B. T. Keeney and K. Heide, "Gender Differences in Serial Murderers," *Journal of Interpersonal Violence*, Vol. 9, No. 3, September 1994.

Robert D. Keppel and Richard Walter, "Profiling Killers: A Revised Classification Model for Understanding Sexual Murder," *International Journal of Offender Therapy and Comparative Criminology*, Vol. 43, No. 4, 1999.

Rachel MacNair, "Psychological Reverberations for the Killers: Preliminary Historical Evidence for Perpetration-Induced Traumatic Stress," *Journal of Genocide Research*, Vol. 3, No. 2, 2001.

W.H.J. Martens, "Marcel: A Case Study of a Violent Sexual Psychopath in Remission," *International Journal of Offender Therapy and Comparative Criminology*, 43(3), 1999.

Susan McWhinney, "Petit Treason: Crimes Against the Matriarchy," in Amy Schroder (ed), *Critical Condition: Women on the Edge of Violence*, San Francisco: City Lights Books, 1993.

Roy Meadow, "Management of Munchausen Syndrome by Proxy," *Archives of Disease in Childhood*, 60 (1985).

Roy Meadow, "Munchausen Syndrome by Proxy: The Hinterland of Child Abuse," *Lancet*, 2 (1977).

Roy Meadow, "Munchausen Syndrome by Proxy," *Archives of Disease in Childhood*, 57, (1982).

R. T. Mulder, et al., "Antisocial Women," *Journal of Personality Disorders*, No. 8 (1994).

Alexandra Przyrembel, "Transfixed by an Image: Ilse Koch, the 'Kommandeuse of Buchenwald,'" *German History* Vol. 19, No. 3. (2001).

K. Ravenscroft, Jr., and J. Hochheiser, *Factitious hematuria in a six-year-old girl: A case example of Munchausen syndrome by proxy*. Presented at the Annual Meeting of the American Academy of Child Psychiatry, Chicago, 1980.

D. A. Reiger, J. H. Boyd, et al., "One Month Prevalence of Mental Disorders in the United States," *Archives of General Psychiatry*, No. 45 (1988).

L. N. Robins, *Deviant Children Grow Up*, Baltimore: Williams & Wilkens, 1966.

M. Rutter, "Antisocial Behavior: Developmental Psychopathology Perspectives" in D. M. Stoff, J. Breiling, and J.D.D. Maser (Eds), *Handbook of Antisocial Behavior*, New York: Wiley, 1994.

M. Sigal, I. Carmel, D. Altmark, and P. Silfen, "Munchausen Syndrome by Proxy: A Psychodynamic Analysis," *Medicine and Law*, 7 (1988).

John M. Steiner, "The SS Yesterday and Today: A Sociopsychological View," in Joel E. Dimsdale (Ed), *Survivors, Victims, and Perpetrators: Essays on the Nazi Holocaust*, Washington, D.C.: 1980.

R. Warner, "The Diagnosis of Antisocial and Hysterical Personality Disorders: An Example of Sex Bias," *The Journal of Nervous and Mental Disease*, No. 166 (1978).

Janet I. Warren and Robert R. Hazelwood, "Relational Patterns Associated With Sexual Sadism: A Study of 20 Wives and Girlfriends," *Journal of Family Violence*, Vol. 17, No. 1, March 2002.

R. A. Wesheit, "Female Homicide Offenders: Trends Over Time in an Institutionalized Population," *Justice Quarterly*, Vol. 1, No. 4, 1984.

NEWS ARTICLES, GOVERNMENT DOCUMENTS, INTERNET SITES, AND OTHER SOURCES

Amnesty International Execution Alert: February 7, 2000 (http://www.ccadp.org/bettiealert.htm).

CBC News, Canada: "B.C. woman waiting for beating death trial arrested for assault," http://www.cbc.ca/story/canada/national/2004/02/11/ellard_bc040211.html.

Church of Scientology, GS-C Comm; GS-G; D/G Intell U.S., *Compliance Report Re: Manson, Bruce Davis,* 22 June 1970—see: http://bernie.cncfamily.com/sc/Manson_Scientology.htm.

"Information on the Infamous Concentration Camp at Buchenwald," 14 February 1945, in U.S. vs. Josias Prince zu Waldeck, *et al.,* War Crimes Case No. 12–390 (The Buchenwald Case), War Crimes Office, National Archives and Records Service, 1976, Record Group 153, Records of the Judge Advocate General, National Archives, (Washington, D.C.).

Los Angeles County case number A-252156, Statement of Charles Manson, November 19, 1970.

Harland Manchester, "Jane Toppan, Champion Poisoner," *American Mercury*, 49: 340–346, March 1940.

Mind of a Killer CD, Kozel Multimedia, 1995–1998.

New York Times, October 18, 1948, K. Sitte, Letter to the Editor.

New York Times, October 22, 1948, "Clay Stands Firm in Ilse Koch Case."

New York Times, March 10, 1993, A. Quindlen, "Gynocide."

SECONDS, http://web.archive.org/web/19981206222051/ and http://www.sni.net/central/manson/man/interview1.html, 19 December 1997.

Bill Trent, "The Girl Who Was Involved in One of North America's Most Bizarre Mass Murders," *Weekend Magazine, St. Thomas Times Journal,* Ontario, Canada, July 24, 1971.

James Tyson, "Woman's Pending Execution Revives Death Penalty Furor," *Christian Science Monitor,* January 16, 1996.

United Kingdom Parliamentary Papers, 1850 Volume 45.

U.S. Department of Justice, Bureau of Statistics, *Female Homicide Offenders 1976–2002,* http://www.ojp.usdoj.gov/bjs/homicide/gender.htm.

ENDNOTE REFERENCES

INTRODUCTION

1 Eric W. Hickey, *Serial Murders and Their Victims* (3rd Edition), Belmont, CA: Wadsworth/Thomson Learning, 2002, p. 213.

2 Peter Vronsky, *Serial Killers: The Method and Madness of Monsters,* New York: Berkley, 2004, pp. ix–xix.

3 Hickey, p. 213. (Statistics rounded off.)

4 Michael D. Kelleher and C. L. Kelleher, *Murder Most Rare,* New York: Dell Books, 1998, pp. 287–288.

5 Hickey, p. 215.

6 A. Frodi, J. Macaulay, and P. R. Thome, "Are Women Always Less Aggressive Than Men?" *Psychological Bulletin* 84 (1977), pp. 634–660.

7 Hickey, p. 215.

8 U.S. Department of Justice, Bureau of Statistics, *Female Homicide Offenders 1976–2002,* http://www.ojp.usdoj.gov/bjs/homicide/gender.htm.

9 Stacey L. Shipley and Bruce A. Arrigo, *The Female Homicide Offender,* Upper Saddle River, NJ: Pearson-Prentice Hall, 2004, p. 3.

10 Ann Jones, *Women Who Kill,* New York: Fawcett Columbine, 1981, p. 14.

11 Susan McWhinney, "Petit Treason: Crimes Against the Matriarchy," in Amy Schroder (ed.), *Critical Condition: Women on the Edge of Violence,* San Francisco: City Lights Books, 1993, p. 48.

12 Patricia Pearson, *When She Was Bad: How and Why Women Get Away With Murder,* Toronto: Random House Canada, 1998, p. 229.

13 James Tyson, "Woman's Pending Execution Revives Death Penalty Furor," *Christian Science Monitor,* January 16, 1996, p. 3.

14 Amnesty International Execution Alert: February 7, 2000 (http://www.ccadp.org/bettiealert.htm).

15 http://www.clarkprosecutor.org/html/death/US/smith746.htm.

16 Hickey, p. 224.

17 Nancy C. Jurik and Russ Winn, "Gender and Homicide: A Comparison of Men and Women Who Kill," *Violence and Victims,* 5:4 (1990), pp. 227–242.

18 As reported by Patricia Pearson in *When She Was Bad,* p. 30.

19 D. Cameron and E. Frazer, *The Lust to Kill: A Feminist Investigation of Sexual Murder,* New York: New York University Press, 1987, p. 1.

20 Jane Caputi, *The Age of Sex Crime*, London: Women's Press, 1987, p. 2.

21 Jane Caputi, "The New Founding Fathers: The Lore and Lure of the Serial Killer in Contemporary Culture," *Journal of American Culture, 13*, 1–12, 1990, p. 2.

22 Ann Jones, *Next Time She Will Be Dead*, New York: Beacon Press, 1994, p. 81.

23 Ann Jones, *Women Who Kill*, p. xviii.

24 Ann Jones, *Women Who Kill*, pp. 12–13.

25 Quoted in Susan McWhinney, p. 48.

26 Jane Caputi, *The Age of Sex Crimes*, London: Women's Press, 1987, p. 8.

27 Mary Daly, *Beyond God the Father: Toward a Philosophy of Women's Liberation*, Boston: Beacon Press, 1973, p. 194; A. Quindlen, "Gynocide," *New York Times*, March 10, 1993, p. A19.

28 Jane Caputi, *The Age of Sex Crimes*, London: Women's Press, 1987, p. 2.

29 J. Radford and D.E.H. Russell (eds), *Femicide: The Politics of Women Killing*, New York: Maxwell MacMillan International, 1992.

30 Lynda Hart, *Fatal Women: Lesbian Sexuality and the Mark of Aggression*, New York–London: Routledge, 1994, p. 141.

31 See Jane Caputi and J. Radford, for example.

32 See Vronsky, *Serial Killers*, pp. 23–29 for a detailed treatment of the "5000 victims" myth.

33 Hickey, p. 242.

34 U.S. Department of Justice, Bureau of Statistics, *Female Homicide Offenders 1976–2002*, http://www.ojp.usdoj.gov/bjs/homicide/gender.htm.

35 Belinda Morrissey, *When Women Kill: Questions of Agency and Subjectivity*, New York–London: Routledge, 2003. p. 19.

36 McWhinney, p. 50.

37 Lynda Hart, p. xiii.

38 Ronald M. Holmes and Stephen T. Holmes, *Murder in America*, Thousand Oaks, CA: Sage Publications, 1994.

39 S. A. Egger, "A Working Definition of Serial Murder and the Reductions of Linkage Blindness," *Journal of Police Science and Administration, 12*: 348–357, 1984.

40 V. Gerbeth, *Practical Homicide Investigations*, Boca Raton, FL: CRC Press, 1996.

41 B. T. Keeney and K. Heide, "Gender Differences in Serial Murderers," *Journal of Interpersonal Violence*, Vol. 9, No. 3, September 1994.

42 Helen Morrison, Forensic Psychiatrist, Evaluation Center, Chicago, *Mind of a Killer CD*, Kozel Multimedia, 1995–1998.

43 Deborah Schurman-Kauflin, *The New Predator: Women Who Kill*, New York: Algora Publishing, 2000.

44 Ronald M. Holmes and Stephen T. Holmes, *Serial Murder* (2nd Edition), Thousand Oaks, CA: Sage Publications, 1998. pp. 42–44.

45 Vronsky, pp. 258–267.

46 Patricia Springer, *Blood Rush,* New York: Pinnacle Books, 1994.

47 Robert D. Keppel and Richard Walter, "Profiling Killers: A Revised Classification Model for Understanding Sexual Murder," *International Journal of Offender Therapy and Comparative Criminology,* Vol. 43, No. 4, 1999.

48 See Hickey and Kelleher and Kelleher.

49 K. E. Cole, G. Fisher and S. S. Cole, "Women Who Kill: A Sociopsychological Study," *Archives of General Psychiatry,* 19, 1968. pp. 1–8.

50 Wayne Wilson, *Good Murders and Bad Murders: A Consumer's Guide in the Age of Information,* Lanham, NC: University Press of America, 1991.

51 Kelleher and Kelleher, p. 9.

52 Associated Press, June 1, June 21, 2006.

53 Hickey, p. 221.

CHAPTER ONE

54 Vronsky, pp. xii–xvi.

55 Robert K. Ressler, Ann W. Burgess, John E. Douglas, *Sexual Homicide: Patterns and Motives,* Lexington Books, Lexington, Mass.: 1988, pp. x–xi.

56 Schurman-Kauflin, p. 57.

57 Hickey, p. 139.

58 Hickey, p. 215.

59 Keeney and Heide, p. 389.

60 Hickey, p. 137.

61 Keeney and Heide, p. 389.

62 Schurman-Kauflin, p. 61.

63 Gitta Sereny, *Cries Unheard,* New York: Henry Holt, 1998, p. 109.

64 Hickey, p. 144.

65 Hickey, p. 221.

66 Hickey, p. 221.

67 Hickey, p. 225.

68 R. A. Wesheit, "Female Homicide Offenders: Trends Over Time in an Institutionalized Population," *Justice Quarterly,* Vol. 1, No. 4, 1984, p. 478.

69 Hickey, p. 217.

70 Wesheit, p. 478.

71 Keeney and Heide, p. 391.

72 Ressler, et al., *Sexual Homicide,* pp. 16–19.

73 Patricia Pearson, pp. 17–18.

74 Ilsa M. Glazer and Wahipa Abu Ras, "On Aggression, Human Rights, and Hegemonic Discourse: The Case of a Murder for Family Honor in Israel," *Sex Roles* 30:3/4 (February 1994), pp. 269–302.

75 Otto Pollack, *The Criminality of Women,* New York: A. S. Barnes, 1961.

76 Ressler, et al., *Sexual Homicide,* p. 34.

77 Ressler, et al., *Sexual Homicide*, p. 29.

78 Ressler, et al., *Sexual Homicide*, p. 29.

79 Schurman-Kauflin, p. 87.

80 Schurman-Kauflin, p. 88.

81 For references, see: Martens, W.H.J., "Marcel: A Case Study of a Violent Sexual Psychopath in Remission," *International Journal of Offender Therapy and Comparative Criminology*, 43(3) 1999, p. 392.

82 Jack Olson, *The Misbegotten Son: A Serial Killer and His Victims*, New York: Delacorte Press, 1993, pp. 491–505.

83 Joel Norris, *Serial Killers*, New York: Doubleday (Anchor Books) 1989, pp. 246–247.

84 *Daniel M'Naghten's Case*, 8 Eng. Rep. 718, 722 (H.L. 1843).

85 Richard L. Jenkins, "The Psychopath or Antisocial Personality," *Journal of Nervous and Mental Diseases*, No. 131 (1960), pp. 318–334.

86 Hervey Cleckley, *The Mask of Sanity*, (5th Edition), Privately Printed, 1988. p. 191. http://www.cassiopaea.com/cassiopaea/psychopath.htm.

87 American Psychiatric Association, *Diagnostic and Statistical Manual of Mental Disorders, Quick Reference Guide* (4th Edition), American Psychiatric Association, Washington D.C.: 1994, pp. 649–650.

88 Shipley and Arrigo, p. 44.

89 John Bowlby, *Attachment and Loss: Volume 1. Attachment*, New York: Basic Books, 1969, p. xiii.

90 M.D.S. Ainsworth, et al., *Patterns of Attachment: A Psychological Study of the Strange Situation*, Hillsdale, NJ: Erlbaum, 1978.

91 American Psychiatric Association, p. 118.

92 Shipley and Arrigo, p. 47.

93 D. A. Reiger, J. H. Boyd, et al., "One Month Prevalence of Mental Disorders in the United States," *Archives of General Psychiatry*, No. 45, (1988), pp. 977–986.

94 L. N. Robins, *Deviant Children Grow Up*, Baltimore: Williams & Wilkens, 1966.

95 *CBC News*, Canada: "B.C. woman waiting for beating death trial arrested for assault" http://www.cbc.ca/canada/story/2004/02/11/ellard_bc040211.html.

96 R. Warner, "The Diagnosis of Antisocial and Hysterical Personality Disorders: An Example of Sex Bias," *The Journal of Nervous and Mental Disease*, No. 166 (1978), pp. 839–845.

97 R. T. Mulder, et al., "Antisocial Women," *Journal of Personality Disorders*, No. 8 (1994), pp. 279–287.

98 M. Rutter, "Antisocial Behavior: Developmental Psychopathology Perspectives" in D. M. Stoff, J. Breiling, and J.D.D. Maser (Eds), *Handbook of Antisocial Behavior*, New York: Wiley, 1994, pp. 115–123.

99 Shipley and Arrigo, p. 51.

100 R. T. Mulder.
101 Shipley and Arrigo, p. 52.
102 G. Cote and S. Hodgins, "The Prevalence of Major Mental Disorders Among Homicide Offenders," *International Journal of Law and Psychiatry*, No. 15 (1992), pp. 89–99.
103 Shipley and Arrigo, p. 65.
104 Keppel and Walter, p. 435.

CHAPTER TWO
105 Vronsky, p. 53.
106 *The Bible*, Mark 6:21–29.
107 Vronsky, pp. 43–45.
108 See for example, Shelley Klein, *The Most Evil Women in History*, London: Michael O'Mara Books, 2003.
109 Vronsky, pp. 45–49.
110 Laszlo Turoczy, *Ungaria suis cum regibus compendio data*, Nagyszombat: 1729.
111 Michael Wagener, *Beiträge zur Philosophischen Anthropologie (Articles on Philosophical Anthropology)* Vienna: 1796.
112 Raymond T. McNally, *Dracula Was a Woman: In Search of the Blood Countess of Transylvania*, New York: McGraw-Hill, 1983.
113 McNally, p. 66.
114 State Archives of Hungary, Budapest, *Thurzo, F. 28, Nr. 19*.
115 State Archives of Hungary, Budapest, *Thurzo, F. 28, 2.19*.
116 Peter Haining, *Sweeney Todd: The Real Story of the Demon Barber of Fleet Street*, London: Robson Books, 2002, p. 10–11.
117 T. Edwards Clark, M.D., *The Galaxy*, Volume 6, Issue 3, Sept. 1868.
118 Geoffrey Best, *Mid-Victorian Britain 1851–1875*, New York: Schocken, 1972, p. 224.
119 *Punch* (17), London: 1849, p. 214.
120 Judith Knelman, *Twisting in the Wind: The Murderess and the English Press*, Toronto: University of Toronto Press, 1998, p. 24.
121 Vronsky, pp. 23–29.
122 Quoted in Knelman, p. 52.
123 *Times* (London), 21 September 1846, p. 4.
124 Béla Bodó, "The Poisoning Women of Tiszazug," *Journal of Family History*, Vol. 27, No. 1, January 2002, pp. 40–69.
125 Quoted in Knelman, p. 67.
126 *United Kingdom Parliamentary Papers* 1850, Volume 45, pp. 447–463.
127 Katherine Watson, *Poisoned Lives: English Poisoners and Their Victims*, London: Hambledon and London, 2004, p. 47.
128 Mark Seltzer, *Serial Killers: Death and Life in America's Wound Culture*, New York–London: Routlege, 1998, p. 1.

129 Harold Schechter, *Fatal: The Poisonous Life of a Female Serial Killer,* New York: Pocket Books, 2003, p. 4–5.

130 Schechter, p. 17.

131 Kerry Segrave, *Women Serial and Mass Murderers,* London: McFarland & Co, 1992, p. 252.

132 Schechter, p. 66.

133 Harland Manchester, "Jane Toppan, Champion Poisoner," *American Mercury,* 49: 340–346, March 1940.

CHAPTER THREE

134 Source: www.queerculturalcenter.org/pages/wuronos/intro.html (obsolete); see also: Tracy L. McKee, *Good Girls Do It Too! A Look at the Representation of Women Who Kill in Made-for-TV Movies,* MA Thesis, Concordia University, Montreal: 2000, p. 6

135 See photos in Sue Russell, *Lethal Intent,* New York: Pinnacle Books, 2002.

136 Ian Brady, *The Gates of Janus,* Los Angeles: Feral House, 2001, pp. 87–88.

137 Aileen Wuornos statement, January 16, 1991.

138 Shipley and Arrigo, pp. 128–129.

139 Schurman-Kauflin, p. 118.

140 Phyllis Chesler, *Patriarchy: Notes of an Expert Witness,* Monroe Maine: Common Courage Press, 1994. Quoting Andrea Dworkin, back cover.

141 *New York Times,* January 8, 1992, p. A1.

142 Chesler, pp. 85–160.

143 Chesler, p. 86.

144 Chesler, p. 95.

145 Vronsky, p. 258.

146 Vronsky, p. 276.

147 Chesler, p. 86.

148 Hickey, p. 215.

149 http://www.phyllis-chesler.com/bio.php.

150 Chesler, p. 95.

151 Chesler, p. 103.

152 Chesler, p. 104.

153 Chesler, p. 104.

154 Russell, p. 160, p. 499.

155 Chesler, p. 127.

156 Russell, p. 457.

157 Chesler, p. 127.

158 Chesler, p. 105.

159 Resler, et al, *Sexual Homicide,* pp. 46–47.

160 Dolores Kennedy with Robert Nolin, *On a Killing Day,* New York: SPI Books, 1994, p. 251.

CHAPTER FOUR

161 Chesler, p. 86.
162 Jerry Bledsoe, *Death Sentence,* New York: Onyx Books, 1998, p. 119.
163 Velma Barfield, *Woman on Death Row,* Nashville, TN: Oliver-Nelson Books, 1985, p. 89.
164 Barfield, p. 90.
165 Bledsoe, p. 127.
166 Bledsoe, p. 133.
167 Bledsoe, p. 136.
168 Barfield, p. 26.
169 Barfield, p. 28.
170 Barfield, p. 54.
171 Barfield, p. 59.
172 Barfield, p. 69.
173 Barfield, p. 69.
174 Barfield, p. 84.
175 Barfield, p. 86.
176 Daniel J. Blackburn, *Human Harvest,* New York: Knightsbridge, 1990, p. 153.
177 Blackburn, p. 152.
178 William P. Wood, *The Bone Garden,* New York: Ibooks, 1994, p. 68.
179 California Department of Corrections (Parole) Probation Report, Dorothea Puente, June 1982.
180 Wood, p. 116.
181 California Department of Corrections (Parole) Probation Report, Dorothea Puente, June 1982.
182 Wood, p. 18.
183 http://www/crimelibrary.com/notoriousmurders/women/puente/4.html.

CHAPTER FIVE

184 Kelly Moore and Dan Reed, *Deadly Medicine,* New York: St. Martin's Press, 1988, p. 148.
185 Peter Elkind, *The Death Shift,* New York: Onyx Books, 1989, p. 19.
186 Elkind, pp. 22–23.
187 Elkind, p. 67.
188 *New York Times,* "Contempt Asked in Baby Deaths Inquiry," November 4, 1983; *New York Times,* "Investigators Near End of Inquiry into Deaths of Infants at Hospital," April 11, 1984.
189 Steven J. Boros, M.D., and Larry C. Brubaker, "Munchausen Syndrome by Proxy: Case Accounts," *FBI Law Enforcement Bulletin,* Washington D.C.: June 1992.
190 Roy Meadow, "Munchausen Syndrome by Proxy: The Hinterland of Child Abuse," *Lancet,* 2, (1977), pp. 342–345.

191 Roy Meadow, "Munchausen Syndrome by Proxy," *Archives of Disease in Childhood*, 57, (1982), pp. 92–98.

192 Roy Meadow, "Management of Munchausen Syndrome by Proxy," *Archives of Disease in Childhood*, 60, (1985), pp. 385–393.

193 Kathryn A. Hanon, "Munchausen's Syndrome by Proxy," *FBI Law Enforcement Bulletin*, Washington D.C.: December 1991.

194 M. Sigal, I. Carmel, D. Atmark, and P. Silfen, "Munchausen Syndrome by Proxy: A Psychodynamic Analysis," *Medicine and Law*, 7 (1988), pp. 49–56.

195 K. Feldman, D. Christopher, and K. Opheim, "Munchausen Syndrome/Bulimia by Proxy: Ipecac as a Toxin in Child Abuse," *Child Abuse and Neglect*, 13, (1989), pp. 257–261.

196 K. Ravenscroft, Jr., and J. Hochheiser, *Factitious hematuria in a six-year-old girl: A case example of Munchausen syndrome by proxy.* Presented at the Annual Meeting of the American Academy of Child Psychiatry, Chicago, 1980.

197 Joyce Egginton, *From Cradle to Grave,* New York: Jove Books, 1990, p. 340.

CHAPTER SIX

198 Hickey, p. 213.

199 Kelleher and Kelleher, p. 107.

200 Kelleher and Kelleher, p. 108; Hickey, p. 216.

201 Janet I. Warren and Robert R. Hazelwood, "Relational Patterns Associated With Sexual Sadism: A Study of 20 Wives and Girlfriends," *Journal of Family Violence,* Vol. 17, No. 1, March 2002, pp. 75–89.

202 Warren and Hazelwood, p. 79.

203 Warren and Hazelwood, p. 87.

204 Emlyn Williams, *Beyond Belief,* London: Pan Books, 1967, p. 119.

205 Emlyn Williams, p. 120.

206 Vronsky, pp. 165–185.

207 Colin Wilson and Donald Seamen, *The Serial Killers,* Virgin Publishing, London: 1992, p. 238.

208 For the definitive account of both Bundy's and Clark's childhoods, see Louise Farr, *The Sunset Murders,* New York: Pocket Books, 1992.

209 Jennifer Furio, *Team Killers: A Comparative Study of Collaborative Criminals,* New York: Algora, 2001, p. 105; *Globe and Mail,* March 3, 1993, page A6.

210 According to the testimony of Karla Homolka as to what Paul Bernardo told her of the encounter.

211 Stephen Williams, *Karla: A Pact with the Devil,* Toronto: Seal Books, 2003, p. 85.

212 Patrick Wilson, *Murderess: A Study of Women Executed in Britain Since 1843,* London: Michael Joseph, 1971, p. 94.

CHAPTER SEVEN

213 http://www.imdb.com/name/nm0831471/bio.

214 Christopher Browning, *Ordinary Men: Reserve Police Battalion 101 and the Final Solution in Poland* (2nd Edition), New York: HarperPerennial, 1998, p. 48.

215 Rachel MacNair, "Psychological Reverberations for the Killers: Preliminary Historical Evidence for Perpetration-Induced Traumatic Stress," *Journal of Genocide Research*, Vol. 3, No. 2, 2001, pp. 273–282.

216 "Information on the Infamous Concentration Camp at Buchenwald," February 14 1945, in US vs. Josias Prince zu Waldeck, *et al.*, War Crimes Case No. 12–390 (The Buchenwald Case), War Crimes Office, National Archives and Records Service, 1976, Record Group 153, Records of the Judge Advocate General, National Archives (Washington, D.C.) [cited as Buchenwald Case].

217 Vronsky, pp. 185–186.

218 Alexandra Przyrembel, "Transfixed by an Image: Ilse Koch, the 'Kommandeuse of Buchenwald,'" *German History*, Vol. 19, No. 3. (2001), pp. 369–399.

219 Michael Kater, *The Nazi Party*, Cambridge, Mass: Harvard University Press, 1983, pp. 148ff and 254.

220 http://yad-vashem.org.il/odot_pdf/Microsoft%20Word%20-%206088.pdf.

221 See Christopher Browning, *The Origins of the Final Solution: The Evolution of Nazi Jewish Policy, September 1939–March 1942*, Lincoln, Nebraska/Jerusalem: University of Nebraska Press/Yad Vashem, 2004.

222 Przyrembel, p. 376 and pp. 386–387.

223 Yehoshua R. Buchler, "'Unworthy Behavior': The Case of SS Officer Max Taubner," *Holocaust and Genocide Studies*, Vol. 17, No. 3, Winter 2003, pp. 409–429.

224 Ernst Klee, Willi Dressen, Volker Riess, *"Those Were the Days": The Holocaust as Seen by the Perpetrators and Bystanders*, London: Hamish Hamilton, 1991, p. 197.

225 PS-1919, *International Military Tribunal*, Vol. 29, 1948, p. 145.

226 Przyrembel, pp. 383–384.

227 K. Sitte, Letter to the Editor, *New York Times*, October 18, 1948, p. 22.

228 "Clay Stands Firm in Ilse Koch Case," *New York Times*, October 22, 1948.

229 George C. Marshall Research Foundation, Virginia. Videotaped interview with General Lucius Clay, cited by http://www.nizkor.org/features/techniques of denial/clay-koch-03.html.

230 Daniel Patrick Brown, *The Beautiful Beast*, Ventura, CA: Golden West Historical Publications, 1996, p. 25.

231 Brown, p. 27.

232 Germain Tillion, *Ravensbrück*, Garden City, NY: Doubleday, 1975, pp. 69–70.

233 See for example, Yehoshua R. Buchler, " 'Unworthy Behavior': The Case of SS Officer Max Taubner," *Holocaust and Genocide Studies*, Vol. 17, No. 3, Winter 2003, pp. 409–429.

234 See Robert Jay Lifton, *The Nazi Doctors: Medical Killing and the Psychology of Genocide*, New York: HarperCollins, 1986.

235 Lifton, p. 208.

236 Raymond Phillips, *Trial of Joseph Kramer and Forty-four Others (The Belsen Trial)*, London: William Hodge and Company, 1949, p. 706.

237 Theodor Adorno, *The Authoritarian Personality*, New York: Harper & Row, 1950.

238 Zygmunt Bauman, *Modernity and the Holocaust*, Ithaca: Cornell University Press, 1989.

239 John M. Steiner, "The SS Yesterday and Today: A Sociopsychological View," in Joel E. Dimsdale (ed), *Survivors, Victims, and Perpetrators: Essays on the Nazi Holocaust*, Washington D.C.: 1980.

240 Ervin Staub, *The Roots of Evil: The Origins of Genocide and Other Group Violence*, Cambridge: University of Harvard Press, 1989, p. 18.

241 Church of Scientology, GS-C Comm; GS-G; D/G Intell U.S., *Compliance Report Re: Manson, Bruce Davis*, 22 June 1970—see: http://bernie.cnc family.com/sc/Manson_Scientology.htm.

242 Ed Sanders, *The Family*, [Revised and Updated Edition], New York: Signet Books, 1989, p. 22; and also see Joel Norris, pp. 162–163.

243 John Gilmore and Ron Kenner, *The Garbage People*, AMOK Books, Los Angeles: 1995, pp. 23–24.

244 John Cashman, *The LSD Story*, Greenwich, CT: Fawcett Publications, 1966, p. 31.

245 Paper presented by Dr. Robert L. Bergman, Head of U.S. Public Health Service for Navajos, Annual Conference of the American Psychiatric Association: 1971.

246 Dr. Sidney Cohen quoted in Edward M. Brecher, *Licit and Illicit Drugs*, Little Brown and Company, Boston: 1972, p. 350.

247 Interview with *SECONDS*, http://www.sni.net/central/manson/man/interview1.html, December 19, 1997.

248 Jess Bravin, *Squeaky: The Life and Times of Lynette Alice Fromme*, New York: St. Martin's Griffith, 1998, p.46.

249 Lawrence Schiller, *The Killing of Sharon Tate*, New York: New American Library, 1970, p. 70.

250 Lawrence Schiller, p. 82.

251 Susan Atkins (cowritten by Bob Slosser), *Child of Satan, Child of God*, Logos International: 1977.

252 Life Term Parole Consideration Hearing of Charles Manson, 1992.

253 Vincent Bugliosi, *Helter Skelter*, New York: Bantam Books, 1975, p. 374.

254 Clara Livsey, *The Manson Women,* New York: Richard Marek Publishers, 1980, pp. 204–206.

255 Bill Trent, "The Girl Who Was Involved in One of North America's Most Bizarre Mass Murders," *Weekend Magazine, St Thomas Times Journal,* Ontario, Canada, July 24, 1971.

256 http://www.cielodrive.com/.

257 Quoted in Vincent Bugliosi, pp. 222–223.

258 Los Angeles County case number A-252156, Statement of Charles Manson, November 19, 1970.

CONCLUSION

259 http://www.trialrun.com.

260 Kim Iannetta, e-mail to author, March 24, 2006.

261 See J. Reid Maloy, *The Psychopathic Mind: Origins, Dynamics, and Treatment* (2nd Edition), Northvale, NJ: Aronson, 1992.

AFTERWORD

262 http://en.wikipedia.org/wiki/ATWA.

INDEX

Page numbers set in boldface indicate tables.